AMERICAN ESPIONAGE

AMERICAN ESPIONAGE

From Secret Service to CIA

Rhodri Jeffreys-Jones

THE FREE PRESS
A Division of Macmillan Publishing Co., Inc.
NEW YORK

Collier Macmillan Publishers
LONDON

For my mother
and
in memory of my father

The Free Press
A Division of Macmillan Publishing Co., Inc.
866 Third Avenue, New York, N.Y. 10022

Collier Macmillan Canada, Ltd.

Library of Congress Catalog Card Number: 77-74854

Printed in the United States of America

printing number
1 2 3 4 5 6 7 8 9 10

The photographs in this book have been reprinted by permission
from

Daily Telegraph Magazine, London
Harper & Row, Publishers, New York, and
the Longman Group, Harlow, England
Popperphoto, London
Princeton University Press, Princeton, NJ
Tate Gallery, London
Wide World Photos, New York

Library of Congress Cataloging in Publication Data

Jeffreys-Jones, Rhodri.
American espionage.

Bibliography: p.
Includes index.
1. Intelligence service—United States—History.
2. Espionage—United States—History. 3. Secret
service—United States—History. I. Title.
JK468.I6J45   327'.12'0973   77-74854
ISBN 0-02-916360-9

Contents

Preface and Acknowledgments

On learning that I was writing a book about American espionage, most people showed great interest in the project and a matching curiosity about its feasibility. They wanted to know whether official documents about espionage had been destroyed, either in the interest of security or because they contained embarrassing information. They were curious about the mechanisms whereby certain categories of evidence may have been withheld from historians or made available in a piecemeal and unreliable fashion. My friends and acquaintances were also eager to find out whether government agencies had placed invisible impediments in the way of research. Had there been unaccountable delays in travel arrangements, blocked visas, or vanishing fellowships? Finally, I was asked whether the custodians of private collections had denied me cooperation, for fear of casting discredit on family members.

I reassured my questioners, and disappointed a few of them, by explaining that, to the best of my knowledge, no significant obstacles were being put in my way. By way of preface to a book of this kind, it is appropriate to give the substance of that explanation. To begin with the last question, I suspect it is true that material in a very small number of private collections in the United States, Spain, and Britain was withheld from me. But this may have had nothing to do with espionage. Private material is, from time to time, denied historians working on any recent subject. Involvement in espionage is not always regarded as a shameful matter to be swept under the carpet. Indeed, a few of my correspondents were proud of having been connected with espionage, an activity which they regarded as exciting, romantic, and patriotic; these individuals willingly volunteered information.

In researching for this book, I experienced no significant obstruction from either past or present officialdom. Government officials have carefully preserved intelligence records, along with other archives, from the Spanish–American war of 1898 to the formation of the Central Intelligence Agency in 1947. There is, on the other hand, a legal provision today which protects "information or material . . . pertaining to cryptography, or disclosing intelligence sources or methods."[1] However, it covers only records up to thirty years old and did not impede my research. Archives over thirty years old are protected only when access might imperil national security, or when "disclosure would place a person in immediate jeopardy."[2] In the former case, it is the custom in the National Archives to place withdrawal cards in files from which sensitive documents have been removed. These cards carry a description of the missing material, which is usually self-evidently nonessential as far as the historian is concerned. In the case of missing files on individuals under investigation or on secret agents in the field, the historian is undoubtedly, though justifiably, deprived of a source of fascinating material. Fortunately, I had decided to write not an anthology of anecdotes but a book about espionage policy with a few anecdotal illustrations, so the restriction on personal data imposed no great hardship.

The researcher's ease of access to materials shedding light on the history of espionage reflects a general conviction in America and several other democracies that all citizens in a free society should, wherever possible, have the right of access to government-held information. Ironically, President Richard M. Nixon, later forced to resign because of his participation in the cover-up of the Watergate scandal, restated the right when he provided for the reform of the classification system of federal documents. His executive order of March 8, 1972, established a system for the mandatory review of classified documents upon request by any private citizen.[3] Nixon, furthermore, kept tape recordings of his White House conversations, a practice which led to the early ventilation of information prejudicial to his political survival but which also suggests his possible desire to help future historians.

Nixon's opponents in public life were, of course, more noted than he for their advocacy and practice of the freedom-of-information principle. This is evident not only from their determined exposure of the Watergate cover-up but also from the action of the *New York Times* in publishing extracts from the "Pentagon Papers," the misappropriated military documents showing up the follies of successive Democratic and Republican administrations in escalating American participation in the Vietnam war. New York District Judge Murray I. Gurfein indicated in his opinion when he "refused to enjoin the publication of the Pentagon Papers at the request of the President" that "matters of history, though sometimes a source of political embarrassment, ought to see the light of day."[4] For this same reason, Judge Gurfein agreed in principle to supply me with information essential to the satisfactory completion of Chapter 13. On being assured that I had secured the declassification of papers relating to "K Project" and therefore already understood the outline of this bold American attempt to introduce democracy to the Balkans in the later stages of World War II, Judge Gurfein supplied me with the identity of the secret emissary, "K."[5] In writing this book, in short, I was assisted by the fact that Americans of every political hue regard knowledge as part of the public domain, subject to the proviso that its ventilation will not prove injurious to national security or unjust to individuals.

Free access to information is of little help if one is unaware of its existence. This book would never have been written without the kind promptings of people whose guidance eventually convinced me that there was scope for more than the occasional article. I am grateful for more than intellectual assistance, however. I would like to thank the director and Administrative Committee of the Charles Warren Center for Studies in American History, Harvard University, who awarded me a fellowship during the academic year 1971–1972; the Committee of the United States–United Kingdom Educational Commission, who granted me a Fulbright travel fellowship for 1971–1972; the Overseas Policy Committee of the British Academy, who gave me an Overseas Visiting Fellowship in 1975; the Executive Committee of the Carnegie Trust for the Universities of Scotland, who also made a grant toward the expenses of my research visit to America in 1975; and two University of Edinburgh committees, which gave me generous support throughout the period 1971–1976: the University Travel and Research Committee, and the Faculty of Arts Postgraduate Studies Committee.

The librarians and archivists at several institutions gave me invaluable help. I am grateful to the staffs of the University Library and the National Library of Scotland, Edinburgh; the Widener Library, Harvard University; the Massachusetts Historical Society, Boston; the Boston Public Library; the State Historical Society, Madison, Wisconsin; the University and Hoover Institution Libraries, Stanford University, California; and the Joseph Labadie Collection, University of Michigan Library, Ann Arbor. The following individuals were so painstaking and generous with their assistance that I would like to thank them individually: Judith Schiff of Yale University Library; Ian McClymont of the Public Archives of Canada, Ottawa; William R. Emerson of the Franklin D. Roosevelt Library, Hyde Park, New York; Ruby J. Shields and Deborah Newbeck of the Minnesota Historical Society; John C. Broderick of the Library of Congress; Hannah Zeidlick and Delmar H. Finks of the U.S.A.

Center of Military History Library, Washington, D.C.; and John L. Walford and Nicholas G. Cox of the Public Record Office, London. In addition, it is a pleasure to express my warmest appreciation of the advice given to me by Ronald E. Swerczek and Timothy K. Nenninger of the National Archives, Washington, D.C.

Numerous friends gave me additional advice. At the Charles Warren Center two of the 1971–1972 fellows, Dragan R. Zivojinovic, now of Belgrade University, and Charles E. Neu, now of Brown University, directed me to sources which proved indispensable to my research on espionage. At the University of Edinburgh, I received further academic advice and help from Donald Rutherford, Philip Wigley, and Angus Mackay. My godmother, Lily Pincus, supplied me with psychological data; Sidney Fine of the University of Michigan gave me inspired archival guidance; my father-in-law, Joseph L. Minkiewicz, advised me on Polish history and made translations from his native tongue and Russian; Sir Stephen Runciman as well as Judge Gurfein helped me to understand K Project; my colleagues Owen Dudley Edwards and George A. Shepperson bombarded me with references and, in undertaking the organization of the Scottish Universities American Bicentennial Conference in June, 1976, contrived to relieve me of certain administrative duties at a crucial time. I am grateful to each of the foregoing.

Harvard University paid for a research assistant to help me during the academic year. I would like to thank him: Brian Ibsen worked harder than I had a right to expect, displayed an original flair, and continued to help after the expiration of his contract. My gratitude is also due to David Fisher, my former graduate student now resident in British Columbia, who voluntarily supplied Canadian materials. My wife, Janetta C. Jeffreys-Jones, collaborated with me in several ways in preparing this book for publication—reading and speculating about archival material, translating from German, helping with proofreading and indexing, and looking after our daughter Gwenda. I am most grateful for her help.

A team of readers criticized, with unvarying tact, the near-final manuscript: Victor Kiernan, Victor Rothwell, Paul Addison, Faith Pullin and Katy Day of Edinburgh University, and C. Duncan Rice of Yale University. Gladys Topkis of The Free Press combined editorial concentration with courtesy and patience in dealing with me. To all these readers, I pay appreciative tribute.

I gratefully acknowledge permission to republish portions of articles which have appeared in the *Journal of American Studies, Canadian Review of American Studies,* and *American Quarterly.*

Research for this book was a pleasurable enterprise because of the warm hospitality afforded to my wife and me in the United States. We received sincere welcomes not only from Charles and Deborah Neu of Providence, Duncan and Susan Rice of New Haven, Gene and Mary-

Ellen Rischer of Washington, D.C., and Alan and Caroline Dodge of Newburyport but from many others as well. In Britain, William R. Brock of Glasgow University gave me constant and much appreciated support and encouragement. Finally, it gives me pleasure mixed with sadness to acknowledge the hospitality and support extended over many years by Oscar and the late Mary Handlin, of Cambridge, Massachusetts.

1

The CIA Foreshadowed: Espionage from Washington to McKinley

Against a background of controversy both recent and ancient, the Senate Select Committee to Study Governmental Operations with Respect to Intelligence Activities in April 1976 published a conspicuously balanced report.[1] Some of its recommendations, to be sure, reflected past disagreements about American espionage. For example, the report demanded closer congressional supervision of the Central Intelligence Agency (CIA). It deplored the use of journalists as agents and requested that the attorney general oversee the agency's counterespionage work. Senator Frank Church, the committee chairman, insisted that there should be fewer covert operations, perhaps none at all.

Such implied criticisms were carefully offset, however, by encouragement. The intelligence report suggested that the CIA director should be more fully empowered and that U.S. ambassadors should help the agency to perform its duties. Senator Church personally declared for the view, often challenged in preceding decades, that a central intelligence organization should have the authority to collect and distribute information as well as to analyze it, and that it should be active in counterintelligence.[2] His declaration drew attention to the signal refusal of his committee, controlled though it was by Democrats, to excoriate a Republican administration.

The recommendations of Church's committee, critical or otherwise, may be considered in the light of short-term factors. It is arguable that the CIA became the target of attack as a result of revelations during the 1960s and

1970s—the unmasking of covert military operations in Southeast Asia, the discrediting of executive privileges in consequence of the Watergate affair, and specific allegations against the agency, such as those concerning the use of poisons and assassination attempts.[3] More recent events and considerations helped to bring about a less biased appraisal of CIA activities. The assassination of Richard Welch, a CIA agent in Athens, had a sobering effect on some of the supporters of wholesale exposure in that it seemed to stem from the leaking and publication of the names and addresses of American spies in Greece.[4] Political prudence, too, set in during the early months of 1976. It was an election year, and those Democrats who believed that voters have memories found it difficult to forget that the CIA had advised against escalation of the Vietnam war, and that this good advice had been ignored in 1964 by a Democratic president, Lyndon B. Johnson.[5] The Republican incumbent, President Gerald R. Ford, was proving to be disconcertingly flexible and, after assessing the public reaction to Vice President Nelson Rockefeller's report on intelligence services, had advanced his own plan for moderate reform.[6] The Democrats knew they were vulnerable on the question of congressional privilege, because so many of the secrets to which congressmen were privy had been leaked to the press. One inference that they feared might be drawn from this was that Congress was not fit to supervise the CIA. Finally, Senator Church released balanced statements as an individual not only because he was no muckraker but because he was sensitive to the political climate in a year when he himself was an aspirant for the Democratic presidential nomination. There is, then, no shortage of plausible short-term reasons for the Senate's circumspection regarding the CIA in the spring of 1976.

Church's restraint reflected long-term as well as short-term considerations. This book is a history of intelligence and, therefore, of the attitudes ultimately exemplified in the 1970s. The book was begun well before the outbreak of debate over the CIA. It is not, then, specifically directed to the controversies of the 1970s. The history of intelligence is treated in its own right as a subject of intrinsic interest. Precisely for this reason, because the book treats past problems on their own merits, not according to present criteria, it may prove to be an example of useful history. To this end, some of the unraveled threads of history have, in the final stages of writing, been drawn together to form a warp for present-day interpretations.

The main focus of this book is on the half-century before the establishment of the CIA, from 1898 to 1947. These were formative years for the development of continuous central intelligence. So many events took place in this period that it would be impossible to discuss them all thoroughly without sacrificing coherence. For example, the activities of the Federal Bureau of Investigation in Latin America in the late 1930s and early 1940s were extensive enough to deserve a separate volume, but because they constituted a departure from the mainstream history of U.S. intelligence they are but lightly touched on here. Similarly, specific incidents such as the sinking of the *Maine* and the attack on Pearl Harbor invite special attention. But, in spite of the fact that American archivists provide what must be uniquely unrestricted access to most intelligence files up to 1947, no new evidence has come to light concerning these events. This book therefore dwells on the significance of hitherto neglected subjects, such as the Russian reports of the Anglo-American spy W. Somerset Maugham. By throwing new light on obscure parts of the American intelligence story and fusing them with existing knowledge, it will be possible to advance broad interpretation in place of particularized history.

The search for broad perspective soon illuminates the significance of the period 1898–1947. Before 1898, there had been many spying ventures. Military espionage during the Revolution and the Civil War was extensive. However, in these periods it developed no great strength beyond the confines of U.S. territory and failed to result in permanent peacetime institutions. Reformed during the war with Spain, the Secret Service became such an institution. Its most useful work was in the field of military counterintelligence, but it was run by civilian officials under the Department of the Treasury. In a civilian-dominated democracy like the United States, the vesting of intelligence functions in civilian hands meant an upgrading of espionage. This process was aided in 1898 by another factor which also became a permanent feature of American espionage, State Department involvement.

State Department involvement in espionage led in due course to a greater emphasis on processing and distributing information in the interest of national security, as opposed to simply gathering it. Indeed, the political scientist H. H. Ransom complains that by now the word "intelligence" has "loosely expanded in common misuse" to include even covert or paramilitary operations. His meaning may be demonstrated with reference to the CIA's Bicentennial publication *Intelligence in the War of Independence,* which contains sections on "covert action" in 1775 (Colonel Henry Tucker's raid on the Royal Arsenal at Bermuda) and "wartime special operations" (such as James Aitken's sabotage efforts in English dockyards, 1776–1777).[7] It may be objected that such modern terminology is inapplicable to revolutionaries whose activities were necessarily clandestine because directed against the then overwhelming might of the British Empire; nevertheless, it is clear that by the 1970s CIA officials regarded covert action as an intelligence activity. Even if CIA historians were wrong in claiming that recent covert actions have Revolutionary antecedents, it is worth noting that military intelligence (which has always involved behind-the-lines operations in wartime) was put on a formal footing before 1898 and, like State Department intelligence, gradually improved its bureaucracy in the few decades after the Spanish war.

Any satisfactory account of American espionage, the process of acquiring information in the interest of national security, must dwell on associated phenomena and their antecedents.

In the history of American espionage, the main importance of the year 1947, when the CIA was founded, is that people thought it was important. Popularly regarded as a modern invention, the CIA has become an unparalleled issue in American and world politics. The CIA controversy has been fanned by the agency's indulgence in extensive covert actions in peacetime and by America's new and daunting position as the strongest military and economic power in the world.

It is not generally realized that the CIA controversy is unprecedented only in its intensity, not in its form. This oversight is partly the fault of historians. According to an interwar writer on espionage, Richard W. Rowan, historians have shunned the topic of espionage because of "the character of spies, the nature of their work, and the often unsavory motives of those who have been the chief beneficiaries of espionage and the intrigues of political secret agents. Spies, in short, are a veritable insecticide upon the Great-Man treatment of history. . . ."[8] The neglect of espionage as a serious historical subject has meant that there has been little discussion of a significant debate in American history.

Although Americans, perhaps to a greater degree than, say, Russians or South Africans, have always respected the need for foreign intelligence, they have, in a typically democratic manner, criticized the instruments of espionage. Indeed, one of the best guides to the changing patterns of the history of intelligence is the changing nature of the criticism leveled at it. Considered in relation to the critical criteria of the 1970s, attacks on espionage from Colonial days to the late nineteenth century demonstrate that the modern generation is not the first to have become aware of the dangers of an intelligence system.

If the criticisms of the 1970s are reduced to general principle, it is arguable—and demonstrable by reference to the narrative in succeeding chapters of this book—that practically every one of them had its precedents in the half-century before the founding of the CIA. This indicates that, in some respects at least, the CIA is indistinguishable from its twentieth-century antecedents. Furthermore, identification of four main areas of criticism suggests that the CIA was foreshadowed even before 1898.

The CIA has been attacked in the 1970s because of its authority, its methods, its alleged inefficiency, and its objectives. Some critics have been dissatisfied with the degree of centralization that has taken place in American intelligence. The CIA seemed to be spreading its octopoid tentacles into every branch of espionage, even into domestic politics. To not a few, the organization was too powerful. Worse, it was accountable to the wrong overlord.

At this point, the critics have diverged. Some have argued for a new type of accountability—for example, to the attorney general for counterintelligence purposes. Others have called for greater congressional control, and still others have maintained that existing rules should be more strictly applied. The last group includes a former director of the CIA, Richard Helms. Specifically, Helms has deplored the failure of his subordinates to obey an executive order from President Richard M. Nixon demanding that the CIA destroy its cache of poisons. Helms testified before the Church committee that CIA employees were trained to accept oral directives as "orders written in blood." Their failure to obey the president and destroy shellfish toxin was therefore deplorable.[9] The testimony of Helms and others indicates that doubts about the authorization of clandestine activities have been both varied and pervasive.

Equally diverse are the criticisms levied against the methods of the CIA. In the 1970s, these were activated by principles which have always inspired Americans: moral integrity, humanity, civil liberties, and the right to privacy. Because morality and privacy interest most people and because journalists try to write for a wide audience, the CIA's apparent defiance of these principles attracted much attention. In February 1976, President Ford called for legislation to protect the privacy of telephone calls and letters.[10] In the same month, the French Communist newspaper *L'Humanité* accused the CIA of using "models" to seduce and corrupt the party's officials in Paris.[11] The Church committee rather more prosaically condemned the CIA's recruitment methods, specifically the agency's use of journalists, academics, commercial publishing houses, and religious leaders. The Senate committee's reservations were based on the view that the use and payment of such agents might corrupt the communications media even if it increased the knowledge available to the CIA.[12]

Two criticisms directed to the methods of the CIA deserve special attention. One concerns the method of murder. In October 1975, Sidney Gottlieb told the Church committee, in a leaked statement which attracted much adverse publicity, that the CIA had intended in 1961 to poison the Congolese premier, Patrice Lumumba. The assassination of Lumumba by other means and by parties unknown forestalled the attempt, but Gottlieb could testify with authority about the original intention because in 1961 he was head of the CIA's chemical division, which had made up the unused lethal dose and dispatched it to the Congo (now Zaïre).[13] Irrespective of whether or not the CIA was ever successful in assassinating an unfriendly foreign official, the fact that it intended to do so in at least one case sets it apart from American espionage organizations prior to the 1940s in an important respect. Although the Spanish nobleman and spy Ramon de Carranza hinted in 1898 that the Secret Service murdered Spanish agents in captivity, and although the British side of Anglo-American intelligence used murder in World War I, U.S. intelligence as such almost certainly stopped short of this particular method for several decades after it had achieved permanent bureaucratic form.

Another method-oriented criticism that deserves special attention was expressed by Secretary of State Henry Kissinger, who articulated a spreading malaise when he criticized the methods of the CIA's critics. Harking back to the early 1950s, when Senator Joseph McCarthy had destroyed the reputations, the livelihoods, and in some cases the lives of worthy citizens merely by questioning them before a Senate committee investigating Communism, Dr. Kissinger complained of a new McCarthyism.[14] He thus drew attention to witch-hunting, a pursuit that forms part of a long and continuous tradition in America.

Adverse comment on the CIA's efficiency drew attention to a different set of problems. For example, there was growing concern in the 1970s about the leakage of secret information, both from intelligence sources themselves and from Senate and House committees set up to investigate them privately. In addition, the debate over efficiency caused certain phenomena already under discussion to be seen in a new light. The size and authority of the CIA were questioned, not in relation to their influence on the Constitutional rights of citizens or the morality of clandestine operations abroad but in connection with results. Soldiers, statesmen, and defense-conscious congressmen expected intelligence sources to be able to predict any threat from Russia or from other countries and movements within the Communist orbit. In September 1975, the House Select Committee on Intelligence, under the chairmanship of Otis G. Pike, exposed the CIA's failure to warn about the Yom Kippur war, the joint Egyptian–Syrian attack on Israel in 1973 which had such severe repercussions on Middle East politics, the petroleum industry, and the economy of the West.[15] In 1976, the CIA was again the target of criticism when Russia took the West by surprise in the Angolan civil war.

It is notable that charges of inefficiency centered on foreign intelligence failures, such as that in Angola. By contrast, criticism of immoral intelligence practices was, if not exclusively concerned with domestic transgressions, at least preoccupied with them. The application of different standards at home and abroad is partly explained by the fact that different people applied them. The CIA was beset with two groups of critics, one of which worried about inefficiency overseas, the other about morality at home. It would be an evasion, however, to explain away ambivalent standards purely in these terms, for the two groups of critics were not mutually exclusive. Although there was a widespread sense of shock at disclosures about certain CIA activities abroad, there was undoubtedly a much deeper revulsion about the agency's reported malpractices in the United States. It is a natural human reaction to protest more strongly when one's own ox has been gored.

In an interview with the *Chicago Sun-Times* in September, 1975, President Ford commented on the objectives of the CIA. He tried to justify former President Nixon's use of the agency in Chile on the ground that Chile, "the first democratic system in Latin America," was being undermined by Communists. Ford maintained that his own administration had refrained from using the agency in Portugal, where Communists were also threatening to take over, because "they had not had democracy in Portugal for almost half a century."[16] The president clearly wished to convince his audience that he thought covert retaliatory methods were in order where the objective was the frustration of totalitarian attempts to subvert established democracies. This had been the case in Chile but not in Portugal. The Ford administration remained consistent in professed outlook when the Turin daily newspaper *La Stampa* published leaked excerpts from the censored Pike committee report on intelligence showing that the CIA had subsidized anti-Communist parties in Italian elections since the 1940s.[17] The administration stood by the CIA's covert action in defending an established democracy against what most Americans would have regarded as totalitarian subversion.

Ford's expressed position on intelligence objectives echoed that of President Woodrow Wilson sixty years earlier. Wilson had been incensed at the espionage activities of Germany in the United States, which he presented in inspired propaganda terms as an attack by an autocracy on an established and neutral democracy. During World War I, he therefore supplied the State Department's intelligence men with challenging retaliatory objectives. It was this war, not World War II or the cold war, that introduced American spies to far-flung "counterintelligence" activities, as they were defensively called (the German term *Abwehr* is analogous), and to complex and confused situations. Their response to the ideological issues of antiimperialism in 1917–1918 and "Moscow Gold" in the 1920s, which will be dealt with in Chapters 8 and 11 below, laid the shaky groundwork for the mistakes of a later age. The debate that began to take place over American intelligence objectives was a virtually indistinguishable part of the progressive reappraisal of foreign policy in general. It was a twentieth-century—indeed, a post-1915—phenomenon. In this respect, criticism of intelligence objectives may be set apart from criticisms of the CIA's authority, methods, and efficiency, several varieties of which were at least partly foreshadowed in the quarter-millennium prior to 1898.

A brief perusal of colonial society is sufficient to reveal that the contrasting values later applied to intelligence methods had the deepest possible American roots. Twentieth-century concern with privacy, on the one hand, and prurience, on the other, was based on colonial rather than "Victorian" attitudes. Historian David H. Flaherty has shown that seventeenth-century New Englanders, like most people in every society, valued and expected privacy in sexual relations.[18] Like so many of their descendants, colonial Americans were also concerned to protect the privacy of correspondence. An early eighteenth-century manual on good manners warned: "Touch not, nor look upon the Books or Writings of any one, unless the Owner invite or desire thee. . . . Come not near when another reads a Letter or any other Paper."[19]

The countervailing Puritan urge to pry into the private affairs of vulnerable victims, such as the unmarried mother, is devastatingly described in Nathaniel Hawthorne's novel The Scarlet Letter (1850). The most celebrated colonial exposure was, however, the affair of the Salem, Massachusetts, witchcraft trials of 1892. In The Devil in Massachusetts (1949), psychohistorian Marion L. Starkey drew attention to several features of the trials, notably the small number of "witches" actually accused in Salem and the disproportionately sensational response to their trial and execution. "The Salem story," she observed, "has the virtue of being a highly individualized affair. Witches in the abstract were not hanged in Salem but one by one were brought to the gallows such diverse personalities as a decent grandmother grown too hard of hearing to understand a crucial question from the jurors, a rakish, pipe-smoking female tramp, a plain farmer who thought only to save his wife from molestation, a lame old man whose toothless gums did not deny expression to a very salty vocabulary."[20] Because the Salem accused were a few individuals, as opposed to an anonymous multitude, Starkey pointed out, they found many sympathizers subsequently.

Though provocative, Starkey's views do not supply a complete explanation of the Salem witchcraft hysteria. The trials may just as easily be regarded as the product of rigid theocracy, of political difficulties which were the aftermath of James II's ill-fated reign, of economic uncertainties, Indian warfare, or simply as an American expression of an international phenomenon to be found in more widespread form in Catholic Europe. Starkey's interpretation does, however, help to focus attention on aspects of the Salem affair that identify it as the forerunner of later witch-hunts, both official and private. The pursuit of witches in Salem is an instance of a tendency, by no means exclusively American, to affix blame for real or imagined evils in society by attacking small and vulnerable minorities, such as Black Muslims in recent times. Further, it is significant that the Salem prosecutors ultimately came under attack from their contemporaries. Subsequent investigators of the affairs of relatively innocuous individuals, be they Massachusetts divines, private detectives, public agencies, or congressmen, have met a similar fate.

The first prominent critic of the efficiency of American intelligence operations was George Washington. During the French and Indian war, which began in undeclared fashion with Washington's Western skirmishes in 1754 and reached its climax in North America in 1759, the young officer deplored the intelligence incapacities of white men. In the beautiful but inscrutable vastness of the virgin continent, the British forces were unable to find the enemy, long at home in the wilderness, let alone fore-stall their attacks. Washington resorted to an aboriginal solution, remark-ing that "small parties of Indians will more effectively harass the enemy, by keeping them under continual alarms, than any parties of white men can do. For small parties of the latter are not equal to the task, not being so dexterous at skulking as Indians; and large parties will be discovered by their spies early enough to have a superior force opposed to them."[21]

During the war for independence twenty years later, Washington used numerous spies. They were white Americans in the main, because they operated in the settled areas of the Eastern Seaboard as well as, on a limited scale, in London and Paris. Washington maneuvered his small army away from the perilous brink of contact with superior British forces by keeping himself informed about enemy movements. Military spies like Nathan Hale have consequently won an accredited place in the American pantheon. Washington realized, however, that it was not in the best in-terest of American intelligence to acknowledge its heroes immediately and publicly. To have done so would have imperiled his agents and en-dangered the prospect of using intelligence successfully in future conflicts. The achievements of Washington's spies awaited public recognition until the publication of James Fenimore Cooper's factually based historical novel *The Spy* in 1821.

During the war for independence, therefore, the Revolutionary pa-triots took special care not to admit the existence of their commander-in-chief's intelligence service, not only so as to protect the cover of the agents concerned but also to avoid tarnishing the public image of their cause. It was deemed good propaganda to impute clandestine methods only to the enemy, thus implying that Britain was unscrupulous and had to use underhanded tactics to succeed.

It was in a spirit of righteous vengeance that the Revolutionaries executed the British intelligence officer John André (though it should be borne in mind that death has always been the automatic sentence for enemy spies captured in wartime). Americans' indignation was far more vehement, however, when it was discovered that one of their own, Benedict Arnold, was a spy and, worse, a traitor. Treason from within and fear of it later accounted for the persecution of many persons less culpable than Arnold and lay at the root of domestic surveillance—politi-cal as well as military—in the United States. In America, as elsewhere, the condemnation of enemy spies rested on the viewpoint that although all spies are immoral, enemy spies are absolutely immoral.

The French Revolution and its aftermath in the 1790s fed the Ameri-can distrust of foreign agents. France had been an ally during the Ameri-can Revolution, and many Republicans in the United States, under the leadership of Thomas Jefferson, admired the Gallic radicalism of the

1790s if not the vindictive executions that accompanied it. The Federalists, however, remembered that France had had a king when LaFayette joined Washington; portraits of the royal family still hung in Congress; the administration of John Adams favored the French revolutionary principle of *Liberté* but shuddered at the thought of *Egalité* and positively recoiled at the mention of *Fraternité*. For the American Republic remained conservatively nationalist compared with social-revolutionary, internationalist France. The Federalists simply could not identify the agents of Jacobinism with Washington's patriot-spies. They began to formulate reactionary intelligence objectives for the United States, but, interrupted by a century of isolationism, their plans remained embryonic.

Twentieth-century intelligence objectives were foreshadowed by the Federalist response to a slave insurrection in Santo Domingo. In 1799, some passengers disembarking from a brig in Charleston Harbor were arrested on suspicion of being emissaries from the French *Directoire*. Secretary of State Timothy Pickering, formerly a supporter of the French Revolution but a zealous convert to Federalism and by 1799 "armored in rectitude" in his defense of law and order, was the instigator of the arrests, fueled by information received from the U.S. consul at Hamburg.[22] Early in the history of the republic, then, a secretary of state had perceived that the line separating covert information and covert intelligence was thin, and that the consular service could be used for surveillance.

Armed officials alerted by Pickering found reportedly subversive documents concealed in tubs on board the Charleston brig, and the affair came to be known as the Tub Plot. The climate of the times produced the rumor that the arrested passengers were *Directoire* spies sent to conspire with Republican politicians, and the Federalist press made the most of the issue. The Alien and Sedition Acts of 1798, which had led to the imprisonment of some seventy outspoken critics of the Federalist administration and which had been attacked by Jefferson and James Madison, now appeared to be retrospectively justified. Ultimately, it emerged that the arrestees had arrived to stir up, not treason in America but revolt against the *Directoire* in Santo Domingo, where the Federalists were themselves encouraging the rebel (and traitor in French eyes) Toussaint L'Ouverture. The Charleston spies had been arrested by mistake. The Federalists' objective was, in fact, to encourage unofficially a black revolt which would weaken the social-revolutionary *Directoire* and frighten Republican slave owners in the Southern states. Their plan had gone wrong, and the Tub Plot discredited for many years any method of federal surveillance, whether through laws or through customs officials. For a hundred years, the United States, in contrast to Britain and France, remained free of laws or intelligence agencies which might have been ideologically oppressive. By the same token, however, America became vulnerable, in the absence of a counterintelligence service, to foreign covert penetrations such as those effected by the Fenians and British intelligence (discussed in Chapter 2).

Foreign intelligence work was not neglected, however. This was partly because the U.S. Constitution of 1787 gave the president greater authority in foreign than in domestic affairs. As the nineteenth century wore on, Congress developed doubts about the nature and desirability of that authority. As a result, the debate over foreign-intelligence authorization grew fierce in the nineteenth century; compromises were struck, only to be forgotten in the heat of future arguments, of which the current CIA controversy is but the latest.

In 1793, Congress established a contingency fund for the use of the president. It was understood that the money could be spent on intelligence work and that the chief executive would not have to account for it publicly. George Washington used the fund to finance intelligence work in Spain by David Humphreys, the U.S. consul safely stationed in Lisbon, Portugal. During the next seventy-five years, presidents used their executive power to send secret agents to Mexico, Canada, the West Indies, Latin America, Europe, Turkey, the Far East, Hawaii, and elsewhere.[23]

If the diplomats of the United States pursued an isolationist policy in the nineteenth century, they pursued it in an informed and cosmopolitan manner. The expertise of the nineteenth-century American spy was, it is true, open to question by modern standards. There was as yet no training, no continuity, no agency at the disposal of the chief executive. At times, there was but indifferent talent at the disposal of the president, whose calls on the services of a spy were too infrequent to provide constant employment and an attractive career for capable men and women. On the other hand, the president was not plagued by job seekers who might have invented artificial intelligence needs. Whatever the merits of the system, they failed to preserve the executive from criticism. Congressional discontent arose because, in an attempt to move outside the trammels of senatorial advice and consent, several presidents used executive agents for purposes of diplomacy instead of for information. Thus in 1831, President Andrew Jackson incurred censure for his use of nonaccredited agents in negotiating a treaty with Turkey. The debate over authorization had began in earnest.[24]

A decade later, the former Jacksonian Senator James Buchanan defended the decision to send special agent William S. Murphy to Latin America with undefined functions. Buchanan, who was soon to become secretary of state in President James K. Polk's cabinet and later president himself, argued that to have the Senate nominate and confirm secret agents would defeat the object of sending them—and soon, he reluctantly admitted, spies would have to be sent to both Cuba and Santo Domingo.[25] Those who feared that Spain's ejection from Cuba would lead to the extension of the Southern slavocracy to that island listened to the expansionist Buchanan with dismay. His opponents failed, however, to exploit the weakness in the position of Buchanan and other custodians of American foreign policy. They could not or would not insist that spies should be kept distinct from accredited diplomatic envoys.

Foiled in his attempt to clarify to his own satisfaction the distinction between unofficial diplomats and spies, Buchanan made the best of it. He used the ambiguity as a smoke screen if things went wrong in Latin America or in the Senate. If unofficial diplomats embarrassed the United States or struck unfavorable bargains with foreign governments, they could be disowned as if they were spies (spies of every nation operated on the understanding that they would be disowned if things went wrong). If senators objected that they had not been given the opportunity to consent to diplomatic appointments, Buchanan and later secretaries of state protested that the envoys in question were mere spies. Buchanan's formula worked well where peace negotiations were concerned, because the Constitution is vague on peacemaking powers (as the Senate discovered again in 1919 and during the Vietnam war). Amplified by Polk, the formula served the interests of the administration during the war with Mexico from 1846 to 1848.

Moses Y. Beach was the prosperous publisher of the *New York Sun,* a newspaper which was to have a continuing association with American intelligence. In November 1846, in the wake of General Zachary Taylor's triumphant advance on Monterey, Beach went to Mexico as a secret agent with instructions from Buchanan to seek an honorable peace. The Democrat Polk no doubt hoped for favorable annexations and desired to limit the glory that might be heaped on Taylor, a Whig, were further U.S. victories to follow. Beach, being English born, was able to use a false British passport during his journey. He nevertheless received an official letter of appointment from the secretary of state, instructing him to negotiate but enjoining him from revealing the purpose of his mission to anybody except the U.S. consul in Mexico City. The $2,609.05 which Beach received for personal expenses came from State Department funds, not from the presidential purse.[26] Buchanan therefore anticipated the role of future secretaries of state who acted as paymasters for presidentially sponsored clandestine activities.

When Beach claimed that he was on the verge of a favorable settlement and Buchanan agreed, Polk wondered how the resultant draft treaty should be presented to Congress. His ambiguous diary entry on the subject reads: "I will waive [Beach's] authority to make it, and submit it to the Senate for ratification."[27] Beach, though at first welcomed by General A. L. de Santa Anna as a peace emissary, was eventually accused by the Mexicans of being a spy and *agent provocateur.* When General Winfield Scott's army landed at Vera Cruz, Beach had to leave suddenly. By this time, Polk was protesting—for the benefit of his audience in the Senate but also in an attempt to reassure posterity that he had not double-crossed the Mexicans by attacking them in the middle of negotiations—that he had not given Beach "diplomatic powers." He had made Beach a secret agent "that he might collect and furnish useful information to his government."[28] In the antebellum years, the national executive thrived on intelligence ambiguities.

The Civil War produced a significant shift in espionage emphasis. Though the Confederate states sent several agents to Europe, the war was chiefly a civil conflict, fought out on the American mainland. Spying for the Union was therefore the duty of the U.S. Army. Although every army grouping had its reconnaissance unit, the first attempt at systematic espionage was entrusted to Allan Pinkerton, a cooper who had turned detective on accidentally discovering that he could make money by solving criminal mysteries and who in 1850 established the first successful detective agency in America. He was working on a case in Baltimore in 1861 when he claimed he had learned of a plot to assassinate Abraham Lincoln as the president-elect passed through that city on the way to his inauguration. Lincoln changed his itinerary in order to avoid harm. After further conferences with Lincoln and General George B. McClellan, Pinkerton organized the U.S. Secret Service, with headquarters in Washington. He sent agents into the heart of the Confederacy and set up a counterespionage network in the North.

Pinkerton's reign was relatively brief, for he resigned in November 1862 upon the removal of his friend and protector General McClellan as commander-in-chief of the U.S. Army. By that time, however, he had firmly established America's first federal intelligence agency and ensured that it would have counterintelligence as well as offensive functions.[29]

After some months of confusion, La Fayette C. Baker took over the direction of the Secret Service. In 1856, Baker had taken part in the San Francisco Vigilante movement, a lawless attempt by the controlling but threatened Bay City elite to keep the Irish-Democrat element in its place. After making a name for himself during a daring espionage raid on Richmond, Baker rose to be a Brigadier-General in the Union Army. As head of the Secret Service, he showed scant regard for due process and allowed his agents to make arrests and searches without warrants. Disregard for such niceties may have assisted Baker in his detective work, but he was also endowed with legitimate gifts in that field. Though Baker's men failed to prevent Lincoln's murder, they did apprehend the assassin, James Wilkes Booth. Shortly afterwards, Baker fell from favor and, upon the conclusion of hostilities, the Secret Service was temporarily disbanded. President Andrew Johnson turned against Baker on discovering that he maintained an espionage system in the White House. Baker thereupon hit back at Johnson and was an adverse witness during the hearings to impeach that unfortunate president. In a revelation of some import for the future of the Secret Service, its former chief was accused of having forged some of the letters incriminating Johnson. Baker died in 1868.[30]

Ironically, the menace of forgery was responsible for the revival of the Secret Service soon after its temporary disbandment. Forgery had always been a lucrative pastime, but Reconstruction governments were forced to take note of it for special reasons. Speculation and economic instability were rife in the years after the war. At a time when scoundrels in high places were abusing their legitimacy to defraud the public purse, crimi- nals with an artistic flair felt more inclined than usual to indulge it in a profitable fashion. They were the nonrespectable counterpart of the "greenback" agitation, a demand for monetary inflation which began with Western farmers in 1867 and became a widespread organized movement in the 1870s. Politicians were forced to act by a proliferation of forged greenback Treasury certificates (issued from 1862 onward to finance the war) and Treasury bonds. Because of these factors, the Secret Service was reorganized, not under the War, but under the Treasury Department.[31]

During the next twenty-five years, the Secret Service developed tech- niques which were to be of use to the government during the war with Spain in 1898. Its agents became expert in the detection and, possibly, the practice of forgery. They developed into a professional corps of detec- tives whose techniques were easily adaptable to the contingencies of espionage. For this reason and for others discussed in the next two chap- ters, the Secret Service once again shot into prominence in 1898.

In the meantime, doubts about the presidential use of diplomatic agents had rekindled. In 1893, debate broke out in earnest, but president and Senate reached an accommodation at least on principle. In that year, President Grover Cleveland had sent a secret commissioner, J. H. Blount, to Hawaii. The commissioner was reported to have taken a hand in the revolution aaginst Queen Liliuokalini which ultimately led to Hawaii's annexation by the United States. The antiimperialist Senator George F. Hoar, of Massachusetts, averred that Blount's appointment was uncon- stitutional.[32] Hoar had been blooded in Constitutional debate during the fight over the Reconstruction amendments adopted to help the blacks at the conclusion of the Civil War. The experienced senator observed that the president

> may to aid him in the performance and exercise of his executive
> powers, if convenient, appoint a mere agent as a messenger, or
> spy, or a person to gather or convey information. But such a per-
> son, so appointed, could be in no sense an officer of the United
> States, could take no office, could exercise no official function, and
> could do no act whatever which could have any binding force on
> the United States, or any of the people, merely because he had
> done it.[33]

A century after Congress had established a contingency fund which might finance spies, a senator had made the distinction in principle so necessary to the uncontroversial operation of secret intelligence. He could not have foreseen that, with the growth of intelligence from 1898 on, the distinction would be ignored in practice.

For more than eighty years following the Hoar compromise, the debate over intelligence authorization flared up with regularity. Its scope broadened. The controversy came to embrace not only senatorial rights in the field of diplomacy but also the methods and operational scope of simple spies. The discussion of authorization took in covert operations, the desirability of overlap between surveillance at home and abroad, the permissible degree of centralization under one agency, and the importance of organizational distinctions between the collection, evaluation, and dissemination of information. After 1898, the debate grew more serious because of the increasing perception of the need for a peacetime intelligence capacity. The CIA provoked criticism in part because the scale of its operations seemed to have exceeded that necessity. CIA troubles also arose, however, because the agency was the offspring of a shotgun wedding between equally reluctant parties—the Department of State and the strange hybrid creature, modern American counterintelligence. So, to the paternity of that celebrated child, the CIA, there have emerged a not altogether surprising number of claimants. One can make one's choice, in the absence of a historical blood test, from such candidates as Pinkerton, Ralph H. Van Deman, Polk, Gordon Auchincloss, William J. Burns, J. Edgar Hoover, William J. Donovan, Adolf A. Berle, and Allen Dulles. But the first case deserving of serious examination is that of John E. Wilkie and his Treasury men.

2

Rivals of the Secret Service

From the recesses of a photograph taken in 1899 he peers at the curious historian with intent, bespectacled eyes set over a manicured mustache, authoritative jowls, an abrasively colorful bow tie and a very smart, if far from quiet, Harris tweed jacket.[1] John E. Wilkie was a man of sartorial and practical boldness. He was characteristically immodest about his achievements as American spymaster in the Spanish war of 1898. Yet, at the same time, he shunned fame and notoriety. Cultivating obscurity for sound professional reasons, he remained little more than a name to most of his contemporaries.

Wilkie not only disposed of America's clandestine enemies in the course of hostilities but stole a march on the domestic rivals of the Secret Service. Soon after the sinking of the *Maine* in February, 1898, when it became "apparent that a conflict with Spain was inevitable," Wilkie sent a letter to the secretary of the treasury, the venerable, white-whiskered Chicago banker Lyman J. Gage, proposing the creation of an "emergency" or "auxiliary" force within the Secret Service division of his department.[2] "I respectfully request," wrote Wilkie, unobtrusively inserting the thin end of a multibillion-dollar wedge, "that the sum of five thousand dollars be allotted to this Division from the fifty-million-dollar defense fund, said five thousand dollars to be employed in defraying the expenses of such special investigations as we may from time to time be called upon to make."[3] Gage "at once approved" the application and sent Wilkie, in the company of Assistant Secretary Frank A. Vanderlip, a former financial

editor of the *Chicago Tribune,* to see President William McKinley.[4] Mc-
Kinley approved the five thousand dollars without hesitation; within
weeks, furthermore, the President from Ohio increased the amount to
fifty thousand dollars.[5]

As we shall see in the next chapter, Wilkie made the most of his early
financial backing, building the Secret Service into the pivotal intelligence
agency of its day. There were both positive and negative reasons for his
success. On the positive side, he was undoubtedly assisted by the high
regard in which McKinley and most of his business-dominated cabinet
held Secretary Gage. McKinley had hardly known Gage prior to including him in his cabinet. The banker had incurred the hostility of some
conservatives for his sympathy with labor radicals and the enmity of
some reformers for his conservative monetary views. The president, however, felt increasingly drawn to Gage because of his personal charm and
experienced an ever warmer glow of satisfaction when his Treasury selection solved one fiscal problem after another. Gage put American finances
on a sound basis in the Spanish–American war, and his known sympathy
for labor must have lessened potential hostility to Secret Service investigators among the many patriotic working people who cooperated with
Wilkie.[6]

There was, in any case, good reason for resorting to Gage's department. Treasury offered appropriate facilities in its Coast Guard, as well as
its Secret Service. Since 1895, coast guard cruisers and revenue cutters
had operated against insurrectionists attempting to leave American shores
for Cuba. These filibusters were dispatched by the *Junta,* the general
legation of the Cuban "republic" in the United States.[7] It was a simple
matter to redirect the vigilance of the Treasury Department toward
Spanish activities. The assets of the Treasury Department may be added
to the influence of Gage as factors strengthening Wilkie's claim to quick
and continuing presidential support.

Wilkie's personal qualities also commended him to McKinley and his
circle. He did not have extensive experience in espionage or detection
work, although he had once worked as a special crime reporter for the
Chicago Tribune. What commended him to his superiors was his essential
soundness. He came from the right part of the country, had worked also
as a financial journalist for the *Tribune,* and had engaged in banking and
steamship business during a visit to London.[8] This background made him
not only the natural consort and choice of men like his friend Vanderlip,
and Gage and McKinley, but also the consort and choice dictated by
wisdom. For the success of the Secret Service owed much to the fact that
an intimate and leak-proof clique was at its center.

Though the Secret Service enjoyed immediate success, it suffered from
some chronic drawbacks which suggest that the Treasury men became
preeminent partly by default. One of the Secret Service's deficiencies was

that it did not supply political intelligence. Its exclusive concern with military and naval information was no great drawback once hostilities had begun, but it is conceivable that a proper appraisal of Spain's intentions in the spring of 1898, liberal and appeasatory as they were, might have averted the conflict in the first place. More serious as a wartime consideration was the Secret Service's practice of centralizing the information collected without attempting to evaluate or disseminate it.

A further drawback was that the Service eschewed offensive spying in favor of counterespionage. In some respects, it is true, its net was far flung, covering the two-ocean war theater. Wilkie ran a major intelligence operation in Canada. In the fall of 1899, Assistant Secretary Vanderlip triumphantly exposed a plot to sell inferior merchandise to Cuban consumers; his revelation that Massachusetts businessmen had flooded the island with circulars "inviting the 'come-ons' to come to Boston to purchase the green goods" was based on the work of Secret Service men who had discovered the fraudulent nature of the trade and indicates that Treasury agents operated in Cuba as well as in the northern dominion.[9] Yet, on the whole, the special force of 1898 was created to protect U.S. territory. Even in the pursuit of that limited goal, the Treasury men suffered from a crucial incapacity, the lack of a diplomatic back-up service to extricate them from difficult situations.

None of the several other possible choices was, however, satisfactory. The "Pinkerton" solution was one to which the government might have turned. The Pinkerton Company, in its antebellum days, was based in Chicago, a frontier trading city with no proper police force, but after 1865 it broadened under the direction of its founder and his two sons, Robert A. and William A. Pinkerton, to become the widely established Pinkerton National Detective Agency, the leading American private detective organization by the late nineteenth century.[10] It was a free-enterprise business in both practice and outlook. The Pinkerton family's firm opposition to anarchism, Communism, and socialism would have commended them not only to McKinley's cabinet but also to most subsequent cabinets. Had the Pinkertons been taken on in 1898, there would have been an intriguing twentieth-century rivalry between the state-run spy systems of Germany and Russia and the privately run American detective agency. The Pinkerton Agency would have taken on subcontracted work and, in that respect, would have resembled the various departmental field agencies which in fact performed government spy work in and after 1898—the Treasury's Secret Service, the Justice Department's Bureau of Investigation (later known as the FBI), and the Army and Navy intelligence services.

The government was deterred from considering the use of Pinkertons in 1898 because the detective dynasty had been charged with inefficiency, fabrication, class bias, and lack of patriotism. Several charges of inefficiency had been made about Allan Pinkerton's period of government service in the Civil War. In 1872 and 1895, President Lincoln's friend and biographer Ward H. Lamon published works in which he claimed that the Baltimore assassination plot supposedly foiled by Pinkerton in 1861 had been invented by the detective himself in order to further his ambitions.[11] Secondly, Pinkerton senior was charged with having betrayed the identity of Timothy Webster, a clever Northern agent who acquired the secrets of Richmond by posing as a Confederate spy; Webster was executed in April 1862 after his chief had contacted him through couriers known to the Southerners.[12] Finally, Pinkerton's dismissal as Secret Service chief at the same time as the replacement of his patron, General McClellan, had been no accident. McClellan had been overcautious as commander-in-chief because he tended to exaggerate the strength of enemy forces. Pinkerton had done nothing to embolden him, since, as the historian Peter J. Parish puts it, the detective "made it his business in peace and war to provide his clients with the kind of information they wanted."[13]

Pinkerton's subsequent career and the reputation of his agency confirmed the wisdom of McKinley's decision to use other means of intelligence in 1898. To begin with, the former secret service chief was the first to make money on a large scale through labor espionage, becoming well known for his hostility to labor organizations from the 1870s onward. During the Civil War, Pinkerton had referred with contempt to Confederate spies in Washington, D.C., who enjoyed immunity from molestation because of their "entree to the gilded salon of the aristocratic traitors."[14] But his youthful radicalism, like that of his Scottish compatriot Andrew Carnegie, was democratic republican, not leveler.[15] Workers regarded Pinkerton and "Pinkerton men" as their enemies. The bloody and unsuccessful attempt of the Pinkerton Agency to break the Homestead Steel Strike of 1892 reinforced this outlook.[16] It would have been impolitic for the standard bearers of the Republican party to rely on Pinkerton men in 1898. Such reliance might have been misplaced in any case. Counterespionage was a most important aspect of secret service work in the Spanish war. Events were to show that the success of counterespionage depended on public cooperation, and the Pinkerton Agency had become too unpopular to inspire such help.

It is conceivable that, in spite of these limitations, the Pinkerton men might have worked for the government. There was a precedent within the span of the post-Homestead years, for in 1894 Robert A. Pinkerton, in charge of the New York office of the agency (Allan Pinkerton having died in 1884), had supplied an operative to Richard Olney, Democratic attorney general and future secretary of state, for secret work in the South.[17] The New York office was strategically situated for Atlantic coast counterespionage in 1898; the McKinley administration may have turned away from Pinkerton men only because of the increasingly serious nature of complaints delivered to the War Department. In January, an early complainer averred that Robert Pinkerton was working for Spain and protested the rumored possibility that William Pinkerton, head of the Chicago office and successor to his father's dynasty, would become head of the Secret Service.[18] There is, however, no evidence that the government took heed of this first complaint (though it was passed on to the Secret Service itself). It may be surmised that little weight was attached to a letter from an anonymous New Yorker, "one who loves his country, and Great Grand Father at Bunker Hill," who perhaps merely presupposed from the Pinkertons' labor record that they would work for Spain against freedom.[19] There was, in any case, no reason why even Robert Pinkerton should have been disqualified from service for having worked for Spain prior to the outbreak of hostilities. Indeed, such experience would have been a special qualification for work in American counterespionage.

Suspicions that Pinkerton agents continued to work for Spain after the declaration of war in April 1898, however, ensured that American espionage would remain permanently on a state footing. These suspicions were never confirmed or even acknowledged by the Secret Service itself, but they did cause concern in official circles. They were induced, in the first instance, by the interception of a letter, dated June 6, 1898, addressed to the head of Spanish intelligence in North America by a spy in Pennsylvania, which referred to assistance received from Pinkerton men.[20] Perhaps because of the elusive nature of the author, his letter was ignored.

A few days later, Assistant Secretary of the Interior Webster Davis received a more disturbing letter from a Kansas City businessman, who disclosed: "I have just learned that a friend of mine here has information which convinces him that seven men, now in the employ of the Pinkertons, are using their efforts to advance the interests of Spain."[21] The businessman's informant was Harry C. Dunlap, who had worked for the Pinkerton Agency for two years. Dunlap claimed that Pinkerton agents were observing American forts along the Atlantic coast. Such surveillance was certainly a Spanish objective, and it was known that Spanish intelligence agents in Canada had retained the services of a detective agency. The accusation tied in with the earlier accusation against Robert Pinkerton, in charge of the Eastern operations of the Pinkerton Agency. On the other hand, many Americans, Dunlap included, had perhaps become excited about the prospect of coastal bombardment, and there was a scarcity of objective opinion about Pinkertons. Why should the government heed unsubstantiated allegations? No doubt in this case officials were moved because the source of the defamatory information was a businessman. The Department of the Interior official passed on to George

D. Meiklejohn of the War Department his "communication from a very worthy gentleman, citizen of Kansas City," expressing "no doubts that the information will be of some importance to your Department."[22] The letter ultimately found its way into the secret service files.

Thus the Pinkerton Agency did not supply American intelligence needs in 1898 because it was in bad odor, largely as a result of its failure in the Civil War and its reputed Spanish association. These encumbrances did not, however, afflict the prospects of rival detective agencies. A number of these had emerged since the Civil War to compete with the agency which by the 1890s had supplied an eponym for private investigation. Founded in 1873, the Thiel Detective Service Company provided national coverage. Boston had been served by the James R. Wood Detective Agency, Inc. since 1879; New Orleans—a center of Spanish intrigue—by Boylan's Detective Agency since 1880.[23] McKinley might well have turned to one or several of such agencies, but he did not.

"Pinkerton" had become an eponym because workingmen considered that all detective agencies shared the antilabor outlook of the Pinkerton family. The free-enterprise detective industry did, in fact, owe its growth not to the righteousness of the private eye or to divorce work (which came later, with the changed attitudes of the Progressive era) but to the good money to be made from bad industrial relations. It was partly because they derived nourishment from that ideological mainspring of the Populist-Progressive period, the fear of violent class revolution, that detective agencies proliferated and prospered between the industrial recovery of the late 1890s and the recession in President Wilson's first administration. The notorious detective James Farley was reputed to have made a million dollars out of strike-breaking work by 1914.[24] Relatively minor agencies like the Manufacturers Information Bureau Company opened branches in several cities.[25] By 1915, William J. Burns had built an agency with twenty offices in the United States and one in London. There were about 270 agencies engaged in labor work by 1914; it is understandable that workingmen regarded all private agencies as forms of "Pinkertonism" and that trade unionists and socialists zealously attacked detective agencies.[26]

By the end of the nineteenth century, many states, under pressure from the Knights of Labor, the Populists, and the American Federation of Labor (AFL), had passed "anti-Pinkerton" laws. This was but the beginning of a tradition that influenced not only contemporaries but also later historians. Thus the U.S. Commission on Industrial Relations between 1912 and 1916, and the LaFollette Committee in the 1930s, gave sympathetic hearings to the critics of labor spies and armed guard agencies.[27] Jack London, Robert Hunter, and Sidney Howard were socialist politicians and writers in the vanguard of the onslaught on the despised "finks." Their imprecations reinforced the idea that the private eye was an effective ancillary to employers and to probusiness government in their fight against strikers and socialists.[28]

Detectives themselves strengthened this impression. Allan Pinkerton anticipated political antisocialism when in 1877 he advertised the services of his men to employers who feared the Communist, who "leaves his slimy trail and wields with deadly effect his two powerful levers: secrecy/combination."[29] Burns evinced a similar attitude a third of a century later when he maintained that the AFL, regarded by many as a relatively conservative institution, was waging a "masked war" against society.[30] This ideological outlook was, to a degree, a response to McKinley's assassination by an anarchist in 1901 and to the Bolshevik success in Russia in 1917. The Justice Department as a result subcontracted counter-revolutionary work to private detectives in World War I. Burns, who had been trained under Wilkie in 1898 and applied secret service methods to his own agency, became head of the Bureau of Investigation (it became known as the FBI in the 1930s) from 1921 to 1924 partly because of his antiradical record.

At the same time, a distrust of private agencies survived in government circles, so that Burns's appointment in 1921 was unusual. Burns himself delivered, by implication, a blistering verdict on his private competitors: "I render daily reports, and on these reports place the amount of money expended each day, which no other agency does...."[31] Many of Burns's competitors were solely concerned with making money and were willing to encourage radicalism to that end. A government that took on such help would have been encouraging the very tendencies it sought to suppress, at the cost of gratuitously alienating labor. Furthermore, the enemy in 1898 was conservative, not revolutionary, and it was in that year that precedents were set for modern American intelligence. There was no room, during the Spanish war or later, for the opportunistic, mercenary spy.

The war of 1898 did provide scope for military intelligence work, both Army and Navy, and military intelligence enjoyed certain advantages over Pinkertonism. Civil War memories enhanced rather than tarnished the martial image. There was vociferous hostility to the Army among a good number of working people because of its role in breaking the American Railway Union during the Pullman strike of 1894, but the Navy was not unpopular. Indeed, ever since novelist Herman Melville's popularization of the successful campaign against flogging in the 1840s, the U.S. Navy had enjoyed the reputation of being humane toward ordinary seamen.[32] Naval reorganization in the last two decades of the nineteenth century had proceeded apace and the maritime branch of the U.S. armed forces by 1898 included an offensive espionage service. This comparative state of preparedness of the clandestine branches of the armed forces had come about because of the drawing-board rivalry of the United States with a great military power, Britain.

Fenianism awoke American statesmen to the danger of penetration, not in itself, but in the reaction it provoked from British intelligence. In 1866 and 1870 the Fenians, a military wing of the Irish-Americans desiring Irish independence, invaded Canada. The preparatory activities of this group had not been observed by any American agents and might have embarrassed Anglo-American relations in a manner beyond the control of the American government. The Fenian invasions came to nothing only because they were observed and, in 1870, actually directed by the British agent Thomas Miller Beach (alias Henri Le Caron).[33] Beach operated on American soil on behalf of the British goevrnment in a manner which was not immediately harmful to the United States. But it was patently the case that, for all American politicians knew at the time, he might have been infinitely dangerous.

The American government simply could not afford to ignore the intelligence activities and contingency planning of rival powers. In October 1886 Lord Charles Beresford submitted to the British Admiralty a paper called "Reorganization of Foreign Intelligence Committee now Naval Intelligence Department." Beresford complained of Britain's lack of naval preparedness in view of the fact that "France, Germany, Russia, Austria, and Italy have a regular Head-quarters' Staff at their Admiralties, whose duties consist solely in organizing plans of the most elaborate description for war preparations. These plans are kept to hand in the Office, and corrected in detail every three months...."[34] The United States did not figure in Beresford's list of well-prepared rival powers, yet, like Britain, it faced an array of naval intelligence services in other countries.

The Royal Navy's Intelligence Department, formed after Beresford's promptings, suffered from low pay and low morale.[35] Nevertheless, British naval and military intelligence had serious contingency plans for war against the United States. These reached full maturity in the 1890s, when the growth of the U.S. Navy coincided with Anglo-American diplomatic disputes.[36] Major-General Sir John Charles Ardagh, director of British military intelligence from 1896 to 1901, proposed a plan for cooperation with the Royal Navy in defense of the Great Lakes and Canada. Lieutenant Colonel Percy Lake of the Canadian Militia advised him on Canadian military potential. Ardagh insisted that a British-Canadian campaign, in order to succeed, would have to be offensive rather than defensive.[37] There were, then, real dangers in imperial rivalry with Britain. As late as 1904, the London War Office received a study of Anglo-American war strategy from its military attaché in Washington.[38] It is true that British intelligence continued to suffer from low morale; Ardagh complained on his resignation in 1907 that he had been "a *vox clamantis in deserto.*"[39] This is, however, the occupational hazard of a spy chief operating in a civilian-dominated society. It should not be allowed to obscure the realities of U.S.–British rivalry before 1917.

The Lords of the Admiralty commented on Ardagh's plea for the defense of the Great Lakes in 1896: "In view of the rapid increase of the American Navy and the impetus given toward perfecting the defensive arrangements of the Country, . . . the proposal, regarded as a policy, can only have a temporary value."[40] The British were aware that the Americans were catching up in military strength. By the 1880s, the gore of Gettysburg and other Civil War battles was receding into memory, and new imperial strategies were afoot. In the field of offensive intelligence, the United States may have lagged behind some countries, but it was clearly coming abreast of Great Britain.

The development of American naval intelligence accompanied and helped to shape the emergence of a great U.S. battle fleet in the late nineteenth century. Rear Admiral Stephen B. Luce campaigned for Navy reform in the 1870s and 1880s. He complained in 1877 that "the naval officer whose principal business it is to fight is not taught the higher branches of his profession."[41] To remedy the situation, he was instrumental in the creation, in 1882, of the Office of Naval Intelligence (ONI), "for the purpose," according to a departmental order, "of collecting and recording such naval information as may be useful to the department in time of war, as well as in peace."[42] In 1884, a further Navy Department order established the naval War College. Naval officers were thus to be furnished with both raw intelligence and the educational background to interpret it; administratively, the link between espionage and education was to continue as a permanent feature in the American armed forces.

From the outset, there was opposition to naval postgraduate education and intelligence. Old-fashioned naval officers saw no need for it. More serious, Congress at first refused to appropriate funds. Representative Hilary A. Herbert of Alabama referred contemptuously to the "alleged war college but really a dancing school" envisaged for Newport, Rhode Island.[43] The War College and ONI had been established by department orders without the consent of Congress and without proper staffing arrangements. Captain Alfred T. Mahan won good publicity for the War College in the 1890s following the publication of his influential book, *The Influence of Sea Power upon History, 1660–1783* (1890). The young Theodore Roosevelt, then a mugwump civil service commissioner recently frustrated in his desire to become assistant secretary of state, backed him up by campaigning among his friends on the Hill in behalf of the War College.

ONI, by comparison, remained a backwater under the discreet guidance of Lieutenant T. B. M. Mason. As the years went by, Roosevelt became convinced of the relative importance of ONI, an institution which he came to regard as more practical than the academic War College. In 1897 the future president, by then assistant secretary of the Navy, wrote to Lieutenant Commander William W. Kimball, who was noted for his recent creation of a U.S. submarine flotilla, that the War College "performs an invaluable function; but it is a pedogogic function, and this means that the War College must ultimately stand under the Bureau of Naval Intelligence and not above it. . . . The Chief of the Office of Naval Intelligence has got to be the man on whom we rely most for initiating strategic work. . . ."[44]

As the Spanish war approached and Roosevelt laid his own precocious plans for naval action, he consulted Mahan, Kimball, and naval intelligence officers. His War Board was, however, an informal arrangement.[45] It was not until 1899, in the aftermath of the Spanish war, that Congress appropriated funds to establish a clerical staff for ONI. For this reason, ONI did not supply the overall intelligence coordination which suddenly became necessary in 1898. On the other hand, Mason had managed to poach a few clerks from other offices, and a few more had been smuggled in under annual "Increase in the Navy" appropriations bills; ONI was probably the Secret Service's nearest rival in 1898.[46]

The year 1885 was in some ways the turning point in the history of military intelligence in the United States. That was the year the Military Information Division (MID; subsequently known by several different titles in the wake of successive reorganizations) was founded. It is possible to regard the emergence of MID, however, as one of several milestones along a well trodden road. Military intelligence had not remained static in the United States since 1789, when the Constitution had called for a War Department whose total personnel, when established, consisted of the secretary, Henry Knox, and one clerk whose duties did not include spying. Secretary of War James Monroe sent military observers to Europe in 1815, a precedent followed by Secretary Jefferson Davis during the Crimean war in 1855 and by Secretary William W. Belknap during the Franco–Prussian war in 1870–1871. In the Mexican war of 1846–1848, cavalry officers such as Robert E. Lee, P. G. T. Beauregard, George G. Meade, and George B. McClellan developed the art of reconnaissance, which played so important a part during the Civil War and was kept alive by anti-Indian scouts during the Plains wars of the 1870s. The American army had not remained completely ignorant of foreign military developments, nor did it neglect the aboriginal skills identified by George Washington in the context of the French and Indian wars of the 1750s as "skulking."[47]

In 1880, General William T. Sherman instructed all officers traveling abroad to make military observations and report them to the adjutant general. Soldiers noted with envy the formation of the ONI in 1882. The

Army and Navy Journal in 1885 commented on the unsatisfactory neglect of information reaching the adjutant general's office and called for a system of collation. The formation of MID immediately afterwards was a response to these pressures. It was not, however, a very sure response. In 1892, the infant MID was saved from the annihilating embrace of the expanding Signal Corps only because the adjutant general's office, threatened with a slight paring of its bureaucracy, suddenly awoke to the significance of espionage.[48] The most that can be said about the fledgling MID is that an attempt had been made to systematize Army intelligence hitherto gathered on a haphazard basis.

The attempt failed. There was no general staff or war college to back up MID until after the turn of the century. The American people had a long history of suspicion toward standing armies and associated phenomena. Organizational inertia and states' rights agitation strengthened resistance to the establishment of a vigorous general staff which might handle intelligence reports from all quarters.[49] MID was no better equipped to supply central facilities and the ingredients of counterespionage, so essential in 1898, than was ONI. On the other hand, MID was in a better position to cooperate with the Secret Service in some respects. For example, there was liaison between Army intelligence and the service in Tampa, Florida, where Spanish agents tried to infiltrate the armed forces embarking for Cuba.[50] While it is true that until the 1890s MID relied almost exclusively on secondary sources of information, such as State Department reports and newspapers, there are indications that it was at least becoming capable of handling purely military information. In anticipation of war, MID opened a file on Cuba in 1892. By the spring of 1898, MID chief Arthur L. Wagner (later director of the Army War College) had assembled eleven officers under his direct command. He was also able to call on the help of forty National Guard intelligence officers spread throughout the nation and of sixteen military attachés overseas. His MID officers, together with ten civilian clerks and two messengers, were crammed into a tiny four-room suite in Washington, D.C. The total congressional appropriation for intelligence work in Washington and overseas was a mere $3,640. But at least a start had been made.[51]

Army and Navy agents in the field performed several valuable services in 1898. From London, they sent back military gossip about Spain. In Cuba, Andrew S. Rowan of MID penetrated Spanish lines and contacted the insurgent leader, Calixto Garcia.[52] Victor Blue, a future chief of staff of the Pacific fleet, crossed the Spanish lines three times on the same island. In Spain itself, penetration was effected by a Spanish-American graduate of West Point whose identity the authorities never disclosed According to one version, he was Aristides Moreno, later in charge of counter espionage on General Pershing's staff at Chaumont in 1917–1918.[53] This agent claimed to have elicited, by exploiting the hospitality of the

Spanish Admiral Camara at Cadiz, the intelligence that Spain did not intend to bombard the Atlantic coast of the United States. The story was potentially revolutionary, for America had lavished great expense on the fortification of her shores. However, there is evidence that the Spanish authorities suspected the allegiance of the American agent. Camara may well have made use of his ingenuousness by feeding him false information.[54] The story of military field intelligence in 1898 is the familiar one of bravery and mixed success.

The most significant peacetime extension of military intelligence prior to 1898 was the establishment of the attaché system. A director of ONI maintained in 1920 that the office, "from its inception, has been based on the proposition of having naval attachés abroad to collect information."[55] Similarly, an Army historian has averred that the War Department was unable from its own resources to supply even "a minimum coverage of foreign military developments" until the designation of the first full-time military attachés in 1889.[56] The development of the attaché system brought about a substantial improvement in peacetime intelligence collation and illustrated the way in which the offensive intelligence branches of the armed forces came to rely on the State Department for cover.

When Congress appropriated funds in 1889 to send military officers abroad as attachés, it was against the background of the prior adoption of this system of observation by other powerful countries. Spain had sent attachés to America immediately after the Civil War. (One of them walked off with a plan of the Atlantic coastal defenses in 1898.) France and Russia soon followed suit, to be joined by Peru in 1871 and by other nations great and small thereafter. The attachés were frequently posted to New York, where every immigrant was a potential spy, rather than to Washington. The attraction of the suddenly fashionable method of espionage was that attachés received diplomatic appointments, being officially responsible to their country's ambassador in a nation under observation. Thus the attaché enjoyed diplomatic immunity while his assistants could be given cover within the embassy in the form of apocryphal appointments As a special correspondent of the *Boston Herald* put it, "The accomplices he corrupts and the spies he employs may be hanged or shot, but the attaché goes free. . . ."[57]

During President Benjamin Harrison's administration, Secretaries of State James G. Blaine and John W. Foster (the latter a grandfather of Allen Dulles of the CIA) experimentally allowed the appointment of attachés overseas. From 1893, at the beginning of President Grover Cleveland's second administration, Hilary A. Herbert—by then secretary of the Navy and a convert to the need for better intelligence—and Secretary of War Daniel S. Lamont put the American attaché system on a regular basis. By the close of the century, U.S. intelligence officers were culling military information in Paris, Berlin, London, St. Petersburg, Vienna, Peking, Tokyo, Rio de Janeiro, The Hague, Lima, Lisbon, Berne, and Caracas. The United States now had a permanent corps of military and naval officers abroad whereas previously it had sent investigators overseas only in troubled times. At home, MID and ONI collated and sometimes published the resulting information. It arrived, however, via State Depatment channels, thus enjoying the same immunity as the attachés and conferring potential power on the secretary of state [58]

But ONI and MID, like "Pinkertonism," suffered from several limitations which prevented them from occupying, singly or together, a central position in American intelligence in 1898. To their incapacity in counterintelligence, their lack of funds, and their limitations in field-agent expertise was added their heavy dependence on the Department of State. Yet it may be argued that any intelligence agency, the Secret Service included, would have had to depend on State for cover, deplomatic immunity, or extrication from embarrassing situations. The selection of the Secret Service may best be understood in the light of the few intelligence options open to McKinley. He could, as has been noted, have used a private agency. He could have allowed the Department of State to develop its own intelligence force (an experiment tried in the 1920s and 1940s). He could have allowed State to coordinate various existing agencies (the World War I solution). Finally, there was a more conservative solution, constituting, nevertheless, a logical first step and using existing resources. The president could have allowed a single especially appropriate agency to become ascendant, with the backing of the State Department. This was what happened to the Secret Service in 1898. Wilkie's Treasury men were chosen because of their counterintelligence capability, investigative expertise, and uncontroversial reputation. It was they who, equipped with these qualities, faced up in the Spanish–American war to the determined spy ring organized by an aristocrat from Seville.

3

The Montreal Spy Ring
of 1898

Ramon de Carranza was well connected in the Spanish Admiralty, thirsted for action on the high seas, despaired of victory without his own vigorous presence off the shores of Cuba, and despised the profession to which wartime necessity had consigned him. For the young lieutenant was a spy. His aristocratic background had helped him become naval attaché in Washington, a post congenial enough in peacetime but carrying the responsibility for espionage work upon the outbreak of hostilities. Carranza's aspirations to glory led him to loathe his intelligence role during the war of 1898. Yet he performed it diligently. He might have had an influence on the course of hostilities but for the vigilance of the U.S. Secret Service and (that constant nightmare of the spy) the indiscretions of his superiors.

Whatever the ultimate fate of Carranza's spy network, its initial potency should not be underestimated. Indeed, the activities of Wilkie's men in 1898 are best understood in the light of the very considerable challenge facing them. The situation confronting American counter-intelligence in the Spanish war was clearly exploitable by the enemy. It was the more problematic because the nature of the Spanish challenge was indefinite. In spite of tactful disclaimers from the countries involved, Spain in 1898 continued to expect aid from Catholic and monarchist Europe.[1] This may have accounted for her choice of Montreal, in French Canada, as a center for intrigue.

Reports to the effect that Spanish agents were about to raise the holy banner among the Catholic masses of North America reached the attentive ears of Wilkie but were as lacking in substantiation as stories about Iberian plans to sabotage installations and poison troops in the United States.[2] For other undercover operations there was firmer proof. A pro-Spanish element was willing to cooperate with Carranza in cities like Tampa, Florida, where strife was to continue in the Latin American community long after the guns of imperial Spain had been silenced. During the war itself, Spanish counterinsurgency flourished in New Orleans, Mobile, Key West, and Tampa.[3] A member of the Cuban revolutionary *Junta* reported at length to the Secret Service about the extent of Spanish activity in New Orleans. The report, sent via a U.S. customs official on June 8, 1898, intimated that there were Franco-Iberian sentiment and activity in New Orleans; that money was collected before the outbreak of hostilities to furnish Spain with a gunboat; that the reactionary Spanish Society included several former army officers; and that resources were still being sent to Spanish forces through the coastal towns of Mexico.[4]

The Secret Service obtained proof of another danger to national security when it began to intercept letters bearing suspicious addresses, such as the one from Agnes Harrison of Santa Cruz, posted to Spanish premier Praxedes Sagastes the day after Congress authorized war, describing the coastal defenses of San Francisco and explaining how they could be circumvented.[5] A real possibility of Spanish naval bombardment existed prior to Admiral William T. Sampson's blockade (from May 10) and ultimate destruction of the second Spanish fleet at Santiago de Cuba. In April, Spain's four armored cruisers capable of speed were a threat to Eastern seaboard towns. The fear that Spanish shells might rain on American civilians and their property was exaggerated, but it is a fact that Segismundo Bermejo, minister of the Spanish Admiralty, ordered the destruction of naval bases along the American coast.[6]

There was considerable scope within the United States for Spanish subversion. But Spanish military espionage in 1898 was directed from Canada. Luis Polo y Bernabé, the Spanish ambassador in Washington, left for the neutral dominion four days before the declaration of war on April 25. Secret Service operatives, two of them in an open manner and another pair unknown to Bernabé, supervised the ex-minister's removal to Toronto. It is not surprising that Wilkie saw through Bernabé's advertised intention of traveling directly on to Spain.[7]

Exactly a month passed between the arrival of the leading figures in the Spanish party in Canada and their departure from home. The Iberian officials, with the assistance of a Canadian detective agency, used the intervening time to establish an information bureau initially located in Toronto. Carranza, who had accompanied Bernabé to Canada in April, justly complained that his job in running the bureau was made unnecessarily difficult by the blunders of his superiors.[8] Barnabé soon moved his suite and the information bureau from Toronto to the Windsor Hotel in Montreal. The conspicuous nature of his error is shown in the identity of other guests at the hotel. Representatives of the Carlist faction, secret service agents, and journalists who mercilessly pursued and identified everyone else jostled shoulders with Spanish spies on the back stairs.[9]

When Bernabé and his party finally sailed for Liverpool on May 21, Carranza and his aides accompanied them. At various ports along the St. Lawrence, the spies discreetly left the ship and traveled back to Montreal, where Carranza had rented a house on Tupper Street. This attempt at subterfuge was fully described in the Canadian press, from whose columns it also appears that a secret service agent—appropriately named Tracer—was a witness to the proceedings.[10]

Impeded though he was by poor morale, bungling officials, and "the most extraordinary vigilance" exercised by Wilkie's men, Carranza tried to obtain information that would be of use to Spanish naval officers and generals.[11] One of his gambits was to dispatch secret agents to gain information about coastal defense and naval strategy. The first of Carranza's spies to be caught was a naturalized English immigrant, George Downing. Downing had been a petty officer on the *Brooklyn*, the Navy cruiser which was later instrumental in the destruction of the Spanish fleet at Santiago. He undertook to obtain information of a strategic nature from the Navy Department and from government navy yards, but Carranza made the mistake of briefing Downing in a hotel room of typical nineteenth-century design. It formed part of a set of connecting rooms which could be rented individually or as a suite. On this occasion Carranza occupied just one of the rooms, with the door leading to the other chamber locked against entry but not against sound waves. On the other side of the door, an American agent was making notes, a summary of which soon reached Wilkie. On May 7, Downing was arrested in Washington in the act of mailing a letter about Navy movements. Two days later, he was found hanging from the bars of his cell window. Wilkie maintained that the remorseful traitor had committed suicide; Carranza conceded that Downing, one of his "two best spies," might have hanged himself, but added, "or else they did it for him."[12]

Not long after this Spanish attempt to obtain information of naval significance, a letter was intercepted, posted from Wyncote, Pennsylvania, addressed to Carranza in Montreal, and signed "J. Henry Balfour." Balfour, if that was his name, referred to previous information he had sent to Carranza and went on to describe in detail the sea approaches to Philadelphia, the hazards of attempting a bombardment, and the potential damage that might be inflicted on the commercial area of the city. Balfour may have been a crank independent of official Spanish espionage, but American counterspies, who had trapped and cross-examined less dangerous operators than Balfour, never discovered anything more about the elusive correspondent.[13]

Carranza was a naval lieutenant, but his brief included Army intelligence. In pursuit of information that would assist Spanish commanders in the field, he employed further secret agents with special functions. He tried to engage men who would enlist in Tampa and San Francisco with the object of joining American land forces in Cuba and the Philippines, learning about U.S. military dispositions, crossing the lines to the Spanish side, and telling all. Needing men with military experience, Carranza appealed to a Canadian detective agency, which in turn referred him to one Frank Arthur Mellor.

A native of Kingston, Ontario Mellor was a former artilleryman who knew which soldiers would be open to offers. A bigamist and a reckless pugilist (one of his wives said he would have taken on heavyweight champion Robert Fitzsimmons), he knew how to exploit other men's weaknesses. He soon got two members of the Kingston battery drunk and bribed them to spy for Spain. One of them "whose name," in Wilkie's words, "might have been Atkins" (he was also known as Prentor), was to go to San Francisco and enlist for the Philippines. But Atkins sobered up and decided "he'd be blowed if he'd fight against White men for any ... foreigner."[14] Pausing only to get drunk again, Atkins staggered into the consul's office in Kingston on May 11, where he made a full statement. Learning that he had been double-crossed, Mellor took prompt action. He beat up Atkins and frightened him into leaving for Liverpool. But Mellor's brutal action came too late. When details of Atkins's confession reached Wilkie via the Department of State, they compromised Mellor.[15]

In addition to recruiting others for spy work, Mellor himself had attempted to enlist at Tampa in the American forces destined for Cuba. He used the identity of a Montreal barman, who promised silence and cooperation in exchange for a woman provided by Mellor. The Army refused to accept Mellor, so he tried to justify his pay by sending strategic information to Carranza. Wilkie's suspicions had already been aroused by Atkins's story, and Secret Service men were watching Mellor in Florida, waiting only for proof before arresting the suspect. At this point, the "Secret Service of the Dominion of Canada" (possibly a name of convenience for British intelligence) provided Wilkie's men, via diplomatic channels, with the current alibis and letter box numbers of Mellor's controllers in Canada. Armed with this information, the U.S. postal authorities intercepted a telegram Mellor sent to Carranza on May 24, and although the coded and pseudonymous message could not have been used in court without revealing details of Canadian cooperation, Mellor was at last placed in custody.[16]

Proof of the case against Mellor was now sought with further

Canadian help, this time unofficial. An estate agent enabled American spies to enter Carranza's house at 42 Tupper Street, Montreal, on May 27 while the Iberian master spy was at breakfast. The spies seized a letter allegedly written by Carranza to his cousin, Admiral J. B. Ymay. As we shall see later, the letter became the center of a diplomatic controversy, Carranza claiming that a version of the text later released by the Secret Service contained interpolations and substitutions damaging to him and to the Spanish cause. According to Wilkie and Ralph D. Redfern, a U.S. Secret Service agent who claimed the credit for having stolen the document, the U.S. version of the "Carranza letter" was genuine and compromised Mellor by referring to the date of his arrest. In the event, Mellor was neither convicted nor released. On August 12, 1898, ten days after the protocol of peace, he became another victim of the prison system, dying of typhoid at Fort McPherson.[17]

In his statement at the Kingston consulate, Atkins had implicated a second member of the local battery, for whom, he claimed, Mellor had also bought drinks and who had also been paid to spy for Spain. But the evidence against this second man, Frederick James Elmhirst, appears to have been slender. Elmhirst did in fact join the Third U.S. Cavalry at Tampa, where he was placed under arrest on June 6 and confined to the county jail. Captain W. S. Scott of the Bureau of Military Intelligence in Tampa interrogated the suspect. He reported that there was virtually no evidence against Elmhirst, who impressed Scott "as a man who is not guilty, though he is an intelligent fellow and possibly has made up his mind to stick to his statement"; Elmhirst maintained that his accusor, Prentor-alias-Atkins, was "a worthless, drunken individual"; it was possible, Scott thought, that a great injustice was being done; Elmhirst deserved at least an early hearing and should be transferred to proper quarters at Fort McPherson.[18] To Scott's complaint, Wilkie replied only that Elmhirst would respond to "a good, hard sweating."[19] Guilty or innocent, Elmhirst was held at McPherson until peace was assured, then released. Elmhirst was the last Spanish emissary from Montreal (or innocent man) to be apprehended by the Secret Service.

When the British government received a photocopy of Carranza's letter, which indicated the existence of an Iberian spy ring in Montreal, it ordered the expulsion of the Spanish officer from Canada. There, according to Wilkie, the story ended.[20] But it is by no means clear that the discrediting of Carranza put a stop to all Spanish espionage centered in Montreal. Because Carranza accused a Canadian detective, Joseph Kellert, of stealing his letter, the Spanish spymaster was detained by legal proceedings until the end of June. One of his colleagues, Juan Du Bose, resisted deportation until early July.[21] On July 5 and 13 a certain "Bonilla," presumed to be Bonilla Y. Martell, the Spanish consul in Montreal, sent coded messages to Victoria, British Columbia. War

Department cryptographers failed to crack the code, which was a new one, but they and Secret Service officials reasoned that the messages probably contained information, forwarded by spies south of the Canadian border and destined for Manila, about U.S. military intentions in the Philippines.[22]

As late as February 5, 1899, the day before the Senate approved the peace treaty with Spain, the Secret Service was trailing Spanish agents traveling between New York and Montreal. This final commission of the war was undertaken by Secret Service agent Owen Owens, who suffered the indignity of being approached at a critical moment by a *New York Sun* reporter and asked whether he was the Secret Service man who was checking on the Spanish agents.[23] In spite of what the modern agent would regard as primitive methods employed by Carranza, his failure should be regarded in the perspective of the overall hopelessness of the Spanish war effort and the comparable mistakes committed by the U.S. "emergency men."

Whatever the operational mistakes of the Secret Service, they did not impair its effectiveness in 1898. The Service owed its success in part to a calculated willingness to overlook Constitutional and legal niceties. On foreign soil, intelligence men got away with improprieties—indeed, felt encouraged by domestic opinion to indulge in them. At home, however, they were aware of skating on thin ice. As Wilkie himself admitted, the Secret Service "existed for the purpose of suppressing counterfeiting, and its operations are limited to that field by the phraseology of the appropriation bill to which it owes its existence."[24] Nevertheless, in the course of exposing the Montreal spy ring, Service operatives broke into a private Canadian residence, stole a letter from that residence, interfered with the U.S. mails, and caused at least one man—Elmhirst—to be confined for the duration of the war without evidence of guilt, indicating a willingness to disregard a suspect's civil liberties.

As the expanded Service became a fixture of the Washington bureaucracy, other abuses crept in. For example, whereas the selection of operatives for the Service was subject to civil service rules, the wheels of bureaucracy soon became checked in the mire of patronage. Senator Henry Cabot Lodge tried to obtain a Secret Service position for a friend as early as May 10, 1898. It is unclear whether or not he succeeded in this or later attempts to place his man in the special force, but it may be significant that by 1919 the Massachusetts statesman was receiving confidential information from Secret Service sources.[25]

The most widespread activity of the Secret Service was the surveillance of suspects. Its agents investigated well over a thousand individuals out of the many more reported to various government departments by zealous members of the public. Many of these suspects had strong sympathy with Spain and had expressed themselves indiscreetly.

Wilkie later revealed that "such persons were watched for a while, and then, if necessary, warned that the Government was aware of their sentiments and intentions, and that any attempt on their part to make a move against the interests of the United States would be followed by arrest." Six hundred men and women who appeared to Wilkie's men to show continued signs of subversive intent were put under "close surveillance for longer or shorter periods."[26] In the course of surveillance, Wilkie ominously but cryptically observed, "there were revealed a great many interesting things that had nothing whatever to do with the Spanish-American war."[27] The special force chief claimed that no class or profession was immune from suspicion: "There were [under close surveillance] professors, diplomats, doctors, merchants, cigar-makers, marines, electrical experts, government employees of foreign birth and uncertain antecedents, capitalists, milliners, dress-makers, society women and servants."[28]

Inevitably, such surveillance led to the invasion of those rights which guaranteed the individual his privacy. In particular there was a lack of regard for the rights of any suspect who spoke a Latin tongue. "It was believed," Wilkie wrote with retrospective evasiveness, "that every large center of population was infested by foreigners of anarchistic tendencies who might seize the opportunity [of the war] for the execution of plots against the officers of the Government or against the welfare of the community at large."[29] For example, Mrs. E. R. Larbig of Brooklyn, New York, insisted in a letter to Wilkie that Spanish and Irish residents were preparing the great American cities for invasion. She knew this was so because Spanish sympathizers had moved into the boarding house where she lived "as reduced circumstances compel one to economize rent money." Mrs. Larbig concluded on a resounding note: "I am an American tracing my decent back to the 'Mayflower'; one of my mother's family fell at Bunker Hill; and one of my paternal great-grand-something was with Washington at Valley Forge. So you can judge what sort of a patriot I am."[30]

Americans were oversuspicious of Catholics of southern European origin, and much of the Secret Service's time and manpower was wasted on wild-goose chases after perfectly innocent Spanish or Italian immigrants. One such chase which led to the detention of an innocent man was the pursuit of Edward G. Montesi, who had emigrated to the United States from Italy at the age of fourteen, in 1870. In 1898, he intended to sail on the English steamer *Tartar Prince* to revisit his native land. He was by now an American citizen, with the Stars and Stripes tattooed on his right arm and a box of handkerchiefs embroidered with the Cuban flag in his luggage. Montesi's wife, her maid, and their two daughters were to accompany him as saloon passengers. At midday on June 11, a crowd of friends gathered on a Brooklyn pier to see the family off.[31]

Shortly before the *Tartar Prince* sailed, Secret Service agents Martin Kastle arrived on board with customs officials and three soldiers. An informant with a grudge against Montesi had alleged that the Italian was a Spanish courier, and Wilkie had sent Kastle on the midnight train from Washington. In order to avoid demonstrations by Montesi's friends or any unfavorable press publicity, Kastle waited for the steamer to sail before acting. He then arrested Montesi without preferring a charge, searched his luggage, read his private correspondence and evesdropped on private conversations between the Italian and his wife. Kastle found nothing of an incriminating nature. Nevertheless, he ordered the *Tartar Prince* to drop anchor off Governor's Island and took the entire Montesi family and their luggage ashore. There Kastle met the inevitable reporter from the *New York Sun,* who suggested that the Montesis be put straight back on the steamer and given a warm send-off. Kastle refused, and the innocent Montesis (who were released the next day without being charged with any crime) missed their boat.[32]

Lieutenant Carranza may have been aiming at a weak spot in the American outlook of 1898 by selecting Englishmen as spies. The Spanish agent who signed himself Balfour told Carranza that Philadelphians "have shown a disposition to embrace and gush over me as I have informed them I am a pronounced Britisher. Americans are great gushers over the British at present as our government and people are pretending great sympathy with them in the fight against good old Spain."[33] That Wilkie's men did not fall into the trap is demonstrated by their apprehension of three British spy suspects. With few exceptions, the outlook of the Secret Service agents seems to have been free of bias. But in their harassment of innocent Catholics they reflected public demands, which were the more strident because of the heightened nationalism of a people at war.

By committing crimes in the name of national security, the Secret Service men of 1898 set a precedent. Some of the grosser intrusions of privacy can be ascribed to the unavoidably bureaucratic nature of a now centrally administered intelligence system operating in a large country. In the Montesi case, for example, operative Kastle repeatedly but unsuccessfully tried to contact Chief Wilkie by telephone and telegraph in order to obtain the authority to release the unjustly detained family.[34] His failure to obtain clearance was symptomatic of the injustices that could occur as a result of the new system of surveillance. That the number of abuses perpetrated by the Secret Service was small is attributable to the fact that bureaucratization had not been taken far. In 1898, as in 1917, central intelligence was entrusted to an informally convened clique. However, in both the Spanish and the German wars, procedures were established which assumed uncontrollable dimensions with the formation of more impersonal surveillance organizations in the future.

The excesses of the Secret Service were partly an accidental consequence of incipient bureaucratic procedure. There was, however, public
support for both the new institution as such and for the methods it used.
There can be little doubt that the extralegal activities of the service,
undertaken on presidential authority, would have been intolerable had
the country earlier been divided over its war aims. But in the summer
of 1898 the country was united. The taxpayers' toleration of expenditure
on an agency for surveillance was implied by their virtual lack of
criticism of the agency and by their active support. The Secret Service
chief complained that he was flooded with applications from cranks who
wanted to become operatives.[35] Nor did Wilkie have any difficulty finding
informers among the American people. Appeals for action by the Secret
Service poured in from every section of society, whether Eastern house-
wives, Midwestern businessmen, or Tennessee miners. Patriotic zeal
encouraged the continued efforts of the emergency force.[36]

It is arguable that, in showing a disregard for legal propriety, the
Secret Service men were giving the American public what it wanted.
The late historian Richard Hofstadter suggested that the general war
hysteria of 1898 occurred because of a national psychological crisis.[37]
Whether or not this is true, many Americans unreasonably expected
Wilkie's men to persecute scapegoats for America's ills, or their own.
Letters from people informing on their neighbors tended to reflect per-
sonal problems such as declining status, nostalgia, and an inability to
cope with newcomers, particularly Catholics from southern Europe.

In spite of its reasonably efficient performance, the Secret Service almost immediately showed signs of giving up its new-found authority in
intelligence matters. The Department of State, the intelligence giant of
the future, took a hand in the affairs of 1898 as soon as the Secret Service
came into contact with diplomatic problems. These arose out of the
suspicion that Mellor, unsavory and guilty though he may have been,
was the victim of a frame-up. Captain Scott of Military Intelligence even
doubted that Mellor was a spy.[38]

In 1898, the Secret Service had a recent history of incidents involving
letters. Before the presidential election of 1888, Sir Lionel Sackville-
West, later Lord Sackville, British ambassador to the United States between 1881 and 1889, foolishly wrote a letter to an unscrupulous correspondent previously unknown to him endorsing the incumbent Grover
Cleveland. The letter, though marked "private," was promptly published
by the Republican press. The British were already in bad odor because of
the Irish question (Irish nationalists on both sides of the Atlantic regarded the rejection of the 1886 Home Rule bill with bitterness), Cleveland lost the election, and Sackville-West was recalled at the request of
the United States, to be replaced, after an interval of British disgruntle-

ment, by Sir Julian Paunceforte.[39] It was after a second letter incident
of this kind that Luis Bernabé had replaced Depuy de Lome as Spanish
ambassador early in 1898. The press had published a letter by de Lome
containing indiscreet remarks about McKinley and America. According to
the Cuban *Junta,* a patriotic Cuban secretary stole the letter, and it is in
fact most unlikely that the Secret Service was involved in either the Sackville-West or the de Lome affair.[40] Nevertheless, both incidents created
preconceptions about the crudity of American methods which the Secret
Service only enhanced by its theft of the Carranza letter.

According to Wilkie, an American agent stole the Carranza letter,
having entered the spy's Tupper Street house on the pretext of wishing
to rent it. The letter, seals unbroken, was entrusted to an American railroad engineer, who took it as far as Vermont, then mailed it to Wilkie in
Washington. On receiving the letter, Wilkie ordered his Montreal agent to
disappear, "to make it absolutely certain that his identity should not be
discovered," waited a week (no explanation given), then made public a
translation of the text (a full version appeared in the *New York Herald* on
June 5) and gave the State Department a photocopy to show to the British
ambassador in Washington.[41] Carranza claimed that parts of the letter
had been forged and other sections badly translated; perhaps Wilkie had
sought to hasten the end of Carranza's spy ring by committing the crime
of secret forgery as well as that of publicly admitted theft.

Since the matter had been made public, the British government was
obliged to respond. The British ambassador in Washington, the increasingly popular and successful Sir Julian Pauncefote, communicated the
contents of the letter as published to Joseph Chamberlain, Britain's secretary of state for the colonies and the cabinet member responsible for
Canada. Chamberlain had married the only daughter of W. C. Endicott,
secretary of war in Cleveland's first administration (the engagement was
kept secret during the controversial campaign of 1888), and the historian
A. E. Campbell has remarked that Anglo-American cooperation was, at
the end of the nineteenth century, "an axiom of British policy."[42] Nevertheless, American truculence in recent disputes over British interests
meant that London was by no means certain to follow the wishes of
Washington.

In the event, Chamberlain telegraphed the governor general of
Canada, Lord Aberdeen, with a decision that favored the United States
in principle: "The Law Officers of the Crown advise that Carranza should
be requested to leave British territory, if the facts are as stated."[43] Britain
and America were about to close ranks in favor of Anglo-Saxon (as opposed to Latin) imperialism. Sir Wilfred Laurier, the Canadian premier,
was obliged to explain to Chamberlain, using Aberdeen as an intermediary, exactly how legal proceedings constituted an obstacle to the immediate departure of Carranza. Joseph Kellert, chief of the Metropolitan

Detective Agency, Montreal, whom the Spaniard had accused of stealing the letter, sued Carranza and Du Bose for damages stemming from false arrest and obtained against them a writ which, under the laws of the province of Quebec, prevented potential debtors from absconding; Du Bose, in turn, threatened to sue the British government; later, several parties concerned with the Tupper Street theft, including Kellert himself, agreed that the Canadian private detective, and not a Secret Service agent, had organized the break-in.[44]

Chamberlain, though forceful in his request for Carranza's deportation, asked that the facts be verified. In a successful attempt to allay Britain's doubts, Secretary of State William R. Day now performed the role of intermediary. He arranged a call by Pauncefote on Wilkie to inspect the original of the Carranza letter. Pauncefote stated that the purpose of this visit was "to establish the fact whether any interpolation had been made." The British ambassador took with him, not a forgery expert, but Calderon Carlisle, legal adviser to the British embassy and a Spanish scholar. Carlisle confirmed that the Spanish text put before him had been correctly translated by the Americans. To Pauncefote it was "manifest" that "there was no erasure or interpolation whatever in the letter."[45]

The British reaction to the Carranza letter caused diplomatic friction and endangered Britain's position as a neutral power. Spanish indignation over the deportation demand may have reflected dismay at the dishonor imparted to Carranza rather than a firm position on the merits of the case, but it was serious nonetheless. Spanish protests to the British might well have taken effect against the background of Anglo-American differences in the 1890s. In 1898 there had been talk of war in defense of the Monroe Doctrine when British Guiana (now Guyana) laid claim to some disputed territory on its boundary with Venezuela, on which gold had been discovered. More recently, there had been controversy over the propriety of allowing sulphur shipments of use to the U.S. war effort to pass through neutral Canada. The British needed allies and went out of their way to placate the United States over such issues. Nevertheless, it was a tribute to the effectiveness of State Department pressure that Britain was prevailed upon to remain firm in its request for the departure of Spanish officials from Canada.

In the absence of any Alien Act in force in Canada, and in light of the seeming inapplicability of either common law or imperial legislation, Aberdeen asked the Foreign Office for advice. Legal experts replied that the royal prerogative would have to be invoked.[46] It was at this stage, on June 11, 1898, that the British prime minister and foreign secretary, Lord Salisbury, authorized his ambassador in Madrid to inform the Duke of Tetuan, the Spanish minister for foreign affairs, that Carranza's withdrawal was to be requested. The British ambassador, Sir H. D. Wolff, was instructed to say that Her Majesty's government looked "for the co-

operation of the Spanish government . . . feeling that Carranza's proceedings were unknown to his superior officers in Madrid,"[47] thus plainly
inviting the Spanish government to make the usual disavowal of a spy
caught in the act. But Tetuan refused to take the bait. He said he believed
Carranza's claim that the letter as published was a counterfeit. Stub-
bornly, the Duke raised a further question. If the British believed the
letter to be genuine, why did they demand the recall, not just of Carranza,
but of Captain Juan Du Bose as well? Du Bose, formerly chief attaché at
the Spanish embassy in Washington, had stayed on with Carranza in
Montreal but was not compromised by the published version of the
stolen letter.[48]

Du Bose assured Tetuan that Carranza was as innocent of espionage
as he, but Chamberlain reflected the intransigence of the British government when he told Aberdeen that the lieutenant's expulsion was the only
alternative to the "adoption of most painful measures."[49] The pro-Wash-
ington partisanship of Salisbury's Foreign Office stood out so starkly
against the background of recent Anglo-American discord that it attracted
adverse comment. Spanish newspapers complained about the Canadian
expulsions. They averred that Englishmen were sending news to the
United States from all parts of Spain. The Spanish press also pointed out
that the former U.S. consul in Cadiz was now in Gibraltar, the British
rock which gave so fine a view of Spanish fleet movements in the straits
below, and was making regular telegraphic reports to his superiors at
home.[50] According to Spanish journalists, it was unjust to expel Carranza
from Montreal while leaving the American consul in Gibraltar free to
pursue these activities. In Westminster itself, the expulsion request was
regarded as legally anomalous. The attorney general had to deny, in
answer to a parliamentary question, that expelled Spanish officials would
be entitled to sue for damages.[51] When Laurier succumbed to pressure
and demanded the departure of Du Bose as well as of Carranza, the chief
attaché agreed to leave, but he retained the right to take legal action
against the British government. As his legal adviser, H. C. Saint-Pierre,
put it: "Du Bose se propose de reclamer des dommages-intérêts du gouv-
ernement britannique plus tard. Il n'est guère probable que je sois son
avocat à cette date."[52]

The last sentence is not a very firm expression of faith in Du Bose's
innocence, but Du Bose's possible complicity in espionage does not detract
from the force of his indignation against American methods. He pointed
out that theft was acquiring the appearance of habit where Americans
were concerned. Letters had been stolen from the Spanish officials de
Lome and Carranza, and "in 1888 the publication of a private letter
fraudulently obtained from the present Lord Sackville, then Her Majesty's
Minister in Washington, caused the retirement from his post of that
distinguished diplomat." On the additional charge of forgery, however,

Du Bose remained relatively silent, restricting himself to the observation that Carranza's letter had been addressed not to the Spanish minister of the Marine (as the Americans claimed) but to a relative in the Spanish naval department.[53]

A year passed without any new revelation about the Carranza letter. Then, in the columns of the *Montreal Star,* a twenty-three-year-old English immigrant to Canada with a record of criminal activity in the United States made a confession. George F. Bell of Montreal claimed that it was he who had broken into 42 Tupper Street and delivered the Carranza letter to Wilkie. Using captured Spanish stationery, Wilkie had employed an expert to forge a new letter. Bell had kept quiet for a year for fear of prosecution for theft, but now he was speaking out because Wilkie had paid him only $50 instead of a promised $1,000 plus expenses. The *Star* of July 8, 1899, published the full text of both "Carranza letters," one called "George F. Bell's version" and the other "the Washington version." In a full discussion of the Tupper Street theft, the *Star* tended to give credence to Bell, in spite of the Englishman's record as an alleged if unconvicted counterfeiter and his admission that he had offered his services to Spain as a double agent. The *Star* was inclined to accept Bell's version of the Carranza letter because it seemed to be confirmed in a textually exact manner by Carranza's original allegations concerning interpolation. The *Star* story was reprinted by the *Boston Evening Transcript,* which two days later carried a refutation by Ralph D. Redfern, still working for the Secret Service in Boston. Redfern stated that the honor of stealing the Carranza letter was his, not Bell's, and that the original and genuine document was still on file in the Secret Service office in Washington. The *Transcript* of July 8 and 10, 1899, preferred the Redfern story and "the Washington version."[54]

The letter may have been on file in 1899, but it had certainly disappeared by 1973. There is a possibility that in the family archives in Seville there survive other letters by Carranza that might illuminate Secret Service methods and throw a sidelight on the war that proved to be the turning point in modern Spanish history. In spite of intercession from a high quarter in the Spanish government, the Carranza letters, if there are any, remain for the time being closed.[55] Sufficient evidence does exist, however, to make one point clear. In 1898, the State Department had to step in to secure full benefit for the United States from the intelligence work of its Secret Service. This was a signpost to the future.

4

The State Department Takes Over

In the summer of 1915, President Woodrow Wilson and his secretary of state, Robert Lansing, vested overall control of American espionage in the State Department. Wishing to enjoy the end product of intelligence work without sharing the stigma attached to it, they delegated chief responsibility for espionage to Lansing's subordinates in the State Department. These subordinates, following what is probably the optimum procedure for an intelligence system, filtered and evaluated information before supplying it to the chief executive.

The State Department controlled espionage after 1915 because of the delicate diplomatic questions involved. Before America entered World War I in 1917, the Wilson administration tried to preserve every appearance of neutrality and to ensure that U.S. secret agents did not seem to be operating exclusively against either the Allies or the Central Powers. From 1917 on, Wilson was confronted with another dilemma which affected U.S. war aims and the conduct expected of American secret agents: that of antiimperialism. The State Department attempted the impossible: U.S. spies were deployed against the internal enemies of the British empire, but America posed as the enemy of imperialism everywhere; at the same time, harassed American diplomats tried to reassure the British that U.S. propaganda was directed against the Austro-Hungarian and Ottoman empires, not Ireland and India.

These pressing and unenviable requirements gave the State Department its authority over intelligence activities in World War I. Its officials depended upon the agents and bureaucratic machinery of various existing agencies to do most of their work. What the State Department itself provided was the coordination, evaluation, and dissemination of information and overall planning. These functions gave it an authority which in the 1920s led some officials to doubt the desirability of centrally directed espionage.

The State Department's control over espionage reflected and accentuated the predominance of political over military considerations, important though the latter were. In 1898 the Secret Service and in World War II the Office of Strategic Services (OSS) concentrated, if by no means exclusively, on military intelligence. The contrasting arrangement made for World War I started a shift toward a system whereby political intelligence would be ascendent over military intelligence, just as civilians control soldiers generally in American society. The arrangement survived until 1942 and has been partially reinstated since World War II.

The opposition of one set of political ideas to another was a reason for the initially slow growth in U.S. intelligence capability when war broke out in Europe in 1914. For an illustration of the origins of this opposition, one can turn to the agrarian politics of the 1890s. In 1896, delegates to the Democratic national convention in Chicago thrilled to the intonations of a speech which was to leave a lasting imprint on the American mind. William Jennings Bryan, candidate for the presidential nomination, the "Boy Orator" from Nebraska, echoed fears of "a vast conspiracy against mankind" expressed in the Populist platform four years earlier. In his speech at Chicago he hurled at the defenders of the gold standard his now famous injunction: "You shall not press down upon the brow of labor this crown of thorns, you shall not crucify mankind upon a cross of gold." He described his opponents as "the few financial magnates who, in a back room, corner the money of the world."

Bryan won the nomination but failed to attain the White House. Ultimately, nevertheless, he did receive the opportunity to apply his homespun principles to the making of foreign policy. Bryan became secretary of state in 1913 as a reward for his support of Wilson's nomination by the Democratic party in 1912. President Wilson never warmed to his first secretary of state even though Bryan, like himself, was a declared opponent of conspiracy and war.

President Wilson stood for reelection in 1916 on a pacifist platform. As the man who had kept America from falling over the brink, he won. By this time, however, Bryan was no longer a member of his cabinet. Wilson had protested to the German government over the U-boat sinking in May 7, 1915, of the British passenger ship *Lusitania* with the loss of 128 American lives. Perhaps foreseeing America's entry into the European holocaust, Bryan resigned in June because of his disappointment over the president's belligerent language in addressing the Germans. According to a memoir written by his wife, he had for some time before the *Lusitania* disaster shown the familiar symptoms—restlessness and sleepless nights unsoothed by hot baths and special diets—of a man troubled by conscience.[1] Historian Ernest May has written that during "the early stages of the war at least the sources of American policy did not lie in intelligence reports or public opinion polls; they lay in the consciences of the Secretary of State, William Jennings Bryan, the Counselor of the Department of State, Robert Lansing, the President's friend and adviser, Colonel Edward M. House, and, above all, of President Woodrow Wilson himself."[2] The departure of Wilson's original choice as secretary of state ushered in a period of war "preparedness," a policy made irresistible by the fact that the president became a political prisoner of the hawks, leaving the doves demoralized and leaderless. The last Populist having relinquished office; the State Department was poised as never before to take an undercover initiative overseas and, as a necessary prelude, to assume the supervision of intelligence operations at home.

From the latter part of 1915, the State Department increasingly concerned itself with intelligence matters. Wilson and Lansing, now his secretary of state, had a keen initial interest in espionage. After June 1915, they no longer had to contend with the scruples of Bryan, and revelations of German intrigue on American soil indicated an urgent and genuine need for the coordination of counterintelligence. Wilson and Lansing set up an espionage organization under the office of the counselor to the Department of State. The counselorship, occupied by Lansing prior to his elevation, was the second-ranking office in the department.

In theory, Lansing had both the authority and the experience to direct the development of an intelligence system. In practice, he did not. The secretary failed, like his predecessor, Bryan, to become fully attuned to Wilson's moods. He was too independent for the president. Lansing's slight but persistent disenchantment was betrayed by his habit of sitting back during cabinet meetings, making pencil sketches of his colleagues. In spite of his prominent position, the secretary was too withdrawn to be an indispensable link in the intelligence chain.[3] He displayed an occasional strong interest and backed up espionage in principle, but his participation was spasmodic, and he sometimes displayed poor judgment. Normally Lansing left day-to-day espionage, as well as the development of an intelligence system, to his counselor, Frank L. Polk.

In 1845, President James K. Polk had saturated Mexico with spies as a prelude to war.[4] His kinsman Frank L. (whose great-grandfather, Revolutionary soldier William Polk, had been James K.'s first cousin) perpetuated and consolidated this tradition. Frank Polk was born in New York City and educated at Groton and Yale. He served in Puerto Rico in the war of 1898 and then took up law. As an independent Democrat, Polk became interested in municipal reform. As president of the New

York Municipal Civil Service Commission and as a political campaigner, he opposed the Tammany machine and attempted to reduce its influence on public policy. In 1914, Polk championed the anti-Tammany candidacy of the young reformer John P. Mitchel, who was running on a Fusion ticket for the New York mayoralty. Mitchel received the endorsement of President Wilson and won the election.

The new mayor made appointments which reflected both his reforming zeal and his enthusiasm for preparedness. For example, Arthur Woods, his police commissioner, battled not only against crime but also against German plotters; Woods's surveillance methods included telephone tapping, an unpopular practice which in 1917 contributed to the defeat of Mitchel in his bid for reelection. In another move designed to combat corruption and of significance for the development of American espionage, Mitchel appointed Polk the city's corporation counsel. Seated in an automobile with Mitchell that spring, Polk was shot through the mouth by a deranged blacksmith, whose bullet had been intended for the mayor. Polk survived to become America's World War I spymaster.[5]

In recognition of Polk's outstanding services as counselor of the Department of State, Congress agreed in 1919 to create for him the special post of under secretary of state, in which office he remained until June 1920 in order to give the new Republican secretary of state, Bainbridge Colby, time to get oriented to his job. As counselor, Polk advised the Wilson administration on the legal aspects of American neutrality which arose from the European war. At the same time, he supervised the work of various government agencies in the field of counterespionage and in investigating alleged violations of American neutral rights by belligerent powers. As war approached, Polk became coordinator of those agencies created or developed for the purpose of gathering intelligence data abroad.[6] In 1916, the counselor had kept in close touch with the French and British embassies, educating himself in the problems of domestic surveillance which the United States would encounter should it enter hostilities. The British had a man in America, Sir William Wiseman, whose special task it was to watch Germans, Austrians, Irishmen, and Indians who might prejudice the interests of his country. In March 1917, on the eve of America's entry in the war, it was a short step for the State Department to set up formal collaboration with Wiseman.

Although under Polk the espionage bureaucracy flourished in several government departments, he was primarily a coordinator, responsible for liaison more than for administrative empire building under the State Department. His system was superior to that of 1898 in that it allowed the sinister hand of the spy to be regulated by the dexterous hand of the diplomat. The system consisted of a typically American division of powers. The State Department, answerable in public and to the public through the president, decided on intelligence policy and coordinated resources. Other departments retained the enabling powers—namely, the legions of trained agents and the money to back them. During the 1920s, 1930s, World War II, and the formative years of the CIA, the Polk model never ceased to command the respect of at least a powerful minority of public servants. Yet, ironically, Polk at the end of his tenure began to introduce innovations which provoked opposition both from jealous military sources and from the guardians of democratic tradition. When Lansing was in Paris for the Peace Conference in the first half of 1919, Polk secretly established the "American Black Chamber," a cryptographic unit with a developing capability for breaking foreign codes.[7] Following Lansing's break with Wilson and his long-expected resignation in February 1920, Polk took another important step, establishing a "foreign-intelligence section" under the State Department which would continue the work of spy coordination in peacetime.[8] Polk probably timed his initiatives to coincide with Lansing's absences because the secretary of state, while quite willing to use secret methods secretly, virulently denounced them in public. It would have been embarrassing for Lansing to have to persuade his fellow cabinet members to support covert methods which President Wilson had so often condemned.

A good deal of wartime espionage work fell on the receptive shoulders of Gordon Auchincloss. Auchincloss was appointed assistant counselor in May 1917. His office was at first located in New York, a natural center for foreign intrigue because of its port and the cover provided by large numbers of immigrants. When international or offensive espionage became more important, Auchincloss moved to Washington. One of the assistant counselor's advantages was that he knew the Treasury Department and its Secret Service because he had performed government tax work. Like Wilkie in 1898, he enjoyed a natural compatibility with his superiors. In common with Polk, he had gone to Groton and belonged to the Links and Piping Rocks clubs in New York. He was the son-in-law of Colonel Edward House.

Polk, Auchincloss, and House constituted an intimate and watertight intelligence triumvirate. The inner circle was assisted by Richard Crane, who had particular responsibility for liaison with Polish and Czech agents and was private secretary to Lansing. Crane had good contacts with the president and enjoyed the inevitable Ivy League background. Mutual backgrounds made for collective discretion. Polk indirectly commented on the Americans' secretiveness when he complained in 1920 that the British secret service "had been carried on with a brass band."[9] There were few secrets within the State Department group, and even fewer leaked from it.

From 1915 on, the State Department gradually asserted its authority over the various American intelligence services. The diplomatic repercussions of the smashing of the Montreal spy ring of 1898 had illustrated the danger of allowing intelligence operations to proceed independently of the official arm of American foreign policy. The Secret Service could not be trusted to be diplomatic in anticipation of foreign responses to domestic events. The Japanese government, for example, was sensitive to any slights to Orientals on the West coast. Blissfully unaware of potential foreign reactions, the Secret Service was compiling tables of the "nativities of forgery convicts."[10] In Washington, furthermore, Congress remained as watchful as ever of any unofficial clandestine moves. President Theodore Roosevelt's appointment of representatives to the Franco-German conference in Algeciras, Spain, and of agents to Santo Domingo had sparked off a lively debate in the Senate in the winter of 1905–1906. The president's use of Commander Albert C. Dillingham as an agent and his show of force in Santo Domingo in 1905 were applications of the "Roosevelt Corollary" to the Monroe Doctrine, a punishment of "wrong-doing" (in this case nonpayment of debts) in the Western Hemisphere, and were particularly controversial. The debate, between Senators John C. Spooner and Augustus O. Bacon, ranged over the responsibilities, duties, and powers of the president and the Senate in conducting foreign relations. Spooner asserted that the president and his secretary of state had the power to withhold information from the Senate and to appoint agents without the Senate's advice and consent. Bacon had to give ground and in 1914 himself conceded President Wilson's right to send secret agent John Lind to Mexico.[11] Wilson ultimately proved to be tragically insensitive to congressional criticism when he quarreled with the Senate over the League of Nations, but in 1915–1917 he was wise enough to let the State Department assert control over the Secret Service. The takeover was only logical in that the capability of the Secret Service did not extend very much beyond counterespionage. In World War I, counterespionage not only yielded pride of place to international intelligence; it had to be integrated with it.

The State Department modified some of the actions of the Secret Service and in some cases acted as a court of redress. Its main role in intelligence matters was, however, coordination. The gradual assertions of control in this respect are revealed by entries in Polk's diary. In 1916, before President Wilson's public conversion from pacifism to belligerence, the second-in-command at the State Department claimed no direct authority over the Secret Service. On June 16, Polk noted in his diary: "Saw [Secretary of the Treasury] McAdoo re Secret Service."[12] William Gibbs McAdoo had married the president's daughter, Eleanor, in 1915, and, politically, the honeymoon was not yet over. Gradually, however, the State Department took on increasing responsibility for central intelligence. Polk recorded on March 3, 1917: "Went to Congress re money for Secret Service."[13]

Power was as ever a perquisite of the purse strings. On March 30,

Auchincloss recorded a visit to his New York office "at my request" by W. J. Flynn, head of the Secret Service.[14] Auchincloss regularly supervised the efforts of the Secret Service to impede the international flow of German funds. Another of Polk's subordinates, Paul Fuller (a New York attorney who had secretly negotiated with the Mexican partisan, Francisco "Pancho" Villa, on behalf of Wilson in 1914), supervised Secret Service operations in Cuba.[15] After the war, Polk continued to keep an eye on even the anticounterfeiting operations of the Secret Service, insofar as they extended to Cuba.[16]

During World War I, the State Department secured the cooperation, not just of the Secret Service, but of all the major intelligence organizations. Continued factionalism in Army intelligence made the supervision of military espionage easy as well as necessary. One example occurred after President Theodore Roosevelt had demanded an improvement in reconnaissance. By 1909, the Army was the less than enthusiastic overlord of the Heavier-Than-Air Division, U.S. Aerial Fleet, consisting of Aeroplane Number 1. The Signal Corps soon expanded its empire by taking over the resultant First Aero Squadron and, during the punitive expedition against Pancho Villa in 1916, used it for courier instead of surveillance purposes. This sort of behavior both invited and justified State Department intervention.[17]

Military intelligence as an autonomous institution continued to be the victim of byzantine struggles in the Army and War Department. In 1908, following Secretary of War Elihu Root's establishment of a general staff, the "Second Division," having earlier emerged, merged, and submerged, finally reemerged. Modeled on the French "Deuxième Bureau" and commonly designated G-2, the division oversaw the organization which, after several administrative and nomenclative changes, once more became the Military Intelligence Division (MID) on August 26, 1918.[18]

The man who dominated military intelligence thinking during this period remained, for most of the time, in the wings. Ralph H. Van Deman was born in Ohio in 1865 and graduated from Harvard in 1889, having read law and medicine. He served in an intelligence capacity in Cuba in 1898 and in the Philippines from 1901 to 1903. According to his unpublished memoirs, Van Deman worked effectively against Filipino guerrillas and Japanese secret agents; however, the future espionage coordinator at this time made an enemy of General Franklin Bell, who was later to impede Van Deman's attempts to achieve autonomy for himself and military intelligence. Van Deman's own candid account relates how the Philippines Department's military intelligence division induced a U.S. citizen to part with correspondence and other documentation concerning his questionable relationship with the Japanese government, on the understanding that the citizen himself would be cleared; Philippines MID, however, refused to return the borrowed materials. Bell, then provost marshal of the Philippines Department, felt that Van Deman was behaving in an ungentlemanly fashion and ordered the return of the documents. Van Deman had Bell overruled, and Bell, according to the Harvard man's memoir, harbored resentment.[19]

Not long after Van Deman's clash with Bell, an official investigation of Army intelligence operations in Venezuela disclosed "the fact that most of the information could better be collected by clerks at a small salary rather than by highly paid and highly educated officers."[20] By this time Bell was chief of staff, and his actions ensured that military intelligence was kept from developing antonomously from 1908 to 1915. Early in 1916, as part of America's preparedness campaign, Van Deman was at last put in charge of military intelligence and began to revitalize it. He remained in the job for two years but gradually alienated his superior officers by demanding independence from the general staff and the right of liaison with other intelligence agencies. In June 1918, he was supplanted by a new intelligence chief, General Marlborough Churchill, and ordered to France.[21]

Over the years, histories of military intelligence, both confidential and published, have stressed its inadequacy on the eve of America's entry into World War I.[22] Certainly dissension continued, making Army espionage susceptible to State Department guidance—a susceptibility much resented by Army historians. Yet complaints by the Army and its agents bear the hallmarks of propaganda. Their "histories" were the pleas of expansionists who had tasted the fruits of bureaucratic victory. The MID and its immediate precursors (the Military Information Section, later Intelligence Section, later Branch, and finally Division) underwent the following budgetary expansion:[23]

	1916	1917	1918	1919
Officers	2	17	282	110
Civilians	1	192	159	140
Total employees	3	209	441	250
Estimated funds (excluding Army salaries)	$11,000	*	$1,000,000	$2,500,000

* No updated estimate available.

$2½ million (though but the partial budget of one of several American espionage organizations) was a sum worth fighting over.

General Churchill, on taking over the MID, produced a wall chart making his swollen organization look rational in function and subordinating everything to his own authority. His chart consisted of 104 little boxes, many of them subdivided, but conforming to a basic skeleton (see Figure 1).[24]

There were many more boxes on the negative side than on the positive. This may have been partly a precaution against the chart's falling into the wrong hands. For the positive branch was responsible for offensive espionage, an activity demanding conditions of maximum security. M.I.5, for example, supervised the activities of military attachés, whose spy networks took operational risks in wartime. M.I.8 contained the subsection "Solutions of Codes and Ciphers."[25] To take charge of this section, Van Deman had looked for a man with the ability to break enemy codes, steal a march on British expertise, and convince his superiors of the need for cryptanalysis. He found him in a young code clerk at the State Department. The new cryptology chief, H. O. Yardley, had learned the arts of mathematical deduction as a teen-aged poker player in the saloons of his native Worthington, Indiana.[26]

The weight of MID administration undoubtedly fell on the sinisterly named negative branch. The negative branch covered a variety of areas, from prison camps to a clippings bureau, from sabotage to motion pictures, from conscientious objectors to the problems of Negro soldiers. Its main official emphasis was on "counterespionage," a term which, in some of its applications, was a euphemism designed to encourage the impression that the United States was pacifist and defensive rather than warmongering and offensive. Subsections like "Counterespionage in Switzerland, Greece, Russia, Far East" speak for themselves. Nevertheless, MID did spend time and money spying on people in the United States.

E. R. Warner McGabe, the assistant chief of staff, G-2, remarked in 1940 that the War Department took over counterespionage activities in World War I "due to the inability of the civil authorities to meet the situation at that time."[27] In fact, however, the FBI, as it became known in 1935, was already emerging. Every counterespionage agency perceived a golden opportunity in World War I. The expansion of the MID, like that of other services, was a response to wartime nationalism and confidence as well as to need. There was, therefore, duplication of effort even during the war. The overenthusiastic hounding of apparently subversive radicals known as the Red Scare of 1919 was in part a result of the operation of a variant of Parkinson's law, which dictates that it is impossible to get rid of government bureaucracies in a democratic society: large counterintelligence agencies, deprived of one enemy by the surrender of Germany, refused to become redundant—they simply invented another enemy.[28]

The functions of MID as expressed in Churchill's chart seem obscure and overlapping because the chart did not properly acknowledge liaison, although there were in fact five liaison offices. One of the lower-echelon offices under M.I.4, "Counterespionage: Sabotage, Propaganda outside

Figure 1.

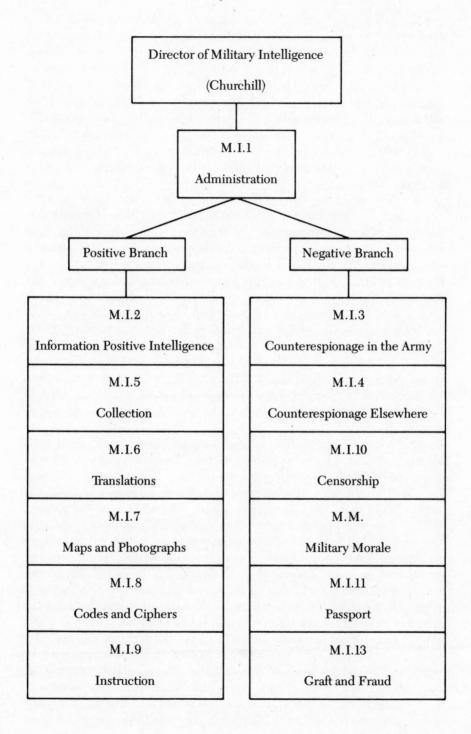

the Military Service in the U.S. and Abroad," purported to liaise with the Department of Justice, the Office of Naval Intelligence, and the Department of State. But the nature of the chart disguised the fact that the whole section, being subdivided geographically, followed the organizational plan of the State Department, which was divided into regional bureaus. As late as May 21, 1917, the Secretary of War had prohibited intelligence liaison even within the Army; MID and its bureaucratically isolationist predecessors were easy prey for the State Department, which was closely knit internally and ambitious externally.[29] Polk and Auchincloss were able to initiate coordination with Army intelligence at every level, and did so.

On the whole, the Navy behaved rather more discreetly than the Army. Like the State Department and the MID, the Office of Naval Intelligence began its reorganization just after the resignation of Bryan. Secretary of the Navy Josephus Daniels was one of six cabinet members who had lunched with Bryan on the day of his resignation.[30] Eighteen days later, on June 26, 1915, he had approved "a general plan for obtaining information."[31] The plan envisaged an expansion of the attaché system; liaison with the Department of State had already been implemented; further reorganization of ONI was "under detailed consideration."[32] On January 2, 1917, the director of naval intelligence reported in categorical terms that "the work of the Office of Naval Intelligence in preparation for war is making steady progress."[33] Whatever the shortcomings of American intelligence in the Wilson years, no one could justly accuse the ONI of having been taken by surprise when the United States went to war in April, 1917.

There were times, in 1917, when Congress must have thought itself surrounded on all sides by mercenary patriots. The director of naval intelligence, Roger Welles, joined the general bleat for more money. He wanted more staff for the naval attaché offices in London, Paris, and Madrid. The naval coding room, he complained further, was severely undermanned, having a mere fifty-seven employees to deal with up to thirty messages a day. He pleaded with the reluctant Daniels to allow him to commission civilians so that they could take on confidential work restricted by security regulations to Navy officers. Welles already had a list of candidates, heavily weighted with graduates of Harvard University. The extent to which ONI cooperated with the State Department is indicated by the names of referees for some of the civilian candidates—such as Frank Polk, Walter Hines Page (ambassador to Britain), and Charles Warren (one of the State Department's legal advisers as well as assistant attorney general).[34] Polk and Auchincloss received the willing cooperation of ONI from top (Daniels, Welles) to bottom (naval dockyards security men).[35]

Through the office of the counselor, the State Department coordinated the espionage activities not only of MID and ONI but of many other organizations. Most federal departments cooperated, as did many local officials, such as city police. The counselor also coordinated, directly or indirectly, the work and informational product of private organizations purporting to be patriotic in character, such as the American Protective League (late nineteenth-century nativist in origin), and private detective agencies. Outstanding in the second rank of intelligence organizations were two additional national bodies, the Justice Department's Bureau of Investigation and The Inquiry.

Attorney General Charles Joseph Bonaparte (the grandson of one of Napoleon's brothers) established the Justice Department's Bureau of Investigation in the teeth of congressional opposition. The *Washington Evening Star* reminded its readers in 1908, the year of the bureau's founding, of the French police minister Joseph Fouché, who was "used by Napoleon to intimidate everybody else in the French Empire, and grew so powerful that he intimidated the Emperor himself by reason of the State secrets he held."[36] The House and Senate appropriations committees reported against the proposal for a bureau, and Congress further prohibited the Justice Department's practice of borrowing secret service detectives. Congressmen attacked the central intelligence systems of Russia, France, and Britain, and Bonaparte admitted under cross-examination that there were "inherent dangers [in] any system of detective police."[37] The attorney general nevertheless established his Bureau of Investigation during a congressional adjournment, pleading that Congress itself had forced his hand by denying him the facilities of the Treasury Department.[38]

Historians have given considerable attention to the development of the bureau in some of its aspects. William Preston, Jr., has described its cooperation with Department of Immigration officials in arresting radical dissenters during World War I and the Red Scare.[39] Max Lowenthal has provided an account of the development of the bureau's antiradical division under J. Edgar Hoover and the successive directorships of William J. Flynn (1919–1921, formerly head of the Secret Service) and William J. Burns (1921–1924, trained with the Secret Service in 1898 and head of the private detective agency bearing his name).[40] By the 1920s, the Justice Department's Bureau of Investigation was clearly a part of the American espionage establishment. It remains to add that, by 1917, the bureau was providing a counterespionage service for the Department of State. Its agents subcontracted some surveillance work to private detectives but, far from being dependent on the Secret Service, the bureau operatives had in several respects supplanted the Treasury men as the eyes and ears of Washington.

Following the Bolshevik seizure of power in Russia on November 7, 1917, President Wilson established a group of experts, called The Inquiry, to determine American war aims and a strategy for the anticipated peace negotiations. Under the guidance of Colonel Edward House, and the administration of Sidney Mezes (director), Walter Lippmann (secretary), and Isaiah Bowman (executive officer), the New York-based Inquiry was largely academic in character, but by 1918 it employed 150 researchers of diverse backgrounds and formed part of the American intelligence network. In September 1918, Carlton Hayes of M.I.4 circulated a memorandum on The Inquiry which illustrates the liaison which existed between the House team, MID, and the State Department.[41] Hayes pointed out that there was already liaison between M.I.2 (MID's evaluation and dissemination section) and The Inquiry. He advocated further cooperation between House's team and M.I.4 because The Inquiry dealt with ethnic leaders who

> all come sooner or later to New York and they can talk (and do talk) more freely with the semi-official "Inquiry" in New York than with the official Department of State in Washington. The "Inquiry" keeps memoranda of all such conferences, and these memoranda should be a veritable mine of useful information to the Counter-Propaganda sub-section of M.I.4. At the same time, the "Inquiry" would appreciate very much a "tip" now and then from us about this or that foreigner or foreign-born leader who is known to us as "suspect" or "positively disloyal" but who is able, at least temporarily, by the use of a smooth tongue to "put something over" the "Inquiry."[42]

The Hayes plan was put into effect.[43] Although The Inquiry had more to do with research than with espionage, it did provide cover for some investigations which flowed into the mainstream of State Department intelligence.

The diversification of American espionage after 1915 obscured from popular vision its increasing tendency toward centralization under the State Department. By keeping a low profile, the department encouraged the illusion of business as usual. For example, the British decision to use Pinkerton men in neutral America brought back memories of Spanish tactics in using a Canadian detective agency in the 1890s. The Britons' hounding of Lajos Trebitsch is a case in point. Trebitsch was a Hungarian Jew who agitated as a socialist in Cleveland and later attacked the Entente in several speeches. Imprisoned for forgery at the request of the British government, he escaped only to be pursued by Pinkerton agents.[44] The State Department was not conspicuously involved in the harassment of Trebitsch but probably supplied the coordination. The inevitability of the State Department's involvement is even clearer in the case of his brother, Ignaz T. Trebitsch-Lincoln. Trebitsch-Lincoln was a British member of parliament before business difficulties induced him to move to the United States, where he became a German secret agent. He was extradited to Britain and languished in Parkhurst prison, Isle of Wight, from 1916 to 1919. This was achieved with the discreet cooperation of the State Department, but, to all appearances, his arrest in the United States was reminiscent of the swoops of 1898 or earlier. He was held at gunpoint by a deputy marshal and five other men, all from the Secret Service and the Pinkerton Agency.[45]

Yet, in spite of appearances, there was no possibility that the experiment of the Civil War would be repeated; William A. Pinkerton himself acknowledged that "prior to 1914" his agency had worked in England, France, Russia, and Canada.[46] The agency was unreliable because it worked for Britain when Americans were supposed to be neutral, and the former Pinkerton detective William Reimers (alias Steinhauer) had organized a German spy network in England, destroyed by British M.I.5 as soon as war broke out.[47] It is as certain that the Pinkerton Agency was discredited as it is that the Secret Service was directed from the State Department. Central intelligence was all the more potent for being anonymous. Discreet State Department control of espionage was to be an enduring legacy of World War I.

5

Counterespionage and the Stirrings of a Police State

The year of the "Red Scare" was a time when part of America's elaborate intelligence network went into action against radicals and U.S.-domiciled aliens. Such was the maltreatment of certain minority groups in 1919 that public opinion—impelled by sympathy for the underdog, among other factors—turned briefly against intelligence services in the 1920s. More enduringly, liberal historical opinion fastened onto the surveillance excesses of 1919 and produced theories such as that which ascribes nativism to irrational anxiety.[1] Preoccupation with the counterspies' treatment of radicals and aliens has led to the neglect of two considerations. First, there has been a reluctance to consider the extent to which America's counterespionage machinery posed a threat to society as a whole. Second, there has been a tendency to overlook the possibility that American counterspies' focus on Reds and foreigners was the result of underemployment: their oversized bureaucracy had been constructed as a response, not to the limited socialist offensive of 1919, but to the massive German penetration of 1915–1918.

The attack on German spies was no overreaction by a nervous, conservative people. In its original inception, if not in all of its ultimate consequences, it was a rational response to a real threat. It is true that German espionage in the United States suffered from many handicaps; it was lampooned at the time for its too rigid "efficiency" and its lack of adaptability to the American scene.[2] Nevertheless, German spies displayed ability and constituted a potentially effective force.

The kaiser's agents were directed from Germany by the head of secret service there, Colonel Walter Nicolai. Because of difficulties in communication and for reasons of liaison, their orders frequently came through diplomatic channels. This presented the German ambassador to the United States, Count Johann von Bernstorff, with an opportunity for intrigue which he seized with eagerness. Under von Bernstorff in theory, but actually under Nicolai, were three spy coordinators. The senior of these, Dr. Heinrich F. Albert, was privy councillor to the German embassy and fiscal agent of the German empire. He had authority over the worldwide German spy network outside the "ring of steel" thrown around the Central Powers by the Allied navies. From his offices in the Hamburg-American Steamship Company premises in New York, Albert supervised commercial espionage activities in the United States. Captain Franz von Papen, Germany's military attaché and a future chancellor in the period of the Weimar Republic's decline, looked after clandestine operations such as sabotage from a suite of offices on Wall Street disguised as an advertising agency. Captain Karl Boy-Ed, the son of a Turk and of the German biographer and novelist Ida Boy-Ed, was the naval attaché. He devoted himself to such activities as gun running to troubled British imperial terriotries. Known as "Germany's Beau Brummel," Boy-Ed was handpicked by Admiral of the Fleet Alfred von Tirpitz and returned first-rate naval intelligence to the Supreme Naval Command at home.[3]

At the beginning of the war, Nicolai sent a special agent to America, but without much success. The multimillionaire Captain Franz von Rintelen was dispatched with orders to try to isolate the United States commercially from the Allies in Europe. He was, further, to encourage anti-Yanqui feeling among the Mexicans and to recruit Irish-American longshoremen to sabotage Allied ships sailing from New York. Von Rintelen failed because his superimposition on a preexisting network led to resentment. Jealous of von Rintelen, Boy-Ed and von Papen blew his cover by describing his activities in indiscreet messages. The alerted American Secret Service allowed von Rintelen to sail for Europe but the British having been apprised of his identity in advance, took him into custody in home waters. Disillusioned with his German superiors, von Rintelen settled in England after the war. In World War II, he worked against the Nazis.[4]

The departure of von Rintelen left German espionage under the direction of four men protected by diplomatic immunity—Albert, Boy-Ed, von Papen, and the ambassador himself. The direct involvement of the German ambassador in North American espionage clearly called for State Department intervention. Beginning in 1915, the counselor received the top-carbon copies of reports submitted by Secret Service Chief Flynn to Secretary of the Treasury McAdoo. The State Department, in turn, fed into Flynn's intelligence picture British-supplied information about secret agents operating on behalf of the Central Powers in America. The necessity of preserving the appearance of correct diplomatic posture—in spite of the administration's rampant Anglophilia—presented a delicate diplomatic challenge. If the German spy network were to be fully exposed and broken up, it would be necessary to supply proof of its existence. But who would supply it? The State Department did not wish it to be known that the Secret Service was operating extensively and one-sidedly against the Germans. The British could have supplied the necessary documentation, but they were deeply engaged in a cryptographic cat-and-mouse game at which the Americans, too, were soon to be adept. They wanted the Central Powers and, for the time being, the American government to remain in ignorance of the fact that they had broken the German codes; the British were unwilling to own up to being in a position to supply the Americans with the information which would have led to the prosecution and expulsion of compromised German diplomats. Even if the British and Americans had been less inhibited, there was good reason to let the German spy network continue, since its operators were known and could be watched to advantage. President Wilson therefore contented himself with demanding the recall, in the fall of 1915, of von Papen, Boy-Ed, and Albert. Their subordinates and von Bernstorff himself were left alone. The Secret Service preserved its operationally useful incognito because its agents made only limited court appearances; the president retained, for the time being, the appearance of neutrality; the German spies were allowed to run.

The partnership between State Department and Secret Service produced good intelligence. For example, by the fall of 1915, State had been made aware of German strategic thinking through its surveillance of von Bernstorff's agents. The Secret Service kept a particular watch on Captain Hans Tauscher, because Flynn at first mistook him for "the head of the German espionage system in this country."[5] Flynn's error led to the indictment of Tauscher on rather flimsy evidence for attempting with Irish assistance to blow up the locks on the Welland Canal system in Canada. Acquitted on this charge, Tauscher was nevertheless considered by the German government for a deferred decoration in recognition of his American work, performed not on behalf of von Papen, whose agent he nominally was, but for the German arms corporation, the Krupps Company.[6] Tauscher's work as the Krupp representative was not illegal, but it was more significant from the diplomatic point of view than his possible implication in the Welland Canal plot.

In May 1915, State Department official Leland Harrison received on behalf of Lansing, then counselor, a report by Flynn on Tauscher. He put it into a file chillingly labeled "Human Espionage Activities." According to Flynn's report, Tauscher had established surveillance over a pair of British-Canadians registered as guests on the seventh floor of the Home

Club Hotel in New York City. The Germans installed relief teams of two male spies and their "wives" in the suite next to the visitors. One of these was Sir William Mackenzie, a leading Canadian financier and creator of the Canadian Northern Railway Company, who was in town to purchase arms. Von Papen's spies discovered that the owner of the hotel was an American capitalist capable of acting as an intermediary in arms deals. The Secret Service report did not reveal the identity of the capitalist, designating him in every instance "Mr. ***." Whatever his identity, its significance did not escape Tauscher, and the Germans decided for good reasons to take action at the highest level.[7]

The naval blockade imposed by the Allies was proving to be highly effective. Commerce with the Central Powers fell from a value of $170 million in 1914 to $1 million two years later. The value of trade with Britain, France, Russia, and Italy in the same period increased from $825 million to $3,250 million. Shortage of weapons and ammunition was a strategic consideration for both sides in the costly battles on the Western Front. Von Rintelen and Albert had realized the vital necessity of achieving through commercial means what the U-boats were failing to accomplish on the high seas—namely, the throttling of the ammunition supply line running from the factories of America to the weary but persistent Allied soldiers. Their plan was to buy up munitions corporations; Albert, for example, arranged for the purchase of the Bridgeport Projectile Company.[8] They would then produce military goods for German-aligned forces (such as the Indian revolutionaries), take orders from the Allies and fail to fill them, and use the pocket-companies as a means of obtaining information from the War Department. Tauscher laid his plans, with the cooperation of von Papen, according to the same strategy.

Flynn's report recorded that, soon after Mackenzie's arrival at the Home Club Hotel, "a prominent man of affairs in New York" asked Mr. * * * to buy up the Union Metallic Cartridge Company on behalf of the Allies. After fourteen further meetings, the businessman turned up early in May, accompanied by none other than Count von Bernstorff, who apparently hoped to remain unidentified. Mr. * * * instantly recognized the count. In the words of Flynn's report, Mr. * * * "said he addressed the Count 'How do you do Count,' whereupon he reddened up." Their disguise having failed, the Germans now made a direct approach to Mr. * * *. Would he purchase Union Metallic for Germany, and, if so, what would be his fee? Mr. * * * stated that $5 million would be a reasonable commission, and the Germans agreed to pay. They suggested that Mr. * * * might subsequently purchase the Winchester and Remington Companies.[9]

Unfortunately for the Germans, their American intermediaries now began to get cold feet. As for Mr. * * *, the sinking of the *Lusitania* made him unreceptive to even more lucrative German approaches. He decided to entice Tauscher's agents into a snare by feigning continued interest in a deal with the Germans. When von Bernstorff put his head into the noose, Mr. * * * concluded that, "knowing Secretary McAdoo as well as he does, . . . it was his duty as an American citizen to advise him over the long distance phone."[10] Another German spy ring had been blown, but the State Department was too discreet to close the noose and demand the recall of von Bernstorff. By watching his secret service at work, it was possible to deduce many things. It was, for example, in full knowledge of Germany's actual desperation (as distinct from diplomatic protests) that the U.S. government allowed weapons to flow unimpeded, except by U-boats, to the Allies.

Knowing in advance that their suspicions were justified, Secret Service men applied even more rigorous surveillance techniques. American citizens found themselves suspected of crimes they had never heard of. Archibald S. White, of the financial firm White & Co., was settling down to a good morning's work on Saturday, June 12, 1915, when the Treasury men knocked on his door. Under interrogation, he denied having acted as von Bernstorff's intermediary in arms deals but finally confessed his sympathy with the views of Bryan, who had resigned as secretary of state a few days earlier. But where, asked his "interviewers," was his wife? In the Adirondacks, White replied, with her Japanese valet and the "Captain."[11]

White was probably in no position to know that Captain Tauscher was being hunted down, that the Secret Service was "tapping" his wife's telephone calls, and that Mrs. White was one of von Bernstorff's mistresses and agents. The American authorities, in contrast, were in the process of becoming fully apprised of the activities and private lives of von Bernstorff and his lady friends. Secret Service Chief Flynn later recalled how the service's specialist in telephone tapping had led wires from the German and Austrian embassies to a specially rented apartment. "When a receiver was taken down in the embassy," Flynn remembered, "a light flashed in the Secret Service apartment. When a phone bell rang in the embassy one rang in our apartment. Four stenographers worked in relays. . . ."[12] Treasury officials supplied the State Department's undercover specialist Leland Harrison in September 1915 with a 200-page transcript of the ambassador's most revealing telephone calls.

The German ambassador foolishly used his mistresses as agents and allowed them to become jealous of each other. In an effort to placate his women, von Bernstorff became loquacious on the telephone and let slip information which was harmful to his professional plans. Since the British were listening in on and decoding his wireless and telegraph messages and the Secret Service was transcribing his telephone calls, the German ambassador kept very few secrets. Von Bernstorff fell prey to the technology of American counterspies (whom the Germans generally underestimated) as well as to the superior guile of his women friends and acquaintances. The son of an ambassador to Britain, he had been projected into the Washington maelstrom with insufficient diplomatic experience of his own, his previous appointment having been to diplomatically unimportant Egypt, at that time virtually a British protectorate. Perhaps he was overwhelmed by his duties or by the family aristocratic tradition; he was certainly intimidated by his wife, whose taunting faithlessness is revealed by the following telephone tap transcript:

AMBASSADOR: ... I have both cars standing here idle. But say, do you think your friend is a recruiting officer?

COUNTESS: I do not think so.

A: I only ask because we have information that a considerable number of recruits are going on that steamer, and you know that recruiting in this country is against the law. If they go on their own hook, of course, it is all right, but recruiting among Americans in this country is against the law.

C: Well, I don't see how he could do it, he wouldn't have time, you know [laughing].

A: Well, that is what I ask.

C: I want to tell you, if that steamer is attacked, I shall never speak to you again in all my life.[13]

Instead of trying to get his wife's lover torpedoed, von Bernstorff tried to salvage some of his lost pride by running after other women.

In December 1915, the State Department allowed the Secret Service to make a further arrest but, having thereby obtained its intelligence goal in the form of confiscated papers, refrained from pushing its case in the courts. The arrest exposed still further an Austrian spy network whose existence was already known to the Secret Service. Dr. Constantin Theodor Dumba, the Austro-Hungarian ambassador in Washington, had organized the ring with the assistance of his counselor, Baron Erich Zwiedinek von Sudenhorst, and his country's consul-general in New York, Dr. Alexander Nuber von Pereked. Dumba's plan was to encourage the development of labor unrest in American steel plants employing Hungarian, Slovak, and German workers. For example, he wished to finance socialist propaganda along the lines of Upton Sinclair's famous novel *The Jungle*.[14] Dumba was undone when the British interrupted a courier bearing messages from him to the Austrian foreign minister. Not all of these messages were in code, and it was safe for the British to ask President Wilson to confront Dumba with his misdemeanor. Dumba withdrew in September 1915, leaving Zwiedinek as chargé d'affaires.

What the Austrians failed to realize was that they were vulnerable from another quarter. It was probably the Americans themselves who had advised the British about Dumba's courier. When World War I began, Czech-Americans who objected to the sway of Austria-Hungary over their land of origin had begun to spy on the diplomatic envoys of its imperial overlords. To his cost, Dumba had remained blind to his manifestation of radical nationalism. After his departure, the appointments secretary to von Pereked, as well as the doorman at the Austro-Hungarian consulate general in New York, had continued to pass information to the patriot Czechs, who duly informed Guy Gaunt, the British naval attaché, and the American Secret Service.[15]

On December 10, 1915, Secret Service men apprehended an employee of the consulate, cryptically referred to by the Hungarian surname "Angyal" and variously described as a secretary and as a diplomat, and confiscated her papers. Angyal was accused of participating in sabotage and blockade running in breach of the conventions of neutrality laid down in the Austro–American treaty of 1870. The imperial chargé, Zwiedinek, voiced his objections to the State Department through Counselor Polk. Zwiedinek asserted that Angyal was innocent and consul general Von Pereked entirely correct in his behavior; further, Angyal was protected by diplomatic immunity and should not be prosecuted. Polk doubted whether stenographers enjoyed diplomatic immunity; Zwiedinek referred to the arrested employee as a clerk. In the meantime, Angyal refused to appear before a grand jury. Later events were to show that von Pereked was indeed blockade busting, but on this occasion the Austro-Hungarians were successful in obtaining relief from Secret Service harassment. Angyal went free; the Americans had what they wanted, her papers.[16]

The Secret Service served the State Department well during the period of America's neutrality. Its agents made swoop after swoop, yet never fully alerted the Germans to the methods being employed against them. The vulnerability of the Germans is illustrated by an insertion in the "Lost and Found" column of the classified section of the *New York Evening Telegram* for July 27, 1915: "Lost—On Saturday, on 3:30 Harlem elevated train, at 50th St. station, brown leather bag containing documents. Deliver to G. H. Hoffman, 5 East 47st., against $20 reward."[17] Unless the insertion was a smokescreen, the Germans were unaware that the briefcase, carried by their spy chief, Dr. Heinrich F. Albert, had been snatched and made off with at high speed by secret agent Frank Burke, a veteran of counterespionage in the Spanish-American war, who had followed Albert until the German nodded off to sleep on the train. In the hands of Flynn, the stolen documents proved a mine of information on Central Powers intelligence. The federal government decided to let the press have some carefully selected details of the exposed intrigue: since the matter was public, Wilson was able to demand the recall of von Papen, Boy-Ed, and Albert. Yet in spite of all this, the Germans remained ignorant of Burke because American sources managed to convey the impression that British intelligence had brought off the coup.[18] Von Papen wrote to his wife: "Unfortunately they stole a fat portfolio from our good friend, Dr. Albert, in the elevated. The English secret service, of course."[19] The American Secret Service had covered its tracks.

American intelligence is revealed at its most calculating in the case of the von Igel raid. Wolf von Igel had been secretary to von Papen before the military attaché's demise and in 1916 took over von Papen's duties as director of the war intelligence center in Wall Street. In von Papen's old office rested a modern and virtually impregnable safe containing the organizational details of the former attaché's extensive spy organization. Following the exposure of their leading spies and the arrest of Tauscher, the Germans became nervous about the contents of the safe and decided to make them absolutely secure by moving them to the embassy in Washington, where they would be protected by diplomatic immunity. On the morning of April 18, 1916, von Igel laid out the contents of the safe on a table ready for packaging. At that precise moment—the coincidence is truly remarkable—four Justice Department agents arrived to take von Igel in for questioning. As one of them held the office guard at gunpoint, another executed a flying tackle on von Igel as he desperately tried to shovel the evidence back into the safe. The two other agents went to the heart of the matter, pouncing on the mass of evidence, weighing seventy pounds, which provided every last detail, down to the telephone numbers, of German and German-American agents in the United States.[20]

The von Igel raid supplied American authorities with proof, which could be used if needed, of German conspiracies in the United States. The timing of the raid, as well as Secret Service records, suggest that the Department of State already knew a good deal about what was going on. But the acquisition of a mass of evidence in 1916 meant that it would be unnecessary to reveal the extent of previous American surveillance; nor would it be necessary to reveal the extent of secret Anglo-American collusion prior to the raid. The Americans could claim to have learned everything from the von Igel papers, nothing from the British. This was to be important in the future, for, apart from details of sabotage and arms conspiracies, the von Igel papers threw light on a politically sensitive issue, the plans of German intelligence to foment rebellions in India and Ireland. (Indeed, the Easter Rising in Dublin broke out almost immediately. In a careful analysis, the historian A. J. Ward has suggested that the arrest of the "rebel" Sir Roger Casement on the west coast of Ireland on April 21, 1916, was not the result of intelligence passed on by the American authorities as a result of reading the von Igel papers. The State Department did not receive the relevant materials until the afternoon of that day. Furthermore, the British, though they quelled the Rising, were unprepared for it.)[21] The von Igel raid made it possible for American intelligence, in a period when President Wilson was campaigning for reelection on a peace ticket, to lull von Bernstorff and his agents into a renewed sense of unsuspecting security about other serveillance, past and present.

Von Bernstorff clearly believed that the Americans would not divulge to the British the "secrets" contained in the von Igel papers. He resisted pressure from Berlin to fire von Igel and replace him with someone more competent, on the ground that if von Igel's diplomatic immunity were removed he could be prosecuted in the courts and the evidence in his papers used openly against him and to Germany's detriment. He argued that von Igel had made valuable contacts among Irish-Americans and arms manufacturers and that time would heal the resentment which had grown against him: "The judicial authorities are waiting for the State Department's decision before proceeding further. Of late there has been an inclinaton to let the matter drop."[22] He recommended that Germany say nothing until after the 1916 presidential election; he wanted no scandal that would impair Woodrow Wilson's chances of reelection on a pacifist platform. After the election, Germany should bring the strongest possible pressure to bear on the Americans to return the confiscated papers to their rightful owners.[23] Von Bernstorff was encouraged in his belief that the State Department was not exploiting information contained in the von Igel papers by the fact that at the time, the press obtained no official leaks concerning Germany's financing of the Easter Rising in Dublin.

Early in 1917, the British confessed to the Americans with wholly disingenuous modesty that they had partially broken the German codes. Their motive in doing so was to draw the United States into the war on the side of the Allies. They correctly believed that the publication of the notorious Zimmerman telegram would help them win this objective. The Germans had been trying to involve Mexico in an anti-American conspiracy for some time; in January 1917, German Foreign Secretary Alfred Zimmerman supplied proof of his country's design. An intercepted code message from Zimmerman to the German ambassador in Mexico opened as follows:

> We intend to begin on the first of February unrestricted submarine warfare. We shall endeavor in spite of this to keep the United States of America neutral. In the event of this not succeeding, we make Mexico a proposal of alliance on the following basis:
> Make war together, make peace together, generous financial support, and an understanding on our part that Mexico is to reconquer the lost territory in Texas, New Mexico and Arizona.[24]

Thus were the conquests of James K. Polk to be endangered after sixty years. The British passed the message on to Frank L. Polk, who showed it to Wilson and Lansing. The press obtained a copy of the note on March

1, 1917, and war became a near-certainty. Not content with gaining this end, the British sought to obscure the means by which the note had been decoded. Every effort was made to convince the Germans that a duplicate uncoded copy had been picked up by the Americans.[25] The cat-and-mouse game was by no means over.

In the fall of 1917, the American government deemed it prudent, in the light of armed hostilities and the strength of public feeling, to make disclosures from the von Igel papers. Leland Harrison of the State Department had objected to their earlier publication for fear that there would be a public reaction against the espionage activities of the government.[26] In the spring of 1918 the British government, delighted with the discredit being thrown on Irish revolutionaries, supplied Lansing, through America's London ambassador W. H. Page, with many more decodes indicating German-Irish conspiracy.[27] When Admiral William R. Hall, the British cryptographer, sent on a final batch of messages in May, it was agreed that "in order to give the appearance of consistency in respect of previous disclosures of German telegrams, all of which have been made by [the United States] government, Hall would, in communicating the documents to higher authority for publication, have to intimate that after exchanging information with the American secret service for over a year he is now in a position to decipher German messages himself."[28] American intelligence was good in World War I, and won the reputation of being even better.

Efficacious though the State Department–Secret Service combination was, it did not entirely meet the requirements of the Wilson administration. MID and ONI had begun to reorganize in 1915; Bureau of Investigation agents had already seen service against the von Rintelen ring on the instructions of Lansing.[29] But a further expansion was to occur. In the spring of 1917, Justice Department agents were pressed into more urgent and widespread service, and, with the approach of hostilities, various branches of military intelligence budded and burst into leaf. Why?

Two factors explain the boom in American counterespionage in 1917. The first is that there is a great deal of difference between making contingency plans for war, which is what happened in 1915, and preparing for an actual war, which is what transpired in 1917. Both Wilson and Lansing became acutely worried about possible penetrations of America's security cloak by German agents. For example, they corresponded about John Ewing, a loyal Democrat from Mobile, Alabama, who had been made American minister to the Republic of Honduras. Ewing had access to American naval codes and had on one occasion lost the key to his diplomatic pouch. One of his daughters had married an Austrian, M. H. von Liebe, whose father was a field marshall and whose brother was in the Austrian submarine service. The couple had left for a honeymoon in Chile. A German was paying attention to another Ewing daughter.[30]

Ewing himself was a likable man but ill: "A year ago," according to an ONI report, "he was nearly dead from drink and though now he does not drink his mind in not particularly active." The report continued. "When questioned as to what transpired at a conference several hours before, he is unable to remember the conference."[31] Against the background of this kind of situation, the State Department put effective pressure on the ONI to tighten up security.[32] Similarly, President Wilson personally warned Secretary of War Newton D. Baker about the danger from "alien enemies" in war-production factories in November 1917, and sought his advice on the problem.[33]

The second factor explaining why the government stepped up counter-espionage operations in 1917 is its desire to make arrests and furnish documentary proof of German undercover operations. Stories of enemy espionage made excellent propaganda, especially when they were true. The *New York Sun,* which had pioneered the technique of the "human interest story" in the 1870s and focused attention on Spanish spies in 1898, was one of several papers ready at a moment's notice to publicize allegations of German intrigue.[34] John P. Jones of the *Sun* took a year off from other duties to work on Austro-German spy-plot stories and in 1917 combined them in the first edition of his book *The German Spy in America.* Theodore Roosevelt supplied a preface dated February 27, in which he pronounced: "I have read the galley proofs of your book, and I wish to say, with all emphasis and heartiness, that you are doing this country a great service in publishing it." Roosevelt, a leading advocate of American preparedness, attacked those of his compatriots who were pacifists, claiming that their opposition to the war was "directly instigated by German intrigues, and paid for by German money."[35]

Woodrow Wilson could not afford to be upstaged by Roosevelt, his Progressive opponent in the 1912 election. The former pacifist needed German spying to establish himself as a patriot. Wilson presented German intrigue as one of the chief provocations leading to America's entry into World War I. The president's Flag Day address of June 14, 1917, is one of many prominent instances of his stress on the espionage theme. He remarked of the Germans:

> They filled our unsuspecting communities with vicious spies and con-spirators, and sought to corrupt the opinion of our people in their own behalf. When they found they could not do that, their agents dili-gently spread sedition amongst us and sought to draw our own citizens from their allegiance—and some of these agents were men connected with the official embassy of the German government itself, here in our own capital.
>
> They sought by violence to destroy our industries and arrest our commerce. They tried to incite Mexico to take up arms against us, and to draw Japan into a hostile alliance with her. . . .

And many of our own people were corrupted. Men began to look upon their neighbors with suspicion, and to wonder in their hot resentment and surprise whether there was any community in which hostile intrigue did not lurk.[36]

By the fall of 1917, in the name of national defense, the Wilson administration had set up a system of domestic surveillance as efficient as that of 1898 and, in that it embraced contingents from the Department of Justice, more pervasive. For this reason, sections of the American people were subjected to investigation in a manner deplored by the upholders of traditional liberties. In their harassment of radicals and suspected radicals as well as of "enemy aliens," Bureau of Investigation officials often ignored the spirit of the Fourth Amendment to the Constitution: "The right of the people to be secure in their persons, houses, papers, and effects against unreasonable searches and seizures shall not be violated."[37] After the Bolshevik take-over in Russia, Communists and anarchists particularly were subject to arbitrary arrest and deportation, but between 1917 and 1920 no radical could go to bed at night without fearing the pre-dawn raid.

Wilson's liberal Democrats had been righteous in the cause of reform; their moral certitude was just as strong when directed against radicals. The attack by the center on both right and left is evident in the career of A. Mitchell Palmer, Progressive legislator turned repressive attorney general. It was Palmer who, in an attempt to extinguish what he inaccurately perceived as a "prairie-fire" of revolution, authorized the legally dubious "dragnet" raids, or mass arrests, of January 2, 1920.[38] The Palmer raids were more extreme than anything undertaken by the Secret Service in 1898 and directly provoked the creation of the American Civil Liberties Union. Assistant attorney general Charles Warren extended more dangerously the requirements of ideological conformity when he conspired with Leland Harrison to link the names of academics critical of Wilson's views with pro-German revolutionary conspirators. Warren was a leading authority on the Supreme Court, and his widow ultimately enshrined his name in the Charles Warren Center for the Study of Liberty at Harvard University, which, ironically, subsidized books critical of the Wilson administration's disregard for civil liberties, among others.[39] In spite of his libertarian views—or, perhaps, precisely because he so strongly resented any challenge to his liberty-loving America—Warren indulged in such excesses of opinion as the view that Charles Beard, author of *An Economic Interpretation of the Constitution* and an outspoken critic of conspiracies from 1787 to 1917, was "tainted with pro-German pacifism."[40]

The penchant for intrusion and undercover persecution was an unsavory aspect of Wilsonian liberalism, but it was by no means confined to its practitioners. Senator Henry Cabot Lodge of Massachusetts was the leading critic of Wilson's foreign policy, and a Republican. He used his influence as chairman of the Senate Foreign Relations Committee to exploit federal undercover resources for his conservative political ends. Thus Lodge recruited the American and French secret services in an unsuccessful attempt to discredit Norman Hapgood, an outspoken journalist and President Wilson's appointee as minister to Denmark.[41] Lodge's action was potentially significant in that the Senate has the Constitutional right of "advice and consent" over all of the executive's major diplomatic appointments.

That it would be a mistake to portray Lodge as the undoubting harbinger of a never-to-be-consummated police state is shown by his response to the apparent harassment of one J. T. L. Jeffries. Jeffries had led the undergraduate preparedness campaign at Harvard in 1914–1915.[42] He defended Lodge's belligerent stand during the *Lusitania* crisis, electioneered in the senator's hawkish campaign in 1916, and in 1918 found himself on active service in France.[43] But he was soon sent home because of emotional instability; investigation showed that he had enlisted against medical advice and that he suffered from a persecution complex of paranoid proportions.[44] Jeffries wrote several letters to Lodge complaining that he was being refused promotion from second to first lieutenant, that his estate off the South Carolina coast had been occupied by traitors, and that letters to his mother in Boston were going astray or being tampered with.[45] After his commitment to a mental hospital, Jeffries alleged that MID and a "nouveau riche [Boston] Democrat close to President Wilson" were trying to ruin his Army career by labeling him a German spy.[46]

Lodge was indifferent to the mail censorship so hotly resented by Jeffries. He dismissed Jeffries' complaint, saying that postal delays were common to men and officers serving abroad. However, he showed sensitivity toward Jeffries' problems in correspondence and went to the trouble of acquiring relevant documentation from the adjutant general to satisfy himself that his constituent and supporter was not being victimized by a faction within the espionage bureaucracy.[47]

It is significant that not even Jeffries regarded himself as having been persecuted by the State Department. Whatever the excesses of certain branches of American counterespionage, the system as a whole was too pluralistic to permit a thoroughgoing central oppression such as that exercised by autocracies and police states. Some of the component parts of American intelligence were notable for their restraint. In spite of wartime tension and suspicion, Josephus Daniels warned the ONI not to interfere with labor unions in the dockyards.[48] No intelligence agency exploited Count von Bernstorff's mistresses for blackmail purposes.

The State Department itself was more concerned with diplomacy than with social control. Its officials were sometimes prepared to offer redress in cases of individual harassment. One such case arose from the quandary of Russian embassy officials after the Bolshevik take-over of 1917. The United States still recognized their position, yet some of them were naturally homesick. One official, the railroad consultant George V. Lomonosoff, said that he had turned Bolshevik and wanted to go home. He found himself in difficulties: first, he had no commonly recognized passport; second, Secret Service agents seized his effects. On the morning of August 7, 1918, future Supreme Court Justice Felix Frankfurter (at that time adviser to the president and to the secretaries of war and labor) called on Frank Polk to appeal for assistance, pleading that Lomonosoff and his wife were forming a bad impression of the United States. Polk received Mrs. Lomonosoff the same afternoon and undertook to rescue the couple from the clutches of the Treasury men.[49]

The virtue of State Department-coordinated intelligence in regard to civil liberties during World War I is indirectly illustrated by the company it did not keep. Neither ONI nor MID contenanced any help from private detectives. In March 1917, the Val O'Farrell Detective Agency approached Secretary of the Navy Daniels. Detective agencies, which had made money out of strikes, had fallen on hard times because of the improvement in industrial relations brought about by preparedness and war.[50] They now looked to counterespionage for a living. The O'Farrell Agency supplied Daniels with a photograph of a young woman with dark hair, appealing eyes, and a substantial expanse of uncovered flesh. By innuendo, the agency linked the girl with New Yorkers having German names, claiming that she was a secret courier. The agency's representative alleged that bureau of investigation agents were failing to protect national security.[51] Daniels preserved the nation from the assistance of the O'Farrell Agency. His restraint in this respect developed into a consistent policy. In 1920, the director of naval intelligence emphasized that it was the aim of ONI "to use reputable business methods and avoid anything savoring of 'gumshoe' methods."[52]

MID, too, was plagued with offers of assistance. Some came from citizens who were patriotic, influential, but clearly unqualified for detective work. Van Deman and Churchill spent hours fighting off the claims of patronage. After an exchange with one correspondent consisting of about a hundred letters, Churchill pinned on the bundle a black-edged card inscribed *"Requiescat in pace."*[53] The Berkeley, California, police chief was one supplicant who tried to use political influence to get an MID appointment. Van Deman retaliated with cutting remarks to the effect that intelligence work was no game for mere detectives; it had to be linked to general, coordinated strategy.[54]

The final comment may be left to William A. Pinkerton of the agency bearing his surname. He remarked at the end of the war that the "experience we have been through in these past four years should guide us for the future." He recommended the creation of a new, federal force of a thousand "trained detectives that will centralize, connect up and weave together data. . . ."[55] In the opinion of the noted private detective, American intelligence was limited and decentralized. This was not entirely true. In the post-Bryan era, MID, ONI, and the Bureau of Investigation had increased in size and extended their activities. The State Department coordinated their efforts and those of the Secret Service, already a going concern, with its own requirements. But, in one respect, Pinkerton was mercifully correct in his criticism. The State Department did not launch an independent agency capable of initiating a centralized oppression of the American people.

6

Overseas Intelligence in World War I

In 1917, the State Department counselor's main intelligence job became foreign espionage. During the war, the office developed strength and independence in this field, particularly in the Far East and East Central Europe. In Western Europe, however, Americans cooperated with British and French intelligence. This was partly because Polk and Auchincloss were two of the leading anglophiles of the Wilson administration. Their diaries show how, well before the outbreak of hostilities between the United States and Germany, they were on social terms with British and French diplomats but not with Germans.[1] For Polk and Auchincloss, as for many Ivy League alumni, anglophilia was a form of snobbery. Auchincloss patently preferred "top people" to what Polk termed "labor people."[2] London was the world center for top people. It was therefore frustrating for Auchincloss that when he went to London to arrange cooperation with British intelligence, it was judged injudicious for him to appear in society. He consoled himself with daily visits to Sir William Wiseman's tailor.[3]

Consistent with the snobbery of Polk and Auchincloss were their self-inflation and conspiratorial outlook. In the eyes of posterity these characteristics, to which later spymasters were also prone, accounted for some of the most objectionable aspects of American espionage. Auchincloss shared with Wiseman that need for aggrandizement which is commonly found in officials of the second rank who privately suspect that they got that far only because of their connections.[4] Auchincloss made the following grandiose entry in his diary for March 30, 1917: "Sir Wm. Wiseman lunched with me at Mid-Day Club. We went over fairly thoroughly the kind of cooperation that we should endeavor to establish between this country and England. I have asked him for information on certain names and he has promised to give them to me and from now on to deal with the State Department through me."[5] Auchincloss occupied a lowly position in the American diplomatic hierarchy, but mixed with the mighty and found it gratifying to think of himself as a leading intermediary between the United States and England.

In the cryptographer Yardley, admiration for the British was mixed with envy and a desire for emulation through bureaucracy, as well as with an exaggerated sense of the importance of intelligence work. He recalled in his memoir that although British wartime decoders were "no cleverer than our own, those in power in England considered a Cipher Bureau of such tremendous importance that they placed an admiral at its head [Yardley was only an Army Captain]. This man, Admiral Hall, because of the information he obtained from the messages that his enormous bureau deciphered, stood next to Lloyd George in power."[6]

Polk was too senior to indulge in such distortions, yet he, too, revealed a passion for self-importance and conspiracy in labeling his desk diary "Confidential." There was nothing vital to national security, for example, in his unintentionally candid remark that Roosevelt was "flattering about my Spanish War record."[7] Intelligence controllers thought themselves important partly because they were the first with the news. What could be more natural than that they should pose as the guardians of great secrets and embellish their clandestine roles?

The popularity of spy and detective stories shows that mystery has an appeal for everyone; secrecy, however, had a special fascination for the Wilsonian entourage. Ignoring the maxims that prime codes should rarely be used and that secrets should be kept to a minimum, Wiseman and House in 1918 labeled most of their messages "secret" and used code for all of them. Auchincloss classified the texts of counterespionage memoranda and telephone taps as "B-99 reports," followed by a serial number identifying the agent concerned, his cryptographic code, and the nature of his information. In a move that did less to confound German intelligence than to satisfy his own cryptic needs, Auchincloss in May 1917 reclassified all the reports A-99, "followed by the same serial number as on the original report to me."[8]

Auchincloss's enthusiasm for secrecy and cryptography may have been contracted from Admiral Hall's mysterious "Room 40" code breakers in London. In spite of President Wilson's denunciation of German espionage, spying was contagious and fashionable. Contemporary fiction, notably the works of Robert Chambers, featured heroes who were both intrepid and clandestine. The British soldier R. S. S. Baden-Powell, famed for his South African campaigns and for his formation in 1908 of the coast-watching, flag-signaling, hero-worshipping Boy Scouts, in 1915 published *My Adventures as a Spy*.[9]

For whatever reason, Auchincloss was afflicted with the outlook of the hero-worshipping Boy Scout starved of personal acclaim. He was not, like the Scouts, too young to serve, but he found himself tied to his safe desk while others marched to glory and to doom. He noted with awe that Wiseman had been gassed at Ypres.[10] One gets the impression from Auchincloss's diary that he was a small boy being led by the hand if not the nose by Wiseman, who in London "took me to one of the special divisions of the War Intelligence Work where I met Guy Standing the actor, who is a commander in the navy, and who is the right-hand associate of Wiseman's in this country. We wandered through many devious ways before we reached the seclusion of Standing's office."[11] This was not the only adventure awaiting Auchincloss in London. He experienced the culinary delights of the House of Commons chef (the menu meticulously noted in his diary) and nightly visited theaters offering entertainment of the Folies Bergères variety.[12] The American spymaster was a vicarious man.

Although American intelligence came of age during World War I, it leaned for support on the informational services of the Allies. Anglophilia produced a one-sided investment of American resources; francophilia, too, induced Americans to collaborate with Allied intelligence both before and after April 1917. Polk saw the French ambassador, Jules Jusserand, on February 10 and 20, 1917, to discuss American espionage laws and the problem of German agents operating on American soil. Polk promised that he would carefully consider the matter of German espionage and "might take the liberty of asking [Jusserand] for suggestions."[13] After the declaration of war, the Americans continued to take an active interest in French intelligence matters. House shared Wiseman's concern over a British intelligence report which stressed the inability of the French premier, Georges Clemenceau, to resolve the feud between his generals Pétain and Foch, in consequence of which the report concluded that "to this day [June 22, 1918] Foch is inadequately staffed, particularly from the intelligence point of view."[14]

The Americans took the initiative in some matters. They were the chief intermediaries in the secret discussions which led to the formation of a Polish contingent under French command, and the United States had an extensive counterespionage network on French soil. It should be added, however, that the historian Richard W. Rowan was probably right in saying that the chief activity of the U.S. network in France was "spying on other Americans" to discover cases of disloyalty and low morale.[15] Some Americans, such as Colonel Richard H. Williams, brought off offensive military intelligence scoops. Williams used balloons, aircraft, his feet, and native wit to retrieve tactical information from behind the German lines. For the most part, however, the State Department relied on the British and French for information about the Western front.

Even in the case of East Central European intelligence, where the Americans quickly established preeminence, some evidence can be adduced to indicate their dependency. W. Somerset Maugham, the Allies' chief agent in revolutionary Russia, was, though sponsored by the Americans, an Englishman. It was an Englishman, moreover—naval attaché Captain Guy Gaunt—who first recruited the Czech-American intelligence agent Emanuel Voska, about whom we shall shortly have more to say.[16] American information on Russia was, therefore, partly the result of English enterprise. The British took some pains over Russian intelligence, the relevant files in the Foreign Office being presided over by the Scottish aristocrat Philip Kerr.[17] It is not clear whether the scions of the British establishment intended to pass on all information to the Americans, but the State Department did have access to a good number of British reports. For example, Polk in the crucial month of November 1917 received reports from Russia forwarded through the British embassy in Petrograd.[18]

At times, liaison between the United States and His Majesty's government was so close that it is difficult to maintain with certainty that Americans held the initiative even in Eastern intelligence matters. Sir William Wiseman established close relations between the office of the counselor and the Foreign Office in March and April 1917. It was later in the same year that House and Auchincloss ventured overseas to confer with the director of military intelligence in Britain, General Sir George Macdonogh. In 1918, Wiseman forged a link between Wilson's fact finding agency, The Inquiry, and the political intelligence department at the Foreign Office.[19] This was one of the consequences of his successful appeal to the Foreign Office to be relieved of military intelligence work to concentrate on political affairs. The Americans, too, concentrated on political intelligence, which became so important in the context of an ideological challenge from the Soviet Union. Against this background, it is in several cases safest to assume that there was joint Anglo-American responsibility for intelligence rather than domination by one partner.

In the field of cryptanalysis, the British preserved their lead throughout the war. Their advantage owed much to the retrieval of a German naval code book from the wreckage of the light cruiser *Magdeburg*, sunk in the Gulf of Finland by two Russian cruisers in August 1914. W. R. Hall's code breakers in "Room 40" of the Admiralty's old building received the captured code book when Russia sent it on to her trusted ally.[20] Together with further naval codes photographed by a British spy planted, according to Yardley, in the German Admiralty, the book gave Hall's team a flying start on their competitors.[21]

Ostensibly, America's well-funded M.I.8 established an independent cryptographic capability during the war. Yardley's team broke several Latin American codes, and the young cryptographer, displaying a flair for salesmanship, persuaded the State Department to keep him on in various capacities after the completion of his wartime MID work. In 1919, he went to Paris, where, in the dull moments between cocktail parties, he broke codes for the American Peace Commission. Later in the same year Polk, as acting secretary of state, put Yardley in charge of an elaborately secretive peacetime "Black Chamber," which had its headquarters in New York, attracted an MID appropriation from 1921, and cracked Japanese codes in the 1920s.[22] Significant though Yardley's successes were, however, M.I.8 was relatively unsuccessful in breaking the codes of America's main wartime enemy, Germany. For information on German codes, Yardley had to content himself with crumbs from Admiral Hall's table.

The Americans realized only slowly that the British, unlike the Russians, were not willing to share intelligence secrets with their allies. Yardley exaggerated Hall's attitude but did not misrepresent it. The Admiral appreciated the degree to which information confers power and the British were not ready to confer power on the United States. In October 1917, Edward "Ned" Bell, one of whose duties as first secretary in the American embassy in London was to liaise with the intelligence officers of the British government, passed to Lansing via Page the texts of fifty-two German dispatches intercepted by the British.[23] These were helpful for propaganda and informational purposes but would have been even more useful if accompanied by copies of the German codes in British possession. The Americans pressed their ally to deliver these codes. In January 1918, Hall agreed to hand over photostats of codes used for communication between the German Foreign Office and Indian American conspirators in the United States. Bell "received the plunder" one morning and sent it by diplomatic bag to the State Department.[24] This show of generosity by Hall was, however, more calculated than Bell realized: the overlord of Room 40 was aware that Secret Service agents had already captured Indian German code letters and transcriptions.

It is clear that although British intelligence was friendly toward America and willing to encourage its progress along approved avenues, it already regarded U.S. undercover specialists as "the competition."[25] Cryptanalytic information was hard currency, disbursable only in exchange for valued services. In April 1918, Page sent on further materials purporting to show that the Easter Rising in Dublin had been "planned to the last detail" by German and pro-German conspirators. He concluded his covering letter to Lansing with the observation that he was also forwarding a "technical memorandum on the cipher messages enclosed which Mr. Bell has prepared...."[26] Hall had released some code information, but only to enable the State Department to argue, if necessary, that it had decoded German conspiracy messages on its own and had not been spoon-fed by the British with information and opinions on Irish nationalism and Allied war aims. Furthermore, the code information supplied by Hall must have been limited, because in August 1918 Yardley visited London to try to learn more about British code-breaking methods. The British received him cordially, as did the French a little later. Nevertheless, the London cryptographers remained tight-lipped on the subject that interested Yardley, and in Paris the Bureau du Chiffre was no more forthcoming.

Ned Bell had told Yardley in advance what the British attitude would be; Yardley recalled that the first secretary had learned from "secret sources" that "the British Intelligence liaison officers in Washington had warned Colonel French [of the British War Office] of my mission, and that every obstacle would be placed in my path."[27] Yardley thought it would be impossible to outmaneuver his British rivals by bringing diplomatic pressure to bear on them, because he feared that there was an English spy in the American code room in London. The American therefore tried to win Hall's confidence by making himself personally agreeable and by demonstrating his cryptological ability.[28] Hall rewarded Yardley with what he intended to be useless consolation prizes but in fact provided Americans with the beginnings of cryptological expertise.

Fortunately for Yardley, his MID team was able to break some codes because of the inevitable clues provided by British transcriptions, and through sheer diligence and ability. In July 1918, Yardley took "great pleasure" in reporting to the State Department that he was able to read code messages between German officials in Chile and Mexico.[29] Eleven months later, Yardley reported that his team was able to decode German messages between Berlin and Mexico.[30] This may have been because the beleaguered Hall eventually gave Yardley "several copies of a certain neutral government's diplomatic codes."[31] Hall would have been glad to oblige Yardley in the case of Mexico, which was a country outside the main orbit of European power politics. He was much more secretive about the arterial lines of communication which carried Europe's pulsebeat. In January 1919, Yardley wired Bell from Paris: "Am still receiving a great number of German messages exchanged between Berlin and Madrid. I feel very certain that if you can get the verbatim German decipherment of the two enclosed code messages, I shall be able to reconstruct the entire German diplomatic code, and thereby accomplish myself that which the British and French have refused to accomplish for me."[32] It was this vital information that Hall had refused Yardley; the "neutral government" codes were merely a sop.[33]

By the end of January 1919, Leland Harrison of the State Department had worked out a plan, with Churchill of MID, for the perpetuation of

Yardley's cryptographic office and, it followed, for an independent crypto-graphic capability. The undercover expert secured for Yardley a lavish peacetime staff of almost a hundred. He set his heart on making things even easier for the fledgling organization by procuring a copy of the German naval code that would decipher the problematic "messages sent in five letters, some of which are accented." Bell was instructed to do his best with the British, who might relent, in Harrison's view, because the war was over.[34]

The British remained uncooperative. Lansing now concocted a differ-ent plan, designed, like its predecessor, to furnish Yardley with the Ger-man codes. He entrusted Harrison with its execution, and Harrison in turn passed the secretary of state's instructions to L. Lanier Winslow, one of the operational specialists of the office of the counselor. The plan was that the United States should emulate the United Kingdom by sending a secret agent into Germany itself, with the object of bribing officials there to betray their country's codes. Lansing insisted that the job should be divorced from the peace commission and the State Department, that it should in fact be subcontracted to MID. Preferably, a neutral country should be chosen as the base for operations. Lansing suggested specifi-cally that the venture should be entrusted to Colonel Edward Davis, the military attaché at The Hague in the Netherlands. At any rate, the "agent should be carefully chosen" and "no time should be lost."[35] Clearly, the State Department was still dissatisfied with the flow of information coming from Admiral Hall and British intelligence. In the 1920s, the resultant willingness of American diplomats to pay for code information became well known in espionage circles.[36]

Admiral Hall's reticence was meant to further the interests of the United Kingdom and the British empire. Hall and the Foreign Office released information, but only for propaganda purposes and, even then, in a manner that hid from Germany the fact that Britain had the keys to German codes. (The Germans were reported to have broken some British codes but, apparently unable to deduce from intercepted messages that the Allies were privy to their own secrets, refrained from feeding Admiral Hall with misleading information.)[37] The release of information acquired by decoding secret German messages sometimes furthered American interests, but merely coincidentally. To the best of their ability, the British made information work for them. The contents of the famous "Zimmerman telegram," divulging a German conspiracy to draw Mexico into any impending war with United States, were held secret by the British until they were assured of having the greatest psychological effect. The release of information concerning Irish and Indian conspiracies in the United States was even further delayed until the right moment had arrived. To the extent that these conspiracies among potentially disruptive elements were exposed after the entry of the United States into the war, the British manipulation of information was in the mutual interest. However, the news releases were designed to further not only the war effort of the Allies but also the particular interests of the British empire. They were actually harmful to President Wilson's credibility as a statesman, in view of his propaganda for self-determination.

It is significant that, even over the limited number of codes farmed out, the British retained a rigid if theoretical control well into peacetime. Harrison promised Hall in May 1919 that the Americans would make no use of information gained from relevant decoded German messages without seeking prior permission.[38] The British admiral was concerned partly about security, partly about the preservation of Britain's ability to monopolize information—and, lastly, about American naval rivalry; Hall had already extracted a promise that Welles of ONI would not get possession of German naval code 55515.[39] He no doubt hoped that interdepartmental rivalry would induce the State Department to keep its promise not to share British cryptological secrets with the military. That the State Department probably ignored Hall's injunction is indicated by American expertise in breaking naval codes in the 1920s and by the participation of MID in the Black Chamber. Nevertheless, it must be concluded that, for the period of World War I, American cryptographers played second fiddle to their British counterparts, with harmful consequences for Wilson's diplomatic overtures.

It would be only natural to suppose, given the anglophilia of Polk and Auchincloss, their reliance on Anglo-French espionage for information on the Western front, and their involuntary dependence on Admiral Hall's code breakers, that American intelligence was incapable of independent assessment during World War I. This was not, however, the case. Polk's team was not distracted by mere foibles. They may have been snobs, but they were patriotic snobs. They were a small enough and talented enough group to be able to see through complex situations. Being responsible more for liaison and evaluation than for collection, they never allowed themselves to be overwhelmed by confusing masses of detailed evidence. The office of the counselor to the Department of State exhibited the sine qua non of a useful espionage system, a healthy scepticism. The refusal of Polk and his lieutenants to be dazzled by the evanescent brilliance of apocryphal intelligence scoops materially aided the national interest of the United States.

Polk was healthily impatient with hysteria and false information. He could be blunt to unreliable informants: "I warned [F. C.] Proctor [general counsel for the Gulf Oil Companies] that he had so often said something would happen [in Mexico] and nothing had happened that we were not very sympathetic."[40] He did not allow differences of opinion to panic him into seeing Bolshevism everywhere. For example, when military intelligence in 1918 objected to the issuance of a passport to Oswald

G. Villard, editor of the liberal magazine *The Nation*, who had an open mind on Bolshevik Russia, Polk saw no reason why Villard should not leave the country; he "did not agree with his views but thought he could do no harm."[41]

It was Polk who unavailingly pressed on Wilson and George Creel the view, ultimately proved correct, that the Sisson papers were forgeries. Edgar Sisson, a journalist who gave up the editorship of *Cosmopolitan* to help the war effort, had acquired the papers when serving as the Russian representative on the Committee on Public Information, Wilson's propaganda agency headed by the former newspaper editor and future New Deal administrator George Creel. The forged papers indicated that there had been German–Bolshevik collaboration in securing a German-assisted leftward shift in Russia in exchange for Russia's withdrawal from the war. Publication of the papers was an attractive scheme from the American government's point of view, in that it would at one stroke highlight German unscrupulousness and throw doubt on the spontaneity of the Bolshevik Revolution. Because the British had questioned the authenticity of the documents, the Americans sought expert advice. Experts who should have known that revolutions do not stem from foreign conspiracies—such as the historian J. Franklin Jameson, future author of *The American Revolution Considered as a Social Movement* (1926)— pronounced the documents authentic, and in so doing commanded the confidence of Creel and Wilson. The official publication of the Sisson papers followed in October 1918, having the effect of increasing Russian suspicions of U.S. diplomacy and, no doubt, contributing to Bolshevik truculence in the future. It is therefore to the credit of Polk and the authors of intelligence emanating from the counselor's office that the counselor fought against majority opinion in an attempt to prevent publication of the Sisson papers.[42]

The case of the Voska war guilt papers provides another example of effective intelligence work ignored in higher quarters. Emanuel Voska was an immigrant who had been forced to leave his native Bohemia when still a young man for holding nationalist and socialist views unacceptable to the authorities of the Austro-Hungarian empire. He arrived in the United States, where he made a fortune in the marble-cutting industry. During this period, he became an advocate of the creation of a Czechoslovak state. At the outbreak of World War I, he created, with the assistance of Guy Gaunt, a network of hyphenate-American counterspies; Voska was partly responsible for the penetration of the New York spy ring organized by von Pereked on behalf of Austria-Hungary in 1915. When the United States lumbered into hostilities, Voska made an ambitious and successful bid to become involved in offensive intelligence. He operated in East Central Europe, doing valuable work for the office of the counselor and MID under the supervision of Lansing's secretary

Richard Crane and the Anglo-American agent W. Somerset Maugham. The experience hardened Voska's attitude toward Bohemia's ancient oppressor, and when victory came, he needed no second invitation to join in war-guilt investigations.

At the conclusion of hostilities, Secretary Lansing, a member of the American Peace Delegation at Paris, became chairman of a commission to determine responsibility for the outbreak of the war. In the long term the question of war guilt was to be crucial. Germany, being held responsible for aggression, was forced to pay reparations for war damage. The British economist J. M. Keynes and his widening circle of advisers believed this burden to be fatal to the chances of democracy under the Weimar Republic of the 1920s. Germans were understandably bitter on the subject of reparations, since they erroreously believed that Wilson had induced them to capitulate in 1918 with a promise of no indemnities. Arguably, Hitler rose to power with the assistance of a people who felt betrayed.[43] In 1918 and early 1919, the services of the American operational espionage network were placed at the disposal of the war-guilt investigators, coordinated by Creel. The act alone indicated a prejudiced state of mind. Voska, in particular, was entrusted with the job of discovering some proof for the view that the assassination of Austria's crown prince at Sarajevo in 1914 had been a German-Austrian plot to trigger world war.

In February 1919, Voska's plans ran afoul of an alleged indiscretion by his son, Lieutenant Arthur E. Voska, then serving on secondment with the Czech army. The indiscretion arose out of one of the several boundary difficulties which World War I had left in its wake. The coal-rich duchy of Teschen, in the southeast corner of Silesia, had been the subject of dispute between Poland and Bohemia since the ninth century. In January 1919, Czech troops took advantage of the collapse of Austria by occupying the duchy's strategic railroad center, Oderberg. The Czechoslovak minister of national defense ordered the Poles out of Teschen, and the local proclamation was signed by the officers of the occupying Czech forces. Arthur Voska was with the Czech forces as an American observer. He and another Czech-American officer were alleged to have signed the expulsion declaration, causing an incident not only embarrassing to the State Department but offensive to the pro-Polish Wilson. Captain Emanuel Voska had been responsible for delivering orders to his son. If the Americanized son was capable of succumbing to an access of vicarious Czech nationalism, what, official logic demanded, could be expected of the Bohemian born father? The State Department asked military intelligence to investigate the desirability, against this background, of granting the elder Voska's request to return to Prague to continue his war-guilt investigations.

Toward the end of February, Emanuel Voska participated in what the official transcript euphemistically described as a "conversation" with General Tasker H. Bliss. Bliss was one of the American peace commissioners at Paris and as such had a duty to help iron out the problem in Teschen. He had also been military attaché in Madrid (1897), President of the Army War College and, briefly, chief of staff; he knew intelligence work, and Voska may be imagined to have experienced, during their "conversation," the psychological pressures of a person under interrogation. When the interview opened Voska was under the impression that he would have to defend his son. Indeed, Bliss, personally conducting the interrogation, soon applied pressure to what was presumed to be a father's weak spot, unreasonably requesting Voska to prove that his son had not signed the Polish proclamation. However, the experienced Army general disconcertingly opened the interview with the following barrage of questions:

General Bliss: What were the orders you received from General Churchill [of MID]?

Captain Voska: To report to the Committee on Public Information and comply with their orders.

B: You received an order from that Committee to go to Prague, which you complied with?

V: Yes.

B: Apparently from this copy of a letter [author unspecified] addressed to Mr. Sisson, you were engaged in examining certain documents, letters, etc., with the idea of tracing any possible connection between the murder of the Crown Prince of Austria and the German Government.

V: That was only a small part of the work. The chief part of the work was the publication of 2,500,000 pamphlets, mostly speeches.

B: You were supposed to have them published and distributed in those countries? That was your principal work?

V: Yes, sir.

B: Who assigned you to this other work of examining these documents with a view to seeing whether the German Government had been mixed up in the conspiracy to murder the Crown Prince?

V: Mr. Sisson.

B: In writing?

V: No.[44]

Evidently Voska was freelancing with the encouragement of the irrepressible Sisson. Yet there is ground for suspecting—for example, in the use of the definite article in the phrase "the conspiracy to murder" Ferdinand —that Bliss might have been prepared to accept Voska's contention about German war guilt. On the one hand, there prevailed in Army circles a reluctance to admit that Voska was being officially sponsored. On the other, there was the tempting prospect of a dramatic vindication for the Allied war effort.

Churchill was eager to allow Voska to return to Prague to continue his mission (whose precise nature every official refrained from specifying, since it was one of President Wilson's declared and well-broadcast principles that the defeated Central Powers should be treated with magnanimity). The MID chief penciled a memorandum to a State Department undercover specialist: "As Capt. Voska's work for the C.P.I. is not finished and as he evidently had no connection with the proclamation said to be signed by his son, I think he should return as soon as the Commissioners are through with him."[45] Churchill's memorandum went to Allen Dulles for comment before being forwarded to Joseph C. Grew, a diplomat then attached to the peace commission, and to Bliss for a final decision. Dulles, the CIA chief of the 1950s, was in 1919 a typical member of the State Department's undercover elite. He was the grandson of Secretary of State John W. Foster, his mother being Mrs. Lansing's sister. During the war, Dulles had learned what Robert Edwards, member of parliament and chairman of the British Independent Labor Party later described as the "striped-trouser method."[46] Under diplomatic cover in Vienna and Berne, he ran clandestine operations. Early in 1918, he made secret contact with the Austrians to try to obtain a separate peace. Dulles was then given the post of second secretary to the Paris peace delegation, where he worked on the definition of the Czechoslovak boundary. He was sagacious enough to question, when consulted, the wisdom of sending Voska back to Prague.[47]

Dulles's objection was not based on the belief that Voska's claims concerning captured documents would turn out to be spurious but on the conviction that the consequences of gratuitously antagonizing Austria would be unfavorable. He suggested that "it would be inadvisable for Captain Voska to return to Bohemia if there is any other possible way of closing up his work in that country."[48] Grew reported that Voska wanted to return to Prague "to wind up his affairs," which meant paying certain debts and finishing his work for Creel.[49] In the event, Voska was able to finish the war-guilt project to his own satisfaction. On March 19, 1919, he wrote to Leland Harrison (both were located in Paris at the time), reporting: "To-day I received a report from Prague that, finally, the documents which we were after were located in a secret section of the military division in Hofbibliothek, Vienna."[50]

Voska told Harrison that he had obtained access to "letters and documents which will give information as to who is responsible for the war."[51] One of the letters was from Ritter von Bilinski, a Polish conservative entrusted by the Austro-Hungarians with the administration of Bosnia-Hertzgovina until just before Ferdinand's assassination; the author of another letter was Stephen Tisza, the Hungarian premier; Voska already had photocopies of both the Bilinski and Tisza letters. Some letters had been removed from the Hofbibliothek to Prague for duplication; others were being inspected and copied in Vienna. Voska was about to return to the United States and had made arrangements for the original materials to be returned and kept in the office of Edward Beneš, the Czechoslovak foreign minister, "where men assigned by the State Department can inspect the documents."[52] Voska did not want to embarrass his contacts by giving the State Department original documents procured at their peril, not to mention at the cost to him of an offensive grilling by Tasker Bliss. But, whatever their public stance on Voska's mission, American diplomats took pains to get their hands on and keep the captured correspondence. Harrison waited two years before sending it to Bliss.

In March 1921, Leland Harrison was going through his papers prior to leaving Paris for Washington and came across the unreturned Hofbibliothek originals. He sent them to Richard Crane with the injunction that they be forwarded, at last, to Beneš. He explained that in the "early days of the Peace Conference," Voska had been in Czechoslovakia "running down certain documents which, if found, were believed to fix the responsibility of Austria for commencing the War."[53] To piece the evidence together, an Austrian faction was apparently suspected of having conspired with Poles, Hungarians, and the German government to provoke war by murdering the crown prince. State Department officials discounted the theory. Harrison told Crane for his "ear alone that all the information submitted by Voska was carefully gone over by Dr. [James B.] Scott, who, as you may remember, was with Mr. Lansing, our representative in the Commission set up by the Peace Conference, to examine into the question of the responsibility for the war. As a matter of fact, Dr. Scott did not find anything in the way of valuable evidence in the papers."[54]

Harrison was anxious to cover up the affair of the Voska papers because its ventilation would have been most discomfiting for his colleagues. Lansing and Scott had endorsed the finding of their commission to the effect that the Central Powers were guilty in general terms of plotting war, and in particular of conspiring with regard to Serbia. It would have been disagreeable to have to publish evidence showing that there had been no plot behind the Sarajevo assassination but that American spies had tried to find one. Second, the Voska affair was swept under the carpet because of Lansing's strenuous condemnation of secret methods such as those employed, under semiofficial aegis, by Voska. It is not clear whether Lansing knew or would have approved of Voska's errand in Prague. In 1919, the Secretary of State noted that "muttered confidences, secret intrigues, and the tactics of the 'gum-shoer' are discredited."[55] By 1921, Lansing had publicly condemned President Wilson for having conducted the main Paris peace negotiations in secret and in violation of his professed faith in open diplomacy.[56] Lansing was partly inspired by personal pique, for Wilson had ignored him in Paris. But, though he had presided over an expansion in American intelligence and had personally encouraged the development of cryptology, he genuinely felt in 1919 that secret methods, when exposed, discredited the United States. This does not mean that he necessarily discouraged secret agents, but he did advocate, like his Republican successors, that the United States should avoid the appearance of being a party to undercover operations. The Voska letters were suppressed not just because they seemed to clear the Central Powers of guilt over Sarajevo, but also because they had been obtained in the wrong way. The Voska affair demonstrates that American intelligence acquired in the field was not always fully utilized or appreciated.

In the Wilson years, American intelligence was stronger in the East than the West. In Western Europe, America had two powerful allies fully competent, or at least experienced, in the business of espionage. Furthermore, in that sphere of war, intelligence problems were mainly military in character, whereas political intelligence was the particular forte of the Americans, both by virtue of their libertarian tradition and as reflected by the domination of the State Department over MID and ONI. A second reason for the Oriental inclination of American espionage was that the United States is a natural bridge between West and East, both in human terms, because of her myriad immigrant groups, and in geographic terms. Normally, the best way for Clemenceau to meet a Polish leader like Jan Paderewski would have been to take the train through Germany. War with the Central Powers meant that the principal statesmen of Europe could best communicate not via Metz and Berlin, but via Brest and Vladivostock, through the United States. Pianist-composer Paderewski became the friend of Woodrow Wilson, and Americans the brokers of international politics.

The secret moves to mobilize Poles on behalf of the Allied war effort illustrate the way in which the United States, and particularly the State Department, became a fulcrum of discreet power. In August 1917, Roman Dmowski became head of a new Polish National Committee formed at Lausanne. Making overtures to Galicians, socialists, and Jews, the committee tried to unite all Poles in the quest for self-determination. The committee sought recognition from the Allied powers and appointed negotiators to this end in each country. Paderewski was such a delegate in the United States, occupying at first a relatively subordinate position within the embryonic Polish hierarchy. The Lausanne committee, soon relocated in Paris, sent instructions to Paderewski through their representative Count Horodyski, the Foreign Office, and the British consul in San Francisco.

Because of America's advantages in power, cosmopolitanism, and geographic location, this structure of authority changed. One indication of the change was that the other Allied powers refused to recognize the Polish National Committee until the United States did so. Another was that Horodyski made a personal visit to Chicago to deal with the Polish National Department, representing four million American Poles. He implored Paderewski to "wire to your great friend [President Wilson]."[57] Dmowski telegraphed Horodyski from Paris stressing the vital necessity of American recognition and money.[58] In consequence of America's rise in prestige, there was a complementary accretion in Paderewski's authority. He was entrusted with the task of raising money in America for undercover resistance to Germany along the distintegrated Eastern front. When he succeeded, and won American recognition for an independent Poland into the bargain, his ascendancy was assured. In 1918, Dmowski, hitherto a lion of the Polish cause, lunched in Washington at the beckoning of the relatively junior State Department official, Auchincloss.[59] In 1919, it was Wilson's friend Paderewski who became Polish premier.

Although there is some evidence to show that Americans were everywhere followers, even dupes, of British intelligence, a different reading may be made of affairs in the East. In East Central Europe and the Far East, the British were often dependent on the Americans. Voska may have been recruited by the British, but he was played out, under MID, by the State Department. Indeed, there is reason to believe that Washington did not always keep London fully informed about America's undercover intentions; at one stage, for example, Sir William Wiseman plaintively demanded to know "whether Van Deman is playing with [the Poles] or the Bohemians."[60] Voska, after Maugham, was perhaps the Allies' most effective agent in East Central Europe. He was suspected, at times, of putting the interests of Bohemia first and those of the United States second, but he could be relied on to put the interest of every other country third or lower.

Intelligence from Siberia provides another example of British dependence on America. It tended to reach the Foreign Office via the State Department, and not vice versa. In the spring of 1918, the British learned of the execution of German agent Kudriasheff from Wiseman and House, after the news had passed through a chain involving the Cossacks, Admiral Austin M. Knight, the Navy Department, and President Wilson. Similarly, a series of messges about Czech military movements in Siberia reached the Foreign Office only after passing through American sources.[61]

Finally, there is the instance of Maugham's uncelebrated but vital mission as secret agent in revolutionary Russia. In this case, the office of the counselor capitalized on British officials' knack of alienating their own agents. Compton Mackenzie became disgusted with war bureaucracy when in charge of British intelligence in the Aegean: the Scottish novelist later wrote *Water on the Brain,* a satire on the military sleuth.[62] Like

Mackenzie, the English writer Maugham (whose exploits form the subject of the next chapter) showed scant respect for the Foreign Office and military hierarchy. The Foreign Office took its revenge by classifying as undesirable his play *Our Betters,* written when Maugham was on intelligence duty in Rome in 1915. A *New York Times* critic remarked of the play, performed at the Hudson Theater on the eve of America's entry into World War I, that Maugham presented in a particularly "penetrating and unpleasant light" the "rootless American climbers" who bought their way into English society only to "rot there."[63] As a result of the Foreign Office intervention, *Our Betters* was not performed in London until 1923, when it was a great success. Unlike the Foreign Office, the State Department recognized that Maugham was fundamentally pro-American and paid little heed to a lighthearted play written at a time when the United States was firmly neutral. In listening to Maugham at the conclusion of his Russian mission and using his ideas, Auchincloss and his colleagues showed that they had more than mastered their anglophilia; they had put it to work for the United States. They showed a flexibility of outlook which was to distinguish American from British intelligence on more than one occasion in the future.

7

Maugham in Russia

W. Somerset Maugham, the noted English novelist, was chief agent in Russia for the British and American secret services during the crucial few weeks preceding the Bolshevik coup of 1917. Yet the voluminous literature concerning Maugham has paid scant attention to his political activities. Students of belles lettres have never examined critically Maugham's intimation that his sojourn in revolutionary Petrograd was both reluctant and pointless.[1] R. L. Calder echoed the sentiments of his fellow literary critics in characterizing Maugham as "a habitué of the Café Royal who had gone to war" and in maintaining that Maugham's mission "did not succeed, of course."[2]

The distortions of Maugham's memory help to explain the dismissal as a failure of his mission to Russia. Ten years elapsed before he wrote about 1917, and then he cast himself in the fictional role of "Ashenden," the central character in Maugham's semiautobiographical collection of short stories, *Ashenden: or The British Agent* (1928). The protagonist of the stories, like Maugham, operated for part of his clandestine career in Revolutionary Russia. In view of the Bolshevik coup, he considered that "all his careful schemes had come to nothing."[3] It has generally been assumed that Maugham, in the persona of Ashenden, thus confirmed his own failure. In fact, however, it was not part of Maugham's assignment to intervene in Russian politics, except insofar as such action might assist the victory of the Allies. In his retrospective fiction, Maugham gave the

87

Bolshevik take-over an air of finality which he had not conceded to it in 1917.

Maugham valued literary over practical achievement, and could therefore exaggerate his failures as a spy without losing faith in himself. It is possible, too, that Maugham chose to overstress those failures because of a masochistic strain in his personality, a feature which might further account for his acceptance of the dangers of espionage. Masochism may have had something to do with Maugham's ability to work with superiors whom he despised. Ashenden's boss, "R," had blue eyes that "only just escaped a squint . . . they gave him a cunning, shifty look," and the secret agent of fiction repeatedly flattered his chief with remarks such as: "In my youth I was always taught that you should take a woman by the waist and a bottle ["R" being in the act of pouring a brandy] by the neck."[4]

Although Maugham stated that the Ashenden stories were "founded on experiences of my own" during World War I, he carefully obscured the identity of some of his key characters and perhaps for that reason managed to avoid prosecution, the fate that befell Compton Mackenzie.[5] "R" was probably Sir George Macdonogh, the British military intelligence chief. On the other hand, he may have been Sir William Wiseman, the Anglo-American go-between who persuaded the famous writer to serve in Russia.[6]

Wiseman was a friend of the Maugham family and because of his position as the chief intermediary between British and American intelligence in World War I was well placed to approach the writer with the idea of an Anglo-American mission to Russia. For his part, Maugham was considered well suited to the role. He spoke many languages, including Russian.[7] Maugham's contempt for the British establishment and the fact that he served with an ambulance instead of a combat unit in France in 1914 (he had been trained as a doctor) did not mean that he was not a patriotic Englishman. He had already served the British Military Intelligence Department in Italy, Switzerland, and (in a liaison capacity) the United States. Switzerland was an important intelligence center, and Maugham later confessed that his nerves had been put to the test in Geneva in the fall of 1915: "I was engaged in work for the Intelligence Department which the Swiss authorities did not approve of, and my predecessor had had a nervous breakdown owing to the strain it put upon his temperament, more sensitive than mine, to break the law; my colleague at Lausanne had lately been sent to prison for two years. I did not know how political prisoners were treated. . . ."[8] The writer's nerve had stood the test, and his experience in Switzerland, where he had been in charge of his own network, qualified him for further intelligence work.

Maugham agreed to Wiseman's request partly through patriotism. At the same time, it is significant that, following the European and American vogue, he had become a russophile. In particular, he sought inspiration from the raw materials of nineteenth-century Russian playwrights.[9] Maugham was asked to work with the Americans in July 1917, first because the United States was now in the war, second because the West coast was a logical point of departure for someone wishing to arrive in Petrograd anonymously and without molestation, and third because Slav immigrants in America could provide him with useful contacts.

From a personal point of view, Maugham was probably glad to cooperate with the United States. Though he had little patience with Americans who aped the British upper classes, he often departed from his normal iconoclasm when discussing things American.[10] Maugham had a close and probably homosexual relationship in the period of World War I with an American named F. Gerald Haxton. Haxton had been harassed by the British authorities. Perhaps for this reason, Maugham became ill-disposed toward his London superiors, "exalted personages" of whom well-bred men spoke "with acidulous tolerance."[11] The writer formed a liking for many Americans, not all of whom inspired instant delight on the part of his fellow-Englishmen. For example, he described Voska, his Czech-American collaborator, in affectionate terms: "He had a curious gait, somewhat like a gorilla's. . . . He was decently dressed in American reach-me-downs. . . . He seemed to have but one passion in life, if you omit an extreme desire for good cigars, and that was patriotism."[12] The same man was described by the foreign editor of the London *Times* as "thickset, of medium height, unshaven, grimy in appearance and dress, with features of the semi-Tartar type that is not uncommon in Bohemia . . . an unprepossessing fellow."[13] Favorably disposed toward the Americans as well as the Russians, Maugham overcame his initial reluctance to accept the Petrograd assignment.

In order to understand how the State Department came to use a British agent instead of an American, it is necessary to recall the nature of U.S. espionage in World War I. To begin with, the choice of an Englishman would have been acceptable in principle to the counselor's group, infected as it was by galloping anglophilia. More than this, the mission expected of the Allies' chief agent in Russia embraced some provisional political negotiation in addition to spying, its chief component. Maugham was to sound out, on a strictly unofficial basis, the willingness of various power groups in Russia to help the Allies to defeat Germany. The brief which the Senate of the 1890s had conceded to unapproved secret agents was to be exceeded. Extreme discretion was therefore necessary. The effectiveness of the State Department intelligence network in keeping its secrets is indicated by the fact that Maugham was known only by his code name ("S," or "Somerville") until his mission was completed. The clannish character of Polk's group protected it from the pry-ing eyes of senators and journalists (not to mention Germans); the appointment of a pseudonymous Englishman further safeguarded the counselor's plans against intelligent guesswork.

Characteristically, the executors of American diplomacy retained the services of an important British agent only after approaches of an informal and personal nature had been made to him. Wiseman had established contact with the State Department concerning undercover operations and subsequently smoothed over difficulties between the British and the Americans concerning Maugham. Wiseman was officially in charge of the British Purchasing Commission. Unofficially, he had kept an eye on potential friends and enemies of the Allies among the American immigrant communities. As the chief of British military intelligence in the United States, he spent $2,000 a month in New York alone on secret service activities.[14] He had established close links with Colonel House as early as December 1916.[15] An amusing and ironic conversationalist, Wiseman exerted a certain magnetism in the State Department and Foreign Office. Perhaps he exaggerated his own importance as a go-between; sometimes he lowered his credibility by acting like a double agent; on the other hand, there is no doubt that he was a vital intelligence link between the Americans and the British, or that his influence in this particular field was considerable.[16]

Wiseman regularly passed on digests of political information from the Foreign Office to the State Department. He had particular responsibility for transmitting Russian intelligence to the Americans. It is significant, therefore, that Wiseman had faith in the abilites of Maugham and organized his briefing in July 1917. For example, he arranged for Professor Richard Gottheil of Columbia University, former President of the Federation of American Zionists, to instruct the agent about possible cooperation from Jews in Petrograd.[17] Most important of all, Wiseman arranged for collaboration between Maugham and Emanuel Voska.[18] Sir Eric Drummond, of the Foreign Office, instructed the British embassy in Petrograd to forward Maugham's messages to the British consul general in New York. Relayed through Auchincloss or Wiseman, these messages were ultimately to inform the State Department.

Wiseman took every precaution to ensure that the Maugham–America liaison would work smoothly. On July 7, 1917, Maugham asked Wiseman if he would receive a salary for his efforts. He did not need the money, but in Switzerland people had regarded him as a fool because he alone in the intelligence organization which he headed had refused remuneration. Maugham was "not unwilling" to serve without pay but left the matter to Wiseman.[19] Wiseman, correctly perceiving that Maugham did not spurn the dollar as he did the pound, arranged that in mid-July, the author received $21,000 in order to launch his Russian trip.

On July 28, Maugham sailed on the slow boat for Japan. He left Japan for Vladivostock late in August, then (according to his short story "Mr. Harrington's Washing") took the trans-Siberian train in the company of a chance American companion, "Mr. Harrington," whose qualities later led Maugham to the conclusion that the predilection for reading aloud was "the only flaw in the perfection of the American character."[20] Maugham arrived in Petrograd early in September, installed himself in the Hotel Europa, and immediately began to transmit reports to the United States.

The Bolsheviks gradually came to suspect he was a spy. For a while, however, his usual cover worked well; "R" had early impressed on Ashenden that an author was well placed to spy on any country, since he could explain his presence and his curiosity with the "pretext that he was writing a book."[21] The intelligence chief of fiction had added that Ashenden would in any case find useful material for his stories in secret service work. Ashenden was comforted by the fact that when Swiss agents searched his hotel room, they found nothing but literary drafts.[22] In addition to acquiring the material for *Ashenden,* the Maugham of real life wrote three plays when on active intelligence duty: *Our Betters* (written in Rome, 1915), *The Unattainable* (Geneva, 1915), and *Love in a Cottage* (Petrograd, 1917). He also wrote, when in Petrograd, a substantial passage on Russian culture, politics, and society later published in *A Writer's Notebook* (1949). In short, he worked diligently at his cover.

Maugham found his hotel room in Petrograd cold and depressing; it aggravated the tuberculosis which had begun to attack his lungs in similarly frigid circumstances in Geneva. But he enjoyed mixing with Russian society, from the working-class crowds on the Nevsky Prospekt to the viewers at picture galleries, audiences at the ballet, and diners at the international hotels. Maugham appears to have used his real persona to gain access to literary circles, where no doubt he picked up useful political gossip, and to gain introductions to government leaders such as the Menshevik premier, Aleksander F. Kerensky, and his deputy minister of war, Boris V. Savinkov (who was to organize a clandestine resistance to Bolshevism in several Russian cities in 1918). In addition, he somehow gained access to political conventions and met Bolshevik partisans.[23]

In order to review the historical significance of Maugham's intelligence reports, it is convenient to place them in the context of two sets of criteria, his briefing and the accuracy of other contemporary reporters on the Russian scene. Maugham's briefing is of intrinsic interest because of its inexactitude. Drummond gave the most conservative description of Maugham's role in a message to the British embassy at Petrograd: "Mr. W. Somerset Maugham is in Russia on a confidential mission with a view to putting certain phases of the Russian situation before the public in the United States."[24] According to this rather vague description, the English agent was on a pure intelligence mission, with the responsibility of providing propaganda for use in America. Drummond did not want to supply his country's diplomats with information that might prove embarrassing.[25]

In January 1918, Wiseman described the objectives of the Maugham mission for the benefit of his intelligence colleagues on both sides of the Atlantic. Since it was he who supervised the briefing of Maugham, his account carries authority. Nevertheless, it too is sufficiently vague to admit of interpretation. "In July 1917," Wiseman recorded, "it was decided to start an Intelligence and Propaganda service in Russia." Maugham, then, or his fellow agents, were to intervene in the internal affairs of Russia to the extent of disseminating propaganda among the Russian people. Wiseman recalled that the intelligence service was to "expose the German political intrigues in Russia." Just as the Allies intrigued to start a revolt of Slav nations against the Austro-Hungarian authorities, so the Germans were (according to Allied counterintelligence) encouraging Bolshevik revolution in Russia. Maugham was expected to supply the Allies with ammunition for the associated propaganda war. Finally, Wiseman's agents were supplied with the injunction to "ascertain whether it was possible to support the more responsible elements in Russia. No attempt was to be made to support any reactionary movement, but it was thought it might be possible, to some extent, 'to guide the storm.' ..."[26] These were the expressed intentions of Wiseman in July 1917, when the Allies were still officially supporting the Kerensky government.

The interpretation which Maugham placed on his briefing is open to question. In some passages in *Ashenden,* the spy gave himself a grandiose if not wholly imaginary role. He had "unlimited funds" and "no one to give him orders."[27] He labored under the impression that he had executive responsibility, that "he was to suggest a policy and, if it was approved by the exalted personages who had sent him, to carry it out."[28] It is possible that to explain his distaste for espionage and to highlight his associated sense of failure, Maugham exaggerated the achievements expected of him as an agent. Elsewhere in *Ashenden,* however, he admitted that it was impractical to attempt to alter the course of Russian history armed merely with native wit and a skin belt stuffed with dollars, that "he had been sent to do something that was beyond human possibility."[29] Maugham either realized that he could achieve only limited ends and gave himself grandiose airs in *Ashenden* merely for dramatic effect, or seriously deluded himself by reading into Wiseman's instructions a greater challenge than was officially intended.

In assessing Maugham's efficacy, it is not only prudent but necessary to ignore the impossible tasks he set himself. For, although Maugham insisted that he failed, he never specified what he failed to do: if *Ashenden* is to be taken literally, his practical brief was no more than "to see what under the circumstances could best be done." It is only where

Maugham's concept of his mandate coincided with Wiseman's that one can be sure of a criterion for success or failure. Taking a liberal interpretation of Wiseman's brief, one can accept the authenticity of Maugham's claim that he was expected to discover ways and means of diverting German resources to the East. He was wrong in inferring that he was to achieve this objective single-handedly. But there was truth in Maugham's assertions as set out in *Ashenden* that he was to work independently of the British and American embassies and that he was at liberty to deal, if he wished, with "a party that was at daggers drawn with that in office." Maugham was correct in observing that "in the event of a sudden upheaval" he was to be "in the confidence of the new leaders of the country" with funds to back up his professions of cordiality. Maugham's job was to identify the new leadership, to determine its worth to the Allies, and to perform the work of an intermediary.[30] In his short stay in Russia, he succeeded remarkably well.

In his various reports between mid-September and mid-October 1917, Maugham at times made more nonsense than sense out of the confused politics of Revolutionary Russia. It was evident to him that the Russian people were tired of the war and distrustful of their allies. They were alienated by Western suspicions of their own radical tendencies and bored by propaganda lectures. But these truculent Russians were great filmgoers. They might just be revitalized by propaganda newsreels showing "what the Allies and the United States are doing for Russia" and "the life of the working-classes in America, pictures of Washington and New York; and some pictures of German militarism and what that means."[31] It was Maugham's rather naïve hope that the fantasies of D. W. Griffith would restore morale in the land which was soon to acclaim the powerful realism of Serge Eisenstein.

Maugham thought that the Allies should continue to support the Mensheviks because they were "anti-Prussian" and opposed the desire of the Bolsheviks for a separate peace. In an interview on October 18, Kerensky repeated to Maugham what he had previously told Lloyd George, and the British agent agreed to impress the British leader once again with the Russian's views. Kerensky exuded defeatism and bitterness. Where were the military supplies promised by the Allies? Why did the British not replace their incompetent ambassador in Petrograd? Why was the London *Times* so hostile to the Russian cause?[32] Maugham dutifully forwarded these complaints. In his own confidential reports he had already intimated that, even if the Kerensky government still balked at a separate peace, its armed resistance to Germany was chaotic and hopeless. He had also indicated in September that Kerensky was losing support and would probably have to relinquish power.[33]

Knowing that Kerensky was finished, Maugham was true to his brief in regarding support for the Mensheviks as a provisional arrangement.

He looked around within Russia for alternative sources of power. His reports stressed in particular the growing might of the Bolsheviks.[34] Because the Bolsheviks were in favor of a separate peace, Maugham made no attempt to deal with them. Perhaps he would have been wiser to accept the evidence that Russia was about to become Bolshevik and neutral, and that a neutral power, if kept on friendly terms, was no worse than an ineffective ally. But the British agent turned away from the Bolsheviks to the Cossacks and to the Slav nationalist groups forming among Austro-Hungarian prisoners of war in Russia.

Maugham cooperated with Slav nationalists, in both America and Russia, through Voska. Voska, as we have noted, was a socialist in his youth, but, although some of the Slav organizations with which he worked in the United States were Bolshevik in sympathy, most were democratic or liberal-nationalist. These organizations had managed not only to penetrate the Austrian embassy in Washington but also to infiltrate German restaurants as waiters in order to spy on the customers. Such voluntary and on the whole non-Bolshevik activities by the Slavs commended their services to the State Department as a possible way of combating Germany and Austria in East Central Europe.

It was toward this end, rather than in connection with German war guilt, that Voska performed his most effective work for American intelligence. In 1917, he offered to assist the Allies. "Being a citizen of the United States for eighteen years and a Czech by birth," he stated, "I am offering my services to my adopted country with the solemn promise that all my previous experiences, my connections with revolutionary organizations, will be exclusively used to bring about the downfall of militaristic imperialism of the Central Powers through a certain form of revolution in the above-mentioned Empire." Voska asked to be responsible to Wiseman and to his friend Charles Crane, the father of Lansing's secretary Richard Crane, a member of the Special Diplomatic Commission to Russia in 1917, and a man with close political ties to President Wilson. He requested an American army commission, a salary of $10,000, and a budget of $659,000.[35] Voska was perhaps extravagant in some of his claims. For example, he rashly promised to arrange a rising in Austria-Hungary to coincide with the spring offensive of 1918.[36] But he was taken on and instructed to report to Richard Crane, since that official was Washington-based. He provided Maugham with contacts, and the chief agent ultimately recommended that Voska be put in charge of counterespionage among the Poles, Czechs, and Cossacks resident in Russia.[37]

In his search for new leaders with whom the Allies could cooperate, Maugham was most deeply impressed by Thomas Masaryk. An advocate of Czech nationalism, Professor Masaryk arrived in Russia in 1917 to organize the Czech Legion from among prisoners of war. Later he was to go to America, where he influenced Charles and Richard Crane and obtained an interview with President Wilson. Thereafter, he returned to be president of Czechoslovakia until 1935. During the crisis of 1917, he urged Maugham to believe that "the internal and external weakening of Russia means *eo ipso* the strengthening of the Central Powers, which makes it necessary to form independent Bohemian, Polish and South-Slav states as a natural barrier against pan-Germanism."[38]

Maugham enthused over the power of the Czech exile movement, which had "70,000 men admirably disciplined and organized."[39] Neither Masaryk nor Maugham was beguiled into believing that the rhetoric of freedom was a panacea for Slav or Allied troubles. Dollar diplomacy and military force were essential ingredients in any satisfactory solution. Masaryk argued that the Slavs might be induced by cash to fight and to establish what from the Allies' point of view could be buffer states against German power. If the Japanese sent 300,000 men paid for in dollars or by the cession of part of Manchuria, even the Russians might be relied upon to fight. But, Masaryk concluded, Allied victory could be achieved only on the Western front, and there only through massive and timely American participation.[40] Maugham forwarded this analysis to his superiors in New York and Washington.

In mid-October 1917 Maugham made a concrete proposal to Wiseman, who discussed it with his American partners, reminding House and Polk that Maugham had gone to work in Russia with the support of a group recruited from various Slav patriotic organizations in the United States. Maugham suggested a scheme which would cost a half million dollars a year to implement. Propaganda was to be disseminated in order to stiffen Russian resistance to German arms and subversion. He proposed to make use of all societies in Russia which were anti-German in character. The Mensheviks would therefore be supported, but not on an exclusive basis. Since Polish aspirations were by definition anti-German, a special organization, under the direction of the chief agent, would encourage and finance Polish activities in Russia. Each anti-German organization would work in ignorance of the purposes of the other groups, under the central direction of the chief agent.[41] Clearly Maugham believed that manipulation might succeed where idealism would fail.

Wiseman thought that Maugham's half million would be well spent. In a way he expected more of Maugham's plans than the chief agent claimed for them. Maugham and Masaryk aimed not so much at the resumption of full-scale warfare in the East as at the diversion of German troops from the Western front. Wiseman thought in more grandiose terms, being by temperament more akin to Voska than to Maugham. Maugham, he pointed out, had good communications through the Rumanian frontier with Polish soldiers in the German army. Wiseman erroneously supposed that what he termed the "Liberal Party" in Germany was "at heart in sympathy" with Polish nationalist aspirations. A blow might be struck at German morale if, simultaneously with the raising of the Polish eagle on the Western front over American-trained Slav patriots, a mutiny occurred among Polish troops in the German army. Wiseman was more sanguine and less reliable than Maugham.[42]

The Bolshevik coup of November 7, 1917, did not unduly affect the strategies of Wiseman and Maugham. But the coup did mean that Maugham had to leave Russia. Since he had always refused to deal with the Bolsheviks, he was now a marked man, the secret agent of reactionary imperialism. Although Maugham had been expecting something of the kind, he was shocked and depressed by the change of government. He was particularly affected when his American friend of the trans-Siberian railroad journey was accidentally killed in the street fighting. His own health, which had declined in Switzerland, was now so impaired by tuberculosis that he was soon forced to undergo confinement in a Scottish sanatorium. It is understandable that the Ashenden of fiction was "depressed because all his careful schemes had come to nothing."[43] Maugham himself had felt defeated. It was in this mood that "Somerville" slipped out of revolutionary Russia.

But of the people actively concerned, Maugham seems to have been alone in believing, retrospectively, that "his careful schemes had come to nothing." Auchincloss recorded how the schemes of the British agent and his Slav friends had received serious consideration after the Bolshevik take-over. In November 1917 President Wilson sent a delegation, headed by House as his personal representative, to confer and cooperate with the Allied war command. Auchincloss accepted an appointment as unpaid secretary to the mission. On November 7, the delegation's destroyer pulled into Plymouth, England. Auchincloss was immensely relieved, for the ship's rats had not respected his altruism, and the engines had failed in U-boat waters. But it was the day of the Bolshevik coup, and relief soon gave way to anxiety over the state of Russia.[44]

In London, Auchincloss was secretary to the general war command delegation, but he had a special responsibility for intelligence liaison. On November 20, 1917, a meeting occurred in the office of Edward Carson, editor of *The Times*. It was called at the instigation of Wiseman, and Auchincloss recorded in his diary that "the others present . . . were Lord Hardinge, of the Foreign Office, General Macdonogh, the Director of Military Intelligence, Count Horodyski and a man named Maume [sic], who had just returned from Russia."[45] Auchincloss's unfamiliarity with Maugham's name indicates more than a lack of literary cultivation. It shows the way in which Wiseman had shielded the identity of "Somerville" even though the agent was working for the Americans, and it suggests that Maugham's self-abasement was unimpeded by any credit from his superiors, who had praised merely his alias.

Horodyski dominated the meeting of November 20. Wladyslaw H. F. Horodyski (the prefix "Count" was supplied by Auchincloss) was a veteran of pre-World War I secret nationalist societies and a conservative democrat by persuasion. In the pursuit of his professional interests as a librarian and an intellectual historian, he had travelled extensively in the West and was supplied with good cover as a secret emissary of Polish nationalism. In 1917, Horodyski was responsible for liaison between his countrymen in East Central Europe and the Polish National Committee then in process of forming a government in exile based in Paris and Washington. He was especially entrusted with the task of raising a Polish army in countries sympathetic to the Allied cause. He gained the ear of the Allies through his friend Sir Eric Drummond, private secretary to Foreign Secretary A. J. Balfour.

Horodyski proposed a plan which was acceptable to those who had supported the pre-Bolshevik strategy of "Somerville." Horodyski's proposals differed from those of Masaryk and Maugham only in that they went further in terms of action. Horodyski declared that the Allies would have to decide immediately whether to let the Eastern front go and fight it out in the West or to prop up the military resistance along Russian frontiers in an attempt to draw German troops away from the Western front. As a Polish nationalist, he advocated the deployment of the 80,000-strong Polish Army Corps in the East. The Russians were opposed to this, but there was no point in appeasing the Bolsheviks. Second, the Pole suggested that Maugham be sent back to Russia promising support no longer to the Mensheviks but to General A. M. Kaledin of the Cossacks. Maugham was to offer 100,000 Allied troops, money, and ammunition if Kaledin agreed to deploy his Cossack forces against the revolutionaries and the Germans.[46]

Carson asked Auchincloss what he thought of the plan. Auchincloss replied to the editor that President Wilson was committed to support Kerensky and could not in good faith encourage Polish and Cossack activities in Russia. The American was, however, impressed. He thought the desired end could be achieved by channeling resources through Rumania.[47] In the next few days, Auchincloss, now in Paris, dined and talked extensively with Horodyski, Drummond, Wiseman, and Maugham. He formed the impression that, around the Polish nucleus, an army of one-and-a-half million might be built. He resolved to ask the American President, already committed to the principle of self-determination, to support the Polish, Rumanian, and Czechoslovak causes.[48]

On his return to the United States, Auchincloss busied himself with the details of East European resistance to the Central Powers and to

Bolshevism. He was unable to act on various suggestions that Maugham be redeployed. Even if he had been well enough to serve, the British agent might have had reason to suspect that he was on the Bolsheviks' execution list.[49] Maugham's plan was, however, reflected in the projects in which Auchincloss was involved in January 1918. For example, he pursued the idea of sending Voska to work with the Czechs and Slovaks in Europe. In addition, Auchincloss implemented a second aspect of Maugham's strategy by ensuring that the Poles received continuing help from the United States. He actively supported Paderewski when the musical virtuoso represented the Polish National Committee in America.[50]

Paderewski had been active on behalf of the Poles long before Maugham went to Russia. He had first befriended House in November 1915.[51] He was a frequent visitor in Auchincloss's office. Woodrow Wilson had supported Polish independence as early as February 1917, and Paderewski was to lose the confidence of his Anglo-American sponsors only after the failure of his Polish premiership in 1919. Consequently, it may be argued that Maugham merely supplied information to confirm the wisdom of established American policy. However, in a time of inter-national uncertainty, Maugham did provide an independent assessment. The matter of Polish loyalty illuminates the utility of the chief agent. The historian Victor S. Mamatey points out that it was not until the con-firmation of the Treaty of Brest-Litovsk, and Russia's withdrawal from the war, that "the Poles decided overwhelmingly to throw in their lot with the Allies."[52] Paderewski, as the leader of the anti-German Poles, could not be entirely believed or trusted during 1917 on the subject of his people's loyalty to the Allies. Therefore, there was comfort to be found in Maugham's anticipation that the Poles would be reliable.

Maugham had objectively estimated the scale of finance ($500,000 a year) that would be necessary to support all East Central European anti-German movements. Auchincloss pressed President Wilson for the money. In January 1918, Paderewski responded through Auchincloss to an American invitation to estimate how much money the Polish cause needed. Later in the same month, Auchincloss, recorded: "The President sent back the letter I wrote ... with reference to the Polish matter, endorsing thereon that he would advance $30,000 a month for six months towards the expenses of the Polish National Committee. This is more than I expected and is very gratifying."[53] At a time when certain advisors associated with The Inquiry were urging circumspection over the Polish tactic, Maugham and Auchincloss gave their voices to the nationalist cause.[54] That their advice prevailed was due in part to Polish-American pressure, but their opinions were respectable mainly because they were assumed to be more objective than those of Paderewski, Voska, and Masaryk.

The influence of Maugham on American policy toward East Central

Europe must be kept in perspective. The information he provided was not the only intelligence on Russia submitted to the American executive. The President's prestigious Special Diplomatic Commission to Russia sailed under the leadership of former Republican Secretary of State Elihu Root in May 1917. Although Voska was subordinate to Maugham, he probably reported independently through Charles Crane, who was one of the commission's members.[55] Individuals who reported to the State Department and were taken more or less seriously ranged from the socialist W. E. Walling to the ambassador to Russia, David F. Francis. The Inquiry, established early in September 1917, produced a constant deluge of information on foreign problems. On the British side, some distinguished academics between 1917 and 1919 filed reports about Russia with the Political Intelligence Department of the Foreign Office. Philip Kerr, private secretary to Lloyd George and later (as Lord Lothian) ambassador to the United States (1939–1940), prepared synopses of these reports, whose contents may have indirectly influenced American policy.[56] In 1918 and 1919, information about Russia continued to flow to the Allies from such sources as the self-styled British agent Bruce Lockhart, the Midwestern politician Raymond Robins, and the administration's envoy to Moscow, William C. Bullitt.

Yet Maugham was more favored than most. He could not personally press his views on the American executive, but Wiseman ensured that his reports quickly reached the right quarter. Maugham was formally in authority over Voska, the one American agent who might have been expected to attain a stature in the eyes of the State Department superior to that of the Englishman. There was always some doubt about Voska's willingness to put the Allied cause first; he made no attempt to disguise the fact that he was a Czech nationalist with a partisan interest in East Central European affairs. (He may also have been the victim of less rational feelings. He bitterly related how a leading Washington politician asked him whether the 200,000 Chicago Czechs "got along with white people."[57]

Maugham was, as the cliché goes, the right man in the right place at the right time. His Russian reports reached Washington during the weeks preceding the Bolshevik coup, when the true disposition of power in East Central Europe was becoming manifest. Unlike other sources of intelligence, he gave due warning of Kerensky's infirmity, of Bolshevik strength, and of Polish and Czech possibilities. The Root Commission had failed to warn Wilson of the rising Bolshevik power and was ignored by the president.[58] Ambassador Francis, a political appointee inexperienced in diplomacy, was so enamored of Kerensky that Wilson deemed him untrustworthy. Lockhart, a Cambridge University blue installed as British consul general in Moscow, was similarly blind to the faults of Kerensky and had no influence in America.[59] The Inquiry, Wilson's research team commissioned to find possible bases for a peace settlement, started too late. Robins and Bullitt, who took a more practical view of Bolshevism than Maugham, started their uphill struggle to influence the State Department when the die, for better or worse, was already cast. The sources of Kerr and Lloyd George on Russia were not firsthand, and their interest in close communication with the Americans remained weak until the 1920s. It is not difficult to understand the precedence Americans gave to "Somerville's" reports in the fall of 1917 and to his strategy in the spring of 1918.

As his title suggests, the chief agent for the Allies in Revolutionary Russia was one of the main contributors to political intelligence in the United States. The influence of intelligence reports on policy formation was, however, limited by the degree to which statesmen were willing and able to accept them. President Wilson, like Maugham, wished to encourage nationalism. But he suffered from personal and political constraints in some matters, and his inconsistency impaired America's moral leadership, which would otherwise have been so useful to the implementation of Maugham's plans. Because the British entente was a fixed star in the president's firmament, he politely restrained his demands for Irish and Indian independence. Because of his known hostility to Communism, he laid himself open to the charge of interfering in Russia's internal affairs by sending American troops to Siberia in July 1918.[60] It followed that his call for self-determination at the expense of the Central Powers was vulnerable to counterpropaganda. At no stage was German propaganda in East Central Europe less effective than that of the Allies.[61]

Similarly, there were domestic influences at work in America which at times superseded or counteracted the logic of intelligence reports. Immigrant lobbies competed for the favor of the administration. Business and labor interests agitated powerfully on national and local levels, both for and against the principle of a world of free peoples. Wilson could ill afford to allow the State Department to consider the Russian and Slav problem on the basis of intelligence alone and without reference to his own country's politics. Maugham was never more than a tool in the hands of his despised superiors.

On the other hand, the Allies' chief agent in Russia must be counted as successful according to two significant criteria: first, his findings were accurate compared with those of other contemporary reporters on the Russian scene; second, following Wiseman's brief, Maugham sensibly advised the Allies on political and financial methods which might enable them to "guide the storm" in East Central Europe. The reactions of Western Europe and of the United States to the invasions of Czechoslovakia and Poland in the 1930s show how an important element of Maugham's analysis gained general acceptance.

It is also true that, if Maugham can take some of the credit for the realization of East Central European dreams of national freedom, he must share the responsibility for some flaws in the American outlook. On a comparatively trivial level, his suggestion that films should be shown in Russia illustrating the benefits of working-class life in the United States encouraged a naive faith in the universal applicability of American ways. More seriously, while the chief agent refrained from advocating armed Allied intervention in Bolshevik Russia, he failed to suggest a *modus vivendi* with the new regime. He could not have foreseen the collapse of Cossack power in January 1918 or the suicide of Kaledin, but he was wrong in estimating that the Cossacks were at any time a national Russian force in the sense that the Bolsheviks were. The methods Maugham advocated—clandestine and devious financial subsidization of various national "self-determination" movements—continue to be controvercial because of differing interpretations of nationalism and democracy.[62] To assert without qualification that Maugham failed as a secret agent is, however, to accept his own word too lightly. The code name "S" has obscured for too long the contribution of Somerset Maugham to American intelligence.

8

U.S. Secret Agents and Antiimperialism, 1913–1920

In the period from 1918 to 1920, American diplomatic utterances began to acquire a reputation as double-talk. This state of affairs did not come about because President Woodrow Wilson was less scrupulous than his predecessors. It happened because of the high expectations raised, and then disappointed, by a morally ambitious statesman. The nature of postwar disillusionment can be appreciated only in the context of the president's proclaimed ideals. Following the Bolshevik Revolution, Wilson replied to the Communists' direct challenge to Western ideology in January 1918 with his famous definition of war aims, the Fourteen Points address to Congress. Historians have devoted considerable attention to Wilson's failure to press for the principle of self-determination, a war aim mentioned in five of the fourteen points. They have, however, virtually ignored the principle to which Wilson offered pride of place, the first of the fourteen points. It demanded "open covenants of peace openly arrived at, after which there shall be no private international understandings of any kind, but diplomacy shall proceed always frankly and in the public view."

Opposition to secrecy had long been part of the American democratic credo. The very rebellion of the colonies in the 1770s had been launched against the distance-veiled deliberations of the government in London. In the nineteenth century, labor unions had been attacked in the United States as elsewhere as conspiracies, and radical farmers inveighed against Wall Street financial plots; in the twentieth, Progressives, including Woodrow Wilson himself, had called for an end to secret donations to the campaign funds of political parties. Indeed, President Wilson strongly affirmed on a number of occasions America's traditional opposition to clandestine dealings. Early in the campaign, he hinted that the cash for Theodore Roosevelt's presidential bid came from Wall Street. He claimed that his own backers were unsullied and called for public accounting.[1] It was entirely in character for him to condemn and exploit for propaganda purposes Germany's espionage activity in the United States, as it was for him to demand "open covenants of peace openly arrived at."

Wilson's attitude toward secrecy was part of a consistent if impractical theory. The president believed that the Austro-Hungarian empire was ruled by autocrats who remained in power through the practice of deceit. Subject peoples—Poles, Czechs, Slovaks—would have rebelled earlier given the advantages of free speech and could be expected to admire American democracy and freedom, once given the facts by U.S. propaganda agencies such as the Committee on Public Information. Similarly, according to Wilson's war message of April 2, 1917, it was not with the "previous knowledge or approval" of the German people that the kaiser directed his lurking submarines to strike at American shipping from the dark recesses of the Atlantic. The president's opinions on secrecy were linked not only to his convictions about self-determination but also to his views on neutrality. The Germans, according to Wilson, were ashamed of their political system. This was why they used secret service methods in a neutral democracy like the United States, where there was nothing to stop them from using the legitimate organs of free expression. "Self-governed nations," he declared in his war message, "do not fill their neighbor states with spies."

Personnel at the counselor's office clearly shared Wilson's attitude toward Germany's secret operations in neutral countries. Frank Polk personally assured the French ambassador in 1915 that he would "promptly" investigate indications "that German-American firms were sending commercial messages through our Consuls."[2] He demanded that the Swedish ambassador explain why his government permitted Germany to use Swedish wireless stations for secret communications. The ambassador hinted in reply that Swedish dependence on German coal put his government in a dependent position.[3]

The State Department continued to emphasize the principle of neutrality after America joined the war. Auchincloss thought that German violations of neutrality should be exploited for propaganda purposes. When House told him that the German government was carrying on intrigues in Mexico, Argentina, and China through Swedish diplomatic channels, Auchincloss thought "the disclosures are startling and can be used to great advantage."[4] His faith in the potential propaganda value of the revelations was consistent with the American administration's assault on German secret methods and on the Central Powers' disregard for the rights of neutrality, national sovereignty, and self-determination.

Condemn the Germans though they might, the State Department's officials were unable to refrain from sending an agent to Switzerland, like everyone else. Because Switzerland remained neutral throughout the war, it was, like the United States prior to 1917, a means of access and contact between the Allies and the Central Powers. Its common boundaries with the struggling foes meant that the Alpine cantons comprised an entrepôt for spies engaged in a busy two-way traffic; Switzerland became the aerie of intelligence agents and a nest of international intrigue. Auchincloss noted in his diary on February 16, 1918, that Abram I. Elkins, an authority on secret liens and U.S. ambassador to Turkey since 1916, was "to go to Switzerland as a sort of High Commissioner for special commercial work but in reality he is to make reports on conditions in Germany as he is able to observe the same from Switzerland."[5] Just a few months after complaining that Germany had violated American neutrality, the State Department was trespassing against the neutrality of Switzerland. There was nothing distinctive about such duplicity. All major powers behaved in the same way, particularly when they were at war. American deceptions were shocking only because they stood out against a sounding board of exceptionally vociferous idealism.

Wilsonian double-talk about neutrality, secrecy, and self-determination may be explained partly on a chronological basis. Before America's entry into the war, Wilson put humanity first and stuck to his principles. After America's entry, he put his country first and selectively abandoned his principles; in addition to condoning espionage, for example, he tolerated British imperialism in Ireland, Egypt, and India in the interest of harmony between the Associated Powers. This chronological explanation is not, however, entirely convincing, for the President departed from his stated principles both before his war message and after the armistice.

Woodrow Wilson used or condoned secret methods on several occasions that cannot be explained away by the exigencies of a national emergency. In the 1912 campaign, after his politically calculated call for openness had met with the expected lack of response from rival candidates, Wilson entrusted his fund raising to William F. McCombs, a young New York lawyer who became his campaign manager and discreetly accepted money from anybody.[6] As we shall shortly see, Wilson sent secret agents into Mexico as soon as he became president; he was to use military force to intervene in that country and both subterfuge and force to intervene in Russian Siberia in 1918–1920 (an episode discussed in Chapter 9). The president's actions in Mexico and Siberia contradicted his belief in self-determination; his clandestine methods were no different from those he condemned in Germans. When peace came in 1919 and democratic debate recovered its vigor, Wilson soon encountered criticism of his inconsistencies. Above all, as the leading advocate of diplomacy that should "proceed always frankly and in the public view," he was attacked for agreeing to the infamous exclusion of 150 American journalists from the opening session of the Paris Peace Conference.[7]

Woodrow Wilson formed and attempted to apply principles in a world full of intractable moral problems. For example, in the case of Indian revolutionaries collaborating with German secret agents in the United States (discussed in some detail below), there was no way of reconciling his belief in self-determination with his abhorrence for autocratic subversion. To complicate matters, the president—like his subordinates—was subject to the inconsistencies associated with human nature, to changes of mind and temper, and to fits of impatience. Human frailty, as well as the moral complexities of problems confronting him, led Wilson to depart from principle, never more so than in the case of Mexico.

The Wilson administration's behavior toward Mexico demonstrates the selective way in which the principle of self-determination was applied. The Monroe Doctrine of 1823 had condemned the acquisition or retention of colonial territories by other powers but opened the way for U.S. neocolonialism by clearly endorsing America's nonintervention in European affairs and yet implying its responsibility for Latin American integrity. President Wilson intervened in Mexico to restore the constitutional legitimacy of that nation's government without being able to demonstrate the justice of his actions. He therefore used secret agents to disguise his intentions and to negotiate—in violation of the agreement between the Senate and the executive, arrived at during the presidency of Grover Cleveland, that an executive agent could be used as a "mere . . . spy," but not as a negotiator. This was a step on the road that led not only to foreign contempt for Wilson's profession of "open diplomacy" but also to disagreements with Congress over the methods used to negotiate the Paris peace settlement of 1919.

Wilson, who entered the White House early in 1913, applauded the constitutionalist government of Francisco Madero, which had been the outgrowth of the 1910 Mexican Revolution. Condemning Madero's overthrow and execution in February 1913, Wilson worked for the deposition of his usurper, General Victoriano Huerta. To this end, he supported the "constitutionalist" rebel Venustiano Carranza, who began to assume control of Mexico in 1915. Historian Arthur Link described President Wilson's response to the Mexican situation as an "important example of the consequences of oversimplification through too much reliance upon obvious moral principles."[8] Certainly, in the first instance, Wilson supported constitutionalism, which he equated with sovereignty of the people and democracy. His method of support, as Link pointed out, was highly personal. As president of Princeton University after 1902, he had converted the fight for academic reform into a vendetta against the campus old guard; he carried the same blinkered vision into the field of diplomacy. Ignoring normal diplomatic procedures and even the State Department, Wilson made his own decisions about Mexico—with the assistance, between April 1913 and October 1915, of no fewer than eleven executive agents.[9] Very soon, according to historian Howard Cline, the United States "was speaking with three tongues, all different."[10] In an attempt to coerce Huerta, Wilson authorized the occupation of the Mexican port of Vera Cruz without the consent of the Senate. This act of intervention in the early part of 1914 made anti-Americanism once again axiomatic for all aspiring Mexican leaders, Carranza included, and dealt an early blow to the credibility of the Wilsonian principle of self-determination in Latin America.

American relations with Mexico entered a critical phase when Carranza tried to reap for his country some of the benefits of Mexican oil deposits. Wilson had attacked American diplomats for being too concerned with American property interests abroad (an accusation that had given him a reason for bypassing diplomats and using secret methods).[11] But Wilson showed concern for the well-being of American capitalist interests in Mexico when Carranza stated his intention to nationalize subsoil deposits. Perhaps Wilson was antagonized by Carranza's use for propaganda purposes of the offer by Germany's foreign minister, Zimmerman, made public in March 1917, to aid Mexico in the event of war with the United States. At the same time, whatever his principles, he could not afford to overlook the strategic importance of the burgeoning oil industry in Mexico. Production had increased from under 13 million barrels in 1911 to over 193 million barrels by 1920.[12] Prior to the outbreak of World War I, Winston Churchill had announced plans to convert the Royal Navy to oil, with the help of a contract from Anglo-American Petroleum Products. Although not vital to British interests, the contract was important, and as Americans moved toward belligerency with Germany, the State Department had to take heed of the requirements of the Royal Navy.[13] By August 1918, there was concern that the U.S. Navy itself might suffer were matters in Mexico to deteriorate further. Accordingly, Secretary of the Navy Josephus Daniels took up the case of the oil tycoons and demanded war across the Rio Grande.[14]

On August 9, 1918, Wilson met with Daniels and Polk to discuss the Mexican situation. According to Professor Cline, Wilson ruled out direct intervention because it would have borne too close a resemblance to the German invasion of Belgium.[15] Certainly Wilson would have been mindful not only of this but also of the recent reaction to Vera Cruz, of his recent call for self-determination through the Fourteen Points address, and of the desirability of not making additional enemies when the United States was already at war. For these reasons, he would have been inclined to stick to principle. At the same time, it is clear that the State

Department had presented him with an alternative strategy. Earlier on the day when Wilson, Daniels, and Polk met, the State Department counselor had met with James Garfield, the government's fuel administrator, and Bernard Baruch, of the War Industries Board. The three officials considered the problem of Mexican oil in the light of information from their own confidential sources. They evidently decided that labor agitation was at the root of the demand for nationalization in Mexico. Later in the day, during his conference with the president and the secretary of the navy, Polk "declined to be catechized" on the subject of war.[16]

Wilson, by now preoccupied with European problems, agreed to allow the State Department to use its own methods, in conjunction with big business. These methods consisted of blanket surveillance and subtle action. Polk noted late in 1918 a complaint from a worthy of Atlanta who worried that the forthcoming Mexican–American labor conference at Laredo, Texas, would pass a resolution "condemning the attitude of the U.S. on the oil situation—that Gompers was to be present and had hoped that we could stop it." From Polk's account of actions taken, it appears that the State Department was closely in touch with plans for the conference. Polk had identified the radical journalist Lincoln Steffens as the leading troublemaker, so he "had given Lincoln Steffens a passport and he would be out of the way."[17] By the 1920s, American interests owned about half the Mexican oil resources, twice the British holding, and formal Mexican–American relations had improved. The improvement came about partly because of the disappointing yield of the oilfields after 1920, but partly, also, as a result of the substitution of undetected secret stratagems for dangerous vacillation.[18]

If Mexican constitutionalists had few illusions about American foreign policy, revolutionaries from India had none. Just after the United States went to war with Germany, Bhagwan Singh, a disenchanted Sikh, demanded: "Is America in this war for the freedom of slave nations? ... It is but a dream. . . ." The revolutionary went on to say that his party could "have nothing to do with such an idea, for the cause of the evil existing in India to-day is the friendship of America and England. . . . Before she entered the war America never dreamt of being the champion of the freedom of Bohemia and Poland. . . . If she does not liberate the Philippines then she is in the position of the person in the old adage who observes the mote in another's eye. . . ."[19] Dr. Chandra H. Chakravarty, another American-based Indian revolutionary, made a similar complaint about diplomatic double-dealing to State Department undercover specialist Leland Harrison. Chakravarty, though a double if not a triple agent himself, pressed the United States to urge consistency on its allies: "If Germany has no right in Belgium and Poland; Austria in Serbia and Roumania; Turkey in Armenia and Palestine; neither England has any right in Ireland, Egypt and India; Russia in Finland, Ukraine and Turkestan; France in Algeria, Morocco and Indo-China; Japan in Korea and Formosa." Chakravarty's memorandum went into routine circulation. It fluttered in turn on the desks of the secretary of state and the president's research team into peace terms, heralding, like some exhausted seabird, a distant but approaching storm.[20]

The problem of Indian nationalism had become an embarrassment to U.S. authorities before the outbreak of the war. By 1915, a force of Indian workers, perhaps conservatively estimated at 7,000 in number, had settled in California.[21] These workers were mainly Sikhs from the Punjab. The Sikhs had been embittered not only by British rule in India but by the hostile reception afforded to many of them in British Columbia, their point of entry to the North American continent. Migration to California did not solve their problems. The Pacific Coast press fulminated against the "Turban Tide"; in 1908, the Asiatic Exclusion League (formed in 1905 with the primary object of keeping out Japanese immigrants) organized violent demonstrations against the Indians.[22] Not surprisingly, Indian workers became sufficiently conscious to supply radical Urdu-language newspapers with a circulation and to provide a place of refuge to Indian terrorists who, because of their color, would have been easily spotted in white, Negro, or Chinese areas.

With apparent unanimity, the articulate Sikhs, Hindus and Moslems in America demanded independence for India. There was some disagreement over tactics. Lala Lajpat Rai, who arrived in the United States in 1914, founded the India Home Rule League of America, which depended on peaceful persuasion.[23] Lajpat Rai's tactics, however, never won the support or publicity conferred on the Gadar party.

The Gadar, or revolutionary, party was founded at a general meeting of Indian workers in San Francisco on November 1, 1913. It was an acute source of worry to the British, because it sought to set light to the Punjab, one of the military cornerstones of the British Raj in India.[24] The Gadar party soon changed its name to the Hindustan Gadar party in an attempt to convince the American authorities that it did not stand for armed revolt in the United States.[25] American conservatives remained less than enchanted with the group, whose character seemed to be so heavily influenced by its leader, Har Dayal. Har Dayal was an Oxford-educated Hindu who, until his dismissal, held a lectureship at Stanford University. Whatever the declared position of his party, Har Dayal was a living challenge to America's cherished ideals. He was, like the American anarchist Emma Goldman, an advocate of "free love." He ruled out marriage for Gadar members, although, as the Indian historian L. P. Mathur delicately put it, "there was no bar on their falling in love." Har Dayal attended meetings of the American revolutionary organization, the Industrial Workers of the World, and founded the Bukunin Institute of California, which advocated revolution everywhere.[26]

According to Mathur, the Indian revolutionaries chose to operate in North America not only because of the presence there of Sikh cover but also because "in comparison to European countries the revolutionaries were able to act more freely and fearlessly in the United States, the land of democracy and freedom."[27] In reality, the American authorities afforded a colder reception to the Indians than to nationalists from East Central Europe. American statesmen rightly or wrongly believed in the advantages of a good relationship with Britain. Popular prejudice against Indian rebels, created in part by British propaganda, bolstered their policies. Hollywood, which began to flourish after 1913 and was significantly located on the West coast, swallowed information disseminated by the British India Office. From *Hindoo Fakir* (1902) to *Gunga Din* (1939), some thirty-five American movies presented an unfavorable image of Indian nationalism and pictured Indian rebels as immature and untrustworthy. Thus public opinion reinforced the anti-Indian line of the Wilson administration.[28]

Circumspection was forced on the American government, however, by a number of factors. First, it was inhibited by publicly acknowledged principles from restricting the activities of a group of freedom fighters who were not breaking the laws of the United States. Second, any ill-judged action taken against the Indians would have been condemned by the Irish-American nationalists and, after the outbreak of war in 1914, by German and Scandinavian immigrants. Some trade unionists espoused the Indian cause, and, last but certainly not least, William Jennings Bryan was an advocate of Indian independence, with firsthand knowledge of conditions on the subcontinent. In spite of these factors, Har Dayal was arrested under the antianarchist legislation which had been passed following the assassination of President McKinley in 1901. In April 1914, he skipped bail and fled to Switzerland.[29]

The European war brought German support for the "Hindu conspiracy," which now began in earnest. On April 26, 1915, the steamer *Maverick* cleared San Francisco bound for Java, a colony which was Dutch, neutral, and the home of a considerable Indian population. Watched by State Department, Justice Department, and Army secret agents, the *Maverick* put in to the Mexican port of San Jose del Cabo, then made for a rocky, uninhabited archipelago 420 miles offshore. She waited off the isle of Socorro for the schooner *Annie Larsen*, which had, however, already departed as the result of a misunderstanding. As the *Maverick* lay to off Socorro, the *Annie Larsen* was beating her way back up the coast to Aberdeen, Washington, where government spies watched her unload an arms consignment which had been organized and paid for by the German firm Krupps through military attaché von Papen. Apparently, the scheme to transfer weapons from the *Annie Larsen* to the *Maverick*, which would ultimately consign them to the Punjab, had failed, and the Punjabi rioters of 1915 had to do without German weapons. This belief may explain in part the relatively mild American response to the episode. Germany did not have to recall von Papen until December. The State Department, however, was not wholly convinced of the failure of the gun-running phase of the "Hindu–Boche" conspiracy. Its final intelligence report on the episode contained the qualified statement: "The *Maverick* had a cargo of arms and ammunition, or was to have received such cargo from *Annie Larsen*." In the event the *Maverick* sailed for the Orient without changing cargo. As she crossed the Line, she may still have been carrying guns: her Swedish master and first mate may well have drunk a toast to Captain Bluff.[30]

In 1915 and 1916, the Wilson administration pursued a soft line toward the Indian conspiracy. The intelligence services, however, kept the Indians under constant surveillance. In the spring of 1917, they stepped up their activities and began discreet harassment of the Indian nationalist movement. By that time, public opinion as a whole was markedly anti-German. Newspapers were critical of any people, including nationalist groups, who cooperated with the Central Powers. Bryan, vulnerable because of his protest at Wilson's tough line with Germany, and Robert M. LaFollette, the Progressive Senator from Wisconsin, were the subjects of increasingly emotional attack. When secret agents captured some Indian papers in March 1917, and leaked their contents to the press, the *New York Times* headlines ran: "German–Hindu Plot Made Use of Bryan; Pacifists' Words and Those of LaFollette Part of Propaganda for Uprising in India."[31] The surreptitious phase of America's opposition to Indian antiimperial revolt was almost at an end. As soon as the United States entered the war in April 1917, its secret agents threw caution to the wind and moved in on the Indians. Those arrested during the "swoop" were, ironically, charged with violations of America's neutrality laws.

According to a contemporary explanation, supplied by the Department of State and publicized by the press, the Indian revolutionaries were betrayed by an informer. Dr. Chandra H. Chakravarty had traveled to Germany to appeal to Arthur Zimmerman for aid, and the Foreign Minister sent him to America via Mexico, telegraphing Ambassador von Bernstorff in January 1916: "I beg that your Excellency will be ready for Doctor Chak's arrival, and will place at his disposal the necessary funds. . . . Dr. Chak has applied . . . here for instructions to be sent to New York and San Francisco."[32] Chakravarty soon received over $60,000 from von Igel, head of the German military information bureau in New York. The Germans wanted him to exploit Indian discontent in Java, Sumatra, and

British Guiana.[33] None of this information was unknown to the British, who, as we have noted, had broken the German diplomatic code and, when it suited them, passed on some of their knowledge to the Americans.

Anglo-American intelligence let Chakravarty run, and simply by following him around they learned about German conspiracies to encourage self-determination and decolonization in the British empire. They learned, for example, that with the aid of a further infusion of $40,000 from the Berlin–India Committee, the Indian revolutionaries in America had set up liaison with Li Yuan-Hung, the short-lived Chinese president, with a view to running guns overland to British India.[34] Historian L. P. Mathur summed up the attitude of U.S. authorities in 1916 in two apposite sentences: "They regarded the activities of Indians including German-nominated Chandra Chakravarty as something which could be checked at any moment. They termed it an oily revolution with an oily leader."[35] When war with Germany became imminent in 1917, the Americans decided to take action against the underground movement, for which they had dangerously little respect. For this purpose, they used Captain Thomas J. Tunney, head of the New York City bomb squad. When war broke out, Tunney, together with Arthur Woods, Mayor Mitchel's appointee as New York police commissioner, was to go over to MID, working in New York under the supervision of Colonel Nicholas Biddle, a prominent bank trustee. But Tunney was still working, in theory at least, for the New York City police when his men raided the unsuspecting Indians in New York, capturing their papers and, on the same day in early March, placing Chakravarty under arrest.

Soon after Chakravarty's apprehension, with war against Germany looming ever closer, Justice and Immigration officials began intensive surveillance of Indians in New York, Pittsburgh, St. Louis, Chicago, Portland, Seattle, and, above all, San Francisco. They built up a case history on the Gadar party. In the few days before Wilson's war message to Congress on April 2, they sent the Department of State over six hundred reports on suspected Gadar activities. Chakravarty's letters and oral information assisted the investigators, but they also drew on the intelligence picture supplied by the British and some orthodox detective work of their own. On April 6, Congress acceded to Wilson's request for war, and immediately West coast officials arrested more than fifty Indians, charging them rather belatedly with violations of American neutrality. Among the arrested was Ram Chandra, joint architect, with the Germans, of the *Maverick* conspiracy.

In the meantime, Chakravarty was still cooperating with the New York police department. In July, Nicholas Biddle of MID sent Van Deman and the State Department a transcript of the latest interrogation. Chakravarty seemed to be acting as a double agent. Not only was he "singing" a pretty song; he appeared to be uncovering further information on his own initiative in order to please his interrogators. He made new revelations about German codes and code routes, claiming that secret messages were handled under the very noses of British intelligence by the Spanish embassy in London. Chakravarty also blew the cover of a Japanese secret agent, Hideo-Nakiao, who was conspiring with Germany through Mexico to destroy the trans-Manchurian railroad. This would give the Japanese an excuse to stop supplying Russia, and when peace came Germany would in turn boost Japanese influence in the Pacific at the expense of the British.[36] Given the state of Japanese internal politics at the time, a German–Japanese conspiracy was not beyond the bounds of credence, and the State Department put both MID and ONI onto Nakiao, who nevertheless slipped the net.[37]

Although intrigued by his yarns, Chakravarty's interrogators remained extremely skeptical. Was he telling a "fallback" story? Were his tales pure invention, delivered in a deliberate attempt to confuse Anglo-American intelligence? Biddle and Tunney knew that Chakravarty was speaking under duress—he would never talk at all except in the presence of a State Department observer, in whose guarantee of protection the Indian professed faith. It seemed rather unlikely, however, that Chakravarty would be more terrified of the Americans than of his own people. The United States could merely put him in jail. In contrast, the confrontation between Gadar subversives and British intelligence agents in Vancouver had ended in assassinations on both sides, British intelligence agents getting the worst of it when their chief agent, Hopkinson, was killed. Already, Chakravarty had been badly frightened on a dark and foggy night in Washington, D.C., in April 1916, when an automobile appeared from nowhere, knocked the young Indian to the ground, and disappeared without a trace. The driver was probably not an American agent, because Chakravarty was useful to U.S. intelligence; Chakravarty had more cause to fear Indians than New Yorkers. Furthermore, his nationalistic outburst to Leland Harrison in October 1917, which the State Department rightly took seriously, indicated where his heart lay. American agents probably learned much less from Chakravarty himself than from his captured correspondence.[38]

Nevertheless, government agencies and the press made much of Chakravarty's confessions during the Indian neutrality trial at San Francisco. The trial, which resulted in the imprisonment of a number of Indians for the duration of the war, was the occasion of an attempt to justify retrospectively the administration's harassment of a nationalist group at a time when the United States was going to war to further the cause of self-determination. The Department of Justice and Tunney tried to show that Indian nationalism was not spontaneous but was part of a carefully prepared German conspiracy.[39] Many Indians, Chakravarty included, were portrayed as the innocent dupes of German propaganda and machination; it was contended that German disrespect for America's rights as a neutral had been evident throughout the Indian conspiracy and fully justified the entry of the United States into the war.[40]

Given the politically freighted nature of the San Francisco trial, the atmosphere must have been tense indeed when Chakravarty took the stand. The expectant hush had hardly developed when a shot rang out, and the key witness died before uttering a word of evidence. The bullet was fired from a gun smuggled into court by one of his codefendants. It removed the one man who might have challenged the documentation of the prosecution's case. For, although there was no doubt about the existence of the Indian conspiracy, the State Department had kept back the original captured documents, feeding lawyers with photocopies which may have been selected for their tendency to illustrate the German hand at the tiller. What, then, was the motive behind the fatal shot? Was it the natural resentment of a sincere revolutionary against an informer? Was it the retribution of a German mercenary? Were the American or British secret agents afraid of a double cross on the witness stand? The assassin left no clue, for he too was instantly shot dead, by a U.S. marshal.[41]

The attempt to discredit revolutionaries went according to plan. Under the guidance of A. Bruce Bielaski, wartime chief of the Justice Department's Bureau of Investigation, secret agents gathered information to show that those Indian revolutionaries who were not fools were scoundrels. Bureau agents cooperated with other public agencies and with the San Francisco-based Mundell International Detective Agency to collect evidence about the financial and sexual motivation of German-inspired revolutionaries. Banks, such as the Irving National Bank of New York City, supplied confidential information.[42] On the basis of this and other evidence, Ram Chandra, the gunrunner and publicist, was accused of misappropriating Gadar funds.[43] Given the fact that they were operating in a monogamous society, Gadarites had laid themselves open to scandal by accepting the early leadership of the "free love" advocate, Har Dayal. There is no evidence that secret agents laid "honey traps" for Indians or used sexual blackmail. They did, however, listen through walls when Indians entertained their girlfriends.[44] Bhagwan Singh, the California-based revolutionary who had attacked America's war aims as "but a dream," was accused of a lack of revolutionary concentration because, when on a mission to Panama, he "took a prostitute named Augustino Coldbert from the tenderloin district to live with him and spent large amounts of money on her...."[45] When, in 1918, Justice Department agents arrested the newly arrived revolutionary Sailendra Nath Ghose, they took care to do so when he was in the company of a Miss Smedley, his secretary and mistress.[46]

The harassment of Indian revolutionaries helped Wilson's foreign policy in the short term. Carefully released stories of German–Indian conspiracies gave plausibility to one of America's prominent war aims, the abolition of intrigue. Further, there was a disposition in India to believe that Wilson intended to make the British apply the principle of self-determination to that subcontinent. Madan Mohan Malaviya, president of the Indian National Congress, spoke glowingly of Wilson, and the Congress itself elected representatives to the Paris Peace Conference. The Government of India Act of 1919, which increased the electorate to over five million, seemed for a short while to augur well for the development of self-government, and, in the longer term, the pacifist leadership of Gandhi from 1920 implied continuing discredit for the principle of "gadar," or violent struggle.[47]

It would, nevertheless, be misleading to place too much emphasis on the foregoing indications that a trustful relationship would develop between the United States and India. In World War II, President Franklin D. Roosevelt and Secretary of State Cordell Hull recognized this and were particularly careful to thwart British imperialist aspirations wherever possible. They were motivated in part by a desire to further American interests instead, but there can be no doubt that their anxiety stemmed to a large degree from the broken promises of World War I. Nehru had awoken to the danger of American imperialism in the 1920s, when he began to incline favorably toward the Soviet Union. Some of his countrymen had come to the same conclusion earlier when, in the year of the Amritsar massacre (a British general's attempt to discourage unrest by shooting into a protesting Punjab crowd, killing an officially estimated 379), American influence failed to get the Indian Congress representatives a seat at the Paris conference table.[48] In America, the Indians were a godsend to the Irish-Americans, who were able to denounce the proposed League of Nations on general principle, not just because there was no separate seat for Ireland.[49] As for the leading Indians themselves, they were just coming out of prison, where, like so many radicals before and since, they had become receptive to an ideology now managed from Moscow.

Sailendra Nath Ghose was laying the groundwork for cooperation with Soviet Russia even as his countrymen languished in American prisons. Ghose had been a promising scientist in Calcutta and in 1916 won the Sir T. N. Palit fellowship of the University of Calcutta to Harvard. According to a brief biography prepared by J. Edgar Hoover for the Department of State, Ghose missed the first round of Indian conspiracies because the British refused to let him leave India. In 1917, he escaped to the United States, arriving just too late to be arrested in the federal swoops of April 1917.[50] In December, he sent a message on behalf of the Indian Nationalist Party (purportedly Calcutta-based but actually centered in New York) to Trotsky and the Workingmen's and Soldiers' Council of Russia. The message ran, in part:

> Comrades:—Revolutionary India rejoices at the rise of Free Russia with the true ideal of government of the people, by the people, and for the benefit of the people . . .
>
> We gladly extend to you . . . the recognition of the millions of Revolutionary India. . . .
>
> The position of Revolutionary India to-day is such as was the case of Revolutionary Russia in 1905. Thousands of young men are now thrown in prison, others hanged, and others deported to penal servitude at the Andaman islands, and this is not all. The hand of British Imperialism is long enough to have several scores of Indian revolutionists arrested in the United States. . . .
>
> Revolutionary Russia should demand that India should be free and that the Indian people should have an opportunity of self-determination.

The message begged Russia to champion the rights of the Indian people "and specially we beg you to demonstrate your good will by championing the cause of the Indian revolutionists who are facing a trial in the United States District Court at San Francisco. . . ."[51]

Ghose was not exclusively committed to seeking Communist aid. America's clandestine embassy-watchers discovered thirty notes sent by him to diplomatic representatives of various countries with appeals to forward the messages via diplomatic bag to their respective foreign offices.[52] In the spring of 1918, Hoover's Justice Department sleuths arrested Ghose at a time when he had in his possession a decoded letter plotting Indian intrigue in Japan, China, and the United States. Hoover sent the letter to the Army's M.I.8 (Codes and Ciphers) and had Ghose charged under the terms of the Espionage Act of June 1917. Ghose wrote to Secretary of State Lansing saying that his arrest was a ruse to prevent him from delivering to the Americans his invention concerning electric power and radio transmission, which would have been of use in the war effort.[53] Perhaps warned off by their experience with Chakravarty, the American authorities did not rise to the bait. According to J. Edgar Hoover, Ghose "was kept in the Tombs for ten months on $25,000 bail."[54]

On his release from prison, Ghose organized the Friends of Freedom for India and wrote two pamphlets for that organization. In 1925, he was still very active in New York and was even charged with having partially subverted British intelligence.[55] The State Department had contracted a headache which the "aspirin age" did little to cure. For Ghose was by no means alone in his machinations. In January 1923, Santokh Singh and Rattan Singh, two of the Gadarites jailed in 1917, attended the Fourth Congress of the Third International in Russia, where they received assurances of Soviet support. In 1924, an American agent in Riga reported that the Communists were planning a major push in India at the first sign of any weakening in the strength of Gandhi.[56]

In the Berlin of 1917, a cosmopolitan succession of visitors must have gazed from the Pariser Platz at the Brandenburger Tor and dreamed of victory. In the anterooms of the warlords, Indian revolutionaries jostled for position with disaffected Algerians, Egyptians, Flemings, Finns, and others. Symbolizing the dramatic potential of the Berlin nationalists was the Irish-American T. St. John Gaffrey, a founder of the German–Irish Society, which had three hundred members by December 1917.[57] The Irish, however, did not clash overtly with American intelligence. From the Democratic administration's point of view, it would have been unwise to harass in a manifestly aggressive fashion Irish-American nationalists who could, in the right circumstances, appeal to the politically entrenched and numerous Irish-American voters. There was no case for a show trial of Hibernian spies, although the administration hoped that the Indian affair would serve as a warning to the Irish. If the State Department had, nevertheless, pushed forward with a determined penetration of clandestine Irish groups, it would have met with indifferent success. The Irish revolutionaries would have been difficult to crack because of their long experience of evading New York-based British intelligence agents. If they had been caught and thoroughly exposed, the evidence would have shown that they were palpably capable of conducting their own conspiracies, without financial or diplomatic assistance from the Germans. It would have been foolish for Irish-Americans to work too closely with the Central Powers, since that would have endangered their carefully developed cover in the United States.

There was, nevertheless, some German–Irish cooperation, and responses to it varied. Voska, for example, claimed to have been inspired by German activity in Ireland, ascribing his plan for Allied operations in East Central Europe to mere imitation of Central Power designs.[58] More significantly, the State Department acted surreptitiously against the Irish. The secret service raid on von Igel's New York office in April 1916 had revealed evidence of Irish as well as Indian collaboration with the Germans. The American authorities did not release news of the captured Irish documents for some time, for fear that the administration would be accused of unneutral behavior in raiding von Igel's office on behalf of British imperialism. However, the news was leaked on the eve of the Indian trial, in a move calculated to convict by association Irish-American nationalists who by now operated in a country fired by anti-German zeal.[59]

By September 1918, probably acting on the basis of information provided by British agents in New York, Wiseman was confident enough to complain to the Justice Department about the actions of Irish nationalists

The capture of Major John André. This early nineteenth-century lithograph shows an enemy spy of the Revolutionary period in a romantic light, demonstrating that the public's attitudes toward spies are subject to drastic change.

Allan Pinkerton and General George B. McClellan. When President Lincoln replaced McClellan as head of the Union Army, the controversial spy chief lost his job, too. (From an engraving by Ralph Chambers in Pinkerton's book *Spy of the Rebellion,* New York, 1883.)

Left, Thomas M. Beach (alias Henri Le Caron), the British secret agent who penetrated the Fenian organization in the late 1860s and whose activities exposed America's vulnerability to foreign intrigue. (From Beach, *Twenty-Five Years in the Secret Service*, London: Heineman, 1892.) Right, John E. Wilkie, chief of the Secret Service's Emergency Force during the Spanish-American War. (From *The American-Spanish War*, Norwich, Conn.: Charles C. Haskell, 1899.)

The Pinkerton assault on the striking workers at the Homestead steel works in 1892 was largely responsible for discrediting the agency in the public mind and thus led indirectly to the establishment of a government-sponsored intelligence service. (Copyright © 1965 by Leon Wolff. By permission of Harper & Row, Inc., and the Longman Group.)

Count Johann Heinrich von Bernstorff with two friends. The German ambassador's indiscreet telephone conversations with his mistresses were tapped by the Secret Service in World War I. (From a contemporary illustration in the London weekly journal *The Sketch.*)

A German plotter, as seen by a *Life* cartoonist during World War I.

This portrait of W. Somerset Maugham by Sir Gerald Kelly, painted shortly before Maugham's spying expedition to Russia in World War I, was entitled "The Jester" by the artist. (Used by permission of the Tate Gallery, London.)

A contemporary cartoonist's view of the decision to conduct sessions of the Paris Peace Conference behind closed doors despite President Woodrow Wilson's well-publicized opposition to secret diplomacy. (By Nelson Harding of the *Brooklyn Eagle*.)

When Truth Is Kept Within Doors
Lies Come Out at the Window

Left, Sir William Wiseman, the go-between of Anglo-American intelligence in World War I. From W. B. Fowler, *British-American Relations, 1917-1918: The Role of Sir William Wiseman*, Plate no. 1. Copyright © 1969 by Princeton University Press. Reprinted by permission of Princeton University Press.   Right, Frank L. Polk, coordinator of U.S. intelligence in World War I. From W. B. Fowler, *British-American Relations, 1917-1918: The Role of Sir William Wiseman*, Plate no. 4. Copyright © 1969 by Princeton University Press. Reprinted by permission of Princeton University Press.

The U.S. Secretariat at the Paris Peace Conference, 1919. The names of the men known to be involved in intelligence work are italicized. Their period of known intelligence service is shown in parentheses. Seated, left to right: P. H. Patchin; *J. C. Grew* (1920s); A. H. Frazier; *Leland Harrison* (1917-1920). Standing, left to right: G. F. Close; *A. C. Kirk* (1920s); G. W. Minot; J. Garfield; R. E. Condon; C. A. Herter; J. H. Smith; *Gordon Auchincloss* (1915-1919); U. S. Grant III. (National Archives.)

The Current Diplomatic and Political Correspondence staff of the U.S. Commission to Negotiate Peace, photographed at the Hotel Crillon, Paris, in March 1919. Colonel Ralph H. L. Van Deman (seated second from left), who had recently reformed U.S. military intelligence, was relieved of his Army duties in 1929. Allen W. Dulles (standing directly behind Van Deman), who had been a secret agent for the State Department in Switzerland in World War I, resigned from government service in 1927 but returned to service in the O.S.S. in World War II and the C.I.A. from its founding in 1947 to his retirement as Director in 1961. (National Archives.)

Trained with the Secret Service in the War of 1898, William J. Burns established a successful private detective agency that specialized in labor espionage and is still in business. In 1921 Burns became head of the Bureau of Investigation (later called the F.B.I.). He directed the federal agency until 1924. (From Burns, *The Masked War*, New York: George H. Doran, 1913).

 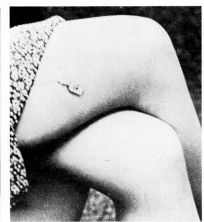

Left, Aerial reconnaissance, first used in World War I, reached an advanced stage in the spy satellite. This sort of development was foreseen in the 1920s, when some experts predicted that the individual agent would become obsolete. (Artist's impression. Wide World Photo.)Right, At the same time, such technological advances as miniaturization facilitated "human espionage," such as this strategically situated electronic ear. (Popperfoto.)

By the 1920s, U.S. military espionage was capable of using such advanced techniques as photo-reduction to facilitate intelligence work. The dot on the "i" in the sample shown here has been removed with a fine instrument, the cavity filled with glue (left), and a piece of microdot film, cut to precisely the same size, eased into place (right). The film negative is not visible to the naked eye. (Ron Startup/Daily Telegraph Magazine.)

Left, William ("Wild Bill") Donovan, Director of the Office of Strategic Services, which took the initiative in many intelligence matters during World War II. (Wide World Photo.)

Below, Allen W. Dulles,, a veteran of U.S. intelligence in World Wars I and II, was the longest serving Director of the Central Intelligence Agency (1953-61). (Wide World Photo.)

in violation of the American Espionage Act.[60] The U.S. authorities refrained from action and allowed the fugitive Irish president Eamon De
Valera to arrive, agitate, and depart entirely unimpeded. Wiseman's
request confirms, however, British faith in American cooperation over the
Irish question. This faith was to be borne out, if not by the actions of the
federal government, then by those of New York City's police authorities,
whose surveillance resulted in the arrest of James Larkin on November
8, 1919. Larkin, general secretary of the Irish Transport and General
Workers' Union and founder of the Irish Citizen Army (which fought in
the Easter Rising of 1916), had been in America since 1914, speaking on
left-wing platforms. He was tried and convicted under the criminal
anarchism laws of New York State and sent to Sing Sing in 1919, being
falsely accused at the same time of involvement in the formation of the
American Communist party. British embassy officials brought pressure to
bear which ensured that Larkin, once incarcerated, would remain in
prison. Protests from Irish trade unionists to the effect that Larkin was
an Irish labor leader, not an American subversive, proved unavailing.[61]

There was a tacit understanding between British and American intelligence concerning the Irish. British intelligence was allowed carte blanche
to work against the Irish in the United States. U.S. secret agents worked
in Ireland, where there were no American voters, and on counterintelligence among returning soldiers. In the latter respect, the Americans
continued to work with the British beyond the armistice. Lieutenant Fanshawe, of U.S. military intelligence, in December 1918 placed under detention a number of American soldiers recently returned from England,
who had uttered such inflammatory statements as "the food those damned
Britishers gave us was not fit to eat." He accused the men of having frat-
ernized with German prisoners of war, of wearing metal rings provided
by the Germans (a method of identification reminiscent of that used by
Spanish spies in the American Army in 1898), and of stirring up trouble
between Britain and America. This trouble was firmly ascribed, in Fanshawe's report obligingly forwarded to Wiseman through the New York
office of the British military attaché, to "Irish sentiment."[62]

In 1919 and 1920, American public opinion shifted once more, and
Irish nationalists again felt the balmy zephyr of popular approval. It became necessary for the State Department to warn the British that the U.S.
government could no longer countenance the sabotage activities of *agents
provocateurs*. Polk represented the State Department view to the British
chargé d'affaires in March 1920, saying that he would have to close the
New York spy office: "I told him I knew that the British officials resented
my attitude . . . but I told him he must realize that my real purpose was
to prevent any awkward incident which would draw an attack on British
officials: that the Secret Service office had been too well advertised in
the past and I urged that they try to cover it up as the Irish and others

were sure to make trouble."[63] In advising the British to go underground, Polk seemed to be condoning foreign clandestine operations on U.S. territory.

The British were not keen on a cover-up operation. Their espionage activities in the United States had acquired a quasilegitimacy, together with relative diplomatic immunity, which they were loath to surrender. They tried to show that the operations of their Secret Service were justified by Irish terrorist activities. But Polk's "information was to the contrary. We had from the most reliable source statements that showed that the trouble had been started by government agents."[64] Unfortunately, the page in Polk's diary indicating the nature of "the trouble" is missing, but he was doubtless referring to the activities of *agents provocateurs* instructed by the British Secret Service. The under secretary of state was adamant in his demands; Polk was blunt enough to complain to Wiseman that the New York branch of the British Secret Service would have to be abolished because it had been indiscreet.[65]

Polk urged on the British that the unionist movement—the campaign to unite the Protestant-dominated "six counties" of Ulster with the rest of Ireland—be dealt with "in a liberal spirit."[66] By 1920, British good will was no longer worth defending without regard to cost. The United States was able to push slightly harder for the principle of self-determination within the British empire, because self-sacrifice, in terms of a possible loss of wartime cooperation, was no longer involved. It was not so unpragmatic, however, as to insist on the absolute disbandment of the British Secret Service in New York.

Reestablished under cover of the British consulate's passport control office, the British spy service continued to harass American-based Indian revolutionaries well into the 1920s, without undue interference from either Democratic or Republican administrations. Larkin was not released from Sing Sing until Governor Al Smith pardoned him in 1923. By this time the labor leader was embittered, and he became Ireland's representative on the Comitern.[67] During World War I, American intelligence had perhaps played a crooked and costly game because there was no other course in sight. But there can be no doubt that, by the 1920s, the Americans had shown themselves to be irresolute over the principle of self-determination and thoroughly inconsistent in their opposition to clandestine methods.

As the second Woodrow Wilson administration drew to a close, its intelligence officials could point with some pride to several developments that had occurred since 1915. For example, the intelligence community had produced useful appraisals and recommendations concerning East Central Europe through Somerset Maugham, Voska, and their collaborators. The United States had for the first time established a code-breaking capability with some potential for future success. Agencies like the Bureau of Investigation and the Secret Service had defended national security when it was threatened by clever and determined foreign secret agents. In selecting personnel for foreign operations and The Inquiry, the administration had drawn on two of America's strongest assets, a cosmopolitan immigrant population and an extensive, lively academic community. A large espionage system had operated with minimal internal friction, largely because the State Department had unchallenged responsibility for liaison, evaluation, and dissemination.

But if the espionage experience of 1915–1920 suggested useful lessons for the future, it also drew attention to some incipient problems. The unfortunate role of federal agencies in the Red Scare was paralleled by the intervention of U.S. agents in Mexican labor politics. This kind of meddling in the domestic politics of foreign countries was to become habitual and, in the long run, detrimental to the interests of both the United States and the other countries concerned. Second, America's quandary over what to do about outlawed and therefore surreptitious Asian revolutionaries whose aims would have been congenial to Thomas Jefferson but were anathema to the British was to be repeated in World War II and thereafter. The World War I experience thus illustrated the difficulty of maintaining a consistent attitude toward espionage: Woodrow Wilson condemned the undercover tactics of the Central Powers, including those directed against British imperialism, but sanctioned secret operations directed against the empires of Austro-Hungary and Turkey. His ambivalent attitude toward espionage was to be shared by many Americans in the aftermath of World War II.

9

The Demobilization of Intelligence As a Fact

Though Ralph Van Deman reached the pinnacle of his career as MID Director in World War I, he maintained an unrelaxed vigilance until his death in 1952. Following his work in the Philippines and his achievement in putting Army espionage on a strong footing in 1918, he held undisputed ascendancy in the field of American military intelligence. In 1941, he once again emerged as the focal point of a large organization. His contribution to World War II was an unofficial counterintelligence outfit based on information supplied by volunteers. It seems probable that Van Deman had been privately compiling a contingency list of suspects ever since World War I. According to historian Richard W. Rowan, a list of 105,000 suspects drawn up by the Navy Department and ordered destroyed by President Wilson, some of whose friends appeared on the list, had fallen into private hands and formed the basis of a secret surveillance system in the 1930s.[1] It is unclear whether Van Deman had access to any such list, but the information in his possession was certainly important, for he was brought into informal intelligence discussions initiated by the State Department in 1941–1942.

Upon the conclusion of World War II, Van Deman turned his attention from Japanese-American spies in California to the problem of Communist subversion. In a period when the American people as a whole were becoming alarmed over the threat of Communism at home as well as overseas, Van Deman once again applied his bureaucratic expertise to counterespionage. Congressional hearings in 1971 brought to light the existence of "Van Deman files" on the personal background of individuals, in the main liberal or left-wing, whom the military intelligence expert had considered to be subversives.[2]

To the layman, Van Deman's interest in subversive groups, whether Filipino nationalist, German autocratic, Japanese imperialist, or international Communist, may appear obsessive. His was, however, no more than the preoccupation of the professional. The enemies he defined were the opponents whom any American of orthodox political outlook might have discerned. If Van Deman grew exceptionally virulent as he grew older, it was in reaction to his treatment by fellow Army officers. He had been kept in the wings until the eleventh hour during World War I. In 1929, he was fired from MID and retired to San Diego. The dismissal of so experienced and unexceptionable an officer, a man with twenty years' active service left in him, invites explanation.

Van Deman's mandatory retirement was less a result of his own tactless truculence and the enmity of his superiors than a symptom, one of many, of the general demobilization of intelligence following World War I. The paring down of the armed forces was a natural accompaniment of peace; in the case of intelligence, however, an argument could be made for continued vigilance as a safeguard against future entanglements. Nevertheless, American intelligence failed to escape the pruning knife.

In the aftermath of World War I invasions of privacy and of the excesses of the Red Scare, there was a reaction—discernible among politicians as well as the people—against intrusive practices. For this reason, counterintelligence suffered a particularly severe bloodletting. This branch of intelligence in any case had outgrown offensive espionage and offered more bureaucratic foliage to be slashed and an opportunity for visible savings to the public purse. It was an ironic result of the demobilization of intelligence following World War I that, since the pruning knife was unevenly applied, the offensive role of American intelligence became relatively more important.

The revulsion against counterintelligence explains specific aspects of demobilization, notably the particularly sharp cutback in MID. The departure of Van Deman was, indeed, a postscript to the chapter which, by 1929, had already been written. The stringent economies of 1921–1922 forced the recall of military attachés from Belgium, Czechoslovakia, Ecuador, Egypt, Holland, Hungary, Sweden, and Switzerland.[3] By 1922 MID headquarters personnel had declined to 90 from a peak of 1,441 in 1918, and the Army's intelligence budget stood at $225,000 instead of the $2.5 million of the final year of the struggle. These figures continued to diminish slightly until 1937, when headquarters personnel numbered 69 with a budget of $267,000.[4] A general staff officer complained in 1937 that by then the total cost of Army intelligence, including the wage bill for military personnel, had sunk to $700,000. He maintained that the U.S.

government spent only $1.5 million on all its intelligence activities. According to his sources, the corresponding figure for Japan was $12 million (Army, Navy, and Foreign Office) and the Soviet Union spent even more, though $10 million went toward internal surveillance. Curiously omitting reference to Germany, the officer was able to advance impressive figures for Britain, France, and Italy.[5]

After the reductions of 1921–1922, those concerned with the welfare of military intelligence continued to be apprehensive. The reaction of the public to the Sacco and Vanzetti trial (in which the two Massachusetts anarchists were deprived of a fair hearing on a charge of murder), to the continued imprisonment of the Irish radical Jim Larkin, and against unofficial enforcers of conformity such as the Ku Klux Klan indicated the growing aversion to authoritarianism in the 1920s. If the respectable middle classes were in the mood to defy Prohibition and its ineffectual enforcement agents, could they be expected to condone the domestic activities of military intelligence? Fearing public reaction against MID and other organs of military intelligence, high-ranking Army officers tried to anticipate further cuts by imposing an internal curtailment of counterespionage activities.

The War Department was apprehensive in 1923 about unauthorized investigations which had already "caused embarrassment."[6] It warned members of the military intelligence section, Officers' Reserve Corps, not to undertake investigations on their own initiative. The Department issued instructions to this effect to all Corps area commanders. A few months later, the *Army and Navy Journal* remained dissatisfied with the situation. It cited several instances in which Army intelligence officers—with one exception men attached to field units rather than to G-2 or MID —had acted like, or presented themselves in the light of, civilian policemen. The *Journal* warned that "the intelligence officer is not a policeman. He is not a diminutive edition of a Burns–Pinkerton detective."[7]

Such warnings went unheeded, and a year later the press got hold of two controversial cases. The first was that of Paxton Hibben, a captain in the Army Reserve. Hibben declared that he was in favor of Senator Robert M. LaFollette, then running on the Progressive farmer-labor ticket for the presidency, and that he advocated diplomatic recognition of the Soviet Union. MID concerned itself with Hibben's views, and the Army conducted a hearing with a view to his discharge. The press reaction was unfavorable. The isolationist *Chicago Tribune*, while deploring Hibben's opinions and regretting his original selection as an officer, warned that the Army would only suffer if it presented him with "the crown of a military martyr." The *Tribune* foresaw "the avid exploitation of an American Dreyfus myth by all the organs of Red or Pink, and the alarm of the 'liberals'."[8]

Just as the fuss over Hibben was subsiding, it was revealed that the current campaign to purge sex from Broadway theatrical productions was based on objections by military intelligence officers to two plays in particular, Ernest Denny's drawing room comedy *Vanity* and the war drama *What Price Glory?* by Maxwell Anderson and Laurence Stallings. The soldiers had concentrated their criticism on *What Price Glory?* High-ranking Army and Navy intelligence officers and two Justice Department officials had attended a performance of the play and submitted a report on it, under the nom de plume "Inspector Peterkin," to Mayor John F. Hylan of New York. The report indicated that the show, sold out on Broadway, contained profanities; furthermore, the play suggested that there were poor discipline and low morale in the Army and the Marine Corps. "Peterkin" complained that marines were depicted as "subject at all times to debauchery and seducements," that intelligence personnel were referred to as "damn Bible scholars," and that, in the first scene, a "captain in full Marine uniform" made love to the only woman in the cast in the presence of his subordinates. MID and ONI considered that the play showed behavior uncharacteristic of the Marine Corps. However, when civilian policemen investigated the charge, they found nothing offensive in the script, concluding that "either it has been misrepresented or it has been very much changed."[9] John S. Sumner, secretary of the Society for the Prevention of Vice, thought the play innocent and suspected a publicity stunt. The Army and Navy intelligence services had exposed themselves to ridicule. The Army felt so threatened that it considered launching an educative program on "Popular Conceptions of Intelligence Duties in Time of Peace." The chief of M.I.4, one of the propaganda sections of MID, wisely warned G-2 against such a course on the ground that it would provoke renewed criticism over the Paxton Hibben affair.[10]

There was less evidence of despondency from ONI than from MID during the 1920s. ONI was less vulnerable to demobilization because it had been less involved in domestic surveillance. Secretary of the Navy Daniels had, in the Wilson period, carefully circumscribed the limits within which ONI was permitted to work; domestically, this meant that naval intelligence was virtually confined to the protection of dockyards. No radicals, let alone politically orthodox civilians, had been subjected by ONI to excesses of snooping and censorship. Unlike MID, ONI was not an obvious target for civil libertarians. Its preservation was demanded on commonsense grounds. Any strategy of national defense was bound to make use of the Atlantic and Pacific oceans, America's natural barriers against aggression. The Navy and its intelligence office would therefore have survived any reasonable reorganization.

Political circumstances, furthermore, made extensive cutbacks in ONI improbable. Senators and Republicans who felt slighted by President Wilson's disregard for senatorial and bipartisan advice during World War I warmed to the organization because it was championed by one of the Wilson administration's most effective critics, Rear Admiral William Snowden Sims. Sims's tactless outbursts had got him into hot water on many occasions, particularly during Wilson's presidency. Secretary Daniels kept extensive files on his indiscretions, including a personal file. For example, in 1910 Sims, who then held the relatively low rank of commander, was rebuked for having remarked that certain Navy rules invented by desk-bound bureaucrats were "generally disregarded in the Fleet with derisive disapproval."[11] The following year, the Canadian-born Sims was publicly reprimanded on the instruction of President Taft for remarking in the course of a speech at a dinner given by the Lord Mayor of the City of London that "if the time ever comes when the British Empire is seriously menaced by an external enemy, it is my opinion that you may count on every man, every dollar, every drop of blood, of your kindred across the sea."[12] Sims was a political liability to the Democrats, who leaned heavily for support on urban Irish-American political machines, because he was blatantly prejudiced against the sons of Erin (he once remarked aloud that Irish-Americans were "asses").[13] To these lapses Sims added the monumental offense, from Daniels' point of view, of charging that the Navy Department had pursued a faulty strategy in World War I.

Upon the outbreak of hostilities with Germany, Sims had become the officer in command of U.S. naval operations in European waters. This expression of confidence in his ability was not reciprocated. So strongly did Sims feel about the strategy pursued by the Navy Department in 1917–1918, that he turned down the distinguished service award offered to him in 1919 by the U.S. government. His gesture was the more insulting because he had accepted high awards from the British, French, Belgian, Italian, and Japanese governments. The Admiral explained the reasons for his disenchantment in a report submitted in 1920 to the Senate's Naval Affairs subcommittee. In World War I, as in the Spanish-American war, the American public had clamored for protection against possible naval bombardment of seaboard cities. Sims charged that, for reasons of politics and incompetence, the Navy Department had directed warships to coastal defense when it should have been obvious that there was no threat and that the Navy's chief priority was to escort convoys carrying men and supplies to Europe. Sims calculated that the Navy Department's unintelligent approach had prolonged the European war, causing a half million additional and unnecessary deaths.[14] The opinion of Sims in the 1920s was that naval reductions should be resisted.

The Senate subcommittee was predisposed to accept Sims's version of past events and his recommendations for the future, at least in part because President Wilson had offended the Senate and rejuvenated Republican party partisanship (which had lain dormant for patriotic reasons during the war) by neglecting to consult either institution in negotiating the peace settlement of 1919. The Senate therefore endorsed Sims's view in 1920, seconded by the Republicans in the administrations of the 1920s.[15]

ONI could derive further comfort from the fact that intelligence was close to the former admiral's heart. He had established a reputation for himself in 1895–1897 as intelligence officer on board the warship *Charleston*.[16] His strategic criticism of American naval war plans reflected his grasp of wide-ranging intelligence. He indicated his continuing interest in this aspect of naval affairs by agreeing to be president of the Naval War College from 1919 to 1922.[17] In Sims, naval intelligence had the most formidable of champions. Any attempt to demobilize naval intelligence would require a firm political hand.

A firm hand did reach out of the weak current of 1920s politics to curtail the ambitions of naval expansionists. Secretary of State Charles Evans Hughes did not exactly suppress America's naval advocates, who never suffered rebuffs comparable to those administered to the military, but he managed to restrain a Navy General Board in full cry. The astutely negotiated agreements reached at the Hughes-inspired Washington Disarmament Conference of 1921–1922 slowed down the race among great naval powers.[18] The reduction of capital ship tonnage construction targets had already been anticipated by a curtailment in intelligence appropriations. When the armistice came, regular officers at ONI were assisted by a temporary force of 306 reservists, in addition to the complement of 18 civil service clerks which antedated the outbreak of hostilities. The Navy had reduced its intelligence back-up staff to 42 in 1920, a dramatic cutback though still an increase of 24 souls over prewar days. The naval appropriation bill of 1920 curtailed the already limited domestic activities of ONI, restricting the office to purely offensive espionage.[19] Although the powerfully supported ONI was never savaged during the 1920s, there was no prospect, in the decade of the Washington conference, for a great revival in its fortunes.

The agencies which had expanded to cope with the problem of internal surveillance in World War I did not shrink to a significant degree, but they changed their function. The Department of Justice's Bureau of Investigation started the new decade under the leadership of William J. Burns, the private detective. At first, his selection seemed to augur well for the unabated continuance of domestic surveillance. As an associate of the "Ohio gang" which frequented Warren G. Harding's White House, he could expect to receive full presidential backing, as well as the support of Attorney General Harry M. Daugherty. As a former Secret Service agent Burns had always taken an interest in radical groups and labor agitators; his past achievements ranged from the arrest of the McNamara brothers, charged with dynamiting the premises of the antilabor *Los Angeles Times* in 1910, to the surveillance of anarchist nude bathers in Puget Sound, Washington.[20] Burns was backed in his antiradical activities by J. Edgar Hoover, head of the bureau's general intelligence division. The bureau seemed poised, at the beginning of Harding's administration in 1921, to step into any vacuum that might be created by the running down of other intelligence agencies.

Peacetime surveillance depended for its momentum on the continuation of a certain high moral purpose. But the divergence from Wilsonian morality so evident in the Department of Justice during Harding's administration provoked opposition to the intelligence activities of the Bureau of Investigation. Daugherty's gang came into increasing disrepute as charges flew to and fro about the sale of patronage, the politically corrupt use of call girls, and the undercover dispensation of the captured secrets of the German chemical industry.

The government had confiscated German dye patents in World War I and turned them over to American chemical firms. The U.S. chemical industry, hitherto limited in scope, benefited further in the war years from specially enacted tariffs, government investment, and the removal of German competition. When Daugherty successfully insisted, soon after becoming attorney general, on being made sole arbiter of the sale and return of confiscated German-owned property, one of the ripest of plums in terms of federal graft had fallen into his lap. It was not long before the odor of putrefaction spread from his office in the Department of Justice: a congressional investigation ultimately accused him of milking $40,000 worth of bonds from the German-owned American Metals Company as his price for transferring its ownership to a Swiss corporation. Daugherty escaped conviction, but not disgrace, by burning the relevant records.[21]

Daugherty's image was not improved by rumors about his house on H Street and another home on K Street which was the headquarters of the Ohio gang. Seekers of political favors would visit the house on H Street in the hope of seeing the president, who frequented the place in pursuit of drink, poker, girls and the comforting company of his old cronies from Ohio. The more gullible bribers would then hand over money, which lined the pockets of the Ohio gang, never reaching the president. Insiders soon got to know of these activities, but Daugherty's immediate unpopularity was by no means confined to a small circle. When the attorney general learned through labor spies of plans for a massive rail strike in 1922, he had used a powerful injunction to crush the stoppage within two days: a ruthless move that aroused the hostility of organized labor. A larger section of the public was already indignant at the graft practiced by enforcement agents of the Prohibition Bureau, which was under the supervision of the Department of Justice. Finally, Daugherty provoked furious and fatal reaction when he asked Burns to investigate his Department's critics in Congress and in the press.[22]

The investigative activities of the Department of Justice were no longer popular by the time Harding died in 1923. Though Harding had remained loyal to the Ohio gang, the elevation of Vice President Calvin Coolidge brought the clean wind of change. The new president dismissed Daugherty in April 1924. Kansas journalist William Allen White remarked of the new attorney general: "When Harlan F. Stone took charge of the Department of Justice, he immediately ordered the spying, telephone snooping, and undercover work of the Department of Justice to cease. A new regime began in that office that day."[23]

The abatement in extrapolice activity was temporary, and the Bureau of Investigation soon regained prestige through the feats of its "G-men" in the gangster era. Nevertheless, the espionage function of the bureau did go into relative desuetude in the 1920s. The same can be said of the private detective agencies retained by the bureau in World War I. Private eyes turned back to industrial relations business and began to realize new profits in divorce work.

Whereas the FBI retained and, later, expanded its residual responsibility for internal security, the Treasury Department's Secret Service bade a final farewell to espionage work in the interwar years. After the assassination of President McKinley in 1901, the service had become responsible for the personal safety of the chief executive.[24] As image building and public exposure became essential ingredients of presidential success, and as rifles and hand guns became ever more lethal but never less available, the protection job grew onerous. Yet the service continued to be burdened with its other traditional tasks as well. These increased when, as a result of World War I, New York became the creditor capital of the world. The increasing complexities of financial life and of international trade added new dimensions to the service's brief of guarding against certain types of fraud. The Treasury Department had to draw the line somewhere and decided to put counterespionage beyond the circumference of its activities.

Gradually, the career profiles of Secret Service agents and directors began to change. Frank Burke, a veteran of Wilkie's force and, as we saw in Chapter 5, the speedy expropriator of Dr. Heinrich Albert's briefcase in 1915, was an example of the old-style agent. With the advent of World War II, President Franklin D. Roosevelt extended the aging sleuth's period of service so that he could help fight against enemy agents.[25] But this was no more than a gesture aimed at morale building. At seventy-three, Burke no longer had the steam, and probably lacked the expertise, to be a modern agent. The younger men in the Secret Service did not have his background of wartime counterintelligence experience. Frank J. Wilson, secret service chief from 1936 to 1946, had made his name as a result of his part in the investigation which led to the conviction of Al Capone for income tax fraud. The career of his successor, James J. Maloney, was based on the pursuit of counterfeiters and the successful protection of presidents.[26] The Secret Service, which had been at the hub of central intelligence in 1898, no longer played a vital part in surveillance activities by 1941.

Bureaucratic changes in the Department of State were less easy to assess, in terms of quantitative reductions, than demobilization of the ONI and MID or mutations in function at the Justice and Treasury Departments. Nevertheless, it must have appeared to most observers after 1918 that successive secretaries of state were dismantling the facilities for civilian espionage. It will be recalled that in 1919 the office of the counselor, responsible for intelligence coordination during the war, became the officer of the under secretary of state. The retitled agency continued to be entrusted with the coordination of intelligence from the Departments of Justice and of the Army and Navy until June 1927, when Secretary of State Frank B. Kellogg abolished the various intelligence-coordinating subunits.[27]

Another casualty followed in October 1929. This was the American Black Chamber, the cryptographic unit which developed with MID during the war and had been saved from extinction in 1919 by Acting Secretary of State Frank Polk. The State Department provided most of the finances for the Chamber in the 1920s. Secretary of State Charles Evans Hughes benefited from its expertise during the Washington Disarmament Conference. Black Chamber experts had broken the new Japanese code, "YU," and were able to give the secretary advance notice of how far the Japanese would be prepared to compromise on capital ship tonnage ratios. The situation was analogous to what might have developed at President Harding's poker table assuming that Daugherty had seen everyone's cards. Hughes pressed the Japanese to their reserve bargaining limit of 10:6 (United States: Japan) from their opening position of 10:7.[28] Eight years later Henry L. Stimson, President Herbert Hoover's secretary of state, withdrew his department's financial support from the Black Chamber, later advancing the view that "gentlemen do not read each other's mail."[29]

One further dissolution which deserves attention is the progressive winding up of the affairs of the chief special agent. In 1919, Leland Harrison was assigned to the office of the counselor as a "diplomatic secretary," his duties including acquiring British and German codes for the Black Chamber and supervising agents and pseudo-agents like

Emanuel Voska. His duties also included the investigation of organizations and individuals, overseas and at home, suspected of subversive activity. To carry out the field work involved, Polk created the Office of the Chief Special Agent.

The new office was an interesting experiment, reminiscent, in that the State Department used its own operational force, of the Federalist arrangement of the late 1790s and foreshadowing developments in the 1940s. But the office, though at least briefly operational in the 1920s, lost ground in the interwar years, as is reflected by the dwindling extent of its front activities. As part of those activities the office for a while provided protection for foreign dignitaries visiting the United States and for some time after that conspicuously concerned itself with hotel and steamer bookings on behalf of foreign officials, State Department personnel, and State Department wives who pined for Paris. The office did less and less in an open way as time wore on—probably, though not certainly, an indication that its undercover activity had all but ceased. The abolition of the office around 1939 was no more than a formality according to the evidence currently available.[30]

The chief special agent did become involved in one investigation, in 1925, which shows that he was still theoretically operational. The Sharp–Ghose affair indicates, however, that State Department espionage dawdled in a halfway house; having developed an independent capacity in World War I, it was still not fully committed to the important goal of keeping the British under surveillance. The affair also throws light on the discontinuity from which State Department intelligence suffered—a discontinuity which was indicated by and led to ignorance of what the British were up to.

The British had failed to comply with Polk's request that they wind up intelligence operations in New York. The acting secretary had conceded their right to "attach someone to the passport office," and this was a privilege they abused.[31] The situation was brought to light in July 1925, when R. S. Sharp, who was in charge of State Department undercover operations in New York City, reported to Chief Special Agent R. C. Bannerman that he had received what he thought was an unacceptable request from agents of the British government. He had been asked to find out about the contacts of J. Edgar Hoover's World War I adversary Sailendra H. Ghose. Undeterred by his term in the Tombs, Ghose was continuing his anti-British activity in the United States. Sharp, however, was reluctant to make an investigation for two reasons which, in the 1920s, sounded convincing—economy, and respect for civil liberties. He did not wish to use the slow method, infiltration, because that would have been expensive. He was opposed to the fast method, a raid to permit the perusal of Ghose's private papers, since this would have involved "violation of the constitutional rights of the man and is hardly practical in view of the instructions that we are to use the greatest discretion in handling the matter." He suggested that British "officials" in New York were much better equipped to investigate Indians than his division was and that they should be asked to utilize their own "extensive organization in New York City" for this purpose.[32]

The incumbent under secretary of state, career diplomat Arthur D. Lane, prompted Acting Chief Special Agent Hall Kinsey to obtain such details as Sharp possessed. Thus encouraged, Sharp alleged that associates of Ghose—indeed, "the controlling elements in the Hindu conspiracy"— were working with Sir William Wiseman, the Englishman who had been the lynchpin of Anglo-American espionage in World War I.[33] Continuing in a vein consistent with other contemporary manifestations of anti-Semitism, Sharp alleged that during World War I and for some years thereafter, "the British Secret Service was honeycombed with English Jews placed there through the power and influence of Jewish financiers surrounding Sir Lloyd George [sic] and the Foreign Office."[34] Wiseman, Sharp wrote, had cooperated with Indians in the war and used the British secret code in the Zionist cause, showing himself to be a "traitor to his own country."[35] Sharp further charged that, in 1925, Wiseman was exploiting unrest in India to advance the interests of the investment banking firm of Kuhn, Loeb, & Co., with which he was associated. But his Indian confederates were now being investigated by a reform element that had developed in the British Secret Service after the fall of Lloyd George in 1922.[36]

Responses to Sharp's report suggest that the State Department had lost none of its skepticism in evaluating incoming information. Kinsey observed to Lane that "a cursory examination of [Sharp's] report seems to indicate that it does not include the more definite information which you wished. . . ."[37] It is probably true that Wiseman had no friendly associations with Ghose; on the other hand, Kinsey had dimissed too lightly another aspect of Sharp's report, that dealing with British intelligence. When Sharp referred to an "extensive" British organization in New York, he had been urgently required to explain "just exactly what organization in New York is referred to."[38] If it was distinct from Scotland Yard, with whom exactly should American officials in London liaise concerning clandestine matters? Replying to this extraordinary question, Sharp pointed out what the most cursory perusal of the under secretary's files would have revealed, that a British intelligence organization operated under the cover of the passport control division of the British consulate's office.[39] The underbriefed Lane displayed great surprise, rapidly culminating in disbelief of Sharp's assertion that "Scotland Yard is not the real inside British [Secret] Service insofar as foreign investigations covering intrigues are concerned."[40] Such a response suggests that the offices of the chief special agent and of the under secretary of state operated at a low key in the field of counterintelligence in the mid-1920s.

However much discredited by his actions in 1919, Woodrow Wilson's public opposition to secret diplomacy received reinforcement in the pronouncements of successive Republican secretaries of state. Notably, Kellogg and Stimson, as well as President Hoover, advocated greater honesty, trust, and openness in international relations.[41] Even private detectives had come into disrepute, largely because of their labor espionage work.[42]

The LaFollette Civil Liberties Committee of the U.S. Senate issued subpoenas in the 1930s summoning representatives of the Pinkerton and Burns agencies to give testimony on their antilabor activities.[43] Clearly spies were losing caste. In the same decade, Senator Gerald P. Nye conducted hearings purporting to show that there had been an American conspiracy, centered on arms manufacturers, to embroil the United States in World War I.[44] By the mid-1930s, there was intense suspicion, inside and outside the Senate, of anything covert. The suspicion may be taken as both a cause and reflection of the rundown in U.S. intelligence facilities.

Those who took a historical view of American intelligence between 1918 and 1941 minimized its extent. Shortly after the outbreak of World War II, historian George S. Bryan wrote: "Americans have liked to think that spying, as an established, normal activity of government, was one of the things that had no place in our national life. The social, political, and diplomatic spy work of European countries belonged, they felt, to an Old World tradition happily left behind."[45] Similarly, General George C. Marshall, Secretary of State at the time of the formation of the CIA, disapprovingly remarked that "prior to World War II, our foreign intelligence was little more than what a military attaché could learn at dinner, more or less over the coffee cups."[46] Allen Dulles, the longest serving director of the CIA, wrote that in "United States history, until after World War II, there was little official government intelligence activity except in time of combat."[47] Both Dulles and Bryan conceded that there had been intelligence activity in World War I; by implication, they confirmed the impression that there was extensive, indeed virtually annihilatory, demobilization after 1918.

Neither contemporary nor later indications of the extent of undercover activity should be taken at face value. Because of the very nature of covert activities, any estimate of their extent may be misleading. Contemporary observers may have exaggerated or underestimated, deliberately or not, the relative extent of intelligence activity before and after World War II. Indeed, it suited Dulles, as it had Voska, to decry America's low level of prewar preparedness. After all, both were beneficiaries of intelligence expansion, in World Wars II and I, respectively.

The evidence presented in the next chapter will in fact suggest that demobilization after 1918 was mythical in several important respects. For excellent reasons, America's interwar spies pretended not to exist, in a way that the conspicuously institutionalized CIA later found to be impossible. Nevertheless, it is undoubtedly true that their quest for obscurity was materially assisted by the demobilization which did in fact occur. Observers of post-1918 American intelligence did not invent demobilization; they merely exaggerated its extent.

10

The Demobilization of Intelligence As a Myth

World War I encouraged rapid social and international change. People living through the relatively stable 1920s in consequence experienced the illusion familiar to the small boy who, his face pressed to the window of a newly stopped express train, imagines that he is moving backwards though the landscape when in fact the train is stationary or may be creeping forward. Just so, the demobilization of intelligence after the war brought a halt to the expansion of the Wilson years, yet failed to eliminate some of the gains made on the pre-1915 system of espionage. The decline of intelligence at the conclusion of hostilities was not so complete or so consequential as politicians sometimes pretended and later observers have unequivocally accepted.

Interwar intelligence is to be compared neither with World War I organizations nor with what happened after 1947. It would be anachronistic to measure the diminutive frame of intelligence in the 1918–1941 period against the looming bureaucratic bulk of the CIA. The CIA is the intelligence agency of a nation which thinks itself, as the term "cold war" implies, embattled. Before the 1940s, Americans regarded war as a temporary phenomenon to be pushed into the background as soon as it was over. Although government intelligence grew inexorably between one peace treaty and the next, the public continued to expect that in peacetime intelligence would be demobilized, along with other military branches. Most of the money and personnel lavished on intelligence in the wars of 1898 and 1917–1918 had been in the field of counterespionage, and it was this part of intelligence that was permitted to run down after 1918. After all, there was no reason to believe that the bureaucracy of one war could be flexible enough to deal with the internal problems of the next. Predictability is a fatal weakness in any intelligence system.

Qualitatively, the American intelligence system of the 1920s and 1930s was by no means uniformly inferior to that of other periods. The dissolution of the American Black Chamber, for example, may be seen as one of the most infamous or most brilliant chapters in the history of U.S. espionage. There is persuasive evidence that Hoover, Kellogg, and Stimson were playing a clever game of bluff in the 1920s, publicly advocating abolishment of the Black Chamber while secretly allowing it to continue.

At this stage, a complication must be introduced. There was a strong suspicion in the State Department that America's own diplomatic codes had been broken, depriving the United States of any intelligence advantage it had hitherto enjoyed. In May, 1925, Secretary of State Kellogg heard from Albert H. Washburn, his minister to Austria, that there had been a security leak. Several Austrian army officers, skilled in cryptography, had found themselves unemployed and out of funds because of the fall of the empire. Washburn's message intimated that one of them, referred to as "Stein," had succumbed to temptation in order to obtain employment and money. Washburn's message ran:

> German secret agent former Colonel secretly got in touch with former Austrian officer on the pay roll of the American Military Attaché here and upon being encouraged under instructions, offered at the second meeting one milliard [i.e., billion] Austrian crowns approximately $15,000 for "cipher tables of the American diplomatic B to P inclusive." Obvious reference is to A-1 or B-1 the existence of both codes being possibly known.[1]

Kellogg took the possibility seriously. In consultation with Lane, he instructed Vienna through a top security cablegram marked "No distribution," but necessarily in B-1 code.[2]

Kellogg preserved a note of skeptical optimism, asking Washburn to "try to ascertain whether agent or agent's principals have copy of code books to which desired cipher tables refer." His next instruction, however, betrayed his real fears: "If not, how is it known that books range from symbols B to P inclusive?"[3] It does appear as if the American diplomatic codes had been partially cracked or captured. Stimson's later stress on open diplomacy was no doubt consistent with his moral leanings at the time, but it may also reflect his awareness that dissolution of the Black Chamber would have had relatively painless consequences, for by then rival powers may have been aware not only of American secrets, but of which of their own secrets and codes the Americans knew. They may already have been operating a double code, one for the benefit of the Black Chamber, another for real business. In practice, the State Department gave away nothing in 1929.

If the State Department had nothing to lose, why did it wait four years before withdrawing support from the Black Chamber? One can speculate that Kellogg did not think of the ruse whereas Stimson did, or perhaps 1929 was a more propitious year for impressing foreigners. Another possibility is that the delay reflects the desire of the State Department to make German secret agents think the Americans were ignorant of their security leak. A sudden rejection of code breaking would have been too easy to interpret. For fear of giving away his knowledge of the leak, Kellogg warned his minister in Vienna to exercise "discretion [over] the advisability of endeavoring to obtain answers" about the extent of German cryptographic knowledge.[4] The Americans could afford a delay in closing down the Black Chamber because they had no immediate fears about any further consequences of the leak; if they pretended for a while to be unaware that their code was broken, the leak might prove useful by allowing them to feed the Germans false information. For top security matters, they already had alternative codes.[5]

Thus the eventual withdrawal of State Department support from the Black Chamber created the appearance of a new openness on the part of the United States but did not in fact result in the death of American cryptography. Almost a third of the Chamber's budget had all along been provided by the War Department. In 1929, the files of the Chamber reverted to the Signal Corps, where William Friedman worked. Friedman, a brilliant cryptanalyst who had helped the Army on a volunteer basis in World War I, joined the intelligence establishment as a salaried employee in 1921. By 1941, under his guidance, the Signal Corps had developed a machine, the famous PURPLE, capable of breaking the Japanese code of the day. The Office of Naval Intelligence had been given such a machine and used it in the period leading up to the Pearl Harbor attack. Furthermore, it was Stimson himself who, as Secretary of War, revitalized code breaking in 1940.[6] One reading of Stimson's change of heart is that he foresaw the scale of America's emergency in 1941 and took precautionary action in spite of his principles. Another possible interpretation is that America had tried to gain an intelligence advantage all along in the post-World War I era and that Stimson engaged in subterfuge in 1929. Such behavior would have been consistent with the actions ascribed to his most brilliant spy by the novelist "John Le Carré," though the conjunction of circumstances in the 1920s may in fact have been purely fortuitous. In the absence of any explicit discussion in the available correspondence of Kellogg and Stimson, we can only speculate.[7]

One of the shibboleths dearest to the hearts of intelligence experts before and after World War II is the opinion that the individual secret agent, like the pioneering frontiersman, is on the way out. In the 1920s, organs of the armed forces joined the State Department in encouraging the view that underhand methods were beyond the pale. The *Cavalry Journal* in 1924 published articles by military intelligence experts noting the "decreasing importance under conditions of modern warfare of the obsolescent secret service and spy systems."[8] It is true that by then certain factors had diminished the relative importance of what the State Department called "human espionage."[9] The contraction in scope after 1919 of counterespionage, which depended on the extensive use of agents, reduced the number of spies on the federal payroll. Internationally, technological advances such as aerial reconnaissance had begun to eliminate the routine work of spies without entirely removing the necessity for using them in making certain assessments of which no machine was capable. However, the too emphatic rejection of secret agents by ONI and MID in the 1920s can only be considered a smoke screen. The fact that spies were largely removed from the direct payrolls of government agencies indicates a purification of the immediate family circle, yet it was a form of disinheritance that only encouraged a league of distant cousins, secret agents in the pay of attachés abroad.

There were several types of attaché, but those most directly charged with foreign intelligence work were under the aegis of the Army and Navy. The priorities of naval espionage reflected what had been implicit in the practically simultaneous founding of ONI and the Naval War College in the 1880s, the necessarily close links between intelligence and educational institutions. (The possible implications of those links for academic integrity were never questioned in the discreet 1920s.) ONI plans entailed spying on the scientific establishments of other powers and the recruitment of academics. The director of naval intelligence, Rear Admiral A. P. Niblack, wrote in a secret report circulated to a restricted audience in 1920: "The State Department is organizing a foreign-intelligence section, and it is proposed later to ask Congress for authority to send out military attachés to certain embassies and legations. The recent war taught the necessity of organizing science in this country, and the National Research Council, under the National Academy of Sciences, is now seeking to organize research in all domains of science."[10]

Niblack displayed the customary American ambivalence concerning methods to be used in extracting secrets from rivals. On the one hand, he assured his security-cleared readers, in a passage which they surely disbelieved, that "the acquisition of information of [sic] any questionable method has been strictly frowned upon."[11] On the other hand, Admiral Niblack was haunted by the fear that the Navy might appear less well informed than the Army. He boasted that the "Navy has developed the art of communications to a degree the Army hardly realizes."[12] ONI

gleaned information in peacetime from naval attachés, tourists, businessmen, journalists, commercial travelers, and code breakers, but also, as
distinct from all these, "agents."[13]

Niblack stressed the importance of the naval attaché as a source of
information and claimed that the U.S. Navy had long been ahead of its
foreign rivals in utilizing this asset. Recently, additional attachés had
been sent abroad, notably to the Latin American cities of Montevideo,
Lima, and Quita.[14] There can be no doubt about Niblack's wisdom in
stressing the role of the attaché in intelligence work. The attaché was a
symptom of the official U.S. friendship being extended to Latin America
in the 1920s. But, more than this, he was the covert employer of military
spies and an intermediary in the deployment of ONI-recruited agents.

The naval attaché, like other attachés, was subordinate within an
embassy to officials of the State Department and subject to dismissal by
them. But ambassadors wanted to avoid direct involvement in spying
or undercover operations. Attachés therefore received their instructions
from ONI. Annually from 1919, ONI issued a document called "Duties
of Naval Attaché." In 1930, a revision by Captain A. W. Johnson, director
of naval intelligence, was approved by Secretary of the Navy Charles
Francis Adams. The document of 1930 showed an ambivalence toward
the use of spies which reflected awareness of the Senate's insistence that
agents beyond the power of congressional approval should not represent
the United States, and the further insistence of the State Department that
embassy civilian officials should not be embarrassed. The Navy Department did not in times of peace "countenance the frequently quoted assertion that a naval attaché is a spy under the protection of international
law. At the same time this should not be interpreted to mean that an
attaché must ignore the use of agents whose employment may be
rendered necessary in the investigation of any questions that bear upon
national defense or loyalty to his own country."[15] The 1930 intructions
warned that the State Department would disown any attaché who was
exposed in his use of dubious methods: "There have been several occasions when foreign attachés have been caught while indulging in
questionable activities that were intended to bring in particularly desirable information. In each case the reputation and career of the officer
concerned did not profit by their [sic] mistaken zeal."[16] The message was
clear: an attaché might employ spies so long as he was not caught.

Captain Johnson gave attachés explicit advice on how to procure information without detection. They were to ensure that all armaments
orders, however small, went through them. This would give them legitimate reasons for visiting munitions factories. They were to cultivate
foreign naval officers, but not headquarters staff or rival attachés, who
might prove too suspicious. In buying secret inventions, attachés were to
avoid correspondence which might betray their purpose and were to

leave the risk involved in delivering documents entirely to the inventors themselves. Again to guard against exposure, Johnson advised attachés never to demand or issue receipts when dealing with their own agents. Agents sponsored by or seconded from ONI (Johnson's report makes it clear that such agents were still operating in 1930) were to be financed from specially opened bank accounts. Local control of ONI agents fell upon the attachés, thus avoiding the risks involved in the 1919 system, whereby a single card index of spies was kept in the Navy Department in Washington.[17]

Although the very use of spies contravened publicly stated principles, their selection was supposed to be consistent with the moral precepts and social expectations of the 1920s. According to Johnson's report, spies might be of either sex, but they should be American, patriotic, and "of good social position."[18] They should be approached through front organizations but would be easy to recruit, since in each European capital "there can always be found a class of typical Americans" who would be "only too glad to offer their services."[19] The instructions of 1930 warned that American intelligence operatives should be on guard against strangers. The attaché should bear in mind that "the use of immoral women as agents is regarded as being very precarious. A woman that will sell herself is usually willing to sell her employer. In addition, women of this type exert a very demoralizing effect upon the men under whom they are placed."[20]

The observation that "if the wife is not contented the husband cannot do his best work" may well be considered in conjunction with these remarks about female prostitutes.[21] It appeared in the 1930 report as part of a very long quotation from a State Department circular of the same year to foreign service officials serving in Latin America. It was applicable to attachés as representatives of the State Department. Apart from their special ability to see through female rivals (though not, presumably, male prostitutes or bisexual operatives), the wives of attachés were expected to be literally their better halves in some cases. Attachés were intelligence, but not necessarily intelligent, officials. Niblack had noted in 1920 that naval attachés were not required to speak the language of the country they operated in.[22] The State Department circular, perhaps expecting, with some reason, that a diplomatic wife would be properly "finished" through mastery of a romance tongue at school, intimated that "she can be of very great assistance to him by learning the language of the country and seconding his efforts. . . ."[23]

The husband's efforts, according to the duties imposed by the State Department, were to be devoted to the cultivation of top people. This gave the wife yet another role, that of society hostess. If, however, she expected to entertain at her dinner table a glittering aristocracy of birth and cultural talent, she was doomed to disappointment. Top people were no longer the same as they used to be. The State Department warned, in the passage quoted for the benefit of naval attachés, that "in the modern democracy political power has passed largely out of the possession of the cultured classes."[24] Diplomatic envoys should remember that "the day of snobbery in diplomacy and of consular aloofness have [sic] passed."[25] Husband and wife should set aside prejudice and make a special effort to entertain both foreign and American businessmen just as if they were their equals. After all, "four billions of dollars of industrial development in Latin America, one and one half billion of loans and eight hundred and seventy odd millions of annual exports to those regions make a total which arrests attention. Antiquated or unsuitable methods must be ruthlessly discarded and right ones adopted."[26]

The profits to be made from the Third World help to explain the State Department's determination to cover up intelligence operations that might impair good relations. The circular of 1930 remarked of Latin Americans: "We want them to know the truth about the ideals we cherish, that as a nation we are not predatory; that the stories of our hunger for land are pure inventions." Having rejected the old imperialism (territorial) in favor of new (economic), the circular proclaimed: "The absence of reprehensible acts on our part is not sufficient to convince a world where traducing one's neighbor is often considered a legitimate maneuver in the competition for trade or political advantage."[27] Positive efforts were being made, such as dismantling the central State Department apparatus for espionage (a gesture directed at foreign nations generally, not just at their intelligence services). Naval attachés were expected to play their part by not being caught bribing foreign scientists and by behaving in a diplomatic manner towards overseas businessmen.

Although there was no shortage of applicants for naval attaché posts in the interwar years, there was no guarantee that those selected would be of outstanding quality. Niblack had complained in 1919 that it was difficult to find qualified men because the pay and allowance for an attaché were insufficient to meet expenses.[28] The position of naval attaché was therefore acquiring the reputation of being a sinecure, open only to those with an independent income. Niblack thought the situation was not likely to improve until directors of naval intelligence were chosen on merit (only about a third of them had had adequate prior experience).[29]

In view of the acknowledged importance of the attaché system in the 1920s and of the attaché's added responsibility of orchestrating spies after 1930, Niblack's observations on the recruitment of attachés have a bearing on any assessment of naval intelligence in the interwar period. First, it is clear that the qualities of the attaché were those of the gentleman amateur. This does not necessarily mean that attachés were exceptionally ill-qualified or stupid—there were other jobs in the diplomatic service that called for men with an independent income, and in any case many affluent people are bright. There is no reason why a man of means and genius should not have been attracted by the prestige of diplomatic service, and the wives of attachés may have been of above-average ability. It is, however, clear that attachés were not chosen for their outstanding qualifications, and it does seem probable that more lucrative jobs in the Navy would have absorbed the officials of higher caliber. Secondly, a man of independent income who was content to spend it rather than increase it had probably inherited his fortune. Naval attachés may therefore have been apt to look down on rising businessmen (accounting for the special State Department warning against snobbery in 1930) and disposed to put business interests at risk through doubtful enterprises. Finally, since salaries were less important to attachés than to poorer people, they survived as a thriving branch of American intelligence in spite of the budgetary restrictions that followed demobilization.

Whatever the limitations of naval attachés, their instructions of 1930 show that they were to be pitched headlong into the world of under-cover intrigue. They were expected to operate at a lower key in peace-time but were already being enjoined to look forward to the next war. When Captain Johnson in his report stipulated that the length to which an attaché could go in a neutral country "depends upon the attitude of the neutral country concerned," he perhaps had in mind the respective fortunes of Central Powers and Allied intelligence in the United States between 1914 and 1917.[30] His report listed ten "elementary principles" regarding wartime espionage work. The first principle was that "personnel for an intelligence system should be assigned before the outbreak of war, in order that selection would not have to be made in haste and without due regard to qualifications."[31] ONI was far from asleep in 1930.

The general qualification which must be made concerning demobilization after 1918 is that, even as it took place, plans were being prepared for rapid remobilization. Prior to 1947, it was one of the principles of American intelligence that, like the flowers in a desert, it would emerge when the rains came. Even in the climate of the 1930s, when a Senate committee headed by Gerald P. Nye blamed American entry into World War I on a conspiracy by "merchants of death"—U.S. arms manufacturers —and when Congress passed neutrality acts which were antimilitaristic and isolationist in character, Army officers did not lose faith in MID's capability for expansion. Successive appropriations acts up until 1937 had limited the number of military attachés to thirty-two. But a general staff officer remarked of MID: "This organization is such that the necessary expansion to meet war requirements can be made by the expansion of present operating sections in, or by the addition of new sections to, the existing branches."[32] The augmentation plans of 1937 provided for an increase in the number of G-2 officers from 20 to 159. Three years later, only 77 officers were planned; this reduction no doubt reflected the relatively small role envisaged for MID, in the context of a new war, in the field of counterespionage.[33] Yet, the general staff officer referred to above summed up the situation when he remarked that G-2 "has certain operating functions, which in time of war will make [it] the largest of the General Staff Divisions."[34] America's skeletal military intelligence service was thought capable of rapidly adding flesh to bone.

The discrediting of Army counterintelligence in the 1920s had not crippled MID's effectiveness. A cutback in personnel can very often lead to improved efficiency; in an intelligence service it means fewer people to share secrets, and fewer leaks. The asset of discretion would not have been wasted on Army intelligence in the 1920s, for it was forging ahead in several fields of technology. Cryptanalysis progressed in M.I.8 under H. O. Yardley, until his embittered resignation upon the withdrawal of State Department cooperation in 1929. Thereafter, the Signal Corps continued to harbor the resilient Friedman. The microdot technique (the photoreduction of secret information so that it can be disguised as a period or the dot on an "i") was known to the Army in the early 1920s. Aerial reconnaissance in World War I had produced a photographic collection which, by 1922, was one of the fastest expanding sections in American intelligence records. By 1928, the War Department was sending abroad assistant military attachés who were specialists in chemical warfare.[35]

Like ONI, MID denied having anything to do with spies. Delivering a lecture at the Army War College in October 1928, general staff officer Colonel Stanley S. Ford complained: "There are some writers who persist in the statement that the United States maintains spies in foreign countries to obtain military secrets. Of course there is no truth in this statement, and officers should deny it emphatically whenever occasion arises."[36]

In the late 1920s, the State Department would have insisted on such denials irrespective of the truth, but in the case of Army intelligence, diplomatic posture may have conformed to reality because of MID's lack of cash. Army intelligence dealt with its relative poverty, and to some degree made up for the absence of a spy network, by exchanging information with other departments and by maintaining an ever growing evaluation system. Colonel Ford remarked that the Departments of State, Commerce, Labor, and the Navy "maintain agents throughout the world, and have furnished to the MID much valuable information."[37] Colonel Ford's successor in 1940 added the Agriculture, Treasury, and Interior departments and the Civil Aeronautics Authority to the list.[38] In 1928, Ford refuted the theory that duplication of work might take place in a foreign capital which harbored agents from so many different departments. He suggested that when a Commerce agent came upon a military secret he should hand it over to the military attaché; the military attaché would let his colleagues know if he stumbled across the business plans of foreign firms, and so on.[39]

The initially confusing mass of military information that poured into the MID did not, according to the Army, suffer the indignity of never being looked at again. It was made accessible and comprehensible. G-2 was proud of the fact that it was the only division of the War Department general staff that was allowed to organize its own records. In the fiscal year 1935–1936, the record section of G-2 indexed over 33,000 papers. Information was fed into a country-by-country intelligence digest. There was a cross-reference framework known as the index guide.[40] All military attachés were "indoctrinated, as it were," in the intricacies of this system before being sent abroad.[41] Each piece of information was assessed for accuracy and interpreted before being classified. Some of the classifications used—"British empire" being allowed to cut across more natural geographic divisions, for example—reflected State Department preoccupations of World War I rather than an open mind about incoming information.[42] On the other hand, MID's observation that evaluation "is a *common sense matter in its essentials*" suggests that the Army's approach to intelligence was at least intended to be pragmatic.[43]

When in March 1922 the United States withdrew its military attachés from eight countries, it singled out for future neglect only Ecuador among Latin American countries. Although attachés were withdrawn from those centers of World War I intrigue, Sweden and Switzerland, they were with the one exception left to continue in Latin American countries, which were now to be the targets of extensive economic diplomacy.[44] However, the effectiveness of the military attaché in pursuit of this end was open to question for the reason that also affected the naval attaché— low pay. In spite of recent increases, the military attaché still required a supplementary private income as late as 1937. In the 1920s, the idea prevailed in the Army that attachés "spent their time drinking pink teas, or sparkling red wines." Colonel J. H. Reeves of the general staff claimed that he had once heard a secretary of war complain that military attachés "were really desired by the State Department as aides to the Ambassador or Minister just to swell the size of the Embassy or Legation Staff."[45]

If Reeves was unhappy about the quality and image of the attaché, he was quite certain about the nature of that officer's job and about the assistance he was likely to receive. According to Reeves, the military attaché would "find the bankers, business and professional men, especially the representatives of large American companies (such as the Standard Oil [Trust], Tobacco Trust, Powder Trust, not forgetting Singer Sewing Machines, and in some countries the missionaries), to be of immense assistance to him."[46] Like the naval attaché, the military attaché was expected to be business oriented.

There was no shortage of applicants for the post of military attaché in the 1920s and 1930s. As in the case of naval attachés, the difficulty was that men without private incomes were excluded. There was one type of post which, however, paid well. This was an attachment to an American military mission. In the 1930s, President Roosevelt strengthened and popularized the "good neighbor" policy toward Latin America. The policy was based on mutual trust, the autonomy of Latin American nations great and small, and a self-denying ordinance by the United States with regard to the "big stick," the use of force to bring Latin American countries to terms. As distrust of the United States faded, Latin American politicians realized that they could ask for American military assistance without loss of face. One device open to them was to pay for American military missions—whose personnel were, therefore, well rewarded. In 1937, there were two such missions, in Guatemala and Brazil. By 1940, there were missions in Argentina, Haiti, Colombia, and Nicaragua as well.[47] The day of the American "military adviser" had arrived.

There were several reasons why a good neighbor policy came to replace the Wilsonian interventions so obnoxious to Latin Americans. American resolve not to intervene in prickly Mexico was considerably stiffened by the realization in the 1920s that that nation's oil asset, whose threatened nationalization had caused dyspepsia in the Department of State, was much more limited in extent than had hitherto been supposed. Ironically, the policy of avowed open dealing with Latin American governments was encouraged by discoveries resulting from code breaking. Yardley's team had broken Latin American codes and revealed the extent to which the United States was distrusted by its hemispheric neighbors; appeals to frankness, including the symbolic abolition of the Black Chamber, were America's response aimed at reducing that distrust.[48] Finally, the Republicans, secure in the knowledge that no one could accuse them of being radicals, put business above politics and gradually allowed trade to develop, with a minimum of strings attached, with any country and any regime. This prepared the way for an improvement in Soviet–American relations in the 1930s and early 1940s, but was also an encouragement to the development of Latin American trust.

The deemphasis on ideology continued in the 1930s under the influence of that most pragmatic of Democratic leaders, President Franklin D. Roosevelt. FDR's recognition of the Soviet Union in 1933 was the natural sequel to Republican trading ventures during previous administrations. If the cold war had its roots in the 1920s, it suffered an important interruption in the 1930s. When Roosevelt called for the revitalization of intelligence, it was without dissimulation; he did so for rational reasons, not in response to a Red Scare. A German spy ring headed by one William Lonkowski had been discovered in New York in 1933. Beginning in 1938, there was an international rash of spy episodes. In Germany on August 4 of that year, the Reich military court sentenced to death Wilhelm Kaschel, a young man from Dresden accused of passing military secrets to an unnamed woman representing an unspecified foreign power. This was the nineteenth German death sentence for espionage since the start of the year. In Britain, the House of Lords was trying to tighten security by modifying the Official Secrets Act. In the United States, Major Joe N. Dalton of G-2 was given credit for breaking a German–Japanese espionage network, a feat that led to eighteen arrests and the biggest trial since World War I. The American public always responded warmly to counterespionage of this kind, and Roosevelt was in tune with public opinion in requesting more funds for Army and Navy intelligence.[49]

In escalating America's spying capabilities, the president faced comparatively few obstacles. He was not encumbered by an entrenched and static intelligence system in the late 1930s. The *Army and Navy Journal* reported that the Army wanted to leave counterintelligence to the FBI but that the Navy was already sending student officers to the FBI school for training. There were still some problems in ONI: its officers served on a rotating basis, so there was a lack of continuity. The creation of a special corps would, however, deprive the officers concerned of experience at sea and of promotion prospects.[50] The failure of counterintelligence to mushroom suddenly in 1938–1939 is an indication of the calm and moderate attitude which still prevailed toward intelligence matters. Necessary steps were, however, being taken. MID personnel and expenditure gradually increased after 1936.[51]

American intelligence, taken as a whole, was relatively limited by 1937 and, in spite of its built-in provision for expansion in periods of crisis, had not reached major proportions when Germany invaded Poland in 1939. Yet, the demobilization of American intelligence between 1918 and 1937 had not left the United States unguarded. American intelligence conveyed to Stalin an unheeded warning concerning Operation Barbarossa, Hitler's surprise attack of June 1941. Passed on through Secretary of State Cordell Hull after verification by J. Edgar Hoover and the FBI, the message had originated with Sam E. Woods, commercial attaché in Berlin between 1937 and 1941. This intelligence scoop appears to be accidental only if one disregards the evidence that ONI and MID had used all the attachés in a given city after 1918, not just their own; Woods was certainly intelligence oriented, for he went on to become an agent with the Office of Strategic Services (OSS) during America's involvement in World War II.[52]

Again, using Friedman's decoding machine, ONI delivered intelligence bearing on Japan's belligerent intentions on the day of the Pearl Harbor attack, December 7, 1941, though not of the precise Japanese plans. The drama of the Japanese raid, intensified by propaganda portraying America as the unsuspecting victim of a treacherous attack, has obscured the achievement summed up by historian David Kahn: "The American cryptanalytic organization swept through this miasma of apathy to reach a peak of alertness and accomplishment unmatched on that day of infamy by any other agency in the United States."[53] It is arguable that the United States failed to avert losses in Hawaii, not because of a failure of intelligence, but because the executive already had too many sources of information.

Demobilization of American intelligence did not mean immobilization. It is worth reiterating that reductions may have encouraged alertness, in that large numbers are so often inimical to security. Conversely, the extensive resources brought into play by the OSS in World War II did not ensure automatic advantages. In fact, they brought at least one disaster. In the early stages of the war the Army's Signal Security Agency had broken the code used by Japanese military attachés. Wireless messages in this code were regularly intercepted from Japanese diplomats in European capitals such as Berlin, Sofia, and Lisbon, and yielded valuable information about German resources and intentions. The Army's possession of the code was a closely guarded secret. In 1943 OSS agents, unaware that the Army already had the code, broke into the Japanese embassy in Portugal to obtain it. The Japanese found traces of the break-in, changed the code, and deprived the Army of its secret source of information. In Kahn's view, the incident "demonstrates the superiority of cryptanalysis over theft as a secret source of information."[54] Though American cryptanalysis owed much to British thefts of German code books in World War I, Kahn's principle rings true. But, at the same time, the Lisbon story suggests a further moral: that any great expansion in espionage unaccompanied by effective liaison constitutes a threat to security.

There was, of course, extensive demobilization of intelligence after World War I. However, the assertion that demobilization was excessive according to the standards or needs of the day is a myth, the invention of unemployed spies and cryptographers like Voska and Yardley and of the institutional propagandists of large-scale intelligence and of the CIA.[55]

11

Moscow Gold

The survival of American espionage after 1918 meant that the State Department continued to exert an unseen influence on events at home and abroad in peacetime. Several of its clandestine policies of the 1920s and 1930s had their origins in Wilsonian thought, and it is clear in retrospect that one of the most important survivals of President Wilson's outlook was his Russian policy. In the sixth of his Fourteen Points, Wilson had demanded that Russia be afforded the opportunity "for the independent determination of her own political development and national policy." He had gone on to assert that the "treatment accorded Russia by her sister nations in the months to come will be the acid test of their goodwill." He had hoped that, left to their own devices, the Russians could reject Bolshevism. Instead, they embraced dictatorship and developed into one of the intractable problems of U.S. foreign policy. Within eight months of his Fourteen Points address, in August 1918, President Wilson had authorized American intervention in Siberia, one of the several areas where Russians were engaged in a bitter civil war to determine their "own political development." On still another issue, Wilson had become vulnerable to the accusation that he lacked candor. In the opinion of Russia's acting commissioner of foreign affairs, George Chicherin, he had "faced the acid test and failed."[1]

The State Department's intelligence men, though relatively sane on the subject of the Red Scare at home, became more and more uneasy, like their president, about the international activities of Soviet-inspired

Communist parties. Their widely shared nervousness prompted policies which, for decades to come, encouraged distrust of America's professions of faith in self-determination. It was founded partly on the actuality of a Soviet drive for power and influence. At the same time, it stemmed from a subjective disbelief that anyone should prefer Soviet to American ways on the basis of visible evidence. The secrecy of Communist operations in revolution-prone countries (usually undemocratic and oppressive of overt reform movements) encouraged the belief that Russia used hidden, unfair methods to gain influence.

It was important for morale, if America were to use conspiratorial methods in defense of capitalism, that Russian tactics should be seen to be unfair. Repression within Russia lent itself to this vision. The Bolsheviks took over the undercover methods of the Tsars. Okhrama became Cheka, later the GYP and OGPU. The *Baltimore Sun* claimed in 1922 that Cheka had so far executed 1,766,118 people—an average of fifty an hour each hour since the revolution.[2] The difficulty was, from a propaganda point of view, that these secret police activities were internal. To justify America's undercover offensive, it was necessary to discover a type of unfair tactic resorted to *externally* by Russian Communists. It was to this problem that "Moscow gold" seemed to provide a solution.

In the 1920s, those who could not believe that Third World peoples liked Communist ideology turned to the theory that they liked Communist gold. The American people were ready for Moscow gold propaganda. Gold had become the inanimate scapegoat for social ills. In 1925, the Bank of England restored the gold standard, regarded by the debtor classes in many countries as a restrictive, deflationary influence. Gold had become unpopular in the United States in the 1890s, when Populist, debt-ridden farmers had demanded the monetization of silver, a measure that they believed would stimulate crop prices. The Populists had praised silver, which existed in abundance in America's Rocky Mountains, as a "gentile" metal: gold was the plaything, according to this particular strain of anti-Semitic thought, of the Jewish financiers of Wall Street and London. Twenty years later, consistency being the last requisite of an irrational creed, anti-Semites emphasized the dangers of the Communist Jewish conspiracy. With a relatively minor adjustment, anti-Semites were able to embrace the hypothesis that Moscow Jews were using their race's legendary monetary skill to insinuate their way into every corner of the world.

Against this background, the office of the counselor opened an anti-communist file entitled "Moscow Gold." The State Department responded to what it thought was an unfair communist challenge in three ways. First, it tried to stop the Soviets' export for propaganda purposes of gold inherited from tsarist Russia, on the ground that it would be subject to litigation in the United States.[3] Second, it resorted to undercover tactics against communists abroad. Third, it deployed the by now unrivaled financial resources of the United States, dispensing what may be aptly termed "Washington gold."

Personnel at the counselor's office were hostile to communism without being hysterical about it; although nervous about Moscow's intentions, they were predisposed to treat with the Bolsheviks in a pragmatic fashion. They had been receptive to the not primarily anticommunist intelligence of Maugham and were prepared to go further than the English spy in accommodating the Bolsheviks once they were in power. Two factors handicapped Polk and Auchincloss in their efforts to persuade their State Department colleagues to be open-minded. One was the outlook of Secretary of State Lansing. The secretary was a conservative, imbued with the values of the legal and financial professions of New York City. His education, if not his advancement, owed something to his patron, Elihu Root, and his father-in-law, John W. Foster, old-guard Republican secretaries of war and state, respectively.[4] Robert Lansing was determinedly antisocialist.

Lansing's intransigence limited his subordinates' room for maneuver. For example, he disapproved of and obstructed the proposal for an international socialist conference to be held in Stockholm in the spring of 1917—well before the Bolshevik triumph—fearing that it would be no more than a German instrument for undermining the pro-Allies Kerensky government in Russia. Accordingly, Polk was detailed to keep a close watch on Sweden.[5] In view of Lansing's weakening position vis-à-vis Wilson, his obstinacy might have been overcome within the State Department but for a second factor. This was the obstacle posed to the flexibility of the undercover men by the Treaty of Brest-Litovsk between Soviet Russia and Germany. It became apparent in February 1918 that no more help for the Allies could be expected from Russia. By making a separate peace with Germany, the Russian communists stimulated a prejudice against their system which lasted well beyond the armistice and affected even the most objective observers in the State Department. In the long term, the United States was constrained to withhold recognition from the Soviet Union until 1933.

In the short term, the counselor's staff became receptive to conservative intelligence. Before recruiting American help, the British intelligence coordinator Wiseman had acquired an unprogressive version of Eastern news through the Russian general staff, and by seeking information from the chief of secret police under the Provisional Government.[6] After Brest-Litovsk, Americans reverted to this same reactionary tradition. Polk gave a sympathetic hearing to bulletins on Russia supplied by Colville Barclay, chargé and counselor at the British embassy.[7] American officals stressed, with Secretary Balfour, those aspects of Maugham's plans that might coincidentally help to bring down the Soviet government.[8]

They cooperated with the anticommunist secret agent R. H. Bruce Lock-hart.[9] Credence was given to the disparagement, by prewar American socialists like W. E. Walling, of Bolshevism's appeal and success; George Creel's attempt to utilize radical socialists, like the Harvard-educated writer John Reed, as American agents in Russia was quickly abandoned. The State Department kept its own men in Petrograd, developed archaic expectations, and waited in vain for word that the time was ripe to move.[10] Lansing and the British right had won the day for hard-line anti-Bolshevism.

Because of Wilsonian propaganda in favor of self-determination and territorial integrity, American intervention in Russian affairs was shameful and concealed. Like their president, Polk and Auchincloss were particularly eager to preserve the appearance of friendship for the Russian people. In June 1918, Auchincloss not only drafted a letter to President Wilson from Lansing suggesting that Herbert Hoover be put in charge of a "Commission for the Relief of Russia" (a proposal adopted in 1921) but claimed that it was his idea.[11] Lloyd George and Winston Churchill were even moved to observe that American opposition to communism was halfhearted, an opinion based on the clandestine, because guilty, American response to Russian affairs.[12] The response is exemplified not only in Auchincloss's proposal to smuggle aid to the anti-German, anti-Bolshevik Cossacks through Rumania but also in the circuitous methods used to further Allied and White Russian causes in Siberia.

America's stated and, no doubt, genuine purpose in sending troops to Siberia was to keep the trans-Siberian and Chinese Eastern railways open and immune to the raids of Red and White forces fighting it out on the steppes. The Allies, and America as an associated power, needed the railroads in order to redeploy Czech forces along the Eastern front. There were, however, two unstated reasons why the United States allowed itself to be drawn in. First, American diplomats felt there was a need to restrict opportunities for Japanese imperialism. Were Japan alone allowed to police the Asian railroads these opportunities would naturally increase. American joint intervention was therefore desirable for this reason. Secondly, the Siberian intervention was a circuitous method of curbing Red power. By manipulating the funding of Japanese–American operations, Polk hoped to undermine Moscow's political and financial strength.

In August 1918, Polk received a complaint from military intelligence via one of his paymasters, Gerald Rathbone, that the White Russians were using American money for purposes other than paying for rails being delivered to them. Polk instructed Rathbone to tell military intelligence they "did not know what they were talking about." Polk then urged him to get supplies delivered anyway. He went on to raise the question of which currency should be given to the White Russians to enable them to pay Americans for supplies. The counselor ruled out the ruble. The

Treaty of Brest-Litovsk had provided for the payment to Germany of 300 million gold rubles as the price of peace; Polk explained that "if we used the ruble, it would raise the value of it and would be of great assistance to Germany."[13] It would have been of even greater assistance to the Bolsheviks, whom, by such unadmitted means, American intelligence men now actively opposed.

Lenin was aware of the clandestine forces ranged against him. Like the Americans, he exploited enemy espionage for propaganda purposes and perhaps exaggerated its dangers. He warned in the spring of 1919 that the

> Whiteguards' advance on Petrograd has made it perfectly clear that in the vicinity of the front line, in every large town, the Whites have a large organisation for espionage, subversion, the blowing-up of bridges, the engineering of revolts in the rear and the murder of Communists and prominent members of workers' organisations. . . . Railwaymen and political workers in all military units without exception must, in particular, redouble their precautions.[14]

White Russians obtained funds from several sources, including, to judge from the Polk–Rathbone correspondence, the American government. On June 13, William Hard of the politically independent periodical *The New Republic* called at the office of the under secretary (as the office of the counselor was called from March 1, 1919). Polk recorded that Hard was "suspicious as to where the money for Russian propaganda came from. Thought it came from advances from this government. Satisfied."[15] Hard was a harbinger of future skeptics who would be less easy to satisfy on the subject of Washington gold.

In March 1919, communists meeting in Moscow formed the Third International. Lenin, the architect of the Bolshevik revolution, declared: "Soon we shall see the victory of communism throughout the world; we shall see the foundation of the World Federative Republic of Soviets."[16] The State Department reacted to this ideological expansionism on a worldwide basis, yet in so doing collaborated with the domestically oriented Department of Justice. The partnership between the under secretary's office and the Bureau of Investigation reflected a fear that revolution would spread not only to undemocratic countries but to the United States. This fear explains some anomalous reactions, including that to Russian gold imports. In 1920, the United States decided not to accept Russian gold. Yet gold was in practice accepted in payment for food shipments during the Russian famine of 1920–1921 and allowed in via third countries for commercial transactions.[17] The real objection was to the importation of Moscow gold to pay for propaganda within the United States. When the Stockholm publisher Ake Bonnier imported $650,000 worth of gold by way of Sweden and the Irving National Bank of New York, W. L. Hurley of the State Department acticipated that the cash would be used "to place contracts for publishing Bolshevik literature in the United States."[18] J. Edgar Hoover coordinated a swoop to confiscate the relevant correspondence, and pressure was exerted on the already anxious bankers.

The Hoover–Hurley partnership facilitated the coordinated surveillance of internal radical groups and their correspondents abroad. The Bureau of Investigation watched ethnic and left-wing groups, Indians and the Sinn Fein, the unemployed and the Harvard Liberal Club. It regularly transmitted to the under secretary's office a "Weekly Bulletin of Radical Activities," whose main bias was domestic, and a foreign oriented "General Intelligence Bulletin." The bureau provided reports and translations of Russian immigrant meetings in the United States and attributed Negro riots and disturbances to socialists and back-to-Africa radicals. The bureau received reports from agents abroad as well as in the United States. These reports were not exclusively concerned with the communist problem. For example, a special dispatch from Berlin in 1921, under the heading "Germany Friendly to Japs Once More," indicated that "following extensive Japanese contributions to German child welfare organizations, Japanese medical students have received invitations to come to Germany for training. The German prejudice against the Japanese, since the war, is gradually lessening, the Japanese gifts having done much to create a friendly atmosphere."[19] The United States took the Japanese threat seriously, and it is significant that in the 1930s President Franklin D. Roosevelt was sufficiently well briefed from Berlin to be opposed to Hitler long before the majority of the Americans perceived the Nazi danger.[20]

The socialist challenge was, however, the main preoccupation of intelligence experts. The following synopsis, dated October 1920, was a typical entry in the general intelligence bulletin received by the under secretary's office: "*Portugal*—Recent reports indicate a plot for the seizure of strategic points—and the formation of a soviet system of government in that country similar to the one in Italy. A movement begun by monarchist sympathizers tends to create the belief that reactionaries were prepared to take advantage of any disturbances."[21] Clearly the State Department was alert to the forces that produced fascist dictators like António de Oliveira Salazar and Benito Mussolini in answer to communist agitation. There is no evidence that U.S. military attachés or other intelligence experts assisted right-wing officers in Portugal or other countries in the 1920s and 1930s—American military advisers were reserved for Latin America—but the State Department encouraged anticommunist forces in other ways. Mussolini, for example, enjoyed an adulatory U.S. ambassador in Richard W. Child, and fascist Italy benefited from Washington-encouraged American capital investment. Even in World War II, the State Department was reluctant to cooperate with clandestine antifascist groups in Italy if they were communist.[22]

Allegations of Soviet–Jewish conspiracy regularly turned up in State Department memoranda and were the more worrying in that they were not entirely fictional. In 1924, State received a report containing such allegations from a spy in eastern Galicia and, taking the matter seriously, passed the information on to J. Edgar Hoover for checking out. Galicia and its capital Lwow (Lemberg) had emotional significance for Poles and, it followed, for Polish-Americans. More than half the population were Poles, about a tenth Jews, and the rest Ruthenians. Lwow had been the scene of heavy fighting in 1914–1915 between the Austrians (the province of Galicia being an integral part of the Hapsburg empire ever since the first partition of Poland in 1772) and the Russians. Then, while the Polish General Pilsudski was away with most of the adult male population of Lwow fighting the Russians and asserting Poland's independence, the Ukrainians attacked the Galician capital. The defense of Lwow, by women and by "Eaglets" (*orlotka:* young boy scouts) small enough to be dwarfed by their rifles, secured the city until the return of Pilsudski's legions and the Ukrainians' retreat in 1920.[23] The defense of Lwow became legendary and Galicia a symbol of Polish nationalist aspirations, whether anti-Austrian, anti-Ukrainian, or anti-Russian in character.

The Galician spy's intelligence report of 1924 averred that the Polish section of the Comintern (as nationalistic in the 1920s as fifty years later) was being starved of funds. The dominant Russian communists were pouring tens of thousands of "gold rubles" instead into pro-Russian propaganda in Galicia. The region had been troubled just before World War I by anti-Semitic violence and murder, occasioned by resentment at the rural credit system allegedly run by Jewish money lenders. Russia saw an opportunity in the resultant sense of grievance on the part of Galician Jews, for, the report continued, "several Jewish organizations in America are interested in the severance of Galicia and White-Russia from Poland and their union with Soviet Russia as a consequence of the persecution of Jews in Poland. On this question negotiations are shortly to commence between American Jews and the Soviet representatives."[24] The Jews in America and Poland were far from any anticipation of that ironic development, Soviet anti-Semitism; to alarmists in the Republican administrations of the 1920s, the situation seemed all too clear.

The seriousness of American concern over the spread of Bolshevism after 1918, when the astringent views of Lansing finally prevailed in the State Department, is indicated by the close watch kept on World War ally Great Britain. Radicalism in the strategic Scottish shipbuilding industry, the "Red Clydeside," sent shivers up many a Wall Street spine. British radicals poked at the sensitive spots in Anglo–American accord. Wiseman noted with alarm the prophecy by pacifist-philosopher Bertrand Russell that the rejection of German peace overtures in March 1918 would result in anarchy and "that American troops will occupy England and intimidate strikers, an occupation (he observes) to which the American army is accustomed when at home."[25] Polk shrugged off any complacency he may have had about the immutability of British society. He resorted to both rising and risen talent in informing himself about British class conflict. In March 1918, he listened to Felix Frankfurter's views on the "labor situation" in England (the future Supreme Court Justice was at the time a Harvard Law School professor and assistant to the secretaries of war and labor); in December, Samuel Gompers, president of the American Federation of Labor, recounted "his experiences in England with the labor people."[26]

The British, on their side, worried over the impact in America of propaganda about the working classes and Americans being used as cannon fodder. Wiseman considered what might be done to counter stories that some 2,000 upper-class military men from Britain were spending the war safely in America, where they were fêted and dined, and about the cowardice of members of parliament when inspecting the front. One aide suggested that counterpropaganda should be disseminated to indoctrinate the Atlantic community against revolution. This would center on the war heroism of the British upper classes, including "a history of what has become of the famous Pole Players who won the National Cup in 1913" and an account of "what the members of the House of Lords have done, and the proportion of those members who served in the War."[27] The truth is that the British upper classes fell in disproportionately high numbers in World War I, but this by no means relieved Americans of anxiety about the threat posed by Irish revolutionary James Connolly and Scottish communist Willie Gallagher to the "England" led by Welsh premier David Lloyd George.[28] Polk therefore kept an eye on Britain, though he used methods which were discreet by comparison with the British operations in New York to which he was to object in 1920.

Some opponents of Bolshevism refused to accept any form of socialism, democratic or otherwise. Americans as well as British conservatives made attempts to tar social democracy in Britain with the brush of Bolshevism. The Labour party had been founded in 1900 with trade union backing. It gradually grew in electoral strength until in January 1924 the party formed a minority government. During this short and unadventurous period of its life, the Labour government tried to improve British relations with the Soviet Union. Its policies were soon put to the test in the general election of October 1924. Four days before polling day —much too late to allow an effective reply—the overwhelmingly Conservative press published a notorious forgery, the so-called Zinoviev letter. According to the letter, Gregori Zinoviev, who occupied a high position in the Third International, was encouraging the communists in the United Kingdom to foment revolution. By implication the Labour party, which had made overtures to the Soviet Union, wanted to make London a satellite of Moscow. Publication of the Zinoviev letter influenced the election, but, when it was discredited, the defenders of capitalism had to contend with a still more embittered working class.

That American intelligence suffered from the same blind spot as British reactionaries is suggested by its attitude toward the one newspaper that spoke on behalf of the Labour party. The labor movement had taken over the *Daily Herald* in 1922. Before that, from 1912 to 1922, its editor had been the social democrat George Lansbury. In 1920, Lansbury visited Soviet Russia and pioneered direct radio news reporting from that country. This was offensive to British Tories and Liberals and prompted an irrational response from Justice–State Department intelligence. An interdepartmental bulletin reported in September 1920: "Considerable interest centers around the investigation being made on the London *Daily Herald*, which is the paper published by George Lansbury for the British Labor Party, which it is admitted is subsidized by the Russian Bolshevik Government."[29]

It is not clear whether Hoover or Hurley believed that the Labour party itself was a beneficiary of Moscow gold. If they meant merely that Lansbury was a communist mercenary, they should have known better. The editor was well known for his liberal, social-democratic views—he was not temperamentally or ideologically attuned to a dictatorship of the proletariat. Lansbury was a rising Labour politician, becoming leader of the Opposition between 1931 and 1935; to regard him as a Bolshevik would have been a serious error in political intelligence. Since the degree to which intelligence reports are taken seriously is open to question, one should be careful about linking them to America's rapturous welcome for Lloyd George in the fall of 1923 and to the eagerness with which the antisocialist views of this played-out political genius were received in the United States. It is certain, nevertheless, that general intelligence bulletin No. 30–12 took the theory of Moscow gold too far in applying it to the Labour party and press in the United Kingdom.[30]

The international affairs section of the Bureau of Investigation's weekly bulletin was at times devoted entirely to Mexico.[31] America's southern neighbor similarly commanded much attention from the State Department's other intelligence resources. In 1921, this attention focused, as it had in the past, on labor troubles. In the wake of President Carranza's abortive attempt to flee Mexico in 1920, which had ended with a burst of machine gun fire in a mud hut, Alvaro Obregon had come to power. Obregon owed his position to an appreciable degree to the support of organized labor, a group whose power in national politics had been enhanced by the Constitution of 1917. The trouble of 1921 emanated from the fact that labor was divided. Obregon received his support from the conservative faction, which was indebted to the influence of the American Federation of Labor, in turn susceptible to the influence of the State Department. Opposed to this faction was a more radical syndicalist group, which advocated social revolution through the means of a general strike. Syndicalists and their sympathizers criticized Obregon for making concessions to U.S. oil companies. The president stood accused of violating that anti-Americanism which was one of the cardinal rules of Mexican politics.[32]

MID's negative branch reported to Hurley in April 1921 that Julia Carranza, the late president's daughter, was conspiring in the state of Coahuila with a group that had already broken out their Winchester rifles and were distributing revolutionary literature. The Julia Carranza group accused Obregon of having "sold out to the Americans."[33] They intended to prevent, in particular, American domination of the oil industry, and to this end were busy securing the support of the Mexican railroad workers, then on strike. The negative branch saw hope in the attitude of Federico Rendon, a leader of those skilled railroad workers who opposed the strike. His Union of Conductors, Engineers, Firemen and Brakemen was against the work stoppage, regarding it as instigated by "reactionaries" attempting to discredit Obregon (who in their view had not entirely capitulated to the demands of businessmen) and fearing the consequences of possible American intervention. In spite of Rendon's opposition to the strike, the negative branch warned against unfounded optimism; plans were already afoot for a general strike in support of the railroad workers.[34]

Twelve days later, the negative branch reported on the frustration of an attempt to introduce the Third International into Mexican politics. According to MID's agents, the "Reds," centered on Tampico, had determined on a general strike in support of an imprisoned revolutionary laborer. MID failed to distinguish between Mexican syndicalist "Reds" and Moscow-oriented communist "Reds," but the distinction was not necessary to the success of the tactics American intelligence decided on. MID supposed that the Reds were "interesting themselves in this movement in order to bring into their organization all the laborers in the oil fields and, thus, as they say, to bring about a separation of Mexican laborers from the so-called 'White Guard', which is made up of American workmen."[35] Reds, to raise consciousness in preparation for the general strike, were holding street meetings and distributing manifestos in Mexico City. It is not clear from the MID report whether its Mexican officers used Army agents or AFL agents, or simply benefited from the tactics of MID-inspired labor spokesmen, in checking the Reds' next move. At the Pachuca convention of the partido Laborista (established in 1919 on the model of the British Labour party) it was anticipated that an attempt would be made to align Mexican labor with the Third International. When the convention met, an American using the pseudonym "Seaman" spoke as an invited representative of his country's labor movement. He supported the Third International and attacked another American, referred to as "Gale," as an apocryphal representative of communism. Gale retaliated in kind, saying that Seaman was no communist. On this cleverly arranged cue, a Mexican rose to defend the Obregon government as the emancipator of the laboring classes. The partido Laborista withheld its support from the Third International.[36]

The surveillance of Mexico is an indication of the seriousness with which the State Department, now under Republican direction, regarded the problem of communism in the 1920s. There was deep concern over the possibility of Bolshevik advances against the various outposts of American capitalism in Latin America. Radicals like Martin Brewster, a member of the Latin American bureau of the Third International, were watched, for the United States could not afford to let Latin America slip away.[37] World War I had overstimulated the U.S. economy, and without the prospect of Latin American trade, the nation would have had to choose between overproduction and unemployment. Latin America drained away manufactured products and exported in return coffee, bananas, rubber, tin, oil, copper, nitrates, mahogany, and sugar. With gentle official encouragement, the antisocialist AFL helped the development of probusiness, job-conscious unionism in Latin American countries and opposed the emergence of class-conscious organizations. The system worked for a decade.[38] By the eve of the Great Crash and Depression of 1929, trade between Latin America and the United States had swollen to a value of $6 billion a year.[39]

To help maintain business stability in countries that traded with the United States, the State Department sought political intelligence from many quarters. In 1927, for example, an agent sent the following warning to the State Department from London: "Our friends tell me that they learned that about a fortnight ago Trades Unions adhering or friendly to the Red International in Latin America received instructions to participate in the Pan-American Federation of Labour with a view to organizing an energetic protest against the so-called imperialism of the United States in Nicaragua, Mexico and China, in opposition to the American Federation of Labour, who were denounced as 'agents of the said Imperialism'."[40] If diction and spelling are to be treated as a guide to nationality, the informant, signing himself "B.A.B.," was British. Ten years after the October Revolution, the State Department was as alert as ever to news from any source, including the "competition," about communist mercenary intensions. Two decades later, its attitude had frozen over to become part of the cold war dogma.

12

Roots of the
Centralization Debate

For any reader of spy fiction, it is axiomatic that the protagonists, invariably male, spend a good deal of time ogling their shapely typists, almost universally female. The typewriter itself has received little attention. The perfection of this machine, which brought stenographers flooding into city offices within a short time span, occurred in the United States in the 1890s. By World War I the departments of Justice and State, in common with other large organizations, were using carbon copies as well as ribbon typescripts. Already the mimeograph machine was in use. Sophisticated code making and code breaking machines printed out their results. Calculating devices were fast reducing their owners to innumeracy, and the age of the computer was no longer a pipe dream.

By making it possible to store and classify information centrally, the carbon copy, the photographic multiduplicator, and, later, the memory bank broke down old specializations. The typewriter of the 1890s and its successors encouraged the process of centralization in American society. And centralization, whether in the shape of a private monopoly like the "Tobacco Trust" or of a government-sponsored conglomerate like the Tennessee Valley Authority, provoked recurrent opposition. The opposition arose both from principle, as one would expect in a country devoted to pluralism and federalism, and from expediency, on behalf of the hosts of displaced experts and unemployed clerks whom centralization left in its wake.

Typewriters and computers were just part of the technology encour-

157

aging rationalization in twentieth-century organizations. Mechanization and automation were to have the same effect in armies as in factories: men were released from physical labor to take part in ever more complex administrative routines. In an age dedicated to efficiency, these routines were performed with economy but increased in number as people expected more and more from society in the way of material goods and social and national security. New bureaucratic procedures released new energies and created more jobs which not only facilitated but demanded central direction.

Technological and bureaucratic improvements were a boon to central intelligence but created a situation that provoked controversy in the 1920s. In that decade, the American public reacted against federal controls imposed in wartime. Machinery for the central direction of intelligence was dismantled both in the State Department and MID (ONI escaping relatively unscathed). After a dormant period, a renewed debate erupted between 1940 and 1942 over the form centralization should take, involving State, MID, ONI, FBI, OSS, and British intelligence. The debate again became acute in the period of the CIA's incubation in 1946–1947, flaring up once more in the 1960s and 1970s.

Why was the debate—apparently about the merely mechanistic issue of how best to organize an intelligence bureaucracy—invested with such bitterness? Its vigorous prosecution stemmed in part from a continuing Jeffersonian distrust of central government.[1] It was also the result of jealousy among various men each trying to preserve his own fiefdom in the intelligence world. This type of behavior is not limited to the U.S. intelligence community. Describing administrative organization in the modern state, the sociologist Max Weber remarked: "When those subject to bureaucratic control seek to escape the influence of the existing bureaucratic apparatus, this is normally possible only by creating an organization of their own which is equally subject to the process of bureaucratization."[2] The tendency toward bureaucratic proliferation and complexity has produced criticism from the watchdogs of public expenditure, and from politicians and journalists concerned about the opportunities for lèse-majesté presented to officials within an increasingly incomprehensible system. Finally, the espionage debate has focused on the crucial question of how best to obtain a clear intelligence picture.

The modern debate over centralization began in the 1920s, against the background of the moral dilemmas faced in World War I, the apparent advance of communism in Latin America and even at home, and confusion over what to do about it. To clarify, as he thought, his vision of world affairs, Secretary of State Frank B. Kellogg in 1927 abolished his department's pivotal intelligence liaison agency, U-1. Between 1919 and 1927, American intelligence had risen from many sources, as if by capillary action, to this one central pool. In their own organizations, MID and

ONI had reflected the regional subdivisions of the Department of State. The Department of State, for its part, made its functional subdivisions (under the supervision of the under secretary of state) conform to military enumeration. Thus U-3 corresponded to M.I.3, dealing, like the MID bureau, with counterespionage. Information from all intelligence services flowed into U-2, U-3, and so on (there were usually about six subdivisions; the numbers kept on changing, possibly for security reasons); these branches then conveyed it to U-1. This central intelligence agency evaluated and disseminated information and transmitted it to the secretary of state. Kellogg was unhappy with the result.

The theory behind the abolition of U-1 in 1927 may be summarized as follows. In the early years of the carbon or photocopy, there had been an enormous accretion in the amount of information made available from various intelligence sources. It became impossible to handle the data. The State Department therefore established a central evaluation system. However, the inflow of information did not abate as the years passed, while back files increased arithmetically in bulk and geometrically in inferred complexity. The tasks of selection and evaluation proved to be beyond the capability of any one team of bureaucrats. U-1 had become inferior, as a source of information, to MID or ONI taken individually, since each of these agencies profited from having less ground to cover. U-1 was an obstacle between the secretary of state and vital information.

The foregoing theory no doubt underestimates the capabilities of central bureaucracy, but it is important historically because it underlay Kellogg's reform of 1927. The secretary of state dramatically announced that "the office designated U-1 is hereby abolished. All correspondence hitherto sent to that office will now be routed to U [that is, the under secretary of state himself]."[3] He left the details of reorganization to the man he had just fired as the chief of U-1, Alexander C. Kirk. Kirk wrote virtually identical letters to Hoover of the FBI, A. J. Hepburn of ONI, and Stanley S. Ford of MID, explaining the new arrangements and the reasons for them. Branches of U with "special functions" would surrender them to geographic State Department divisions; high-priority MID reports hitherto routed via Kirk and U-1 would now go straight to Kellogg.[4]

Kellogg reformed intelligence in a way that ensured that anticommunist espionage would continue to receive special attention. A few days before the abolition of U-1, Kellogg made certain that U-3, the chief special agent's branch of the under secretary's intelligence organization, would continue as an independent operation. The countersubversion agency was in future to be known as the Bureau of the Chief Special Agent (CSA).[5] In practice, however, the function of the CSA was undermined. Kirk explained that "all matters relating to Communists or Communistic activities" would now be the special responsibility of Robert F. Kelley, chief of the Eastern European division of the State Department.

Kelley, who was directly responsible to Kellogg, would take over liaison with MID in anticommunist matters.[6] ONI, too, was expected to take special heed of communism, though there is little evidence that it ever did. A list of ONI personnel was circulated to the regional divisions of the Department of State so that liaison would be possible. All officers in charge of ONI sections were to correspond with their counterparts in State Department regional divisions except for Commander Paul H. Bastedo, responsible for the British empire (Bastedo was to become the U.S. naval attaché in London in 1943, after a period as President Roosevelt's naval aide), and Lieutenant Commander Grayson, in charge of "all matters pertaining to confidential investigation, communism, etc."[7] ONI liked to avoid subjects like communism, but the State Department singled out the problem from all others.

Kellogg's desire to obtain a clearer picture of communism was not the only reason for the reform of intelligence in 1927. The secretary wanted to ensure that his own house was in good democratic order. He was particularly sensitive to criticism about class discrimination. In this connection, Kirk hinted at the controversy centered on the personality of Under Secretary of State Joseph C. Grew.[8] As under secretary from 1924 to 1927, Grew had been responsible for coordinating intelligence work; Kirk, as assistant under secretary, was his aide and confidant. Grew, however, came under fire from the Senate Committee on Foreign Relations and the press for allowing foreign service appointments to be managed by a "Harvard clique." A feature writer for the National Editorial Association complained that Grew was a member of "the inner circle of social diplomats which has set the well-to-do diplomats over the hard-working consuls ... the teahounds of the service are getting all the breaks." Exposed to such criticism, Grew was too weak to withstand the enmity of Kellogg, who distrusted him. After accepting the Turkish ambassadorship, Grew wrote apologetically to Kirk, his now vulnerable protégé: "I received distinct impressions that the Administration wanted me to go...."[9] Grew had fallen prey to democratic feeling and jealousy over patronage.

Apart from considerations of class prejudice and antipathy to the Ivy League, there was a genuine feeling that U-1 was not an efficient mechanism. Kirk honestly reflected this feeling in his letters to intelligence chiefs. Explaining the reform of 1927, he wrote that "the reason for this change is a desire to render certain information received from without immediately accessible to the officers in the Department directly interested in the subject matter thereof and to enable those officers to supervise the distribution of material to Government agencies outside the Department who have expressed a desire to receive such information."[10]

Clearly some State Department personnel entertained strong reservations, from the beginning, about the wisdom of Kellogg's reorganization. Kirk wrote of the dissolution of U-1 in a tone that neatly differentiated between what he regarded as the pious wish of the Department of State and his own view: "It is hoped that no confusion will result from initiating the procedure outlined above. I shall be glad, however, to receive any suggestions which you may care to make...."[11] Kellogg had started what was to be a lasting controversy.

Debate over decentralization affected military intelligence as well as the State Department, but in different ways. Those concerned about military espionage wanted to protect democracy at home in the libertarian rather than the egalitarian sense. Being subordinate to the State Department, military intelligence felt the reforms of 1927 only at second hand. MID and ONI were not central to American intelligence as U-1 had been. Military intelligence officers continued to accept their peripheral, subservient position in the intelligence community until the 1940s, their humility reflecting a passionate civilian opposition to the idea of central military counterintelligence. On the other hand, military spymasters insisted on the principle that purely military espionage should be autonomous and internally centralized.

ONI, having powerful friends, being averse to counterintelligence, and enjoying a scandal-free reputation, survived the 1920s organizationally intact. Indeed, the reform of 1927 by implication endorsed the internal organization of naval intelligence in that Kellogg took the trouble to explain it to various divisions of his department.[12]

The Army did not enjoy a comparable immunity from criticism. Americans inherently distrusted land forces, fearing that a standing army, if improperly controlled, would have the power to defy civilian authority and to oppress or spy on free citizens. The approach of World War I deepened the foreboding. Furthermore, there had been a longstanding campaign within the Army itself against the general idea of unitary national authority. Although the leader of the campaign, Fred C. Ainsworth, had been dismissed as adjutant general in 1912 for insubordination, his supporters fought on within the Army bureaucracy. The National Defense Act of 1916 made provision for war by increasing the number of general staff officers, but stipulated that no more than half of them would be permitted to work in the Washington, D.C., area. This restricted the general staff officers at the War College division (which was then responsible for overseeing espionage) to nine.[13]

Opposition to a central system of military intelligence continued even after America entered the war. The secretary of war permitted liaison between his intelligence service and those of other departments only after stiff debate. Preparing for another battle over centralization in 1944, the historical branch of G-2 concluded that military intelligence was less coordinated in 1918 than it had been at the beginning of the war. The 1944 report noted regretfully that "the war ended in November 1918, just as an adequate organization [MID] was developed."[14] Reorganization of the Army in 1920 did promise permanence for MID, but the struggle was by no means over.

The postwar attack on military intelligence at first lacked direction. In March 1919, for example, the *Washington Herald* welcomed the retirement without pay of intelligence experts who had been given wartime commissions straight from civilian life. The paper argued that America had too many "spy hunters" and reported that counterintelligence experts were applying in droves for jobs at the State Department. With considerable satisfaction, the *Herald* reported that the "State Department has declined to be an asylum for the many lame ducks of the disintegrating Bureau of Military Intelligence."[15] After 1919, criticism of MID became more specific. Although it survived, defenders of central intelligence complained in the 1940s that, between 1919 and 1939, the functions of military intelligence were as a result of continuous disagreement altered "almost annually."[16]

Critics of MID wished to ensure that its ducks, lame or otherwise, did not roost in the State Department or come to exert an influence in civilian life. Because of their opposition, when U-1 disappeared in 1927, M.I.3 was in no position to set up a police state. Military intelligence was allowed to practice internal coordination and to liaise to a limited degree with other agencies, but MID was permitted no opportunity to become the central intelligence agency of the United States. By pouncing on domestic indiscretions of MID such as the Paxton Hibben affair (discussed in Chapter 9), the press saw to it in the 1920s that the military were browbeaten into subservience to the politicians.

Although in later years there was considerable Army resentment against proposals for civilian hegemony in intelligence matters, there is little evidence that senior Army officers intended to invade civil rights in the 1920s and 1930s. Warning against unauthorized investigations, the secretary of war noted in 1923 that "a secret military police operating in time of peace is most obnoxious to the American people."[17] That the highest officials continuously acted in the light of this principle is evident from the subsequent organization of MID. Colonel E. R. Warner McGabe, assistant chief of staff, G-2, described the functions of MID in 1940. He emphasized that the branches of MID were individually in close liaison with the Department of State, a condition of affairs that clearly gave civilians the initiative. The intelligence branch was divided into eight sections, one for aviation and the others geographic—British empire, Latin America, and so on. "The grouping," McGabe observed, "is based on a convenient and logical method. It closely follows the State Department set-up and covers the whole world."[18] MID had accepted decentralization and the overlordship of the Department of State, itself lacking a focal point for intelligence.

McGabe drew attention to MID's disavowal of certain functions which it had undertaken in World War I. These included espionage and counterespionage among the civilian population of the United States, the investigation of fraud and graft which impaired the war effort, and the protection of military–industrial plant against sabotage. "These functions," McGabe said, "pertain to civilian agencies of the government and were taken over by the War Department due to the inability of the civil authorities to meet the situation at that time."[19] In 1940, civilian suspects were simply turned over to the FBI. The Army employed no agents to counteract domestic subversion because such activity would subject the War Department "to a charge of militaristic propaganda which invariably causes unfavorable reaction."[20] McGabe's views were officially those of the Army, being used to "indoctrinate" future officers at the Army War College. It may therefore be argued that Army intelligence officers understood the relation of the military to democratic society. The evidence suggests that they accepted the subordinate role of the military more readily than civilians drafted into intelligence in World War I, or part-time reserve corps intelligence officers in the 1920s, or CIA civilians from the late 1940s.

Although it accepted the essentially nontotalitarian basis of American society in contradistinction to German or Russian society, the Army was not prepared to relinquish its right to centralized, offensive intelligence of the strictly military variety. McGabe noted in 1940 that the espionage section, one of five sections in the counterintelligence branch of MID, "prepares plans for use of agents in case of emergency."[21] Here, in embryo, was a scheme for central, offensive espionage in wartime, for the agents referred to were entirely distinct from the spies recruited in the course of normal peacetime duties by military attachés. Before America's entry into World War II, then, MID was claiming the right to define its own goals and to act independently. In the 1940s, it fought for independence against the OSS and CIA. This action by Army officers was attacked as an attempted incursion on civilian power. However, MID's fight for independence in the 1940s was based not on a desire to encroach on civilian power but on its traditional determination to guard purely military intelligence from tampering by poorly informed civilians.

Adolf A. Berle was theoretically at the nerve center of American intelligence between 1940 and 1944, having been made assistant secretary of state in 1938 on the personal initiative of President Roosevelt.[22] Berle had already enjoyed political preferment in Roosevelt's home state of New York and had been special counsel to the Reconstruction Finance Corporation. Like FDR, he had gone to Harvard and in other respects possessed a background similar to that of Frank Polk, who had orchestrated American intelligence in World War I. Unlike Polk, however, he had a clear and less than optimistic perception of paradox: "Navigating the rapids in the next few months," he noted in February 1942, "is going to be difficult, if not impossible, and it will require pretty careful steering to remain both honest and American, and at the same time see that all of the interests which have marched together are kept together, going in the same direction and for an ultimately victorious, and I hope somewhat idealistic, end."[23]

Even in the face of fascism, Berle was uncertain about the validity of America's mission and the legitimacy of "dirty" operations used in its pursuit. The assistant secretary's uncertainty weakened his resolve to keep the State Department ascendent in intelligence coordination. Like Kellogg before him, he lacked faith in the existing intelligence system but, unlike Kellogg, he paid the penalty for faithlessness, being forced to relinquish control of the high-command post of American wartime espionage. It should be stressed that it was self-doubt that cost Berle control; the State Department's retreat was no adverse reflection on his efficiency, to which Secretary Cordell Hull himself attested. Nor could the assistant secretary protest that he was not properly empowered. He was well connected and carried as much official authority as previous spymasters. He had responsibility for aviation and, for a while, shipping and radio— all related to intelligence operations. Briefly, like Polk before him, he was acting secretary of state. Hull entrusted Berle with the job of negotiating for air bases to protect the "American Empire" after World War II.[24] Yet, in spite of such advantages, Berle failed to gather into his capable hands alone the strings that might control American intelligence. His reticence was symptomatic of a spreading, though not yet prevalent, unease about America's role in world politics and about the purpose and nature of U.S. intelligence. That unease was at the root of the debate over central intelligence from 1946 to 1976. In Berle's case, hesitation was to have an influence on the course of World War II.

On May 31, 1940, Berle went through the elaborate procedure of gaining entry to the office of the security-conscious J. Edgar Hoover. The FBI chief's office had been chosen as the scene for a meeting of the Joint Committee on Intelligence Services, a group which included Berle's former commanding officer, General Ralph H. Van Deman. Van Deman was supposed to be retired but was known to be as interested in domestic surveillance as was Hoover himself. As the meeting progressed, Berle became disturbed at the attempt being made to integrate foreign and domestic spying in the United States. He later recorded that "we had a pleasant time, coordinating, though I don't see what the State Department has got to do with it. . . ."[25]

Berle decided that day that if the State Department were to become involved in intelligence coordination, it would have to assume a dominant position and restrain the excesses of men like Hoover. His first step to this end was to try to put offensive intelligence on a central footing under the direction of the State Department. In another meeting in Hoover's office on June 4, 1940, he converted the FBI and MID to a plan which, he privately hoped, would "transfer some of this paranoid work into positive and useful channels." The committee decided on this occasion that "a secret intelligence service" would have to be set up, which Berle supposed "every great foreign office in the world has, but we have never touched...." The assistant secretary attempted to coordinate activities, and the OSS appeared in 1942. By the time it had been organized, there was already a Joint Intelligence Board, formed at the instigation of the Army and Navy for cooperation with the Allies, and Berle was on that, too, "representing State." But his doubts about central intelligence and his role in it had returned. "Whether we can do anything," wrote the official spokesman for the State Department, "remains to be seen."[26]

Life magazine commissioned a photograph of Berle in 1942 which shows an alert and capable-looking man seeming slightly younger than his forty-seven years. He is, however, nervously fidgeting with what looks like a package of cigarettes. He is surrounded by the reassuring symbols of his profession and status—the wall map behind, the pile of official documents in front, the college ring on his wedding finger.[27] Such details may signify nothing (office portraits were common in the 1940s), but Berle's apparent need for reassurance may imply his own awareness that he had failed to impose his authority on American central intelligence.

Franklin D. Roosevelt was notorious for his skill in exploiting information, in some cases monopolizing the truth and keeping his subordinates in the dark. It must have been demoralizing for Berle to find that the president, having been his patron, established no exclusive line of communication with him concerning intelligence matters (as had existed in the Wilson–House–Polk–Auchincloss chain a quarter of a century earlier). OSS director William J. ("Wild Bill") Donovan later pointed out that Roosevelt had suffered through having had no intelligence coordinator prior to Donovan's appointment in July 1941. The chief executive received information from eight agencies, G-2, ONI, FBI, State, the Customs Service, the Secret Service, the Immigration Service, and the Federal Communications System, and was therefore forced to be his own intelligence officer.[28] It is not clear whether FDR's predicament in this respect was involuntary or otherwise, but the effect was the same as far as the assistant secretary of state was concerned: Berle never came in from the cold.

Personal ambition and institutional pride encouraged the fragmentation of intelligence in World War II. Berle noted that on a day in November 1940, "we started work on organizing the Intelligence Division for the Department. Intelligence is beginning to be interesting in the Department now, so everybody wants to be in on it. The surprising thing is that what they say rarely, if ever, reveals any great knowledge of what it is all about. . . ."[29] Field intelligence work produced some hard-nosed heroes, but it was the glamor of secrecy and surreptitious adventure and the satisfaction of serving one's country without risk that brought men flocking to the portals of America's intelligence agencies. Those who arrived first had often traveled light, unhampered by such intellectual baggage as technical knowledge or multilingualism. Second-rate people, once hired, defended their bureaucratic territory with the unequaled ferocity of the unsuccessful. Just as important in causing dissension was interagency animosity, occasioned by institutional pride and a jealous coveting of government appropriations. Agencies began to produce, instead of information which helped to protect the nation, propaganda known as "promotional intelligence," defined by Army officers as "intelligence that would serve the interests of the producer."[30]

Personal and institutional rivalries beset Berle on several fronts. In September 1940, just a few months after the assistant secretary's involvement in coordination, General Sherman Miles of MID complained to him that the FBI was failing in its job of counterespionage. According to Miles, J. Edgar Hoover had neglected propaganda and failed to effect the penetration of ethnic groups. MID was supposed to leave domestic intelligence to the FBI, but Berle agreed to use his influence to try to set up a new system for domestic surveillance. Miles remained unmollified, and at the end of October there was an open row on the intelligence committee between him and the men from ONI and the FBI, who refused to pass on information to MID which would have saved Miles's staff from duplicating work already done. The following year, MID and ONI made common cause against a new enemy. Roosevelt in July 1941 appointed Donovan to be coordinator of information, responsible for the collation and analysis of intelligence bearing on national security and for special operations. The War and Navy Departments objected because they feared that Donovan would present a military picture that might endanger their supplies of battleships, tanks, and airplanes. The COI, as he was called, reported directly to the president.[31]

Since Donovan had a wide brief and presidential backing, Berle was reduced to little more than an onlooker, keeping himself and the State Department informed. Donovan sometimes even took the diplomatic initiative—for example, sending a young OSS lieutenant, Turner Mc-Baine, to negotiate in Cairo with high-ranking British diplomats over political warfare in the Balkans.[32] This situation, and the feuding it gave rise to, reflected Donovan's personality as much as it did Berle's. Donovan, much decorated for martial bravery, had acquired the nickname "Wild Bill" while serving in General John J. Pershing's punitive expedition against Mexican insurgent "Pancho" Villa in 1916. (He seems to have been called after a contemporary baseball pitcher of erratic delivery.)[33] There was probably an element of irony in the prefix, because the grey-haired, fifty-eight-year-old Donovan who shot into prominence in the 1940s was known to be conservative: a Hoover Republican, a millionaire Wall Street lawyer, and an Irish Catholic. The World War II intelligence chief was, however, known equally for his strong views, decisiveness, and vigor. FDR had listened to him instead of to his defeatist ambassador to Great Britain, Joseph P. Kennedy, when Donovan predicted that Britain would hold out against the Luftwaffe. Britain's Spitfire fighter pilots proved Donovan right. It was for the quality of being frequently and positively right that Roosevelt trusted Donovan. The pragmatic president was able to tolerate his COI's anti-New Deal views whereas loyal supporters of new dealism, like Berle, found such views doubly irritating in the man who had superseded them.[34]

In January 1942, Berle complained directly to Roosevelt about the COI, plaintively saying, "It would be of help to us if we knew exactly what picture the President had of Bill's functions."[35] Berle had confidence in approaching FDR because Donovan had again run afoul of the seemingly inexhaustible jealousy of rival public figures. Hoover of the FBI was particularly incensed. In the first place, Donovan men had encroached on FBI territory, breaking into the Spanish embassy in Washington to photograph code books used by officials of the pro-Axis Franco dictatorship. (Hoover responded by setting off squad car sirens outside the embassy during a Donovan-inspired burglary; FDR was forced to hand over the job to the FBI.)[36]

Berle took up a second issue in contention. This arose out of meetings over which he himself had presided in June 1940, following revelations about the Nazis' clandestine political operations in Latin America. After conferring with Hoover of the FBI, Miles of MID, and Admiral Walter S. Anderson, director of naval intelligence, Berle had won approval from the State Department and the president for the proposal that the FBI should assume responsibility for intelligence and counterintelligence in the Western hemisphere. Hoover set up a Special Intelligence Service which operated between July 1, 1940, and March 31, 1947. His agents worked in Mexico, South America, Central America, and the Caribbean, effectively blocking such Nazi plots as the attempt to set up a puppet regime in Bolivia. So effective was the FBI on the home front that it eliminated enemy sabotage altogether, an achievement that surpassed that of the Bureau of Investigation in World War I. This performance, following on the heels of the successful crackdown on gangsterism in the 1920s and 1930s, meant that the unsavory incidents associated with Attorney General Daugherty were soon forgotten. Hoover's reputation was such that he could expect to receive support for his agents' work in Latin America. But the FBI's mandate in 1940 (issued, of course, prior to America's entry into World War II) had limited its espionage work to civilian matters. The distinction between military and nonmilitary spying became blurred and impossible to observe after Pearl Harbor. Hoover defended his domain with all the tenacity of the entrenched and successful bureaucrat. Referring to Hoover's fight to preserve the good neighbors as a fiefdom of the FBI, Berle noted provocatively that Donovan "wanted to get into South America and I understood that the President had vetoed that."[37]

Berle reminded Roosevelt of yet another sore point. Donovan had trespassed on FBI and State Department territory by investigating ethnic minorities in the United States with a view to recruiting secret agents for work overseas. Because of this initiative, "Bill had got crossways of the Attorney General and Secretary Hull."[38] The assistant secretary's complaint was partly based on principle—he did not want a central intelligence agency embracing both foreign espionage and domestic surveillance—but it also reflected pique; after all, Berle himself had at one time lent a sympathetic ear to MID stories about the FBI's shortcomings in relation to ethnic group penetration.

Roosevelt stood by Donovan, but by the summer of 1942, the COI himself realized that he had taken on, if not too much, too many people. Roosevelt agreed. On June 13, 1942, he issued the military order establishing the Office of Strategic Services. He ordered that the OSS should "perform the following missions: (a) Collect and analyze such strategic information as may be required by the United States Joint Chiefs of Staff; (b) Plan and operate such special services as may be directed by the United States Joint Chiefs of Staff."[39] Again Donovan was to be at the head (as director), and again the brief was broad, if more explicitly geared to foreign military intelligence. The difference was that, under the new scheme, Donovan was responsible, not to the president, but to the joint chiefs of staff.

Even this failed to appease some officers in ONI and MID, who continued to withhold cooperation from Donovan, and the FBI still asserted hegemony in Latin America, Latin Americans and the German Secret Service permitting. The State Department remained unhappy with the situation whereby an undercover agency operating under military aegis could trespass in politics and diplomacy, and later transferred its hostility to early plans for the CIA. Innovatory centralization, in short, failed to prevent discord.

The quarrels within the intelligence community were no mere teapot tempest. They played an appreciable role in World War II. Such is not the impression left by the boastful heroes of the conflict or their credulous biographers, who convey little sense of the seriousness of the rifts within U.S. intelligence, within United Kingdom intelligence, and between American and British intelligence. Anglo–American intelligence harmony in the 1940–1945 period is, perhaps, so often taken for granted because World ar II was in several ways misleadingly similar to World War I.[40] Roosevelt, like Wilson, was partial to the British cause but was more adventurous. He claimed to be risking impeachment by arranging intelligence cooperation with Churchill as early as 1939, when the English statesman was still first lord of the Admiralty and was himself exceeding his authority. Churchill routed his messages to FDR through the American embassy in London, which used a U.S. code, the "Grey code," for transmission. George VI is reputed to have supported secret Anglo-American liaison in defiance of the threat of Nazi retribution (Churchill: "If the Nazis set up a puppet government in Britain, I would be accused of disclosing confidential material..." King: "Then I lose my head at Traitors' Gate, too.")[41] But the real danger to the secret liaison was the possible reaction, given disclosure, on each side of the Atlantic. On the British side, the Foreign Office was uneasy about Churchill's initiative, and Prime Minister Neville Chamberlain may not have been fully briefed concerning it.[42]

In the United States, Roosevelt had good reason to be anxious. The secret correspondence was carried on under the nose of Ambassador Kennedy (who read most of it); the Grey code was suspected of having been sold to German intelligence as early as 1924 (as we saw in Chapter 10, Secretary of State Kellogg became suspicious in May, 1925); finally, the bulk of the correspondence was copied by Tyler G. Kent, an American code clerk in the London embassy who, convinced that Roosevelt was bent on war, was about to turn his copies over to the U.S. Senate and press when, just a week after Churchill became prime minister in 1940, Scotland Yard men arrested him.[43] From the outset, Anglo–American intelligence liaison was in greater danger of exposure and disaster in World War II than it ever was in World War I.

Roosevelt and Churchill appeared to continue to cooperate in intelligence matters after the United States entered the war. They communicated through two intermediaries. Donovan was one. The other was the World War I flying and reconnaissance ace, Canadian industrialist William Stephenson. These two performed the role of Wiseman in World War I. Transatlantic British intelligence, known as British Security Coordination (BSC), continued to operate in New York, from its old office on Wall Street (Passport Control). Stephenson eventually opened new offices at the Dorset Hotel, at Hampshire House—and at Rockefeller Center, where OSS also had its offices.[44] When the British captured one of the latest German "Enigma" code machines, Roosevelt supplied further evidence of his willingness to cooperate. He sent Friedman to help make Enigma work—but only in exchange for American access to the resultant German secret codes and broken messages, an access which Churchill had been most reluctant to grant.[45]

The time-honored cat-and-mouse game was again in progress, but this time it was reputed to have a particularly savage character. According to a story relayed to the Americans by Stephenson, British code breakers working in England in November 1940 intercepted and decoded a German message intimating that the city of Coventry was to be bombed as a lesson to British civilians. Churchill had to decide whether to evacuate the city, saving lives in the short run, or do nothing, in order to shield from Germany the knowledge that Britain had its codes and to save the lives of soldiers in future campaigns, when they would have the advantage of foreknowledge of enemy plans. According to the story relayed by Stephenson to Roosevelt, the prime minister backed his soldiers and sacrificed Coventry, which German bomber crews devastated on November 14. This story was supposed to have convinced Roosevelt of the ruthless fortitude of Britain's resistance to Hitler.[46] Recent research by the former British diplomat Sir David Hunt has revealed that, in fact, Churchill had only four hours' notice of the Coventry raid and took all the life-saving precautions practicable in such a short space of time.[47] The conclusion to be drawn from all this is that the secret Roosevelt–Churchill liaison was leak-prone, dangerous, ungenerous and (through no fault of their own) lacking in candor.

Anglo-American intelligence was rendered discordant by the quarrels originating in several sources. For example, J. Edgar Hoover obstructed British intelligence in America for fear that it might strengthen the OSS, with which it inevitably corresponded.[48] The rifts within and between U.S. and British intelligence are nowhere better illustrated than in the varying responses to the peace initiatives of Admiral Wilhelm Canaris.

Canaris was from 1935 to 1945 head of the *Abwehr,* the German military intelligence organization established in 1920 to continue the work of Colonel Walter Nicolai, the World War I spymaster. Canaris was no easy man to fathom. On the one hand, he was upper middle class, urbanely cosmopolitan rather than obsessively Aryan (he was a lover of Spain and, according to a World War I rumor, of the legendary spy Mata Hari when in Madrid); he was at the same time a contemptuous foe of Hitler's lower-middle-class supporters, his imperialism, and his politically oriented Reich Security Office, which, under Heinrich Himmler, controlled the Gestapo. On the other hand, Canaris had more than a touch of ruthlessness. He was said to have arranged the brutal murder of the revolutionary Rosa Luxemburg in 1919, he supported Hitler as a proponent of law and order, a portrait of his friend Franco hung in his office, and he was said to have persuaded Hitler to help the fascists in the Spanish civil war.[49]

Disputes arose over Canaris because, before and during World War II, he kept offering to cooperate with British and, later, American intelligence to bring about the downfall of Hitler. In 1943, he seemed to be making a strong effort to discredit the Führer by inducing Italy to make a separate peace. Was he serious, or was he trying to penetrate and mislead his intelligence enemies? Opinion on this crucial question split both

British and American intelligence.[50] Ultimately the Americans, who, after all, had made the important peace initiatives in World War I, took Canaris more seriously than the British. In the process, America offended Britain and began to feel her capability as the senior intelligence partner she was to become in postwar years.

Clearly, bureaucratic feuding continued on many fronts after the formation of OSS in 1942. But it is equally clear that the roots of the modern debate about the centralization of U.S. espionage are to be found in the period 1927–1942. The dissolution of U-1 had far-reaching effects on the intelligence community. It untied the knot that had not only bonded various intelligence agencies to State but provided the internal cohesion of the intelligence agencies themselves. The weakening of civilian control over espionage created a power vacuum, doubts arose about the roles of individual agencies like the FBI, about civilian–military relations and about leadership. The dissolution of U-1 may indeed have eased Secretary of State Kellogg's intelligence dissemination problem (centralization has not always resulted in a better espionage flow), but it did create the situation that led to the rise of powerful agencies combining several and sometimes surprising intelligence functions: the OSS, CIA, and Defense Intelligence Authority. This, in turn, raised the question of how to preserve civilian, democratic control over such agencies.

13

The OSS and K Project

The Office of Strategic Services operated for a relatively short period, from June 13, 1942, to October 1, 1945. From its inception, the agency provoked controversy, and there has been continuing disagreement among intelligence veterans and historians about the achievements of OSS. Yet a composite image of the organization has settled in the public mind. It is usually held that in World War II the United States had a mere fledgling intelligence organization to begin with; the OSS was staffed by young men who had to be tutored by the British, a task undertaken with varying degrees of patience. Gradually, however, the OSS came into its own and even began to supplant British intelligence. At the same time, the unenterprising, stuffed-shirt career diplomats of the State Department were shouldered aside. In three years, American espionage came of age, and, so the story goes, the CIA was subsequently made possible as a result of this brief experience.[1]

The OSS image undoubtedly has a factual basis. To begin with, OSS operated on an unprecedented scale. For example, its budget estimate for 1945 was $57 million.[2] This sum excludes money spent on their own improved intelligence services by the FBI, the Army, and the Navy. Whatever allowance one may care to make for the decreased purchasing power of the dollar, the generally larger defense budget, an increase in taxable population, revised attitudes toward deficit spending, the wider scope of World War II operations, and the much larger subsequent budget of the CIA, $57 million is a significant advance on, say, the $2.5

million spent by MID in the last year of World War I. Second, it is true
that the OSS differed from its immediate predecessors (though not the
Secret Service of 1898) in having so little time for protocol. Its officials
often took the initiative in cases where State Department diplomats delayed on account of principles more suited to peace than to war. In this
respect, the OSS was a typical New Deal agency; President Roosevelt,
an unorthodox pragmatist himself, allowed Donovan to operate informally, just as he had permitted General Hugh Johnson to bulldoze
business and labor into a new pattern of industrial relations in the 1930s.
Finally, the OSS exploited its wide-ranging charter by organizing
paramilitary operations and guerrilla aid schemes. There were very few
precedents for these activities.

   The OSS was by no means devoid of novelty. Yet the agency's break
with tradition has been exaggerated. Donovan promised Roosevelt a
secret service staffed by young men and duly produced one. Many of
these young men were intellectuals with no previous experience of
espionage; with the natural pride of the young, they inflated their own
importance in World War II and left unchallenged the view that the OSS
was a giant step forward.[3] Several promising young recruits were sent for
training to London, where they found themselves considered very green.
Literary veterans of British intelligence like Malcolm Muggeridge and
Ian Fleming have perpetuated this impression, together with the idea
that the U.S. recruits became overnight "indistinguishable from seasoned
pros who had been in the game for a quarter of a century or more."[4] Such
observers failed to compare like with like; America, too, had her
"seasoned pros," but they had not been sent to London to learn the
intelligence game.

   America's older generation of World War II leaders, such as Dulles,
Marshall, and Eisenhower, did their best after 1945 to strengthen the
illusion that American espionage had been wholly inadequate in the interwar years. General Eisenhower declared that "the American public has
always viewed with repugnance everything that smacks of the spy:
during the years between the two World Wars no funds were provided
with which to establish the basic requirement of an intelligence system—
a far-flung organization of fact-finders." He poured scorn on the attachés
as "estimable, socially acceptable gentlemen" ignorant of the principles
of spying.[5] Unlike many of the greenhorns taken on by OSS, Eisenhower
was old enough to know better. But it should be noted that, like others
writing in a similar vein, he was enamored of his own part in World War
II victories and regarded the institutions of that period in a warm glow.
Furthermore, World War II veterans often belittled prewar intelligence
because they were professionally disposed toward and interested in securing a higher state of a military preparedness in peacetime.

   For better or worse, OSS represented a continuation of tradition, albeit one that sometimes flowed cyclically rather than evenly. For example, the militarization of intelligence in World War II was a retrogressive step. It was a revival of the system of espionage formulated in the 1880s and reversed in 1898 through the Secret Service–State Department partnership. The World War II reaction against the diplomatic stuffed shirt had its origins in antipathy to the "Harvard clique" that had managed espionage when Joseph Grew was under secretary of state (1924–1927); this antipathy, in turn, was part of a general rejection in the 1920s of the privileged, intellectual tone of the Wilson administrations. But the World War II reaction was not to endure; after 1947, the State Department once again had control over espionage. The revival of State's power within the intelligence community was discreet and inconspicuous, thus failing to undermine the prevailing impression that civilian control had been overturned in 1942 and 1947, but it was real nevertheless and marked a return to the pattern of World War I and the 1920s.

The various divisions and bureaus of OSS followed earlier models. The division of secret intelligence was responsible for overseas espionage and was subdivided on regional lines, following the State Department's organizational principle. One of the division's important bureaus was functional rather than geographic. This special bureau, the labor desk, was clearly a descendant of Wilsonian intervention in Mexican politics, U-3, and the bureau of the chief special agent of the 1920s and 1930s. Another important OSS division was X-2, or counterintelligence, which had its antecedents in the Secret Service, MID's negative intelligence, and the FBI.[6]

The research and analysis division was descended from the office of the counselor and U-1; the foreign nationalities division performed the same sort of work as Auchincloss, Charles and Richard Crane, and Voska in World War I; the censorship and documents division continued the work of World War I's M.I. 10 and its successors; and the morale division combined the functions of MID's military morale branch and George Creel's Committee on Public Information in World War I. The excellent map division continued the fine achievements of MID in the 1920s. The special projects and field experimental units of OSS, dealing with secret weaponry and warfare, were developed on an unprecedented scale in World War II, though it had been recognized in the 1920s that the intelligence community should concern itself to a greater degree with science. The novel maritime division supplied small boats and backed up the major innovations of World War II "intelligence," the special operations division and operational groups organization, supplying small-scale and medium-scale paramilitary units, respectively, to resistance fighters behind enemy lines. The MID had sent a few officers to aid the Cuban revolutionaries in 1898, and the State Department had supplied funds and weapons to its friends in European and Asian civil wars in 1917–1920, but the extensive assistance provided to guerrilla fighters was the one major intelligence innovation of World War II.[7]

When America entered World War II, British intelligence supplied her with a great amount of secret strategic information. This was helpful to the OSS and to the development of postwar American espionage. However, the nature of British–American relations in the intelligence field did not undergo a revolution in World War II. Then, as in World War I, the British intended the relationship to be neocolonial: British intelligence would produce the information, and the OSS and FBI would consume it and take action accordingly (for example, transmitting strategic information to the armed forces or arresting suspected fascist spies). But, as in World War I, the United States developed an independent capability which, as we saw in the previous chapter, led to friction. The friction was greater in World War II than in the previous global conflict partly because the diplomats were not in control on the American side, partly for reasons related to top-level discord (discussed in the previous chapter), and partly because the United States rapidly became the more powerful military partner, and the British did not like playing second fiddle.

British tutelage was a factor in both world wars because the United States entered them late and had to make up leeway in intelligence as in other military and political spheres. In World War II, the United States entered hostilities sooner and continued them longer. Furthermore, in 1941 America already had the embryo of a massive intelligence organization. For these reasons, American intelligence was probably more independent of its British counterpart by 1945 than it had been in 1918. Bill Donovan owed more to an American tradition of espionage than he ever admitted.

OSS leadership drew on the seasoned professionals of peacetime as well as World War I. Even some of the outcasts of American espionage played a role in the 1940s. Van Deman was duly consulted, and Yardley set up code-breaking units for America's intermittent ally, General Tai Li (the powerful Chinese intelligence chief), and for the Canadians, who eventually fired him because they found him "unmanageable."[8] At the top level, Donovan, a millionaire Wall Street lawyer, came from the same sort of background as the intelligence leaders of 1898 and 1915–1920 and had experience with espionage during the Wilson administration. His corresponding official at the FBI, J. Edgar Hoover, was also a veteran of the intelligence community.

American intelligence did not conjure its experts out of thin air in the 1940s. Experienced men filled vital posts and played key roles. The U.S. naval attaché in London, for example, was Paul H. Bastedo, the 1920s ONI official and former adviser to President Roosevelt. In Spain, a delicate area following the fascist victory in the civil war, the British had as ambassador Sir Samuel Hoare, who had been head of an intelligence mission in Moscow in World War I. But America, too, in May 1942 sent an experienced clandestine specialist as ambassador: Carlton Hayes, head of M.I.4 in 1918 and author of the successful plan to use The Inquiry for espionage purposes. Like several intelligence veterans of World War I, ranging from humorist James Thurber (a code clerk with House in Paris) to American historian E. Franklin Jameson (who assessed the Sisson papers), Hayes enjoyed a successful literary career in the 1930s, becoming a history professor at Columbia University. Drawing on his World War I experience and incidentally briefing himself for the next war, he became an authority on the history of nationalism in several countries, including Spain.

Hayes gave friendly support to the fascist regime in Spain. Eventually (in November 1943), he came to an agreement with the OSS whereby he would tolerate counterintelligence operations against German agents in Spanish territories on condition that these were conducted in a quiet professional manner and did not involve Spaniards or give rise to incidents which might impel the already pro-Nazi Franco government to side with Germany. Hayes's misgivings about the OSS reflected his inmate conservatism as much as any real lack of expertise in the men whom he distrusted.

Two experienced men were in charge of an American spy ring in North Africa. One was Robert Murphy, the State Department's representative in Algiers, who in 1941 established a network of "vice consuls" to spy in such cities as Tunis and Casablanca. Later in the same year, Colonel William Eddy of COI took up a post in Tangier, near Spanish Morocco. Eddy was a former MID man and military attaché. Murphy and Eddy believed in encouraging the French *Résistance* and General Charles de Gaulle rather than in appeasing the North African sympathizers of Vichy France. Leland Rounds, one of Murphy's spying vice consuls and, like Murphy and Eddy, an OSS recruit, wanted to encourage the Spanish resistance. Rounds had worked for MID counterintelligence in the 1930s against both Communists and Nazis and tried to launch an OSS expedition to Malaga, in southern Spain, to help the Republicans against Nazi agents and against Franco. He was supported in this and other anti-Franco schemes by Donald Downes, one of Donovan's officials, who had recruited potential secret agents among exiled civil war Republicans. Downes was an Exeter and Yale graduate who had worked for ONI in the Balkans and Middle East. In short, the OSS men whose schemes Carlton Hayes opposed were not ignorant hotheads—they simply disagreed with the ambassador (and with Washington) over politics and strategy. They, as much as Hayes, represented a tradition.[9]

OSS sources of recruitment in World War II reflected strengths which had been exploited to advantage in the Wilson administrations. In his book *The Intelligence Establishment* (1970), Professor Ransom argues that the "melodramatic publicity" lavished on OSS paramilitary operations has diverted attention from the more valuable work performed by intellectuals in World War II.[10] The "100 professors" group was recruited as soon as the OSS became operational and included brilliant young men like historian Arthur M. Schlesinger, Jr., who was soon to win a Pulitzer Prize, and other academics with a bright future.[11] Ransom points out that the entry of academics into intelligence was a natural sequel to their use in helping to formulate the New Deal policies of the 1930s.[12] In fact, President Wilson had already used university professors on a wide scale, both in the research division of the U.S. Commission on Industrial Relations (the federal investigation of 1912–1915 that produced a blueprint for an American welfare state) and in The Inquiry.

The other notable source for new intelligence recruits (as opposed to the "old hands" such as Donovan, Dulles, Friedman, and others already discussed) was the American immigrant population. Bernard Yarrow, for example, recruited into OSS in 1942 and sent to London to liaise with the governments-in-exile of Czechoslovakia, Poland, and Yugoslavia, was a Russian emigré. OSS resistance operations in Greece were managed from Cairo by the head of a leading Greek-American fraternal operation, George Vournas. Yugoslav-Americans similarly worked for OSS; one of these was the left-wing writer Louis Adamic, who worked with the Cairo station; another was John Blatnick, who for eight months fought with General Tito's partisans behind enemy lines.[13] None of these agents acquired the significance of Voska in World War I, but their operations were more extensive than those arranged by Robert Lansing's officials and were based on the same principle.

OSS was innovatory in only a few respects, and these were marginally connected with intelligence proper. It may be argued, of course, that it operated in World War II and that all the good ideas had been thought of in World War I. Yet, in areas where innovation was needed, none materialized. China was one such area, Japan another. Since the United States had both Chinese-American and Japanese-American populations, there might conceivably have been scope for anti-Japanese espionage both on the Asian mainland and in Japan itself. But the OSS had extremely limited success in recruiting agents for such work among its own population.[14] Reasons are not difficult to suggest. Racial prejudice on both sides, U.S. Oriental exclusion policies in the late nineteenth century, hostility to Indian revolutionaries in World War I and, above all, the internment of the essentially loyal Japanese-American population of California in February 1942 all played their part.[15] These factors were beyond the control of the OSS, but the organization invented no way around them and was no match for British intelligence in the Far East.

The success of American undercover operations in World War II should not be underestimated. Even in Asia, the picture was by no means one of unrelieved failure: OSS special operations officers gave successful assistance to the Kachin natives in Burma in their fight against the conquerors from Japan. In Europe, there were brilliant individual successes, of which the most celebrated is that of Allen Dulles. Donovan had at first put Dulles in charge of the New York offices of COI and OSS. But, partly at Dulles' request and partly because Donovan thought the future CIA chief a poor administrator, the head of OSS New York was transferred to Berne. From his Swiss base, Dulles operated spy networks in France, Germany, Hungary, Yugoslavia, and Italy. His agents obtained political and strategic information from Germany, Dulles helped to arrange the surrender of German troops in Italy, and, as we shall see below, he laid some of the foundations of postwar American espionage.[16]

Yet it would be misleading to say that the Dulles mission was innovatory. Not only was he of State Department stock (as we saw in Chapter 2, his grandfather, Secretary of State J. W. Foster, had helped to initiate the attaché system), but he had enjoyed a diplomatic career himself. He had performed intelligence duties at Berne in World War I and continued them at the Paris Peace Conference in 1919. Dulles' later criticism of the inadequacy of espionage between the world wars stemmed partly from pique. In 1927, he had resigned from the State Department to join his brother's New York-based international law firm, Sullivan and Cromwell, because he was unhappy with the relatively small salary attached to what would have been his next posting, at the American embassy in China.[17] His attitude toward pre-World War II espionage was also influenced, of course, by his position as advocate and director of the CIA. Whatever Dulles might have thought, his spell in international business in the 1930s seems not to have dulled his capacity for espionage any more than it impoverished him. Dulles' expertise was invaluable to the OSS.

The story of the clandestine diplomatic operation "K Project" illustrates the OSS at work. The significance of the tale is not comparable to that of the Maugham mission to Russia in 1917, for the Eastern front had not collapsed, and the scale of American operations in World War II limited the relative impact of any one episode on overall strategy. But K Project's history does throw light on the State Department–OSS clash in a particular instance, on the continuing dilemma of Russo–American cooperation, and on the problem posed by an inclination on the part of some Balkan politicians to trust the United States rather than Britain. This last phenomenon, the affinity between Americans and the Balkan states, was problematic because it undermined an accord reached in June, 1942, between OSS and its British equivalent, the Special Operations Executive, whereby SOE would have predominance in India, West Africa, the Middle East, and the Balkans (OSS spheres of influence included North

Africa and partnership in Europe).[18] The K Project story shows how Anglo–American rivalry, Russo–American rivalry, and rivalries within the U.S. intelligence community—phenomena of the World War I and interwar periods—all came into play once again in the course of a World War II undercover operations.

K project, whose details remained classified information until 1975, took shape within the framework of the Western Allies' strategy for victory in 1943–1944. The Russians, who had borne the brunt of so much of the fighting against the Germans, secured an agreement from the Western Allies, at conferences in Moscow and Teheran in October and November 1943, that they would launch an attack through France, opening a second front. In order to soften the German resistance to the envisaged Allied landings in France, the Atlantic partners decided to try to demoralize and weaken their enemy in the Balkans. Donovan and the British were already engaged in psychological warfare through cooperation with Yugoslav and Greek guerrillas. K Project was aimed at Bulgaria.

Major Murray Gurfein, chief of the Psychological Warfare Division, OSS, was responsible for introducing "K" to the American intelligence community. (He later became known for two other acts in his colorful career. Early in 1943, when he was an assistant U.S. attorney in New York, he arranged a deal with the American Mafia whereby criminal syndicates in Sicily would prepare the way for an American invading force and cooperate with ONI, in exchange for the release on parole of gangster chieftain Charles "Lucky" Luciano, born Salvatore Luciana in Sicily, who was serving a 35-year sentence for forcing women into prostitution. A generation later, Gurfein, by then a federal circuit judge, refused to enjoin the *New York Times* from publishing the "Pentagon papers.")[19] Gurfein's introduction of "K" to OSS officials led to a significant attempt to undermine German influence in the Balkans.

All memoranda on the K Project carefully guarded the identity of "K" whose very existence remained generally unknown for thirty-three years. In 1976, the journalist William Stevenson published a book in which he remarked that "Admiral Canaris was known as K within the British Foreign Office."[20] He also observed that "by the time Canaris genuinely sought an escape hatch from a collapsing Nazi empire, his record in the British file marked 'K' made London feel an obligation to let him stew in his own juice."[21] Although such references as these suggest that "K" of the K Project was none other than Canaris, there is no confirmatory "K" file on Canaris either in the Public Record Office, London, or in the Foreign Office library in the same city.[22] The truth is that the Americans operated an agent of their own called "K," who had nothing to do with Canaris. It is possible that, by coincidence, British Security Coordination, operating from the same building in Rockefeller

Center as the OSS, may have dubbed Canaris "K" just at the moment when Americans decided to use the same letter to describe their own agent (Kafka's novels popularized the letter "K" and perhaps suggested it to more than one clandestine hierarchy), or there may have been some confusion.[23] Whatever the explanation, it is now evident that "K" of K Project was one Angel Kouyoumdjisky.[24]

Gurfein came across Kouyoumdjisky in 1942, when working at the OSS office in Rockefeller Center. Kouyoumdjisky, a leading Bulgarian businessman and a former banker, was well connected in Bulgaria, being a friend of King Boris III. He wished to press certain views on the American government and to this end visited OSS and State Department officials in Washington. A number of Washington officials, such as Cavendish W. Cannon, a third secretary at the American embassy in Sofia (and soon to become chief of the State Department's Division of Southern European Affairs), were prepared to vouch for his standing. Impressed by Kouyoumdjisky's knowledge of Balkan affairs, Gurfein introduced him to the head of the New York OSS office, Allen Dulles, and to Dulles' close associate Spencer Phenix.[25]

In spite of personal intervention by Donovan, who visited Sofia in 1940, Bulgaria had fallen into the Axis orbit when King Boris allowed Hitler's troops to cross his country to attack Allied forces in Greece and Yugoslavia.[26] Kouyoumdjisky urged American leaders to believe that this did not signify that the Bulgarian elite were pro-German. He maintained that the Axis alliance had come about because the United States and Britain had neglected Bulgaria when they should have been courting that country through personal representations and a generous economic policy. He had in mind a massive American investment program, such as that actually put into effect for the benefit of Western Europe in later years and known as the Marshall Plan. In his view, American intervention would woo the Bulgarians away from the Nazis and at the same time halt in its tracks the menace of domestic communism (strongly entrenched in Bulgarian Macedonia) and Russian imperialism (by the fall of 1943, Stalin was taking steps to ensure that Bulgaria would fall under his influence, not that of Tito of Yugoslavia, whom he already regarded as a defector from the Communist bloc).[27] According to Kouyoumdjisky, it was not too late for America to make amends for past neglect; significant sections of his country's power elite were prepared to lend an ear to advances from the U.S. government.[28]

At first, Kouyoumdjisky's plans moved slowly. The Americans had no particular economic or strategic interest in Bulgaria and needed time to assess Kouyoumdjisky's ideas and reliability. In June 1943, the OSS moved Gurfein to another assignment in London. For their part, the Bulgarians, subject as they were to German propaganda and to intimidation by fascist security forces, needed some convincing sign that the

Allies might win the war. Events in Italy in the summer and early fall of 1943 therefore had an important effect on Balkan calculations. In July, a consortium of fascists, officers, and monarchists, led by Marshal Pietro Badoglio, Italy's Army commander-in-chief during the conquest of Ethiopia in 1935, overthrew Mussolini and placed him under arrest. On becoming prime minister, Badoglio dissolved the fascist party, declared war on Germany, and surrendered the remnants of the Italian fleet and army to the Allies. These events encouraged Balkan countries to look to the West. The Hungarians approached the Allies in the summer of 1943, the Rumanians later in the same year.[29] Balkan approaches of this kind made an impression on Americans in view of the need for diversionary activity to safeguard the Normandy landings planned for May, 1944.[30] The Balkans now comprised a strategic area, and Kouyoumdjisky was soon to become "K", a significant secret agent for the Allies.

Gurfein was recalled from London in October 1943. He was to be sent on a mission to the Near East, where his job would be to authenticate Kouyoumdjisky's status as a "bona fide agent of the United States," and to provide any necessary liaison. First, however, the OSS had to persuade the State Department of the desirability of the plan. Gurfein recalls that there was high-level support for K Project and general enthusiasm for the idea that a democratic government might be installed in Bulgaria. The trouble was, in the view of State Department planners, that "the small chance of success" might be "outweighed by the negative reaction of Stalin if he found out about the project." The compromise eventually reached at Yalta, whereby the West and Russia agreed to mutually exclusive spheres of influence, was some distance away. Gurfein had no doubt that K Project "would have to be disavowed by the governments involved if friction with the Soviets resulted."[31]

In November 1943, Gurfein requested an interview with Berle. He was about to leave for Cairo, a city which housed not only flies, beggary, and cynicism, but an OSS planning station. Berle recorded that Gurfein "wanted to discuss the possibility of having 'K' emerge as the channel of communications between the United States and Bulgaria in the event of peace feelers."[32] The assistant secretary of state gave Gurfein to understand that he believed in the possibilities of the K Project.[33] However, this was an instance of noncommunication between the diplomatic and intelligence communities, for Berle wrote in a momorandum that he had "promptly endeavored to discourage" the use of "K" as an intermediary and insisted that K Project should be a pure intelligence mission.[34] Berle thus voiced the traditional legalistic objection to the concept of a "bona fide" secret agent with political functions, without exhibiting the flexibility of his predecessors or the candor of an entirely self-confident statesman.[35]

Donovan now discussed K Project with Secretary of State Hull. He obtained permission for Gurfein and Kouyoumdjisky to go to Cairo, but only after the Russians had been informed. Thereafter and, according to Berle, without consulting State, the Army took "K" and his escort to Istanbul via Aden.[36] "K" set up headquarters in Istanbul, where he knew several businessmen and bankers.

From the outset, it was clear that his work was personally and politically risky. Gurfein was unable to establish whether the Germans knew about K Project, but it was ominous that a Gestapo agent moved into the room next to "K's" headquarters at the Pera Palace Hotel. "K" and Gurfein were shadowed in the streets, yet this was so common an event in Istanbul that they could not decide on its significance. In spite of these dangers, if dangers they were, Kouyoumdjisky established contact with Sofia through couriers and through his friend Nicolas Balabanov, formerly the Bulgarian Minister to Vichy France, and now his country's ambassador in Turkey, who had an apartment in Istanbul.[37]

At this point, the British objected to K Project. Anglo-American intelligence had not been going along so smoothly as in World War I. According to Berle, the problem extended further than J. Edgar Hoover's troublemaking; he maintained that American officials had seen no reason for the "very considerable espionage" which the British conducted in the United States in 1942.[38] The officials' attitude had naturally displeased the British. Just after Christmas 1943, Phenix and Whitney Shepardson called on Berle to explain the latest outbreak of British irascibility. Shepardson had worked with House and Auchincloss at the Paris Peace Conference of 1919. He had been the first London chief of OSS and, having been attached for cover to the American embassy in that city, spoke with some knowledge of Foreign Office attitudes. The British, he told Berle, "wished us to have no contacts in the Balkans or Middle East."[39]

Shepardson was probably right in suspecting that the British resented U.S. influence in the Balkans. Anthony Eden, who lodged the objection to K Project in his capacity as foreign secretary, was suspected of British chauvinism. He was lukewarm not only about American approaches to Bulgarians but about Bulgarians as such. The Byzantine historian Sir Steven Runciman, British press attaché at the Sofia Legation in 1940–1941 and a professor at Istanbul in 1943, recalls that Eden was particularly hostile toward Bulgarian officials: one of them, the diplomat Ivan Stancioff, was given refuge by the British ambassador in Ankara, Sir Maurice Peterson, when the Communists took over in Bulgaria, but Eden ordered the expulsion of Stancioff from the embassy in spite of the fact that the exiled Bulgarian no longer represented a hostile power (Peterson ignored Eden's instructions and continued to protect Stancioff).[40] The British foreign secretary was clearly opposed by temperament to American–Bulgarian liaison.

Prime Minister Churchill was just as resentful of accretions in U.S. prestige at the expense of Britain, but was in principle sympathetic to any move that would curtail Russian power. He favored a Balkan strategy —indeed, was suspected of trying to spare the lives of British tommies on the beaches of Normandy by throwing G.I.s into the Eastern fray.[41] But Churchill was certainly not in a frame of mind that would permit him to overrule Eden or to liaise on this issue with Roosevelt behind the foreign secretary's back. Churchill correctly distinguished between Russian communism, on the one hand, and Macedonian or Bulgarian communism, on the other. According to Runciman, there were signs as early as 1941 that Churchill was committed to the support of left-wing Bulgarian guerrilla movements—and, although British soldiers sent to help Balkan resistance forces sometimes complained of lack of government support, it is clear that the prime minister continued to consider the Bulgarian left to be the fascists' most promising enemy. In any case, Churchill, though a keen supporter of monarchy at home, disliked Balkan monarchs and had no confidence in the ability of King Boris or his successor, the Regent Cyril, to carry through a volte-face. There is no reason why Eden's objection to K Project should have angered Churchill.[42]

British–American cooperation in the Black Sea and Eastern Mediterranean countries was as fragile in 1943–1944 as it was to be in the Suez crisis of 1956. The State Department was prepared to ignore what it regarded as silly Foreign Office objections to a sound American scheme and insinuated its own policies through the Straits of Bosphorus. K Project was allowed to continue.

"K's" activities inspired optimism in the Department of State. The Bulgarian capitalist arranged for representatives of Sofia to meet American emissaries in a secret location, and U.S. officials made the necessary arrangements.[43] By this time, Berle was an enthusiastic convert to K Project. He revealed his change of heart in a memorandum on the subject to Under Secretary of State Edward R. Stettinius, Jr. Berle began by asserting that the British-American promise to invade France, given to the Russians at Moscow and Teheran, had been made "on the assumption that, because of bombing and other factors, the German will and ability to resist would have vastly deteriorated by the first of April." Implying that the German fighting spirit had not in fact diminished, Berle expressed the fear that military operations across the English Channel "might be exceedingly hazardous." He concluded that an erosion of German morale by mid-February 1944 was an immediate priority. "The only practicable method of doing this," in the opinion of Berle and his intelligence colleagues, was "to induce surrender and changing of sides by Bulgaria and by Hungary."[44]

Berle evidently based his optimism on a Balkan domino theory. He hoped that, once Bulgaria had fallen into the Allied camp, Hungary, at least, would follow suit. On the basis of what Balabanov had told Kouyoumdjisky, the assistant secretary wrote: "The results of the so-called 'K' project indicate that there is a distinct desire on the part of Bulgaria to change sides." Berle also consulted Cavendish Cannon, who not only knew Turkey but had also accompanied the secretary of state to Moscow in 1943 and had experienced Russian toughness at first hand. Indeed, Berle noted that "the Soviet Government is intensely suspicious and tends to see intrigue in the Balkans as directed against her, even though there may not be the slightest foundation for such an idea." He therefore recommended that the Russians be kept informed of moves by the United States. These should be the establishment of official lines of communication with Bulgaria and Hungary at the "highest level neces-sary" and the preparation of a strike force under American command which would be able to secure the integrity of either or both countries were they to change sides.[45]

K Project failed in its immediate objective. In the first place, Gurfein suspected that Balabanov was, though sincere, oversanguine about the willingness of his colleagues to change sides. Though American officials made preparations for a secret meeting with their Bulgarian counter-parts, "K" was unable to persuade the Balkan politicians to turn up.[46] Their reluctance is understandable in light of the difficulties the Allies were then experiencing in fighting their way up through the Italian pen-insula. The initial landings in Sicily and the south of Italy (with some help from the Mafia) had augured well. But, in the fall and winter of 1943–1944, the Germans seemed to be winning the battle for Italy. In the face of what Eisenhower summed up as "the rivers, the mud, and the enemy," British and American forces made depressingly slow progress.[47] Sporadic local help was no substitute for what had originally been hoped for but never materialized—substantial political and military defections orchestrated by Badoglio. Only later did it become apparent that German resistance was desperate, a manifestation of the "conqueror complex" rather than of enduring military strength.[48] How was the Bulgarian elite to realize this, while still in the grip of Nazi propaganda? Much more obvious to Bulgarian leadership (itself several shades pinker since the death of King Boris in mysterious circumstances in 1943) was the dramatic success of the Red Army. In the first three months of 1943, the Russians attacked west of Kiev and forced the Germans to retreat past the old Polish frontier. It was impossible to ignore the fact that, in Churchill's words, "the whole southern front was aflame and the German line deeply penetrated at many points."[49] Bulgarians were more impressed by the advances of the remorseless divisions from the north than by the conjectural strength of an American striking force which had yet to pass the Straits of Bosphorous.[50] D-Day was more necessary to K Project than K Project to D-Day; the OSS initiative was premature and overshadowed by Moscow. Thus K Project was at the heart of the West's dilemma toward the end of World War II, indicating that one dictatorship had been defeated only at the cost of strengthening another.

K project may be assessed from several perspectives. To begin with, it revealed the rift between U.S. and British intelligence. For this, the British were partly responsible. In refusing to trust secret emissaries from the enemy, they showed themselves to be suffering from an acute attack of bulldog myopia.[51] On the other hand, their refusal to trust Canaris or Kouyoumdjisky may be defended. Just as K and Gurfein were arriving in Istanbul, Canaris was entering into a conspiracy with Franz von Papen, the World War I spy and former Reich chancellor who was now German ambassador to Turkey. According to one theory, von Papen was to be the channel for peace feelers. Hitler believed this theory and eventually had Canaris executed.[52] But Hitler and the Americans may well have been wrong and the British right with regard to the enigmatic admiral. According to *Abwehr* documents, Canaris and von Papen were fearful both of Russian expansion and, in the wake of Allied landings in North Africa, of anticipated Allied penetration through the Dardanelles. They laid plans to sabotage French, British, and American shipping should Turkey join the Allies or let Allied supplies through to the Black Sea and Russia.[53] The documents circulated in connection with this venture were probably genuine in intent rather than mere cover for peace feelers.

The British may have been right, too, if for the wrong reasons, in withholding support from the proposed American mission to liberate Bulgaria both from the Nazis and from the Red Army.[54] The Red Army entered Bulgaria in September 1944 as soon as the Bulgarians had decided to change sides. It is difficult to conceive of an American military intervention that would have forestalled the Soviet action, and later events in Hungary and Czechoslovakia were to show that the Russians were no respecters of mere political sovereignty. Better timing might have saved Bulgaria for the West; K Project took place too soon to take advantage of Allied victories; subsequent plans for military and economic help did not mature fast enough to benefit Bulgaria. Hypothetically, too, greater unity within and between American—British intelligence might have ensured greater success. Practically, however, plans to save Bulgaria from Communism were doomed, even if they were desirable. In assessing K Project, in any case, one should bear in mind the same qualification that is necessary in judging the strategy of "S," or Somerset Maugham, in 1917: its official objective was to embarrass the Germans, not the Russians. The exiled Kouyoumdjisky and Balabanov could console themselves in later years that in this respect, at least, their Balkan plan had worked.

Examined from another perspective, K Project illustrates how American intelligence had stolen the initiative by the end of World War II in at least one significant instance. Americans had shown themselves to be more open-minded than the British (who had developed their siege mentality after the traumatic evacuations from Dunkirk) and more receptive to German undercurrents. From his Berne office (whither he repaired as soon as he could get away from New York) Allen Dulles had made a point of cultivating the German "opposition," already dismissed by the British as unreliable. His patient approach was rewarded. In 1945, General Reinhard Gehlen, the German Eastern front intelligence expert, decided to surrender, not to the British, but to the Americans. Dulles quickly realized the importance to the looming cold war of Gehlen's microfilmed records of German military intelligence operations in Soviet Russia. The United States thus acquired the spymaster and his ready-made spy network for use against the Soviet Union.[55] Dulles' ready appreciation that not all Germans were enemies, so consistent with his opposition to the Voska war-guilt mission and to reparations in 1919, helped America gain an intelligence ascendance.

Power simply compounded the problems of American intelligence. Moral questions—about methods and about the collaboration with Soviet dictatorship—proliferated. They were not in themselves insoluble but, given the nature of democratic society, led to endless dispute and self-doubt. Debate over intelligence intensified and showed up in the power struggle over whether to centralize and, if so, what to put at the center. The need for some form of central intelligence was by and large accepted after World War II. However, there was no such thing as an acceptable blueprint. For the formal unification of collection, evaluation, and special operations under OSS had brought less harmony than the looser, informal World War I system, when the office of the counselor had confined itself, in the main, to the coordination of intelligence and the evaluation of results.

14

The Coming of the CIA

Undercover operations in World War II lacked cohesion because the State Department lost its grip on central intelligence. The divide-and-rule policy of President Roosevelt, the military and technical complexity of modern warfare, and the dazzling piecemeal initiatives of the OSS all contributed to the demoralization of State.

When peace came and with it a new and unproved president, the diplomats struck back. They favored a centralized, peacetime intelligence organization under the control of their own department. Postwar America was, however, distrustful of such a proposal. In the Senate, there were fears that the State Department was selling out to communism. Such fears led to the conviction that Roosevelt's tainted diplomats should never be given powers of central surveillance. In the armed forces, there was a general malaise growing out of the problems of demobilization, the creation of an independent air force, and the unification of strategy under a new Department of National Defense. America's various warriors were not in the mood to surrender intelligence powers to the State Department peacefully. For their part, the diplomats were worried about the effects of reconversion cutbacks on themselves and vitally aware of the powers information conferred in the modern world. They opposed the extension of military powers, which they had accepted in war, into peacetime. They wanted for themselves not just the control they had lost in 1942, but the central intelligence powers which had been created for the OSS.

Because of the strength aligned against them, State Department officials played a waiting game, knowing that they would eventually defeat military opponents who were vulnerable to new postings and legislative opponents susceptible to political reverses. The Army and Navy won the first round when the National Security Act of 1947 established an apparently decentralized CIA, independent of the Department of State but open to military influence, while confirming the eclipse of the FBI's network in Latin America. Gradually, however, the Army in particular came to regard the Act of 1947 as a Pyrrhic victory. Prior to its enactment, State Department lawyers had slightly modified its clauses in a way that seemed harmless at the time. The CIA thereby obtained wider powers than the Army realized in 1947. Furthermore, while State needed information, CIA agents, like their predecessors in American history, needed the department for cover. In the 1950s, the positions of leadership occupied by the Dulles brothers, Allen in the CIA and John Foster in State, confirmed the reciprocal relationship. The enraged Army woke too late to the fact that the State Department had won the day. At the same time, very few had yet been made aware of the CIA's potential for autonomy irrespective of the wishes of diplomats or anyone else.

General Donovan had presented FDR in November 1944 with a plan for centralized postwar intelligence. Donovan's proposed agency would have reported directly to the president, bypassing the joint chiefs of staff. It was to collect information by overt and covert methods, to determine its own objectives, to collate information, and to conduct subversive operations abroad. Donovan excluded responsibility for police work from his proposed brief, but he envisaged a powerful, centralized organization, autonomous from the State, Army, and Navy leaders.

From the beginning, there was some support for his point of view. Assistant Secretary of War for Air Robert Lovett found, at the end of an official investigation, that under the OSS intelligence collection had been good but evaluation and dissemination poor. Donovan's recommendations (leaked to the press by the jealous J. Edgar Hoover) seemed reasonable in this context. The arguments were good enough to convince Hanson W. Baldwin, a Pulitzer Prize-winning military correspondent on the staff of the *New York Times*. Baldwin, who had cooperated with Allen Dulles and others as a semiofficial intelligence expert, crusaded in 1946 on behalf of a central system.[1]

When President Harry Truman disbanded the OSS on September 20, 1945, he explained in a letter to Donovan that the State Department would be taking over the activities of the research and analysis branch and the presentation branch of the OSS. He implied that this was an interim measure, representing "the beginning of the development of a coordinated system of foreign intelligence within the present framework of the Government."[2] The secretary of state soon appointed Colonel Alfred McCormack as his special assistant for research and intelligence.

McCormack's Interim Research and Intelligence Service operated on a grander scale than U-1, its peacetime predecessor of the 1920s, having 900 employees on its payroll. On the other hand, it was modest in scope compared with the 13,000-strong OSS or the CIA of the 1970s, which called on the services of 16,500 people. McCormack's service advised the State Department on intelligence matters, formulated clandestine policy, and coordinated the work of other undercover agencies, to which many former OSS operatives had moved. It therefore met the requirement of the Army and Navy that they should be allowed to continue to collect their own information. The service was nevertheless independent of the Army and Navy in that it reported directly to the secretary of state, not to the joint chiefs of staff or to the president.[3]

President Truman abolished the OSS system of central intelligence because he abhorred anything that resembled the Nazi-style police state. The signing of the United Nations charter in San Francisco in 1945 and the fact that the U.N., unlike its predecessor the League of Nations, would include the United States seemed at the time to indicate that international espionage would become obsolete. One factor that helped to undermine this impression was the report, published in July 1946, of the Joint Committee on the Investigation of the Pearl Harbor Attack. The report indicated that the American intelligence system had provided various clues that would have made it possible to anticipate the time and place of the Japanese assault, but that these had not been properly interpreted or passed on to the right quarter. Although it may or may not be true that Kellogg's decentralization of intelligence produced this situation (and it is ironic that Grew, a victim of the 1927 reoranization, was ambassador to Japan in 1941 and predicted the Pearl Harbor attack), advocates of centralization took heart from the findings of the joint committee. Truman could not afford to ignore the findings, for Democrats had to defend themselves against the charge that Roosevelt knew in advance of the Japanese intention but had allowed the attack on Pearl Harbor to take place in order to rouse public opinion, get America into the war, and do for the economy what the New Deal had not accomplished. Democrats simply had to blame Pearl Harbor on an intelligence failure.

On March 5, 1946, Winston Churchill delivered his "Iron Curtain" speech in Fulton, Missouri. The advent of the cold war dispelled some of the illusions inspired by the creation of the U.N. and forced Truman to press for a revitalized peacetime intelligence agency. But the president had started, and continued to support, tendencies that could be used against him. His own anti-communist rhetoric created a climate of opinion quickly exploited by conservatives, who argued that the State Department and later (according to Senator Joseph R. McCarthy) the CIA itself were infested with Reds. Second, Truman's initial demobilization of central intelligence in 1945 stimulated departmental demands. The

Army joined the ever-outspoken Navy in denouncing tight centralization. The FBI, having lost its Latin American domain, joined the infighting.[4]

The attack by the FBI produced a backlash because journalists considered it to be propaganda aimed at making Hoover the director of a central intelligence system. Syndicated columnists Joseph and Stewart Alsop wrote in the *Washington Post*:

> This country would in fact have what only such nations as Germany, Spain and Russia have heretofore boasted, a secret service with the responsibility for both foreign espionage and internal security, and with the power of internal arrest.... It was for this precise reason that the forceful J. Edgar Hoover was excluded, in the original executive order prepared by the chiefs of the State and War and Navy Departments, from any participation in the central intelligence agency.[5]

However weak the competition, two further factors ensured that Truman would have to give ground temporarily in his plan to entrust intelligence to the Department of State. The first was the personality of McCormack. The intelligence chief's devotion to capitalism and efficiency might be deemed to have flowed naturally from his background as a New York corporation lawyer and as the reorganizer of MID in World War II. But McCormack suffered from a common military failing, tactlessness. His gift for giving offense left his organization helpless in the face of a second factor, the allegation that the Research and Intelligence Service shared the State Department's imputed disposition to be soft on Communism.[6]

The accusation came partly from disaffected State Department officials, but more importantly from Congress. In April 1946, *Times* correspondent Baldwin reported: "Motivated by Red-baiting charges, always good for some votes, that Communists had infiltrated the State Department, the House Appropriations Committee has rejected appropriations for the Department's intelligence unit."[7] McCormack resigned, and the functions of his service were dispersed within the State Department in a manner similar to the decentralization of 1927. In the meantime, by executive order on January 22, 1946, Truman had created a National Intelligence Authority, congenial to military men because of its inclusion of the secretaries of war and of the Navy. The attack from Congress, however, continued unabated into 1947.[8]

As in 1919, Congress had been released from its wartime loyalty and gave vent to pent-up frustration. Republican Styles Bridges, Chairman of the Senate Appropriations Committee, indirectly rebuked the Department of State for impeding the Canadian work of the FBI in 1946 and for failing to stop the spread of Communism into China in 1947. Bridges attacked the proposed National Security Act for its contemplated pooling of intelligence resources, even though the plan had by this time been diluted to the taste of the Army and Navy. The criticism by Bridges and others of his persuasion (notably Clarence Brown in the House) ultimately encouraged the CIA to seek respectability in its own, liberal version of anticommunism. At a later stage, to add further irony, liberal critics were to take a leaf out of Bridges' book and deplore the centralization of American intelligence and the autonomy and abuses to which it had led.[9]

Testifying before the Senate Armed Services Committee on April 1, 1947, Vice Admiral Forrest Sherman described with relish the day in November 1946 when he had called on Navy Secretary James V. Forrestal. Forrestal had summoned a couple of admirals, a general, and Assistant Secretary of War for Air Stuart Symington "to a meeting at his home at which it was agreed to draft a plan for unification acceptable to both the War and Navy Departments, and within the scope of the President's letter of 15 June, 1946."[10] Truman had very astutely decided to spike military jealousies and congressional criticism by permitting the Army and Navy to draft the proposals. In 1947, the bill which Admiral Sherman and General Lauris Norstad initially drew up came before congressional committees for consideration. Forrestal and Sherman defended it for the Navy, Secretary of War Patterson for the Army, and General Carl Spaatz for the Army Air Forces. The State Department merely sent an observer.[11] Critics of the national defense proposals therefore had to take on leaders of the armed forces, only recently sanctified by victory and immune to charges of treason.

Bridges and Brown tried their best. Bridges forced Admiral Sherman to say that "no representatives of the State Department had participated actively in the drafting of the legislation."[12] Four weeks later, in the House, Secretary of War Patterson said the proposals had been drafted "in close collaboration" with the State Department.[13] The legislation survived these contradictions in spite of a severe mauling by the Senate Armed Services Committee, the CIA coming through unscathed except for a slight reduction in the salary of the director.[14] The Army–Navy-sponsored National Security Act of 1947 satisfied the demands of its proposers, leaving intact the facilities for intelligence collection hitherto enjoyed by the Army and the Navy. The newly created CIA did not report to a military board (such as the joint chiefs of staff) but, on the other hand, was not formally subservient to the Department of State. It was responsible to a National Security Council, on which the military was represented, and through the council to the president.[15]

Military advocates of the National Security Act denied State Department influence on the legislation because they genuinely thought there had been none. They did not foresee that minor modifications of the legislation, which Admiral Sherman did not think worth disputing, would have far-reaching effects, including the revival of State Department in-

fluence in intelligence matters and the rise of the CIA as an elite institution. The Army and Navy submitted their consolidation proposal on
January 16, 1947. As the bill went through succeeding drafts, it fell
under the scrutiny of State Department officials and lawyers. The department opposed certain aspects of the draft bill. The first draft proposed a National Security Council composed of the secretaries of state,
national defense, the Army, the Navy, and the Air Force, and the chairman of the National Security Resources Board.[16] State Department officials objected to the fact that the secretary of state would be not only
outvoted five to one but dominated by military men on a body which,
in the words of Assistant Secretary Sprouille Braden, "could develop into
a branch foreign office."[17] The bill as enacted reduced the military vote,
the National Security Council being made up of the president, the
secretary of state, the secretary of defense, and other secretaries and
under secretaries only when appointed by the president and approved
by the Senate.[18]

The State Department lodged an objection to a further aspect of
the draft bill. It focused on the issue of autonomy versus centralization
in intelligence collection. The department's legal adviser, Charles Fahy
(who had been solicitor general of the United States, 1941–1945), remarked in response to the eighth draft of the consolidation bill: "It is
difficult to overemphasize the importance of leaving the great mass of
intelligence which flows into the State Department under the administrative control of the Department of State. It comes from the four corners of
the world through the Foreign Service."[19] In the light of this observation,
there would appear to be grounds for accepting the contention of observers of events in 1947 and later that the CIA formed an intelligence
monopoly at the expense of the State Department.[20] This point of view
overlooks the mutual dependence of state and the CIA in the 1950s. It
is, however, understandable, for the CIA revealed its power as soon as it
went about its business. In 1948, it set up its Office of Policy Coordination, whose nomenclature reflected the wording of the 1947 Act but
whose function was "dirty tricks" and political subversion overseas.[21] The
authority for the CIA's initiatives came from Truman and the National
Security Council, whose dilution the Army and Navy now bitterly re-
gretted. For the council could confer special powers on the CIA under
the provisions of two apparently innocuous clauses of the Act of 1947
listing the duties of the CIA: Sec. 102(d)4: "to perform for the benefit
of the existing intelligence agencies, such additional services of common
concern as the National Security Council determines can be more effi-
ciently accomplished centrally"; and Sec. 102(d)5: "to perform such
other functions and duties related to intelligence affecting the national
security as the National Security Council may from time to time direct."[22]

In later years, critics of the CIA suggested that the crucial subclauses did not reflect the legislative intent of Congress. After some senators had expressed reservations to this effect, Eisenhower established in 1956 a President's Board of Consultants on Foreign Intelligence Activities.[23] Ten more years were to elapse before it became fashionable to criticize the CIA, but journalist Hanson Baldwin was already prepared to announce that he had changed his mind about central intelligence. He claimed in testimony that, in closed congressional hearings in 1947, advocates of a "coordinating, correlating and evaluating agency," rather than a collection agency, had won the debate over peacetime intelligence.[24] Baldwin clearly envisaged and advocated an upgraded equivalent of the 1920s, evaluation-oriented intelligence system. He claimed that victory had been snatched from the jaws of the righteous by the inclusion of the offending subsections, which "made it possible for the CIA to acquire, through directives of the National Security Council, a complete monopoly and dictatorial control of all branches and functions of U.S. Intelligence, including collection and clandestine propaganda and political activity."[25] Twenty years later, the Commission on CIA Activities (the Rockefeller Commission) reported to President Ford on the same point: "It is clear from the legislative history that Congress expected the National Security Council to give the CIA responsibility and authority for overseas espionage."[26] Historical disagreements reflected the debate over centralization in 1947. The one point on which memoirs and reports agree is that the CIA rapidly acquired an intelligence monopoly at the expense of other agencies, as a result of Section 102 of the National Security Act.

Appearances notwithstanding, the CIA did not, in fact, win monopoly powers in 1947. However advanced its laboratories, it could not develop the entire apparatus of high-technology espionage on its own. Military involvement was unavoidable in developing U-2 reconnaissance planes and spy satellites, and military expertise was indispensable in deciphering complex information about Soviet missile dispositions and know-how. During the loyalty crisis of the late 1940s and early 1950s, both the CIA and the State Department became faction-ridden over the desirability of self-imposed purges in order to counter the charges of Senator McCarthy and others that Communists had infiltrated security-sensitive jobs. Although internal debate lessened the potency of the CIA to a degree, it is undoubtedly true that, by the 1950s, the State Department had permanently lost its monopoly over central intelligence. The CIA was the chief beneficiary of the lapse. This is of some significance; the CIA was less accountable for its actions than the intelligence branches of the State Department (through time-honored procedures, the secretary of state was answerable to Congress). Until public reaction set in during the 1970s, the CIA disregarded restraints to which the Department of State had been subject. The margin between intelligence and political operations, increasingly important to senators since the 1840s, became less perceptible as the State Department stepped down. On the other hand, it is demonstrable that the CIA was more dependent on the Department of State than on any other department. The State Department gradually reimposed civilian control over intelligence after 1947, ensuring that the CIA never became a real monopoly.

The continued viability of State Department espionage can be illustrated in several ways. To begin with, the department's spies did not lose their autonomy in 1947. The remnants of McCormack's research and intelligence group (survivors of the wartime OSS) lingered on for a while until they were finally discredited and dispersed by charges of communism.[27] In the meantime, a new group of spies had formed under the State Department. These were refugees from the foreign intelligence sections of G-2. The advent of the CIA caused a drastic pruning of G-2; some of the demobilized experts (such as the captured-documents analysts) found jobs with the CIA; others dropped out; a further group, whose discreet anonymity was dictated by the current political climate, agreed to assist the Department of State.[28] This last group, never discussed in public but known internally as "the organization," supplied information on, for example, Indonesia, France, air-force logistics, and on counterintelligence, which its defenders claimed was an important supplement to the work performed by the CIA.[29]

The autonomy of the State Department was encouraged by further factors. Charles Fahy had been quite right in emphasizing the importance of the Foreign Service, which had traditionally offered cover to military attachés as well as to the State Department's own agents. CIA agents needed diplomatic immunity just as much as any preceding group of spies. In response to a freedom-of-information lawsuit filed by a former State Department aide, National Security Council officials acknowledged in 1975 that the CIA had used the Foreign Service for cover since 1948. George Lardner, Jr., of the *Washington Post* followed up the story with some figures gleaned from "informed sources." From these, it would appear that the CIA had saturated many embassies with its secret agents by 1961, having a total of 3,700 employees working under State Department cover. The CIA commanded a whole floor at the Paris embassy, eleven out of thirteen positions in the political section of the Chile embassy, and fifteen out of twenty in the same section in Vienna. According to Lardner's sources, there was a danger by 1961 that the CIA would shoulder aside the bona fide representatives of the State Department in the execution of their political duties. It is altogether more credible that the CIA increasingly leaned on the Department of State for shelter and support.[30]

When the CIA began to make serious mistakes in the 1960s, its employees were frozen out, the secret agent being no more indispensable at that time than he ever had been. In three important respects, then, the power shift in the intelligence community from State Department to CIA may be qualified. First, the State Department strengthened its position on the National Security Council in 1947; second, the department retained some intelligence autonomy; third, American spies remained, as ever, dependent on diplomatic cover and protection.

The debate over the centralization of American intelligence, which had been suppressed in the interest of a united front during World War II and broke out in earnest between 1946 and 1948, subsided in the 1950s. Secrecy provisions in the Act of 1947 discouraged public debate. Those concerned about the problem of national security were provided with an alternative spectacle in the rise and fall of Senator Joe McCarthy, who focused his main accusations on the possibility of Communist infiltration in the State Department. Allen Dulles, reported to be responsible for the catchall clauses in the CIA legislative charter, was director of the agency from 1953 to 1961. His brother, Secretary of State John Foster Dulles, encouraged rather than resented the power of the CIA.[31] Friction between the Department of State and the CIA, which might well have stimulated public debate, took second place, at the highest level, to fraternal cooperation.

Debate over the CIA revived in the 1960s and 1970s. CIA mistakes inevitably occurred from time to time, and when they "embarrassed" the Department of State (thereby, incidentally, increasing its power in intelligence matters), the agency became fair game for journalists. The loss of a U-2 plane over the Soviet Union and the abortive invasion of Cuba through the Bay of Pigs were two espiodes that stimulated criticism. The Vietnam war differed from previous foreign wars in American history in that it provoked serious dissent at home. Therefore, CIA and FBI domestic surveillance activities, which would have been criticized as inadequate in 1898, 1918, or 1942, in the late 1960s were shocking by their very existence. There occurred one of those periodic revivals of an almost paranoid fear of conspiracies, fed by real evidence of administration plans for secret warfare in Indochina. The CIA had warned against American involvement in Vietnam but, since its advice was not public knowledge, the agency was criticized along with the other institutions of government.[32] Congress joined in the hunt for evidence of executive malpractice. Presidential power had gradually increased since the 1950s in the area of foreign affairs. President Nixon chose a weak secretary of state in William P. Rogers and in relation to Vietnam and other problems conducted a personal clandestine (if effective) foreign policy through Dr. Henry Kissinger, his assistant on national security affairs since 1969. (Kissinger became secretary of state in 1973.) Kissinger, a believer in virtual autonomy for foreign ministers, used executive privilege as a reason for not appearing before congressional committees. Both houses of Congress were as a result in an angry frame of mind by the beginning of Nixon's second term as president. Congressmen turned their wrath on what they regarded as the excesses of Nixon and Kissinger just as their predecessors in the 1890s had protested against extraconstitutional diplomatic representation. Amenable as it was to the executive arm of government, the CIA could not expect to escape the scrutiny of the congressional committee chaired by Senator Church.

Criticism of the CIA reached a crescendo in the 1970s partly because of the political climate. The decade was one of disillusionment with government. The American self-image fed on foreign reactions to the scandals under constant review in newspapers exported from the United States, and assiduously copied by journalists overseas. As in so often the case, the roots of criticism were to be found in much earlier writing and investigations, the work not of outsiders exploiting a popular mood but of insiders arguing a minority point of view which only later rippled outward in distorted form. In this context, it is worth dwelling a little further on the writings of the *New York Times* journalist Hanson Baldwin.

Baldwin offered not only an analysis of the strengths and weaknesses of American central intelligence but an exploration of how they arose. No muckraker on the make, he had been born into a position of privilege. Son of the editor of the *Baltimore Sun,* he received his education at the Annapolis Naval Academy. Switching from the Navy to his father's profession, he won his Pulitzer Prize in 1942 for outstanding reporting of the war in the Pacific. Although he shared the general American assumptions about the iniquities of Communism, Baldwin was a rebel in one, typically journalistic, respect: he had an overriding contempt for the "cover-up," disliked the secrecy provisions of the National Security Act of 1947, and eventually got into trouble for publishing classified information in what he believed to be the public interest. In 1962, the FBI investigated Baldwin after he had published information about Russian missile bases which was still unknown to high-ranking government officials. Therefore, although he shared the State Department and CIA's cold war outlook, Baldwin ranked as an informed and fearless commentator in terms of any assessment by him of American intelligence.[33]

In July 1948, Baldwin published five articles on American intelligence which provoked a lively reaction among OSS veterans and others.[34] The journalist maintained that, on balance, the peacetime intelligence system was a failure. Its inadequacy was conclusively demonstrated, in Baldwin's view, by the failure to deliver information about the Soviet atomic energy program. For Baldwin, the CIA still represented a ray of hope. He recognized the dangers intrinsic in centralization, particularly the scope afforded to "empire builders."[35] The journalist thought the current investigation into the CIA by Allen Dulles, backed by his rising brother, John Foster, would result in a satisfactory pruning of bureaucracy.[36] He ventilated in his articles his conviction that central intelligence should be concerned with evaluation. Baldwin thought the CIA would be able to bridge the conceptual gap between G-2, A-2, and ONI assessments of Soviet military "capability" and the State Department's political assessment of communist "intentions." In other words, the CIA should optimally be capable of explaining why the Soviet Union had the capability for overrunning Western Europe in forty-five days, yet apparently had no intention of doing so.[37]

Baldwin went on to assert that the CIA would be able to reconcile the differing intelligence pictures offered by the Navy, Army, and Air Force. Each service presented its own overall estimate of opposing military strength, emphasizing areas of particular threat. But in the struggle for appropriations, intelligence officers presented figures designed to advance departmental rather than national interests. "The Navy," Baldwin noted, "emphasizes Russian submarine strength; the Air Force, Russian air power; the Army, numbers of Russian divisions."[38] The CIA, if appropriately strengthened, would be able to reconcile service estimates with one another, as well as with political data supplied by the State Department.

The *Times* correspondent made it clear, however, that he did not extend his approval to operational expansion. As early as 1948, he was worried that the actions of the CIA might prove to be a liability in this respect. Already, he pointed out, naïve young CIA operatives in Rumania, Hungary, and Finland had behaved indiscreetly, betraying procapitalist "rings" to the Russian secret police. One lamentable example of overzealous behavior had occurred in the fall of 1947, when "two young and exuberant army officers" inherited from the OSS had been sent by the CIA to Rumania, where they made contact "almost openly" with anticommunist groups and kept written records of the names of the dissidents and of the transactions at supposedly secret meetings. According to Baldwin, these "naive efforts" were "duck soup" for the Russian secret service. The Russians seized the documents and used them in evidence against the conspirators. The American secret agents escaped from Rumania, but the incident was embarrassing for the United States and a tragedy for dissident leader Dr. Juliu Maniu, who was jailed for life. Baldwin argued that overzealous behavior was not limited to a handful of agents: he questioned Allen Dulles' advocacy of a crusade for "freedom" in Communist countries and the CIA official's tendency "to lump together the functions now conducted by the State Department's 'Voice of America [propaganda radio program],' the FBI and the Central Intelligence Agency." In view of such evidence of excessive enthusiasm, and considering the major accretions in CIA power being contemplated, Baldwin recommended a congressional watchdog committee.[39]

Baldwin became increasingly dissatisfied with the intelligence situation after 1947. From the beginning, he had chafed at the situation whereby clandestine agencies were able to issue propaganda, while their critics were muzzled by secrecy legislation. He pointed out to a former FBI official in 1947 that "many of the facts are not available but on the other hand too many of them are advertised to the world with great fanfare."[40] By 1954, the correspondent was quarreling with Allen Dulles concerning the advisability of publishing figures about CIA expenditures *in toto* and on Indochina. (He had trapped Dulles into a discussion by publishing an exaggerated figure—one billion dollars.) He further accused the CIA director of being unenthusiastic about the watchdog committee being proposed by Senator Mike Mansfield. Baldwin told Dulles that, in common with other Americans, he was worried "about the growing police power of the FBI and the powers of other secret agencies of government like the CIA."[41]

When opponents of the proposed watchdog committee dug their heels in, Baldwin trained his journalistic guns on the CIA and, in a closed hearing, opened fire in earnest. He attacked what he deemed to be the poor intelligence record of the agency and, reversing his previous position, attributed its inefficiency to overcentralization. The CIA was too large and had developed a monopolistic tendency. For example, with the exception of a three-year contractual truce beginning in 1951, the CIA had consistently tried to infiltrate and undermine the State Department's secret service, the "organization."[42] In 1948, Baldwin had urged the fusion of State Department and CIA collection facilities; in the light of events since then, he advocated devolution and autonomy.[43] The scope of CIA operations, he maintained, was too wide. He specifically called for the abolition of CIA collection facilities: "combining the functions of collecting of intelligence with that of evaluating the collected intelligence is like letting a member of one of the competing teams umpire a baseball game."[44]

In some of his criticisms, such as his call for the proper costing of intelligence and his attack on blanket cover-ups, Baldwin quietly anticipated the CIA's strident assailants of the 1970s. His call for a congressional watchdog committee to oversee financial and other aspects of U.S. intelligence, a proposal met by the Pike and Church committees in the 1970s, was in fact the recurrent demand of an unheeded minority in the 1950s and 1960s. In 1955, Senator Mike Mansfield acquired thirty-four co-sponsors for his Senate resolution requesting such a system. This strange coalition of liberals and McCarthyites deplored the high-handedness and oversecrecy of the espionage establishment. In the aftermath of the Bay of Pigs fiasco, there were several more demands for congressional supervision of the CIA, the most prominent being made by Representative John Lindsay in 1963 and Senator Eugene McCarthy in 1966.[45]

Baldwin's attack on "promotional" intelligence disseminated by the

Navy, Army, and Air Force helped to persuade Eisenhower to initiate the Defense Intelligence Agency, which started to operate in October 1961. The DIA functioned under the Department of Defense, took over some of the duties of the forces' intelligence branches such as the supervision of attachés, coordinated military intelligence, discouraged "budgeteering," and permitted a greater measure of civilian control over the espionage activities of the armed forces. According to Professor Ransom, however, the centralization of military intelligence did not dramatically improve its quality.[46]

The State Department's "organization," whose treatment Baldwin deplored in the 1950s, fared slightly better in the 1960s. Its staff declined from over 900 in 1946 to 323 in 1966, but it produced important policy-oriented intelligence for the department on such problems as "African Labor Organizations." Its analysts consumed and evaluated information produced by other branches of the intelligence community and continued to look down on "special operations." In 1963, the director of the Bureau of Intelligence and Research within the organization was elevated to the rank of assistant secretary. This, however, did not resolve a controversy within the State Department summed up as follows by Ransom: "Should a functional or regional bureau of the department have its 'own' intelligence specialists, or should there be a separate intelligence bureau within the department?"[47] The problem of State Department intelligence stressed by Baldwin in the 1950s was no nearer to resolution in the 1960s than it had been in the 1920s.

From the historian's point of view, Baldwin's testimony is significant because he returned to the consideration of a problem which had its origins in the period between Kellogg's decentralization of 1927 and the formation of the CIA in 1947. An efficient intelligence system with clear objectives was an urgent priority for a great power. An efficient system was most likely to be achieved by a small group at the hub of an organization in which the evaluation and coordination of intelligence were centralized. But the members of the group would have to be skilled and knowledgeable to be able to select information important enough to send on to the secretary of state and the president. If it was to be leakproof, it would have to be composed of intimate friends and exclude others with a just claim to be privy to its secrets (thus, Wilkie's superiors had been like himself Chicago bankers, and Polk's intelligence coterie fellow Ivy Leaguers). However, as Baldwin's writings and testimony well illustrate, centralization of any kind was at odds with American competitiveness and pluralism, and cliques and secrecy were the very poison of democracy.

15

The Spy in the Mind

The formation of the CIA in 1947 did not represent a sudden break in the history of American espionage. The CIA grew from the practices of the preceding half-century. To begin with, it inherited OSS personnel. Many OSS men left the intelligence community in 1945 as a result of Truman's demobilization. But, just as intelligence veterans reenlisted for World War II, former OSS men returned for both short and long periods of service with the CIA. Some former OSS officers served the United States as ambassadors and in this capacity no doubt assisted the CIA's activities. A few, such as Evron Kirkpatrick, Roy Cline, William Eddy, Robert Joyce, and Fisher Howe, served the State Department's intelligence organization and cooperated, however uneasily, with the CIA. In the footnotes to his well-researched book OSS, the political scientist R. Harris Smith names thirty-six former OSS men who served directly with the CIA or CIA organizations.[1]

As we saw in Chapter 13, the OSS drew many of its characteristics, as well as some of its recruits, from espionage developments since the late nineteenth century. Like the OSS, on which it was partly based, the CIA owed much to two strands of espionage which had produced the main intelligence agencies of the mid-twentieth century. Military espionage traced its lineage from the 1880s through such figures as Van Deman, Donovan, and General Walter Bedell Smith, director of the CIA from 1950 to 1953. Civilian spying was descended from Wilkie through Polk and on to Dulles. The clash between military and civilian intelligence interests and methods is, then, rooted in the early history of institutional espionage. Furthermore, the question of means and ends, centralization, and congressional supervision have been warmly debated since the 1890s or earlier.

It is, of course, true that intelligence activities have been debated with unusual heat in recent years. In spite of the fact that the CIA merely continued existing intelligence traditions, it has been the focus of an unprecedented amount of criticism. In this sense, the year of its foundation was a turning point in the history of U.S. espionage. The year 1947 was also significant because the CIA, a peacetime agency, took on the quasi-military assignments known as "covert actions." Such actions originated in the initiatives of the OSS in World War II and may to a certain extent result from the weakened grip of the State Department on espionage in the 1940s and the centralization of liaison, evaluation, and collection. Just after World War I, Leland Harrison of the State Department had authorized special operations to acquire German codebooks, with the object of improving America's pure intelligence capability; not long after World War II, the CIA was by contrast intervening in foreign countries on its own initiative with political ends in view: the new professionals were sowing their wild oats.

As public servants sheltered by the executive umbrella, spies have been allowed considerable latitude and freedom from investigation. It is doubtful whether the Pinkerton Agency, if hired in 1898, would have gotten away with covert action in later years. Similarly, it is inconceivable that private detectives, if contracted to pursue intelligence goals, would have been allowed also to define them. Yet the power of goal-definition devolved on both the OSS and the CIA. President Franklin D. Roosevelt explicitly charged the OSS with defining its own goals; the Washington correspondent of *Esquire,* Taylor Branch, writes with some force of persuasion that the CIA veterans of the 1970s "consider themselves a true professional élite," responsible for "shouldering burdens for the American people that the people would not want to bear or even hear about."[2] As an agency of the people, the CIA has taken on decision-making powers which would not have been tolerated in government-hired private agencies—powers which, in an earlier age, were the sole prerogative of elected politicians or of government departments responsible to them.

Because of its augmented responsibilities, the CIA has become in the 1970s the target of attacks that might otherwise have been directed at politicians. The CIA has been accused of betraying American ideals of open dealing and democracy by its actions in the Congo, Chile, and elsewhere. Yet, in most cases, the agency claimed to be using the most effective methods at its disposal to defend American ideals and interests against "subversion," the secret tactics of enemies, especially Communists. This dichotomy of ideals stretches back over several generations. It was evident in American attitudes toward "Moscow Gold" in the 1920s, toward German espionage in World War I, and toward British intelligence in the war for independence. The double standards of the CIA in the 1970s are related to contradictory attitudes shared since the beginning of the national experience—for example, in relation to Nathan Hale, Benedict Arnold, and John André.

In short, neither the espionage community nor the controversy surrounding it is a recent phenomenon. There have been important milestones in the history of American espionage, notably the entry of the Secret Service (1898), State Department (1915), OSS (1942), and CIA (1947) into the intelligence field. But continuities are evident with respect to both institutions and attitudes. It may be argued, indeed, that ambivalent attitudes toward the spy are part of a wider American tradition. Epitomized by the actions of the pre-Civil War vigilante mob or the twentieth-century private detective agency, the tradition holds that "law and order" may be maintained, if necessary, by using illegal methods. But the origins of and reactions to espionage may be considered in a still wider context, that of social psychology and popular literature. For the CIA and its antecedents were products of American society, not just of small groups within it. By virtue of his character the spy has provoked complex and disparate reactions. Ambivalent popular attitudes toward the spy help to explain his support, the opposition to his activities, and his fluctuating fortunes.

Since there are many varieties of human ambivalence, it is useful to consider an attempt to define the phenomenon in spies. In the early 1970s, a team of psychiatrists from the Tavistock Institute of Human Relations in London had the opportunity of analyzing the personalities of a number of Arab spies who had been captured by the Israelis and were willing to cooperate in an extensive series of interviews. The London analysts producd a composite picture which provides a starting point for the study of the psychological makeup of spies in general. They described the tensions that can arise when idealistic goals are ruthlessly pursued. They argued that the idealistic spies and guerrillas whom they had interviewed tended to rationalize unscrupulous methods. Up to a point, the spies succeeded in convincing themselves of their righeousness but, thereafter, they sometimes succumbed to anxiety, guilt, and "splitting"—that is, they developed split personalities. "The fully developed state," the psychiatrists maintained, "is one in which on one side of the ego split there is a completely brutalized ruthless pattern of behaviour with violence, cruelty and murder while on the other side is a pattern which would pass for normal loyalty to family and friends, geniality to non-involved people and evidence of an adequate sense of social responsibility."[3]

According to the Tavistock team, the extreme form of ambivalence that they termed "splitting" was to be found more often in spies than in guerrillas or other unofficial partisans. The British psychiatrists argued that spies experienced a dual urge for concealment and public confession corresponding to the psychological characteristics of scopophilia (the desire to hide) and exhibitionism. Because the spy worked alone, he became particularly prone to neuroses. Because he behaved unscrupulously toward others, so, "on the principle of talion," he became suspicious of the intentions of others toward himself and even paranoid.[4]

It would be dangerous to generalize literally on the basis of so selective a group, composed of spies who were (a) caught and (b) willing to be extensively interviewed by psychiatrists. Arab spies against Israel may well be more idealistic and less professional than CIA agents allotted to a variety of assignments in the course of routine careers. The Tavistock analysts may be challenged on the ground that they regarded Arab spies and by extension all secret agents as potentially sick people. On the other hand, if the Arab spies did display amateur characteristics, their composite psychological portrait is worth bearing in mind when considering not just other secret agents, but also the response of the layman to the problem of espionage. In probing for the specific applicability of the foregoing psychological interpretations, it is naturally advantageous to begin with neurotic (but not necessarily atypical) members of society. A good sample of the support for the government snooper is to be found in the crank letters received by John Wilkie in 1898.

As soon as the *New York Sun* broadcast Wilkie's status as chief of the secret service, he began to receive numerous letters. Correspondents usually demanded the harassment of a person or group, particularly in the form of penetrating surveillance. Wilkie's agents deemed some of the writers to be "dopey," others sane.[5] Regardless of such diagnoses, anyone writing to the Secret Service was himself likely to display one or more of the characteristics of a spy, such as scopophilia, exhibitionism, or paranoid suspicions. By 1898, the American spy was beginning to exert charisma.

A good Wilkie operative never ignored the character of his informant. From Pennsylvania, Assistant Operative Charles LaSalle reported the observations of one correspondent's brother that "she was a widow and that she left Renovo about 8 or 10 years ago. That he had not heard from her for about three years and he did not know where she was at the present time. That she was considered to be half crazy, that she had on one or two occasions tried to commit suicide and that she was not a responsible person."[6] The reason for the investigation into Mrs. M. L. McDougall's character was the receipt of a letter from her saying that "she had heard threats made by Dr. Mary Walker and others against the Hon. President of the U.S. and Secretary of War and asks the Secretary to answer and sign himself M. L. Williams and to direct his answer to her at Renovo, Clinton Co., Pa."[7] The unfortunate widow displayed dual characteristics, the desire to pry into another's activities and to emerge from one's own concealment, which might correspond to Freud's paired components, scopophilia and exhibitionism. The contemporary judgment was that she was "crazy."[8] Yet others who denounced their neighbors in similar terms were taken more seriously, even though to the historian they also reveal disturbed personalities.

Anti-Catholicism was a socially acceptable neurosis. It was rooted in anticlericalism and the Reformation and received rational reinforcement in the mid-eighteenth century, when the soldiers of France had their eyes on the middle reaches of the Mississippi. By 1898, it would have been wishful thinking on the part of Spain to imagine that French-Canadians or Mexicans might join with American Catholics in a holy crusade. Nevertheless, there was considerable nativist, anti-Catholic feeling in the United States, stemming from resentment at the influx of "new immigrants" from southern, eastern, non-Protestant parts of Europe. This explains not just the letters sent to the Secret Service alleging Catholic conspiracy but the serious consideration they received. Mrs. McDougall might be dismissed as irresponsible; not so W. G. Hill, President of the Lord's Vineyard and Colonization Company, Chicago ("organized for helping distressed Christians and furnishing them with Homes and Lands, whereby they may be able to support themselves").[9]

Hill's letter advocated more extensive surveillance, stating it to be "of the utmost importance that all these detectives should be men of the highest moral character, well educated, trustworthy in every respect and staunch Protestants; for, in looking for our enemies, we will find them in the papal ranks."[10] In view of the remoteness of any possibility of Roman conspiracy in 1898, Hill's attitude may be described as overly suspicious, if not paranoid. But his assumption was widely shared.

The nature and popularity of spy fiction suggest that the study of espionage should be broadened beyond the scrutiny of agents, agencies, and cranks. There are four points about the spy novel that should be noted at the outset. First, it is often authentic. Such fiction writers as Daniel Defoe, William T. Le Queux, R. Erskine Childers, J. Compton Mackenzie, Graham Greene, Ian Fleming, and Cord Meyer all operated as secret agents; thus some spy fiction shed light not just on abstract, fantastic hero figures but on a significant aspect of human nature.[11] Second, spy novels are about ambivalence, or what we have called splitting. Thus, Graham Greene summed up John Buchan's appeal in terms of the complementary attractions of overt rectitude and secret immorality; "Who will forget that first thrill . . . as the hunted Leithan . . . ran 'like a thief in a London thoroughfare on a June afternoon,' thinking to himself, 'Now I saw how thin is the protection of civilization'?"[12] Third, whether the author is Mario Simmel in Germany or Alistair Maclean in Britain, the spy novel is usually colloquial and contemporary in style; touching on a universal theme, it reaches out to everybody.[13] Finally, this particular art form is by no means confined to the United States. To take the British Isles alone, Ireland has produced Erskine Childers' *The Riddle of the Sands* (1909), Liam O'Flaherty's *The Informer* (1925); England has spawned William T. Le Queux and his hundred thrillers, W. Somerset Maugham, Graham Greene, John Le Carré; Wales, the Welsh-language play *Brâd* (Treason) by Saunders Lewis; Scotland, Conan Doyle and John Buchan.[14] Many spy-story writers—like the wandering Pole, Joseph Conrad—have been cosmopolitan themselves.[15] Spying is part of international human nature, not a distinctive characteristic of the American people.

Espionage is nevertheless a particularly important phenomenon in American history and culture. Because the United States emerged as the most powerful nation in the world in the twentieth century, its spies are of more than usual interest. Because America is a democracy, there has been an open debate even on clandestine subjects. America may be compared with the spy who plucked up enough courage to talk about himself to a psychologist—a nation no more spy-ridden or insane than any other, but more willing to discuss its problems in public. Indeed, the very first successful novel with an American setting was *The Spy* (1821), James Fenimore Cooper's factually based account of the exploits of Harvey Birch, an unpaid patriotic agent in the American War of Independence. In this novel, Cooper's ambivalence toward Birch is clear: the impecunious spy "belonged to a condition in life which rendered him the least reluctant to appear in so equivocal a character."[16]

Cooper was the first of a host of American spy-fiction writers. Most of them were quickly forgotten, if popular in their day, because they drenched their novels with too much contemporary detail and with short-lived passions. Robert W. Chambers was no exception to this rule. Randolph Bourne, an intellectual more than usually alienated from his fellowmen, identified Chambers's appeal in a plaintive letter to a woman friend in 1915:

> My young sister is almost a passionate vulgarian, and takes with really virtuous indignation my deviation from the norms of popular music, the movies, Chamber's [sic] novels, Billy Sunday, musical comedy, tennis, anti-suffragism, and the rest of the combination that makes up the healthy, hearty, happy young normal person of the well-brought up family of the day of the middle-middle class. I find her an index to current America, but we scarcely get along.[17]

Like Bourne's sister, Chambers's numerous spy novels provided "an index to current America." They appeared between the 1890s and the 1920s, a period when modern espionage and security neuroses began to emerge.

Chambers was not an original writer; his spy novels are interesting because archetypal. For example, their collective attitude toward the secret agent is ambivalent. In *The Red Republic* (1896; about the Paris Commune) and *Lorraine* (1897; about the Franco-Prussian war), the spy is a hero; in *A King and a Few Dukes* (1896) and *The Conspirators* (1899) he is at best to be feared, at worst a villain.[18] *A King and a Few Dukes* is about the adventures of a New Yorker in the southern Caspian mountain region and contains many references to Russian spies whose pervasive power is awesome.[19] *The Conspirators* is about a West Point graduate who, assigned from the American Embassy to become aide-de-camp to the Duke of Luxembourg, thwarts the designs of two villainous German spies to reduce the Duchy's sovereignty. The moral of these tales is that a spy can be a hero or a villain, depending on which side he is on. It may be inferred that the very large readership which Chambers attracted found the moral acceptable not only in literature but perhaps also in real life: domestic critics of the self-contradictory policies of Wilson and Lansing toward U.S. and alien espionage were always in the minority.

But is it really safe to generalize from so few examples? Do James Fenimore Cooper and Robert Chambers tell us much about the possible ambivalence of modern spies and of the public attitude toward them? One might argue that their novels were period pieces, that in any case ambivalence is a common literary theme, not a distinctive feature of spy novels. Indeed, an argument can be made for the view that the spy hero of fiction appeals to a wide readership because he is single-minded, not because he is self-doubting. This is true of Ian Fleming's highly popular secret agent, James Bond. To a lesser extent, is it not also true of the main protagonists in novels by Liam O'Flaherty, Raymond Chandler, and Dashiel Hammett? Gypo and his like appeal as private individuals with well-portrayed personalities, not as symbols of psychological splitting.

If fiction reflects reality and the spy of fiction is sometimes portrayed as a man without doubts, it follows that secret agents in real life may also be complacent about their role. Certainly the CIA put up a boldly unrepentant front when it came under attack in the early 1970s. In April 1974, it issued a pamphlet called *The Central Intelligence Agency* listing comments on the CIA by various presidents. Eisenhower remarked in 1959 that "in the work of intelligence, heroes are undecorated and usung," Kennedy in 1961 that the CIA's "successes are unheralded—[its] failures are trumpeted," Johnson that the CIA was striving "for an orderly, just, and peaceful world." Nixon recognized in 1969 that the CIA faced a dilemma: "This organization has a mission that, by necessity, runs counter to some of the very deeply held traditions in this country and feelings, high idealistic feelings, about what a free society ought to be," but concluded that the agency's work was "vitally important." Finally Truman, whose administration had spawned the CIA in 1947, sent a portrait of himself to be hung at CIA headquarters in Langley, Virginia, signed "To

the Central Intelligence Agency, a necessity to the President
United States, from one who knows." If the CIA accepted the\
ments at face value, it was at the cost of considerable oversight:
presidents were speaking to CIA personnel or otherwise encouraging
them, and would not have chosen such occasions for criticism.[20] Truman
would hardly have signed his Langley portrait with the following words,
also attributed to him: "I never had any thought when I set up the CIA
that it would be injected into peacetime cloak and dagger operations. . . .
This quiet arm of the President of the United States has been so far
removed from its intended role that it is being interpreted as a symbol of
sinister and mysterious foreign intrigue. . . . I therefore would like to see
that the CIA be restored to its original assignments as the intelligence
arm of the President . . . and that its operational duties be terminated
or properly used elsewhere."[21] The CIA's selection of presidential quotations suggests a self-congratulatory rather than introspective outlook.

This argument can be taken further. For example, Secretary of State
Henry Kissinger and William E. Colby (CIA director, 1973–1976) showed
apparent insensitivity to criticism by boycotting covert-action hearings
conducted by the Church committee.[22] In a prepared statement to the
House Select Committee on Intelligence in August 1975, Colby declared
that in the twenty-eight years since the inception of the CIA "instances of
wrongful action" by its agents "were truly few and far between," and
admitted that it would be "disingenuous" of him to say that he welcomed
the House inquiry into CIA activities.[23]

Attempts by intrepid individuals to publish information they considered to be necessary to the public interest met with obstruction and
disapproval from intelligence agencies and their official backers, a circum-
stance which led many journalists to suppose that undercover intransigence was widespread. The Daniel Schorr affair provoked considerable
controversy. Schorr, a sixty-nine-year-old CBS television correspondent,
leaked the Pike Report to the Manhattan-based newspaper, *The Village
Voice*. When he refused to disclose to a committee on congressional ethics
how he had obtained the report and defied a subpoena, he was threatened
with contempt proceedings. He based his defense on the First Amendment and escaped punishment when half the ethics committee voted
in his favor on September 15, 1976. Schorr's actions in leaking the report,
standing up to the committee, and holding out against a $150,000 in-
vestigation by twelve former FBI agents provoked both criticism and
praise. Referring to the First Amendment defense and freedom-of-the-
press issue, Congressman James H. Quillen of Tennessee remarked that
"newspapers come and go, but our country remains forever."[24]

Liberal sections of the press, however, defended Schorr. An editorial
in the *New York Times* condemned his harassment and likened his treatment to that of Daniel Ellsberg in 1971. Ellsberg had leaked the "Penta-

gon papers" to the *Times*. At his Los Angeles trial for this offense, Judge Matthew Byrne dismissed the charges against him when it was revealed that E. Howard Hunt and G. Gordon Liddy (two of the men behind the Watergate burglary) had planned a break-in at the office of Ellsberg's psychiatrist and that the government had withheld information necessary to the defense. The Ellsberg trial had produced public uproar; similarly Schorr received several thousand letters of encouragement.[25]

In spite of such indications of public disquietude over quasi-governmental covert operations, the FBI showed continuing intransigence after publication and public discussion of the Pike inquiry. FBI Director Clarence M. Kelley had undertaken to drop surveillance of domestic radicals unless they were engaged in criminal activities, but, hoping perhaps that the storm would blow over, began to make qualifications. On August 15, 1976, Kelley stated that the FBI would continue to investigate the Socialist Workers' party (a Trotskyist group engaged in noncriminal activities) because its alleged connection with the Fourth International made this "a counterintelligence case rather than a domestic security investigation."[26] Kelley's actions may be interpreted to mean that the FBI was prepared to accept reforms, not out of genuine conviction, but because of outside pressure.

The CIA showed a determination to persevere in its old ways and a definite desire to take advantage of a perceived relaxation of public vigilance. A dispute between the State and Justice departments, on the one hand, and the CIA, on the other, in December 1976 resulted in a leak which revealed that the CIA was bugging the telephones of pro-independence politicians from the militarily important Trust Territory of the Pacific Islands. The CIA was technically justified in that the Micronesian officials were foreigners, but an anonymous Justice Department source complained: "It's like bugging your children's telephone."[27] On another front, questions were asked in the British House of Commons about Briddon (Butchers) Ltd., a London corporation which purported to deal in meat and poultry but actually published and distributed CIA propaganda. In 1974, Briddon (Butchers) Ltd. changed its name to the more convincing Rossiter Publications, and by 1976 it was conducting an ever more vigorous business in defiance of important sections of public opinion in the United States.[28]

The CIA resisted the Pike and Church inquiries and, assisted by public reaction to the Welch assassination, appeared to have "weathered the storm." This was the phrase used by the CIA's new Director, George Bush, in September 1976. Bush added: "The mood in Congress is changing . . . no one is campaigning against strong intelligence," clearly regarding this state of affairs as a triumph.[29] Soon after his election in 1976, President Jimmy Carter nominated as director of the CIA Theodore C.

Sorensen, who had been one of Kennedy's advisers at the time of the Bay of Pigs episode. Sorensen, nevertheless, having a perception of public expectations quite different from that of Bush, promised a scaling down of covert operations. But this was not to be the end of the matter.

Opponents of the Sorensen nomination, some of them rumored to be CIA officials opposed to reform, leaked to the press information calculated to weaken the stature of the former Kennedy man. For example, it was revealed that Sorensen had defended Ellsberg's release of the Pentagon papers on the grounds that too many federal documents were classified and that leaking was a time-honored custom; indeed, Sorensen had stated in defense of Ellsburg that he himself had used classified documents in writing his book *Kennedy* (1965). In a spirited rebuttal of his critics before the Senate Intelligence Committee in January 1977, Sorensen said he had never tried to conceal his support for Ellsburg. But after reading his rebuttal statement, he withdrew his name from consideration.[30]

CIA intransigence was divisive in that it provoked so much criticism over issues like the Sorensen affair. But the ruthlessness that is inseparable from undercover activities has not infrequently been accompanied by qualification and opposition within the CIA itself. One should not take at face value the tough defense put up by Republican-appointed FBI and CIA leaders in the face of criticism. It is only natural that they should have extolled their organizations' virtues in the face of attacks in the press and Congress. They had a professional commitment to do so and a duty to defend their subordinates. CIA Director Colby was prepared to reform his agency in response to what he regarded as constructive criticism; for example, he revised the CIA's budgetary control system at the request of the Rockefeller Commission.[31] Other U.S. intelligence officials have, from time to time, experienced genuine crises of conscience. Two of the best-known examples are Victor Marchetti and John D. Marks. Marchetti was a CIA military analyst until he moved to join the staff of the office of the director, where he served from 1966 to 1969. Marks worked for the State Department's Bureau of Intelligence and Research between 1968 and 1970. His experience of liaison with other intelligence services led him to the same conclusion as Marchetti: that clandestine operations and secret interventions in the internal affairs of foreign countries were intolerable.[32] In spite of opposition from the CIA, which forced the deletion of several passages from their original typescript, Marchetti and Marks in 1974 published their exposé, *The CIA and the Cult of Intelligence.*

The case of Philip Agee is no different in its essentials from that of Marchetti and Marks. Agee was a CIA agent for twelve years, acquiring a special knowledge of U.S. intelligence operations in Latin America.

According to his own account, he left the CIA and began to publish the names of American secret agents. He supplied CIA-related information to "revolutionary organizations that could use it to defend themselves better."[33] His book *Inside the Company: CIA Diary*, which contains a 26-page appendix listing CIA agents and front organizations, escaped expurgation because it was published by a major British firm, Penguin, in 1975.[34] The author himself moved to Cambridge, England, to work on his next book, exposing CIA activities in Jamaica and elsewhere. Late in 1976, Home Secretary Merlyn Rees authorized the serving of a deportation order on Agee, on the ground that the ex-CIA agent was endangering British national security.

Agee is to be distinguished from Marchetti and Marks because he writes from a socialist standpoint. He has defined the CIA as "the secret police of American capitalism, plugging up leaks in the political dam night and day so that shareholders of U.S. companies operating in poor countries can continue enjoying the rip-off."[35] Not many CIA agents claim to have become socialists, but Agee's autobiographical book gives an account of the development of a doubting frame of mind in a hitherto orthodox young man which suggests that disillusionment may not be highly unusual. Agee says he joined the CIA "to avoid two lost years in the Army" and in a naïve frame of mind.[36] He maintains that field work in poor countries convinced him that the high-flown ideals of training camp were mere rhetoric. On the one hand, Agee's story and conduct may be regarded as atypical if not improbable and calculated to play into the hands of the CIA's defenders. On the other hand, his account of disillusionment within the "Company" is not incredible: perhaps one should accept the fact that the unquestioning "007" type may not be universal and that CIA "headquarters and stations alike are peppered . . . with officers who long ago ceased to believe in what they're doing."[37]

Eulogizing CIA men at the White House swearing-in ceremonies for Director William F. Raborn, Jr. and Deputy Director Richard Helms, President Johnson claimed that "in two and one half years of working with these men I have yet to meet a '007'." He had met not real life James Bonds, but men of "logic and analysis."[38] Perhaps LBJ exaggerated because he had never come across the CIA's men of action, those responsible for actually carrying out covert operations; nevertheless, his observation that there were many thinkers in American intelligence would be difficult to refute—and thinkers are given to introspection. The journalist Taylor Branch suggested that the CIA professional elite thought it was "shouldering burdens for the American people;" these burdens doubtless consisted, very often, of agonizing choices which few single-minded men would have cared to make.[39]

A powerful case can be made for the view that the CIA of the 1960s and 1970s, far from being a maverick outfit, simply enacted the desires of a torn people who were willing to defend liberty for some even at the cost of undermining it for others. The desire had been evident in the formative years of the CIA, for example in the Alger Hiss trials of 1949–1950.

Although espionage never ceased to interest either politicians or ordinary people from the 1920s to the early 1940s, the main preoccupation of these years was with foreign intelligence. The situation changed in the period of the rise of the CIA, when the spy played on the American mind more than ever before. The Hiss trial made a domestic issue of Communist espionage at a time when Americans were feeling uncertain in the face of the Russian challenge and were looking for a crusade.

Alger Hiss had the credentials of an Eastern establishment figure: Harvard '29, Washington *Social Register*, New Deal and State Department insider, and president of the Carnegie Endowment for International Peace. In 1949–1950, he was brought to trial on a charge of perjury for denying his association with Whittaker Chambers, erstwhile senior editor of *Time*. Chambers alleged that he had acted as a go-between, transmitting State Department secrets from Hiss to the Russians.

Hiss endured two trials. The first, beginning in May, 1949, ended in a hung jury. The situation fomented considerable emotion. Congressman Richard M. Nixon, who made his name by pressing for the Hiss investigation, revealed that Justice Samuel Kaufman's "prejudice for the defense and against the prosecution was so obvious . . . that the jury's 8–4 vote for conviction came frankly as a surprise to me."[40] Early in 1950, a second jury convicted Hiss.

The Chambers–Hiss episode illustrates the psychology of the spy and public reactions to it. The prosecution's case rested on Chambers's testimony concerning his acquaintanceship with Hiss in the 1930s, when Chambers had been a rising Communist journalist. Attention focused, therefore, on the reliability of Chambers as a witness. In the course of the second perjury trial, psychiatrist Carl Binger testified in defense of Hiss. Binger's job was to discredit Chambers. He described the prosecution witness as a pathological liar, an antisocial character with a compulsion to make false accusations.[41] Chambers's personality, in brief, conformed to that of a spy: he was a ruthless man who ultimately made himself socially acceptable by posing as the champion of the common man against an Ivy League traitor.

Dr. Henry A. Murray, a former director of the Harvard Psychological Clinic, supported Binger's testimony in court. He said that he had come across men like Chambers when serving as a lieutenant colonel with the OSS. Chambers was afflicted with a psychopathic spy personality and attracted to the "idea of being a mysterious man with secret knowledge and working as an intelligence officer."[42] Hiss's defense attorney, Lloyd P. Stryker, had by this time already made his point about Chambers:

> In the warm countries, you know, where they have leprosy, some-
> times you will hear on the streets perhaps among the lepers a
> man crying down the street, 'Unclean, unclean!' at the approach of
> a leper.
> I say the same to you [the jury] at the approach of this moral
> leper.[43]

Such remarks were as unkind to Chambers as to lepers, and it is by no means clear that Hiss was innocent (in 1939 he had been investigated in a desultory way for potential disloyalty by Adolf Berle, who had no taste for such work).[44] But it does seem, in retrospect, that Hiss was convicted on the evidence of an unreliable witness.

An American jury voted to convict Hiss because prosecution lawyer Thomas Murphy persuaded them of the reliability of Chambers's evidence. Murphy astutely inferred that Chambers's frailties made him all the more human and credible. Chambers's record of proven mendacity in public affairs was no guide to his present conduct; was there any profound difference, asked the ingenuous Murphy, between occasionally lying to your wife and occasionally lying about political affairs? Conjugal liars were still accounted honest men—why not Chambers in his exposure of Hiss?[45] Such reasoning, combined with skillfully managed if inconclusive documentary evidence, helped to persuade a majority of the jury, and to make Hiss an "American Dreyfus."[46]

The Dreyfus case split French society in the 1890s, but Alfred Dreyfus would never have been convicted in the first place if France had not been deeply divided. In an America which was divided over security problems, Hiss was deprived of his liberty in the name of freedom. In the ensuing unhappy years of "McCarthyism," many citizens accused of having Communist sympathies were deprived of their livelihood and even their sanity in the name of the same cause.

There are many interpretations of McCarthyism. Some historians argue that Senator Joseph McCarthy took advantage of the state of party politics in Wisconsin or the Senate. Others maintain that he had special demonic qualities which made the American people unable to resist his charisma, ready to believe his unfounded accusations about communism in the State Department, and acquiescent in the smear tactics used so irresponsibly by the senator and his supporters. Some conservatives have been prepared to defend McCarthyism.[47] But according to the late historian Richard Hofstadter, McCarthy and his defenders belonged to a "pseudo-conservative" group outside the mainstream of American politics.[48]

To attribute McCarthyism, or for that matter Populism or CIA excesses, to backwater elements is to indulge in escapism. After all, 50 percent of those sampled in a Gallup Poll of January 1954 had a favorable opinion of McCarthy and his activities. The literary critic Leslie Fiedler argued as early as 1955 that McCarthyism was part of a tradition along with Populism, and in recent years historians Richard M. Freeland and Athan Theoharris have pointed to the political use of anticommunism by the Truman administration.[49] McCarthyism and reactions against it in the mid-1950s were extreme manifestations of conflicting beliefs and emotions which affected many decades and many people in American history.

In this context, it is worth noting that several popular fiction writers of the 1950s shared some of the viewpoints of Robert Chambers and Fenimore Cooper. Indeed, the growth of the U.S. spy-fiction industry since World War II has helped to clarify the nature of the American spy novel and to shed light on the outlook of the reading public. Yale historian Robin W. Winks, formerly U.S. cultural attaché in Britain and a spy-fiction critic, has drawn attention to the "moral ambivalence" to be found in modern U.S. espionage novels.[50]

Winks's view may be quite adequately defended against the contention that the reading public consists of single-minded people in search of James Bond. To begin with 007 himself, he is of course a British joke; Ian Fleming's novels are a form of escapism. Graham Greene similarly wrote spy novels as "entertainments," though he failed to keep out introspection altogether. Erskine Childers may have been a single-minded British patriot when he wrote *The Riddle of the Sands,* but he sided with the Irish after the Easter Rising of 1916; O'Flaherty makes it clear that Gypo *should* have been a thinking man, and John Le Carré leaves one in doubt that George Smiley *is* a thinker.

A book which epitomizes the oft-delineated malaise of modern America is Sterling Hayden's *Wanderer* (1964).[51] Cast in the form of a novel, *Wanderer* is nevertheless autobiographical. It is about an impressionable but intelligent spy, Hayden himself. In the book, Hayden reveals a high degree of consciousness about the contradictions and hypocrisy of life. He is sufficiently ruthless in his honesty to convince the reader, in the end, that he is not a likable person. Yet—and here there is an unintended ray of hope, indeed an unexpected laurel wreath, for the spy—Hayden clearly refuses to give up idealism or the search for truth.

As a young man, Hayden was a handsome, six-foot-five-inch dreamer with the archaic ambition of becoming a schoonerman. This he achieved. Thereupon "Wild Bill" Donovan, whose business interests embraced Hollywood and who knew Hayden through Donovan's son, introduced the brilliant but impecunious sailor to movie acting. When war broke out in Europe, Donovan arranged for Hayden to train with the British in England; later he operated for the OSS, sailing between Italy and

Yugoslavia with provisions for the partisans, and participating in land-based undercover operations. In Yugoslavia, Hayden began to sympathize with communism; he joined the U.S. Communist party in 1946 when, in Hollywood circles, it was decidedly chic to do so. In 1951, when the political atmosphere was difficult, he betrayed his former comrades to McCarthy's investigators. Later, he reverted to being a schoonerman and, when the reaction against McCarthy set in, stated his regret at having acted as a stool pigeon.[52]

If Hayden shifted direction with every variation in the breeze, he is at least a weathervane to popular mood. Several passages in *Wanderer* capture the spirit of the times through which its author lived. Hayden well conveyed the desire of OSS chiefs to ape the British style (in OSS headquarters, Cairo, "a bastard version of the Taj Mahal," numerous servants "glided in endless circles"), as well as OSS resentment of British immutability ("a secretary entered with tea—which made it quite clear that this was a British Theatre of War").[53] Hayden remained alert to contradictions of every sort. He retrospectively deplored the years of the Hollywood blacklist, when McCarthyism sent radical writers into exile, "only to find that producers were willing to—very discreetly, of course—buy more than a hundred scripts underneath the table."[54] The sailor–actor eventually decided that he was himself a contradiction, someone "flawed inside" and lacking in identity. Hayden sailed to Tahiti, where he expected to find himself.[55]

Hayden did not behave in an exceptionally cowardly way in view of the widespread terror created by the McCarthy hearings, nor was he a key witness: he is important because his book exemplified the reactions of many Americans to McCarthyism. His case reinforces the point that society is capable of splitting over the issues of loyalty and security. Whether or not it is true that spies in fact are more prone than society as a whole to split-mindedness, it is reasonable to conclude that American espionage, with some of its excesses, is the product of a popular state of mind that seems to be neither ancient nor modern but eternal.

Divided loyalties have produced not just espionage itself, but criticism of it, in individual secret agents, within agencies, and within society as a whole. Society's ambivalence on the issue is as evident in reactions to the Hiss trial as in the reception afforded to Wilkie's operations in 1898. Popular fiction is redolent of conflicting attitudes toward secret agents, in the United States as elsewhere. In recent years, the Ellsberg, Schorr, and Sorensen affairs have produced typically mixed responses. It is true that there have been secret agents in fiction who never seemed to doubt their methods and CIA directors to whom recalcitrance in the face of criticism has seemed second nature. But even the image of the unyielding, bullheaded spymaster has simply goaded the modern critics of American espionage into greater efforts.

The critics of American espionage have in recent years concentrated their attack on two issues. Covert operations are a controversial matter because they seem to be unprecedented and unauthorized. The issue of authorization is, of course, an old one, related to various constitutional, political, legal, and moral debates that started in the earliest days of the republic. There can be no doubt, however, that the permanent American distrust of spies has been stimulated by events since World War II.

The modern phase of the argument over intelligence authorization began in the 1940s. As we have seen, authorities on intelligence like Lovett and Baldwin thought the OSS experience demonstrated the need for better evaluation and dissemination of information. The proposal that the CIA should be authorized to process as well as collect information led to fears within the State Department that a "branch foreign office" would emerge; conservative Congressmen like Bridges and Brown were suspicious of any type of centralization. Ultimately, State Department lawyers drafted clauses in the 1947 Act that give the CIA unspecified but potentially wide powers. These could be authorized, however, only by a governing body in which State was powerfully represented. At will, State could empower, assist, obstruct, or disown the CIA in pretty much the same way that any foreign office treats an individual secret agent. The CIA was fully authorized, yet minimally authorized, and when things went wrong, recriminations began to fly.

The distinguished historian Henry Steele Commager has recently attacked the ways in which undercover operations contravene the Constitution—ways more serious, in his view, than any since the days of Reconstruction. According to Commager, recent presidents have falsely assumed that the Constitution gives the executive a "blank check" in matters of intelligence. He has reiterated the time-honored objection to the abuse of executive agreements and stressed the clauses in the Constitution designed to separate the powers of purse and sword—powers which, he fears, are combined in a nonaccountable CIA. In this sense, Commager has echoed the preoccupation of Baldwin, the journalist who thought the public had the right to know about the CIA's budget. Commager argues that the liberal press—the *New York Times, Washington Post, New York Review of Books, The Nation, The Progressive*—has been exercising the vigilance over intelligence agencies which should be the duty of Congress. The historian remarks that the Constitution gives Congress the power of the purse, and that the State Department is a statutory, not a Constitutional, institution, so that the supine acquiescence of the Pike committee and other investigators in the face of obstruction from the intelligence community is inexcusable.[56] Commager's criticisms show that the traditional Constitutional debate is still alive and a stimulus to the controversy over the meaning of the 1947 legislation.

Covert action and the controversy surrounding it constitute the second feature obtruding against the background of American intelligence since 1898. Though there are precedents for special operations, ranging from antiquity's Trojan horse to Voska's mission to Russia, they came into their own as far as the United States is concerned in World War II.

The modern controversy arises from the fact that paramilitary agents began to work for the CIA in 1948. Their presence in the peacetime intelligence community seemed to reverse the trend toward civilian central intelligence that started in 1898 and to take the idea of the military adviser (applied in South America in the 1930s) one step further. According to Marchetti and Marks, paramilitary agents were disliked by traditional intelligence men.[57] Furthermore, their operations failed in communist or "enemy" countries like China and came to be concentrated in friendly or potentially friendly countries—Cuba, Indonesia, Tibet, Laos, Bolivia, Guyana, Iran, Guatemala, Santo Domingo, Greece, Portugal, Chile, and so on. Commager remarked that "ill-considered interventions in the internal affairs" of such countries had resulted in the "alienation of much of world opinion."[58]

No doubt every malfeasance by the United States is pounced upon by foreign critics, partly because of the high expectations aroused by American ideals and partly because of a natural jealousy of the most powerful country in the world. Even against this background, however, Commager is clearly right in saying that some of the CIA's actions have become a national liability. The CIA has been the scapegoat of the European left ever since 1947: it is now automatically suspected by a wider section of public opinion overseas. For the charismatic spy is as enigmatically regarded by Europeans as by Americans, and the real or imagined exploits of the CIA are irresistible to the journalist and propagandist. In Britain, for example, the Agee deportation case won instant notoriety in many sections of the press. The front page of a popular tabloid, *The Sun*, greeted its readers on November 22, 1976, with the headline "Face to face with a 'spy'; blonde who bugged me, by banned CIA rebel," illustrated by a suitably alluring photograph. For the social-democratic left, "CIA" had become a standard epithet of obloquy.[59] The same can be said for right-wing elements in some countries where the objective of American foreign policy had been to encourage a move toward democracy. In Spain, for example, the news weekly *Possible* reported a rightist accusation that the 1973 assassination of fascist prime minister Admiral Luis Carrero Blanco had been an implementation of CIA policy.[60]

By the 1970s, specific covert actions by the CIA in foreign countries had created a general distrust of some aspects of American foreign policy. Instead of courting and strengthening the potential friends of America, the CIA seemed in some instances to be converting them into enemies. In this sense, special operations are a threat to national security and are therefore inimical to the traditional goals of American espionage. Against this background, objections continue to be voiced at home to covert operations and legal–Constitutional trespasses: if American espionage continues to be a bastion of democracy, democracy remains the scourge of espionage.

Notes

ABBREVIATIONS USED IN THE NOTES

CIR   Records of the research division of the Commission on Industrial Relations, 1912–1915, State Historical Society, Madison, Wisconsin.

EMH   E. M. House Collection, Yale University Library, New Haven, Connecticut.

FDS   Files of Charles Fahy, legal adviser, general records, Department of State, 1946–1947, National Archives, Washington, D.C.

MID   Records of the War Department General Staff Military Intelligence Division, 1917–1941, National Archives, Washington, D.C.

NA   National Archives, Washington, D.C.

OC   Records of the office of the counselor, Department of State, National Archives, Washington, D.C.

ONI   Records of the Office of Naval Intelligence, National Archives, Washington, D.C.

PRO   Public Record Office, London.

RSS   Records of the U.S. Secret Service, National Records Center, Suitland, Maryland.

USDS   Records of the under secretary, Department of State, National Archives, Washington, D.C.

WLP   Sir Wilfrid Laurier Papers, Public Archives of Canada, Ottawa, Ontario.

WOID   Records of the War Office Intelligence Division, Public Record Office, London.

PREFACE

1. Executive order no. 11652, March 8, 1972, explained in pamphlet called *Know Your Rights to Mandatory Review of Classified Documents* (Washington, D.C.: Interagency Classification Review Committee, n.d.).

2. *Ibid.*

3. *Ibid.*

4. Gurfein to Jeffreys-Jones, July 19, 1976.

5. Gurfein to Jeffreys-Jones, July 23, 1976; Jeffreys-Jones to Gurfein, June 30, 1976; Gurfein to Jeffreys-Jones, July 19, 1976.

CHAPTER 1

1. See *Final Report Book 1: Foreign and Military Intelligence,* and *Final Report Book 2: Intelligence Activities and the Rights of Americans* (Washington, D.C.: Government Printing Office, 1976).

2. Senator Frank Church, quoted by Washington correspondent Patrick Brogan in a report to the (London) *Times,* April 27, 1976.

3. *San Francisco Chronicle,* Sept. 18, 1975; *Washington Post* Oct. 11, 1975; Senate Committee on Intelligence, *Alleged Assassination Attempts Involving Foreign Leaders* and *Hearings Vol. I: Unauthorized Use of Toxins* (Washington, D.C.: Government Printing Office, 1976).

4. Brogan in (London) *Times,* April 27, 1976.

5. *The Pentagon Papers as Published by the New York Times* (New York: Quadrangle, 1971), pp. 262, 341, 472.

6. *San Francisco Examiner,* Sept. 16, 1975; (London) *Times,* Feb. 17, 1976; (London) *Observer,* Feb. 23, 1976; *Report to the President by the Commission on CIA Activities within the United States* (New York: Manor Books, 1975).

7. Harry H. Ransom, *The Intelligence Establishment* (Cambridge, Mass.: Harvard Univ. Press, 1970), p. 8; Central Intelligence Agency, *Intelligence in the War of Independence* (Washington, D.C.: CIA, 1976), pp. 16–19.

8. Richard W. Rowan, *The Story of Secret Service* (London: John Miles, 1938), p. 1.

9. *San Francisco Chronicle,* Sept. 18, 1975.

10. (Edinburgh) *Scotsman,* Feb. 19, 1976.

11. Allegations summarized in the (London) *Times,* Feb. 17, 1976.

12. (London) *Times,* April 29, 1976.

13. *Washington Post,* Oct. 11, 1975.

14. (London) *Observer,* Feb. 23, 1976.

15. *New York Times,* Sept. 14, 1975.

16. *San Francisco Examiner,* Sept. 16, 1975.

17. (London) *Times,* Feb. 27, 1976.

18. Flaherty, *Privacy in Colonial New England* (Charlottesville: Univ. Press of Virginia, 1972), p. 81 and passim.

19. *The School of Good Manners* (New London, Conn.: 1715), p. 16, quoted in Flaherty, *Privacy,* p. 119.

20. Marion L. Starkey, *The Devil in Massachusetts: A Modern Enquiry into the Salem Witch Trials* (Garden City, N.Y.: Anchor, 1969; originally published in 1949), p. 14.

21. Quoted in George S. Bryan, *The Spy in America* (Philadelphia: Lippincott, 1943), p. 15.

22. John C. Miller, *Crisis in Freedom: The Alien and Sedition Acts* (Boston: Little, Brown, 1951), p. 146.

23. H. M. Wriston, "Executive Agents in American Foreign Relations" (Harvard Univ. Ph.D., 1922), pp. 326–360.

24. *Ibid.,* pp. 94f.

25. *Ibid.,* p. 107.

26. Anna K. Nelson, "Mission to Mexico—Moses Y. Beach, Secret Agent," *The New York Historical Quarterly,* 59 (July 1975), pp. 234, 238.

27. *Ibid.,* p. 227.

28. *Ibid.,* p. 234.

29. James D. Horan, *The Pinkertons: The Detective Dynasty that Made History* (New York: Crown Publishers, Inc., 1967), pp. 52–61, 64–76, 78–79, 102–110.

30. See Harnet T. Kane, *Spies for the Blue and Gray* (Garden City, N.Y.: Hanover House, 1954), pp. 126–127, and the unreliable La Fayette C. Baker, *History of the United States Secret Service* (Philadelphia: L. C. Baker, 1867).

31. John E. Wilkie, "The Secret Service in the War," in *The American–Spanish War: A History by the War Leaders* (Norwich, Conn.: Chas. C. Haskell & Son, 1899), p. 423; Irwin Unger, *The Greenback Era: A Social and Political History of American Finance, 1865–1879* (Princeton, N.J.: Princeton Univ. Press, 1964), pp. 164, 403.

32. Wriston, "Agents," p. 131.

33. *Ibid.,* p. 132.

CHAPTER 2

1. John E. Wilkie, "The Secret Service in the War," in *The American–Spanish War: A History by the War Leaders* (Norwich, Conn.: Chas. C. Haskell & Son, 1899), portrait facing p. 423.

2. Wilkie, "Catching Spain's Spies," *Boston Sunday Herald,* Oct. 2, 1898.

3. Wilkie, *The American–Spanish War,* p. 424.

4. *Ibid.*

5. *Wilkie,* "Catching Spain's Spies."

6. Margaret Leech, *In the Days of McKinley* (New York: Harper, 1959), pp. 104–105; H. Wayne Morgan, *William McKinley and his America* (Syracuse, N.Y.: Syracuse Univ. Press, 1963), pp. 258–259.

7. G. W. Auxier, "The Propaganda Activities of the Cuban *Junta* in Precipitating the Spanish–American War, 1895–1898," *The Hispanic American Historical Review*, 19(1939), pp. 286, 289–290.

8. *Who Was Who in America* (Chicago: A. N. Marquis, 1943), 1.

9. *Boston Herald,* Sept. 3, 1899.

10. James D. Horan, *The Pinkertons: The Detective Dynasty That Made History* (New York: Crown Publishers, Inc., 1967), p. 25.

11. Norma B. Cuthbert, ed., *Lincoln and the Baltimore Plot, 1861, from Pinkerton Records and Related Papers* (San Marino, Cal.: The Huntington Library, 1949), p. (xvii); Ward H. Lamon, *The Life of Abraham Lincoln: From his Birth to his Inauguration as President* (Boston: J. R. Osgood & Co., 1872), and *Recollections of Abraham Lincoln, 1847–1865,* ed. Dorothy Lamon (Chicago: A. C. McClurg & Co., 1895).

12. Harnett T. Kane, *Spies for the Blue and the Gray* (Garden City, N.Y.: Hanover House, 1954), Chapter 4; Richard W. Rowan, *The Story of Secret Service* (London: John Miles, 1938), pp. 294–295.

13. Peter J. Parish, *The American Civil War* (London: Eyre Methuen, 1975), p. 192.

14. Rowan, *Secret Service,* p. 290.

15. See Herbert G. Gutman, "Five Letters of Immigrant Workers from Scotland to the United States," *Labor History,* 9 (fall 1968).

16. See J. Bernard Hogg, "Public Reaction to Pinkertonism and the Labor Question," *Pennsylvania History,* 11 (July 1944).

17. Olney to R. A. Pinkerton, May 3, 1894, in Richard Olney letter books, Library of Congress, Washington, D.C.

18. Anonymous to secretary of war, Jan. 5, 1898, in RSS.

19. *Ibid.*

20. J. Henry Balfour to Ramon Carranza, June 7, 1898, in RSS.

21. John B. Palmer of the A. T. Lowry Grain Co., Kansas City, to Davis, June 15, 1898, in RSS.

22. Davis to George D. Meiklejohn, assist. sec. of war, June 20, 1898, in RSS.

23. Advertisements in *The Detective* ("Official Journal of the Police Authorities and Sheriffs of the U.S."), 35 (May 1919), p. 8.

24. W. Zumach, "Report on Investigation of Detective Agencies" (n.p.: 1914), in CIR.

25. P. A. Zizelman (eastern manager of the MIB) to general manager, Weltman Bros., New York City, July 14, 1905, in Joseph Labadie collection, University of Michigan, Ann Arbor.

26. Anonymous, "List of Detectives" (n.p., 1914); D. O'Regan, "Conclusion Derived from Investigation of Armed Guards up to September 1, 1914" (n.p., n.d.), Zumach, "Report," *passim,* in CIR.

27. Hogg, "Public Reaction"; "Investigation in Relation to the Employment for Private Purposes of Armed Bodies of Men, or Detectives, in Connection with Differences between Workmen and Employers," *Senate Report*, 52 Cong., 2 sess., no. 1280 (Feb. 10, 1895); U.S. Commission on Industrial Relations, *Industrial Relations: Final Report and Testimony* (Washington, D.C.: Government Printing Office, 1916); U.S. Senate, Committee on Education and Labor (known in connection with industrial investigations as the "La Follette Committee"), *Violations of Free Speech and the Rights of Labor*, Part I, Report no. 6, *Strikebreaking Services* (Jan. 26, 1939).

28. John G. ("Jack") London, "The Scab," *Atlantic Monthly*, 93 (Jan. 1904); R. W. Hunter, *Violence and the Labor Movement* (New York: Macmillan, 1914); Sidney C. Howard, *The Labor Spy* (New York: Republic, 1924).

29. Pinkerton, *The Mollie Maguires and the Detectives* (New York: G. W. Carleton & Co., 1877), p. 15.

30. W. J. Burns, *The Masked War* (New York: George H. Doran, 1913).

31. W. J. Burns to Charles McCarthy (director of the research division, Commission on Industrial Relations), Feb. 16, 1915, in Charles McCarthy papers, State Historical Society, Madison, Wisconsin.

32. H. Melville, *White Jacket: or, The World in a Man-of-War* (New York: Harper, 1950); Harold D. Langley, *Social Reform in the United States Navy, 1798–1862* (Urbana: Univ. of Illinois Press, 1967), pp. 185, 195.

33. George S. Bryan, *The Spy in America* (Philadelphia: Lippincott, 1943), pp. 197–199. See also Thomas M. Beach, *Twenty-Five Years in the Secret Service: The Recollections of a Spy, by Major Henri Le Caron, pseud.* (London: Heinemann, 1892).

34. Beresford, "Reorganization," p. 1: in Admiralty and Secretariat Files, in PRO.

35. Extensive correspondence between Beresford and British Treasury officials, 1886–1887, in letter book containing "Reorganization," Admiralty and Secretariat Files, in PRO.

36. See John A. S. Grenville and George B. Young, *Politics, Strategy, and American Diplomacy: Studies in Foreign Policy, 1873–1917* (New Haven: Yale Univ. Press, 1966), p. 173.

37. Ardagh, "Memorandum," June 13, 1896, in WOID.

38. H. J. Foster, *A Study of the Strategical Considerations Affecting the Invasion of Canada by the United States* (London: War Office Staff, 1904), in WOID.

39. Ardagh, "The Intelligence Division (Confidential)," Feb. 26, 1907, in "Ardagh Memoranda 1896–1901," 2 vols., Vol. II: J. C. Ardagh papers, in PRO.

40. Opinion summarized in secretary to the Admiralty to under sec. of state, War Office, June 4, 1896, in WOID.

41. Grenville and Young, *Politics, Strategy*, p. 16.

42. General order no. 292, March 23, 1882, issued by Secretary of the Navy William H. Hunt, quoted in A. P. Niblack, *The History and Aims of the*

Office of Naval Intelligence (Washington, D.C.: Government Printing Office, 1920), p. 1.

43. Grenville and Young, *Politics, Strategy,* p. 21.

44. Roosevelt to Kimball, Dec. 17, 1897, in Elting E. Morison, ed., *The Letters of Theodore Roosevelt* (Cambridge, Mass.: Harvard Univ. Press, 1951), Vol. I, *The Years of Preparation, 1868–1898,* p. 743.

45. Grenville and Young, *Politics, Strategy,* p. 280, 280n.

46. Niblack, *History,* p. 2.

47. Bruce W. Bidwell, "History of the Military Intelligence Division, Department of the Army General Staff" (unpublished document prepared for the Department of the Army, 1954), Part I, pp. II: 1–2. See also Chapter 1.

48. Bidwell, "History," Part I, p. VI: 1; *Annual Report of the Secretary for War, 1891,* V (Washington, D.C.: Government Printing Office, 1892), 3, 43, ... *1892,* I (1893), p. 7; Historical Branch, G–2, "Materials on the History of Military Intelligence in the United States, 1885–1944" (unpublished document, dated 1955, located in USA Center of Military History library, Forrestal Building, Washington, D.C.), Part I, p. 1.

49. See Walter Millis, *Armies and Men: A Study in American Military History* (London: Jonathan Cape, 1958), p. 176f.

50. See Chapter 3.

51. Bidwell, "History," Part I, pp. VI: 15, VIII: 1.

52. Bryan, *Spy,* p. 200.

53. Rowan, *Secret Service,* p. 740.

54. Compare the evidence on bombardment intentions in Rowan, *Secret Service,* p. 440, and Orestes Ferrara, *The Last Spanish War,* transl. W. E. Shea (New York: The Paisley Press, 1937), p. 136.

55. Niblack, *History,* p. 4.

56. Bidwell, "History," p. II: 2.

57. *Boston Herald,* Sept. 3, 1899.

58. *Ibid.*

CHAPTER 3

1. Raymond Carr, *Spain 1808–1939* (Oxford: Clarendon Press, 1966) p. 385; Ernest R. May, *Imperial Democracy: The Emergence of America as a Great Power* (New York: Harcourt, Brace, & World, 1961), p. 218.

2. *London Spectator,* May 28, 1898; anonymous, undated copy of telegram attributed to "Writer" (apparently an American or Canadian secret agent) sent to the Treasury Department from Canada; "Lena Huhn me Aguirra" of Houston, Texas, to General Ramon Blanco (Spanish commander in Cuba), May 29, 1898 (copy of intercepted letter); Capt. W. S. Scott (in charge of Bureau of Military Intelligence, Tampa) to George D. Meiklejohn, assist. sec. of war, June 29, 1898, all in RSS.

3. Editorials in *Cigar Makers' Official Journal,* 26 (Aug. 15ff, 1901); "Tampa's Capitalistic Banditti," *American Federationist,* 10 (May, 1903); J. E. Wilkie, "The Secret Service in the War," in *The American–Spanish War: A History by the War Leaders* (Norwich, Conn.: Chas. C. Haskell, 1899), p. 430.

4. Anonymous to Lieutenant Commander A. V. Wadhams, U.S. Custom-house, New Orleans, June 8, 1898, in RSS.

5. Harrison to Sagasta, April 20, 1898; dispatch, dated April 28, 1898, of Washington correspondent of Brooklyn *Eagle,* both in RSS.

6. Orestes Ferrara, *The Last Spanish War,* transl. W. E. Shea (New York: The Paisley Press, 1937), p. 136.

7. Wilkie, *The American–Spanish War,* p. 425.

8. R. Carranza to Admiral J. G. Ymay (Carranza's cousin) May 26, 1898, published in Wilkie, *The American–Spanish War,* pp. 433–436. The authenticity of this "Carranza letter" was challenged in several respects (see pp. 37–41 below); the passage in which Carranza criticized his superiors was allegedly an interpolation.

9. Unidentified newspaper clippings, bearing the dateline Montreal, May 21, in RSS.

10. Special report to *Toronto Star,* dated May 23, 1898, in RSS.

11. Carranza to Ymay, in Wilkie, *The American–Spanish War,* p. 433.

12. *Ibid.,* p. 433. See also Wilkie, "Catching Spain's Spies," *Boston Sunday Herald,* October 2, 1898.

13. Balfour to Carranza, June 6, 1898, in RSS.

14. Wilkie, "Catching Spain's Spies."

15. M. W. Twitchell, U.S. consul, Kingston, Canada, to J. B. Moore, assist. sec., State Dept., May 11, 21, 1898; G. W. Cridler, 3rd assist. sec., State Dept., to sec. treas., May 24, 1898; both in RSS.

16. J. G. Foster, U.S. consul general, Halifax, Nova Scotia, to Moore, May 27, 1898; Cridler to sec. treas., June 2, 1898; both in RSS. Foster's reference to "the Secret Service of the Dominion of Canada" is puzzling. The Canadian Northwest Mounted Police had a file on Mellor, according to the (Regina, Northwest Territories) *Leader:* clipping enclosed with letter from D. L. Cavan, Canadian govt. agent, Bad Axe, Mich. to "The Chief of the Detective Department," Washington, D.C., June 6, 1898, in RSS. But the Royal Canadian Mounted Police had no jurisdiction in Eastern Canada in 1898. In the R.C.M.P. and Dominion Police files in the Public Archives of Canada, there is no reference to the Montreal spy ring: I. McClymont to Jeffreys-Jones, January 7, 1974. I am grateful to Dr. McClymont for this information and for drawing my attention to the Sir Wilfrid Laurier papers.

17. Wilkie, *The American–Spanish War,* p. 432; *Montreal Star,* July 8, 1899.

18. Scott to assist. sec. war, June 23, 1898; in RSS.

19. Wilkie to J. Priest (the law officer responsible for the arrest of Elmhirst in Tampa), June 8, 1898, in RSS.

20. Wilkie, *The American–Spanish War,* p. 436.

21. Sir Wilfrid Laurier to Lord Aberdeen, June 7, 1898; Du Bose to H. C. Saint-Pierre, June 23, July 2, 1898, all in WLP.

22. A. W. Greeley, chief signal officer, signal office, War Dept., to assist. sec. war, July 16, 1898, in RSS.

23. Owens to Wilkie, Feb. 6, 1899, in RSS.

24. Wilkie, *The American–Spanish War*, p. 424.

25. Lodge to Dixwell, May 10, 1898; Lodge to C. D. Taft, Feb. 1, 1900; W. Berry to Lodge, July 22, 1919; Lodge to J. J. Jusserand, Sept. 23, 1919 (Lodge papers, Massachusetts Historical Society, Boston).

26. Wilkie, *The American–Spanish War*, p. 429.

27. Wilkie, "Catching Spain's Spies."

28. Wilkie, *The American–Spanish War*, p. 429.

29. *Ibid.*, p. 423.

30. Mrs. E. R. Larbig to Wilkie, May 9, 1898, in RSS.

31. M. Kastle to Wilkie, June 13, 1896; passenger list for Prince line sailing, New York–Azores–Gibralter–Naples–Genoa, June 11, 1898, both in RSS.

32. Kastle to Wilkie, June 13, 1898, in RSS.

33. Balfour to Carranza, June 6, 1898, in RSS.

34. Kastle to Wilkie, June 13, 1898, in RSS.

35. Wilkie, "Catching Spain's Spies."

36. Larbig to Wilkie, May 9, 1898; ninety-eight miners of Embreville, Washington County, Tennessee, to John D. Long, secretary of war, demanding the arrest of one Andrew Henry for sending information to Spain, May 6, 1898; John B. Palmer of A. T. Lowry Grain Co., Kansas City, Mo., to Webster Davis, Dept. of Interior, Washington, D.C., June 15, 1898, all in RSS.

37. Richard Hofstadter, *The Paranoid Style in American Politics* (London: Cape, 1966), p. 148.

38. Scott to assist. sec. of war, June 23, 1898, RSS.

39. Harry C. Allen, *Great Britain and the United States: A History of Anglo–American Relations (1783–1952)* (London: Odhams Press, 1954), pp. 520–521.

40. H. Wayne Morgan, "The DeLome Letter: A New Appraisal," *The Historian*, 26 (November 1963), 37.

41. Wilkie, *The American–Spanish War*, pp. 432, 436; Sir Julian Pauncefote to Lord Aberdeen, June 10, 1898, in WLP.

42. Campbell, *Great Britain and the United States 1895–1903* (London: Longmans, 1960), p. 5.

43. Chamberlain to Aberdeen, June 6, 1898, in WLP.

44. Laurier to Aberdeen, June 7, 1898; Du Bose to Saint-Pierre, June 23, July 2, 1898, all in WLP; *Boston Evening Transcript*, July 8, 10, 1899.

45. Pauncefote to Aberdeen, June 10, 1898, in WLP.

46. Opinion of Richard Webster and Robert B. Finlay, June 10, 1898, in files on "Spanish Espionage in U.S.A.," in PRO.

47. Salisbury to Wolff, June 11, 1898, in PRO.

48. Wolff to Salisbury, June 12, 1898, in PRO.

49. Chamberlain to Aberdeen, June 12, 13, 1898, in WLP.

50. Wolff to Foreign Office, June 16, 1898, in PRO.

51. (London) *Times*, June 17, 1898.

52. Du Bose to H. C. Saint-Pierre, Q.C., June 23, 1898; Saint-Pierre to Laurier, June 23, 1898, both in WLP.

53. Du Bose to Saint-Pierre, July 2, 1898, in WLP.

54. The *Montreal Star* of July 8, 1899, published the full text of both "Carranza letters," one called "George F. Bell's version" and the other the "Washington version." In a full discussion of the Tupper St. theft, the *Star* tended to give credence to Bell, in spite of the Englishman's own record as an alleged if unconvicted counterfeiter and of his admission that he offered his services to Spain as a double agent. The *Star* was inclined to accept Bell's version of the Carranza letter because it seemed to be confirmed in a textually exact manner by Carranza's original allegations concerning interpolation. The *Boston Evening Transcripts* of July 8 and 10, 1899, preferred the Redfern story and the "Washington version."

55. Manuel Fraga Iribarne (Spanish ambassador to the Court of St. James; later Spanish minister of the interior) to Jeffreys-Jones, Jan. 29, 1974.

CHAPTER 4

1. William Jennings and Mary B. Bryan, *The Memoirs of William Jennings Bryan* (Darion: Bryan Memorial University, 1925), p. 421.

2. May, Ernest R., *The World War and American Isolation, 1914–1917* (Cambridge, Mass.: Harvard Univ. Press, 1959), p. 37.

3. Arthur S. Link, *Wilson the Diplomatist: A Look at his Major Foreign Policies* (Baltimore: Johns Hopkins Press, 1957), pp. 26–27.

4. H. M. Wriston, "Executive Agents in American Foreign Relations" (Harvard Ph.D., 1922), pp. 341–343.

5. Lawrence E. Gelfland in *Dictionary of American Biography*, 3rd supplement (New York: Charles Scribner's Sons, 1973).

6. *Ibid.*

7. David Kahn, *The Codebreakers: The Story of Secret Writing* (New York: Signet, 1973), p. 172.

8. *Naval Investigation. Hearings before the subcommittee of the Committee on Naval Affairs. . . . Printed for the use of the Committee on Naval Affairs* (Washington, D.C.: Government Printing Office, 1921), p. 2715.

9. Diary of Frank Polk, April 12, 1920, in EMH.

10. *Annual Report of the Chief of the Secret Service Division for the Fiscal Year Ended June 30th* [1907, 1909, 1910, and 1911] (Washington, D.C.: Government Printing Office, 1907–1911).

11. Henry M. Wriston, *Executive Agents in American Foreign Relations* (Baltimore: Johns Hopkins Press, 1929), pp. 122, 238, 308–309.

12. Confidential diary of Frank Polk, June 16, 1916, in EMH.

13. Confidential diary of Frank Polk, March 3, 1917, in EMH.

14. Gordon Auchincloss diary, March 30, 1917, in EMH.

15. Polk diary, Dec. 27, 1917, in EMH; Arthur S. Link, *Woodrow Wilson and the Progressive Era, 1910–1917* (New York: Harper & Row, 1943), pp. 129–130.

16. Polk diary, Dec. 3, 1918, in EMH.

17. Historical branch, G-2, "Materials," Part I, pp. 2–3.

18. M. B. Powe and E. E. Wilson, "The Evolution of American Military Intelligence" (unpublished manual, dated May, 1973, prepared for use by the U.S. Army intelligence center and school at Fort Huachua, Arizona; personal copy on loan from Mr. Delmar H. Finks of the USA Center of Military History Library), p. 15.

19. Van Deman, "Memoirs" (unpublished, undated ms. in the library of the U.S. Army intelligence center, Arizona), I, pp. 8–15, 23–26, referred to in Powe and Wilson, "Evolution," pp. 13, 16.

20. Powe and Wilson, "Evolution," p. 16.

21. Historical branch, G-2, "Materials," Part I, pp. 3, 5.

22. George S. Bryan, *The Spy in America* (Philadelphia: Lippincott, 1943), p. 229; Emanuel V. Voska and Will Irwin, *Spy and Counterspy* (New York: Doubleday, Doran, 1940), p. 260.

23. Extracted from Historical branch, G-2, "Materials," Part I, Exhibit B: "Headquarters Personnel and Funds Military Intelligence Activities (1885–1944)."

24. "Military Intelligence Division–General Staff" (chart, dated October 1, 1918, in MID).

25. *Ibid.*

26. Kahn, *Codebreakers*, p. 167.

27. McGabe, "The Military Intelligence Division, War Department General Staff" (typescript of lecture delivered at the Army War College, Washington, D.C., 1940), pp. 11–12.

28. C. Northcote Parkinson, *The Evolution of Political Thought* (London: Univ. of London Press, 1958), pp. 243–244.

29. Historical branch, G-2, "Materials," Part I, p. 4.

30. Lawrence W. Levine, *Defender of the Faith: William Jennings Bryan: The Last Decade* (New York: Oxford Univ. Press, 1965), p. 3.

31. Progress report of James M. Oliver, director of Naval intelligence, to chief of naval operations, relative to general board letter no. 425, June 26, 1915, in Josephus Daniels papers, Library of Congress, Washington, D.C.

32. *Ibid.*

33. Progress report of E. McCauley, Jr., D.N.I., to C.N.O., relative to G.B.L. no. 425, Jan. 2, 1917, in Josephus Daniels papers, Library of Congress, Washington, D.C.

34. Memorandum on "Enrollment of officers for the Office of Naval Intelligence and the Offices of the Naval Attachés at London, Paris, and Madrid," enclosed in Roger Welles, D.N.I. to Navy Department, July 17, 1917, in Josephus Daniels papers, Library of Congress, Washington, D.C.

35. A. P. Niblack, *The History and Aims of the Office of Naval Intelligence* (Washington, D.C.: Government Printing Office, 1920), p. 24.

36. Max Lowenthal, *The Federal Bureau of Investigation* (New York: Harcourt Brace Jovanovich, 1950), p. 4.

37. *Ibid.,* p. 6.

38. *Ibid.,* p. 5.

39. Preston, Jr., *Aliens and Dissenters: Federal Suppression of Radicals, 1903–1933* (Cambridge, Mass.: Harvard Univ. Press, 1963).

40. Lowenthal, *FBI.*

41. Carlton J. H. Hayes, "Memorandum for Major Hunt. Subject: 'Colonel House Inquiry' and its Utility for M.I.4 September 4, 1918," in MID.

42. Hayes, "Memorandum."

43. Douglas Johnson (of MID, New York) to Marlborough Churchill, Nov. 20, 1918, in MID.

44. Ignaz T. Trebitsch-Lincoln, *The Autobiography of an Adventurer,* transl. Emile Burns (New York: Holt, 1932), p. 102f.

45. Ignaz T. Trebitsch-Lincoln, *Revelations of an International Spy* (New York: McBride, 1916), p. 283.

46. William A. Pinkerton, "The Bolshevik Problem in America," *The Detective,* 35 (May, 1919), 3.

47. Brian Murphy, *The Business of Spying* (London: Milton House, 1973), p. 47.

CHAPTER 5

1. John Higham, *Strangers in the Land: Patterns of American Nativism, 1860–1925* (New Brunswick: Rutgers Univ. Press, 1955).

2. John P. Jones, *The German Spy in America: The Secret Plotting of German Spies in the United States and the Inside Story of the Sinking of the Lusitania* (London: Hutchinson, 1917), pp. 28, 114.

3. Jones, *German Spy,* pp. 23, 24, 36, 114, 116.

4. Jones, *German Spy,* p. 144; Brian Murphy, *The Business of Spying* (London: Milton House, 1973), p. 53.

5. Flynn, memorandum for the secretary of the treasury, May 12, 1915, in subfile "Human Espionage Activities," contained in Leland Harrison's file, in OC.

6. Bernstorff to "Berlin," Jan. 8, 1917, in file on "German messages intercepted by British and forwarded by Edward Bell and Walter H. Page from London: 1916," in OC.

7. Flynn, memorandum for the sec. of the treasury, May 10, 1915, in "Human Espionage" file, in OC.

8. Jones, *German Spy*, p. 55.

9. Flynn memorandum, May 10, 1915.

10. *Ibid.*

11. Transcript of interview with Archibald S. White, June 12, 1915, "Human Espionage" file, in OC.

12. Barbara W. Tuchman, *The Zimmerman Telegram* (London: Constable, 1959), p. 77.

13. Transcript, June 19, 1915, in file on "Telephone conversations tapped by agents, May 30–Sept. 2, 1915, of calls of Bernstorff, Boy-Ed, Mrs. Archibald White, et al.," in OC.

14. Jones, *German Spy*, p. 237.

15. George S. Bryan, *The Spy in America* (Philadelphia: Lippincott, 1943), p. 226; Emanuel V. Voska and Will Irwin, *Spy and Counterspy* (New York: Doubleday, Doran, 1940), p. 20 and passim.

16. Confidential diary of Frank Polk, Oct. 21, Dec. 2, 10, 1915, in EMH.

17. Clipping in "Human Espionage" file, in OC.

18. Press release no. 31–83, May 31, 1942, in general records of the Department of the Treasury; office of the secretary; general correspondence, in NA.

19. Jones, *German Spy*, p. 55.

20. Jones, *German Spy*, pp. 38, 88–91.

21. Alan J. Ward, *Ireland and Anglo-American Relations 1899–1921* (London: Weidenfeld & Nicolson, 1969), p. 108.

22. Bernstorff to "Berlin," Aug. 26, 1916, in Bell and Page file, in OC.

23. *Ibid.*

24. David Kahn, *The Codebreakers: The Story of Secret Writing* (New York. Signet, 1973), p. 145.

25. Kahn, *Codebreakers*, p. 149.

26. Ward, *Ireland*, p. 152.

27. Enclosures with Page to Lansing letter, Apr. 29, 1918, in Edward Bell's file, in OC.

28. Edward Bell to Department of State, May 10, 1918, in Bell file, in OC.

29. Tuchman, *Zimmerman*, p. 78.

30. ONI report enclosed and discussed in Lansing to Wilson, Aug. 24, 1917, in Woodrow Wilson papers, Library of Congress, Washington, D.C.

31. *Ibid.*

32. Roger Welles (director of naval intelligence) to sec. of the Navy via chief of naval operations, Oct. 10, 1917, in Josephus Daniels papers, Library of Congress, Washington, D.C.

33. Wilson to Baker, Nov. 3, 1917, in Wilson papers.

34. Frank L. Mott, *American Journalism: A History of Newspapers in the United States Through 250 Years, 1690 to 1940* (New York: Macmillan, 1941), p. 376.

35. Both quotations from Jones, *German Spy*, p. 3.

36. Bryan, *Spy*, p. 220.

37. See Max Lowenthal, *The Federal Bureau of Investigation* (New York: Harcourt Brace Jovanovich, 1950); Donald Johnson, *The Challenge to American Freedoms: World War I and the Rise of the American Civil Liberties Union* (Lexington: Univ. Press of Kentucky, 1963); William Preston, Jr., *Aliens and Dissenters: Federal Suppression of Radicals 1903–1933* (Cambridge, Mass.: Harvard Univ. Press, 1963); and Robert K. Murray, *Red Scare: A Study in National Hysteria, 1919–1920* (Minneapolis: Univ. of Minnesota Press, 1955).

38. Johnson, *American Freedoms*, p. 146.

39. For example, Preston, Jr., *Aliens and Dissenters*.

40. Warren to sec. of state, Dec. 18, 1917, in file on "Indian revolutionists, Neutrality investigations," in OC.

41. W. Berry to Lodge, July 22, 1919; Lodge to J. J. Jusserand, Sept. 23, 1919, Lodge papers, Massachusetts Historical Society, Boston.

42. Jeffries to Lodge, May 26, 1918, in Lodge papers.

43. Lodge to Jeffries, June 19, 1918, in Lodge papers.

44. Anonymous physician quoted in Peter G. Harris (for adjutant general) to Lodge, Feb, 26, 1919, in Lodge papers.

45. Jeffries to Lodge, n.d. (but certainly January 1919), enclosing a report purporting to have been written and signed by John F. Douney and others of the Douney Agency, Providence, R.I., on Dec. 9, 1918, in Lodge papers.

46. Jeffries to Lodge, Jan. 23, 1919, in Lodge papers.

47. John M. Dunn to Jeffries, March 7, 1919, in Lodge papers.

48. Josephus Daniels, memorandum to all commandants (aids for information) and all branch offices, "Activities connected with Labor troubles" (Aug. 14, 1918), in ONI.

49. Polk diary, Aug. 7, 1918, in EMH.

50. W. Zumach, "Report on Investigation of Detective Agencies" (n.p.; 1914), pp. 19, 21, in CIR.

51. S. C. Maloney to Daniels, March 24, 1917, in Daniels papers.

52. A. P. Niblack, *The History and Aims of the Office of Naval Intelligence* (Washington, D.C.: Government Printing Office, 1920), p. 6.

53. Correspondence of Robert R. Reed of the New York law firm of Reed, McCook & Hoyt with Churchill, Van Deman, et al., 1917–1918, in MID.

54. August Vollmer, chief of police, Berkeley, to Representative Arthur Elston, U.S. Congress, Dec. 8, 1917; Van Deman to Elston, Dec. 20, 1917; in MID.

55. Pinkerton, "The Bolshevik Problem in America," *The Detective*, 35 (May 1919), 3.

CHAPTER 6

1. For example, the Polk diary, June 19, 1916, in EMH.

2. Polk diary, Dec. 16, 1918, in EMH.

3. Gordon Auchincloss diary, Nov. 15, 1917, in EMH.

4. On Wiseman's background, see Wilton B. Fowler, *British American Relations, 1917–1918: The Role of Sir William Wiseman* (Princeton: Princeton Univ. Press, 1969).

5. Auchincloss diary, March 30, 1917, in EMH.

6. Herbert O. Yardley, *The American Black Chamber* (London: Faber, 1931), p. 149.

7. Polk diary, May 9, 1917, in EMH.

8. Auchincloss diary, May 19, 1917, in EMH.

9. Robert S. S. Baden-Powell, *My Adventures as a Spy* (London: Pearson, 1915).

10. Auchincloss diary, May 29–July 27, 1917 (block entry), in EMH.

11. Auchincloss diary, Nov. 8, 1917, in EMH.

12. Auchincloss diary, Nov. 15, 1917, in EMH.

13. Polk diary, Feb. 10, 20, 1917, in EMH.

14. Arthur Murray (of British military intelligence) to Wiseman (forwarded to House), June 22, 1918, papers of Sir William Wiseman, in EMH.

15. Richard W. Rowan, *The Story of Secret Service* (London: John Miles, 1938), p. 682.

16. Emanuel V. Voska and Will Irwin, *Spy and Counterspy* (New York: Doubleday, Doran, 1940), pp. 20–21.

17. Correspondence between Kerr and J. Y. Simpson of the department of information, intelligence bureau, Foreign Office, between Oct. 1 and Dec. 18, 1917, in the papers of Philip Kerr, Eleventh Marquess of Lothian, Scottish Record Office, Edinburgh, Scotland, United Kingdom.

18. Polk diary, Nov. 27, 1917, in EMH.

19. Fowler, *Wiseman*, p. 200.

20. Barbara W. Tuchman, *The Zimmerman Telegram* (London: Constable, 1959), p. 14.

21. Yardley, *Black Chamber*, p. 150.

22. David Kahn, *The Codebreakers: The Story of Secret Writing* (New York: Signet, 1973), pp. 168–172.

23. Walter Hines Page to Lansing, Oct. 17, 1917, in OC.

24. Bell to Leland Harrison, Jan. 26, 1918, Leland Harrison file, in OC.

25. See John le Carré, *Tinker Tailor Soldier Spy* (London: Pan, 1975), p. 121f.

26. Page to Lansing, April 29, 1918, in OC.

27. Yardley, *Black Chamber*, p. 145.

28. *Ibid.*, p. 148.

29. Yardley to Leland Harrison, July 18, 1918, in OC.

30. Yardley to L. Lanier Winslow, June 14, 1919, Leland Harrison file, in OC.

31. Yardley, *Black Chamber*, p. 150.

32. Yardley to Bell, Jan. 21, 1919, in OC.

33. Yardley, *Black Chamber*, p. 150.

34. Yardley to Bell, Jan. 29, 1919, in OC.

35. Lansing to Winslow, Feb. 10, 1919, Leland Harrison file, in OC.

36. See Chapter 11, below.

37. John P. Jones, *The German Spy in America: The Secret Plotting of German Spies in the United States and the Inside Story of the Sinking of the Lusitania* (London: Hutchinson, 1917), p. 190.

38. Harrison to Winslow, May 14, 1919, in OC.

39. Bell to Harrison, Jan. 26, 1918, in OC.

40. Polk diary, Aug. 8, 1918, in EMH.

41. Polk diary, Nov. 30, 1918, in EMH.

42. Polk diary, Oct. 4, 1918, in EMH; Peter G. Filene, *Americans and the Soviet Experiment, 1917–1933* (Cambridge, Mass.: Harvard Univ. Press, 1967), pp. 47–48.

43. John M. Keynes, *The Economic Consequences of the Peace* (London: Macmillan, 1920); J. W. Hiden, *The Weimar Republic* (London: Longmans, 1974).

44. "Notes of a conversation between General T. H. Bliss and Captain Emanuel Voska, February 26, 1919," in Leland Harrison Papers, Library of Congress.

45. Churchill to Alexander C. Kirk, Feb. 24, 1919, in Leland Harrison papers, Library of Congress, Washington, D.C.

46. Bob Edwards (member of parliament) and Kenneth Dunne, *A Study of a Master Spy (Allen Dulles)* (London: Housmans, 1960), p. 7.

47. Allen Dulles, *The Craft of Intelligence* (London: Weidenfeld and Nicolson, 1963), p. 10.

48. Dulles to Grew, Feb. 25, 1919, in Harrison papers. See also Dulles, *Craft*, p. 11.

49. Grew to Tasker Bliss, Feb. 28, 1919, in Harrison papers.

50. Voska to sec. of state, attention Harrison, March 19, 1919, in Harrison papers.

51. *Ibid.*

52. *Ibid.*

53. Harrison to Crane, March 24, 1921, in Harrison papers.

54. *Ibid.*

55. Robert Lansing, *The Peace Negotiations: A Personal Narrative* (New York: Houghton Mifflin, 1921), p. 221.

56. Lansing, *Peace Negotiations*, p. 217.

57. Horodyski to Paderewski, Sept. 1, 1917, file on "Russia, War, 1917," in PRO.

58. Dmowski to Horodyski, Oct. 2, 1917, in PRO.

59. Auchincloss diary, Oct. 7, 1918, in EMH.

60. Wiseman to Auchincloss, Jan. 26, 1918, Wiseman papers, in EMH.

61. J. Henry Balfour correspondence, including messages, of June, 1918, Wiseman papers, in EMH.

62. J. Compton Mackenzie, *Water on the Brain* (Garden City, N.Y.: Doubleday, Doran, 1933).

63. *New York Times,* March 13, 1917, quoted in Raymond Mander and Joe Mitchenson, *Theatrical Companion to Maugham* (London: Rockliff Publishing Corporation, 1955), p. 117; file on "1917 Maugham, Somerset," in PRO.

CHAPTER 7

1. See Richard Cordell, *Somerset Maugham: A Biographical and Critical Study* (London: Heinemann, 1961), and Anthony Curtis, *The Pattern of Maugham* (London: Hamish Hamilton, 1974).

2. Robert L. Calder, *W. Somerset Maugham and the Quest for Freedom* (London: Heinemann, 1972), pp. 200, 205.

3. W. Somerset Maugham, *Collected Short Stories,* 4 vols. (Harmondsworth: Penguin, 1971), vol. 3 (originally published in 1928, in slightly different form, as *Ashenden*), p. 224.

4. *Ibid.,* p. 44.

5. *Ibid.,* "Introduction."

6. Curtis, *Pattern,* p. 109.

7. W. Somerset Maugham, *A Writer's Notebook* (London: Heinemann, 1949), p. 169.

8. W. Somerset Maugham, *The Collected Plays,* 5 vols. (London: Heinemann, 1932), vol. 3, p. vii.

9. Maugham, *Notebook,* p. 154.

10. See W. Somerset Maugham, *The Razor's Edge* (London: Heinemann, 1944), p. 283 and passim.

11. Maugham, *Stories,* vol. 3, p. 157.

12. Maugham, *Notebook,* p. 140.

13. Henry Wickham Steed, *Through Thirty Years,* 2 vols. (Garden City, N.Y.: Doubleday, 1924), vol. 2, quoted in R. W. Seton-Watson, *Masaryk in England* (Cambridge: At the Univ. Press, 1943), p. 33.

14. Wilton B. Fowler, *British–American Relations, 1917–1918: The Role of Sir William Wiseman* (Princeton, N.J.: Princeton Univ. Press, 1969), p. 19.

15. *Ibid.,* p. 12.

16. *Ibid.,* pp. 12–14, 65–67.

17. Gottheil to Wiseman, July 2, 1917, papers of Sir William Wiseman, in EMH.

18. Voska and others, "Russian Matters" (memorandum dated July 12, 1917), in a selection of material from the Wiseman papers, in Calder, *Maugham*, pp. 274–275.

19. Maugham to Wiseman, July 7, 1917, in Calder, *Maugham*, pp. 273–274.

20. Maugham, *Stories*, vol. 3, p. 197; Sir Eric Drummond to Wiseman, Aug. 29, 1917, Wiseman papers, in EMH.

21. Maugham, *Stories*, vol. 3, p. 10.

22. *Ibid.*, vol. 3, p. 20.

23. Maugham, *Notebook*, pp. 155, 163–164, 173–179.

24. Memorandum dated Aug. 22, 1917, in Calder, *Maugham*, p. 277.

25. Cf. Maugham, *Stories*, vol. 3, p. 156.

26. "Intelligence and Propaganda Work in Russia July to December 1917" (memorandum dated Jan. 18, 1918), in Calder, *Maugham*, pp. 286–287.

27. Maugham, *Stories*, vol. 3, p. 189.

28. *Ibid.*, p. 156.

29. *Ibid.*, p. 189.

30. All quotations from *ibid.*, p. 156.

31. "Summary of Reports Received from Agent in Petrograd, under Date of September 11, 1917," in Calder, *Maugham*, pp. 279–282.

32. Transcript of Maugham's interview with Kerensky, in PRO; private secretary archives, 1917–1924, A. J. Balfour: published in Calder, *Maugham*, pp. 288–289.

33. Cablegrams from Maugham summarized in cablegram from Wiseman to Drummond, Sept. 24, 1917, in Calder, *Maugham*, pp. 282–283.

34. Calder, *Maugham*, pp. 280, 284, 287.

35. Undated memorandum from Voska, Wiseman papers, in EMH. See also Emanuel V. Voska and Will Irwin, *Spy and Counterspy* (New York: Doubleday, Doran, 1940), p. 24f.

36. Cable from Petrograd (probably Maugham) to the British Foreign Office, received on Oct. 6, 1917, the substance of it being forwarded to Wiseman: digest in Wiseman papers, in EMH.

37. Summary of Maugham cablegram of Oct. 21, 1917, in Calder, *Maugham*, pp. 283–284.

38. "Summary of Reports Received from Agent in Petrograd, under date of September 11, 1917," in Calder, *Maugham*, pp. 279–282.

39. *Ibid.*, p. 280.

40. *Ibid.*, pp. 281–282.

41. Summary of Maugham cablegram of Oct. 16, 1917, in Wiseman memorandum of Oct. 21, in Calder, *Maugham*, pp. 283–284.

42. Wiseman memorandum of Oct. 21, 1917, commenting on Maugham

cablegram of Oct. 16, 1917, in Calder, *Maugham,* p. 285. See also Geoffrey Barraclough, *The Origins of Modern Germany* (Oxford: Basil Blackwell, 1957), pp. 439–440.

43. Maugham, *Stories,* vol. 3, p. 224.

44. Gordon Auchincloss diary, Nov. 7, 8, 1917, in EMH.

45. Gordon Auchincloss diary, Nov. 20, 1917, in EMH.

46. Horodyski memorandum, quoted in Gordon Auchincloss diary, Nov. 20, 1917, in EMH; Horodyski to Jan Paderewski, Aug. 21, 1917, in file on "1917 Political, Russia (War)," in PRO.

47. Gordon Auchincloss diary, Nov. 20, 1917, in EMH.

48. Gordon Auchincloss diary, Nov. 28, 29, Dec. 3, 6, 1917, in EMH.

49. See Maugham, *Stories,* vol. 3, p. 221.

50. Gordon Auchincloss diary, Jan. 6, 31, 1918, in EMH.

51. Louis L. Gerson, "The Poles," in Joseph P. O'Grady, ed., *The Immigrants' Influence on Wilson's Peace Policies* (Lexington, Ky.: Univ. Press of Kentucky, 1967), p. 279.

52. Victor S. Mamatey, *The United States and East Central Europe, 1914–1918: A Study in Wilsonian Diplomacy and Propaganda* (Princeton, N.J.: Princeton Univ. Press, 1957), p. ix.

53. Gordon Auchincloss diary, Jan. 29, 1918, in EMH.

54. Lawrence E. Gelfland, *The Inquiry: American Preparations for Peace, 1917–1919* (New Haven: Yale Univ. Press, 1963), p. 141.

55. Undated memorandum from Voska, Wiseman papers, in EMH.

56. Reports of Bernard Pares, professor of Russian history at the University of London, and James Young Wilson, professor of natural science at New College, Edinburgh, summarized in the papers of Philip Kerr, Eleventh Marquess of Lothian, Scottish Record Office, Edinburgh, Scotland, United Kingdom.

57. Voska and Irwin, *Spy,* p. 200.

58. Peter G. Filene, *Americans and the Soviet Experiment, 1917–1933* (Cambridge, Mass.: Harvard Univ. Press, 1967), pp. 18–19.

59. Arthur Walworth, *Woodrow Wilson: World Prophet* (New York: Longmans, 1958), pp. 93, 137; R. H. Bruce Lockhart, *Memoirs of a British Agent,* 2nd ed. (London: Putnam, 1934), p. 177 and passim.

60. See Christopher Lasch, "American Intervention in Siberia: A Reinterpretation," *Political Science Quarterly,* 77 (1962), p. 205, and Robert J. Maddox, "Woodrow Wilson, the Russian Embassy and Siberian Intervention," *Pacific Historical Review,* 36 (1967), p. 448.

61. Summary of Maugham cablegram of Oct. 16, 1917, in Wiseman memorandum of Oct. 21, 1917, in Calder, *Maugham,* p. 283.

62. See George F. Kennan, *Russia and the West under Lenin and Stalin* (London: Hutchinson, 1961), pp. 52–60; N. Gordon Levin, Jr., *Woodrow Wilson and World Politics* (New York: Oxford Univ. Press, 1968), p. 7; and Gerson in O'Grady, *Immigrants' Influence,* p. 278 and passim.

CHAPTER 8

1. John J. Broesamle, *William Gibbs McAdoo: A Passion for Change* (Port Washington, N.Y.: Kennikat Press, 1973), p. 69.

2. Confidential diary of Frank L. Polk, Nov. 26, 1915, in EMH.

3. Diary of Frank L. Polk, Feb. 3, 1917, in EMH.

4. Gordon Auchincloss diary, Sept. 4, 1917, in EMH.

5. Auchincloss diary, Feb. 16, 1918, in EMH.

6. Broesamle, *McAdoo*, p. 69.

7. See Thomas A. Bailey, *Woodrow Wilson and the Lost Peace* (Chicago: Quadrangle, 1963), pp. 125–133.

8. Arthur S. Link, *Wilson the Diplomatist: A Look at his Major Foreign Policies* (Baltimore: Johns Hopkins Press, 1957), p. 19.

9. Larry D. Hill, *Emmissaries to a Revolution; Woodrow Wilson's Executive Agents in Mexico* (Baton Rouge: Louisiana State Univ. Press, 1973).

10. Howard F. Cline, *The United States and Mexico,* rev. and enl. ed. (New York: Atheneum, 1963), p. 143.

11. Link, *Wilson,* p. 25.

12. *Encyclopaedia Britannica,* 14th ed., 24 vols. (New York: Encyclopaedia Britannica, Inc., 1929), XV, p. 384.

13. Peter Calvert, *The Mexican Revolution, 1910–1914: The Diplomacy of Anglo–American Conflict* (Cambridge: At the Univ. Press, 1968), p. 193.

14. Polk diary, Aug. 9, 1918, in EMH.

15. Cline, *United States and Mexico,* pp. 186–187.

16. Polk diary, Aug. 9, 1918, in EMH.

17. Polk diary, Nov. 7, 1918, in EMH.

18. *Ency. Brit.,* XV, p. 384.

19. "Extract from YUGANTAR of BHAGWAN SINGH for July, 1917," in file on Indian revolutionaries, in OC.

20. Memorandum from Chakravarty to Harrison, circulated by Harrison under cover of a letter dated Oct. 19, 1917, in OC.

21. L. P. Mathur, *Indian Revolutionary Movement in the United States of America* (Delhi: S. Chand, 1970), pp. 15–16.

22. Mathur, *Indian Movement,* p. 14; Alexander Saxton, *The Indispensable Enemy: Labor and the Anti-Chinese Movement in California* (Berkeley: Univ. of California Press, 1971), p. 247.

23. Gary R. Hess, *America Encounters India, 1941–1947* (Baltimore: Johns Hopkins Press, 1971), pp. 9–10.

24. T. G. Fraser, "The Intrigues of the German Government and the Gadar Party against British Rule in India, 1914–1918" (London University Ph.D.: 1974), pp. 13, 15.

25. M. Naidis, "Propaganda of the Gadar Party," *Pacific Historical Review,* 20 (Aug. 1951), p. 251.

26. Mathur, *Indian Movement,* pp. 23, 28, 55.

27. *Ibid.,* p. v.

28. Hess, *America Encounters,* pp. 3, 4, 6.

29. Mathur, *Indian Movement,* p. 28.

30. H.T.J., "Summary of Hindu Conspiracy" (April 15, 1918), in OC; Giles T. Brown, "The Hindu Conspiracy and the Neutrality of the United States, 1914–1917" (University of California M.A.: 1941), p. 53; John P. Jones, *The German Spy in America* (London: Hutchinson, 1917), p. 80.

31. *New York Times,* March 8, 1917.

32. Zimmerman to Bernstorff, Jan. 13, 1916, in OC.

33. Brown, "Hindu Conspiracy," p. 54.

34. *Ibid.,* p. 67.

35. Mathur, *Indian Movement,* p. 147.

36. Transcript of Chakravarty's interrogation, enclosed in letter from Biddle to Van Deman, July 20, 1917, in OC.

37. Charles E. Neu, *The Troubled Encounter: The United States and Japan* (New York: John Wiley, 1975), p. 88.

38. Transcript of Chakravarty's interrogation; memorandum from Chakravarty to Harrison; Brown, "Hindu Conspiracy," p. 57; Fraser, "Intrigues," pp. 55ff.

39. Thomas J. Tunney, *Throttled! The Detention of the German and Anarchist Bomb Plotters, as Told to Paul Merrick Hollister* (Boston: Small, Maynard, 1919), p. 99; H.T.J., "Summary."

40. H.T.J., "Summary."

41. Reports of Justice Department secret agents Arthur M. Allen (April 7, 9, 1917) and Don S. Rathbun (April 7, 11, 1917), telegram of U.S. attorney general Thomas W. Gregory to agent-in-charge Rathbun (c. April 6, 1917), all in OC; Brown, "Hindu Conspiracy," p. 56, 76.

42. Reports of Justice Department secret agents Rathbun (March 16, 1917) and L. G. Munson (March 24, 1917), in OC.

43. H.T.J., "Summary."

44. Reports of Justice Department secret agent Bryan, "In re J. S. Ginan Singe, Neutrality" (surveillance of Room 450, Oregon Hotel, Portland, on March 18, 1917), in OC.

45. H.T.J., "Summary."

46. *Ibid.*

47. Hess, *America Encounters,* pp. 10–11.

48. *Ibid.*

49. Speeches of Senator David I. Walsh of Massachusetts, reported in *Worcester Post,* Jan. 30, 1919, and *Fall River Globe,* Oct. 11, 1919.

50. Hoover to W. L. Hurley, July 22, 1921, in under secretary file (continuation of main counselor file), in NA.

51. Enclosed with a covering note from Van Deman to Leland Harrison, May 28, 1918, in OC.

52. Van Deman to Harrison, May 28, 1918. Ghose's fellow-revolutionary, Pulin Behari Bose, may have been the prime instigator of the diplomatic appeals to the Soviet Union and other countries; the Indians naturally couched their correspondence in terms unhelpful to investigating secret agents—and historians.

53. Ghose letter (no addressee, n.d.), decoded and sent to M.I.8 on March 21, 1918, and Ghose to Robert Lansing, July 16, 1918, both enclosed with Hoover to Hurley, July 22, 1921: under secretary file, in NA.

54. Hoover to Hurley, July 22, 1921.

55. R. S. Sharp, special agent in charge of New York division (of State Department counterintelligence) to Hall Kinsey, acting chief special agent, July 11, 1925, in the "Administrative File of Chief Special Agent Bannerman," situated in anachronistically labeled "Office of the Counselor" record section, which survived until June 27, 1927, in NA.

56. Mathur, *Indian Movement,* p. 122; F. W. B. Coleman, legation of the U.S.A., Riga, Latvia, to sec. of State, July 11, 1924, in OC.

57. Alan J. Ward, *Ireland and Anglo–American Relations, 1899–1921* (London: Weidenfeld and Nicholson, 1969), p. 143.

58. Memorandum from Voska, n.d., Wiseman papers, in EMH.

59. Ward, *Ireland,* p. 155.

60. W. B. Fowler, *British–American Relations, 1917–1918: The Role of Sir William Wiseman* (Princeton, N.J.: Princeton Univ. Press, 1969), p. 163.

61. See Emmet Larkin, *James Larkin: Irish Labour Leader, 1876–1947* (London: Routledge, 1965).

62. Anonymous memorandum summarizing Fanshawe's report, Dec. 9, 1918, Wiseman papers, in EMH.

63. Polk diary, March 16, 1920, in EMH.

64. *Ibid.*

65. *Ibid.,* April 12, 1920.

66. *Ibid.,* March 16, 1920.

67. O. Dudley Edwards, "James Larkin: Imprisonment in Sing Sing and a Challenge to Cosgrave," *The Irish Times* (Dublin), April 21, 1976.

CHAPTER 9

1. Richard W. Rowan, *The Spy Menace* (London: Thornton Butterworth, 1934), p. 156.

2. *New York Times,* July 9, 1971, quoted in M. B. Powe and E. E. Wilson, "The Evolution of American Military Intelligence" (unpublished document prepared for use by the U.S. Army intelligence center and school at Fort Huachua, Arizona, May 1973), p. 51.

3. S. Heintzelman (acting chief of staff, G-2), "Report of the M.I.D. for the fiscal year ending June 30, 1922," p. 3, in MID.

4. Historical branch, G-2, "Materials on the History of Military Intelligence in the United States, 1885–1944" (unpublished document, 1944), Part I, Exhibit B: "Headquarters Personnel and Funds Military Intelligence Activities," in USA Center of Military History library, Forrestal Building, Washington, D.C.

5. F. H. Lincoln (assistant chief of staff, G-2), "The Military Intelligence Division, War Department General Staff" (typescript of lecture delivered at Fort Humphreys, Washington, D.C., Jan. 5, 1937), p. 3, in MID.

6. Adjutant general, "Unauthorized Investigational Activities" (War Department, March 13, 1923), in MID.

7. "Duties of Intelligence Officers, U.S. Army," *Army and Navy Journal* (Sept. 1, 1923), in MID.

8. *Chicago Tribune*, Sept. 10, 1924.

9. Both quotations from *New York Sun*, Sept. 25, 1924.

10. Mark Brooke (chief, MI-4), "Popular Conceptions of Intelligence Duties in Time of Peace" (memorandum for the executive officer, G-2, dated Oct. 17, 1924), in MID.

11. Beckman Winthrop (acting sec. of the Navy) to Sims, Nov. 1, 1910, in "Sims' Personal File Nov. 1910–1917, 1918," in Josephus Daniels papers, Library of Congress, Washington, D.C.

12. Taft to Sec. of the Navy G. L. Meyer (the text being incorporated into Navy general order no. 100), Jan. 9, 1911, in Sims's file, Daniels papers.

13. Selig Adler, *The Isolationst Impulse: Its Twentieth-Century Reaction* (London: Abelard–Schuman, 1957), p. 85. Cf. text of the speech in Alan J. Ward, *Ireland and Anglo–American Relations, 1899–1921* (London: Weidenfeld and Nicolson, 1969), p. 247.

14. *Naval Investigation: Hearings before the subcommittee of the Committee on Naval Affairs . . . Printed for the use of the Committee on Naval Affairs* (Washington, D.C.: Government Printing Office, 1921), and biographical memorandum in Sims's file, Daniels papers.

15. Elting E. Morison, *Admiral Sims and the Modern American Navy* (Boston: Houghton Mifflin, 1942), p. 475.

16. Morison, *Sims*, p. 44.

17. *Ibid.*, p. 475.

18. Walter Millis, *Armies and Men: A Study in American Military History* (London: Jonathan Cape, 1958), p. 246.

19. *Naval Investigation*, p. 2716.

20. David Fisher, "Home Colony: An American Experiment in Anarchism" (Edinburgh M. Litt., 1971), p. 137.

21. Andrew Sinclair, *The Available Man: The Life Behind the Masks of Warren Gamaliel Harding* (New York: Macmillan, 1965), pp. 235–236; William E. Leuchtenberg, *The Perils of Prosperity 1914–32* (Chicago: University of Chicago Press, 1958), p. 181.

22. Sinclair, *Available Man*, pp. 258–259, 262.

23. Max Lowenthal, *The Federal Bureau of Investigation* (New York: Harcourt Brace Jovanovich, 1950), p. 298.

24. Charles Schwartz (public relations officer for the Secret Service) to L. H. Titterton (manager, script division, National Broadcasting Company, Inc., New York City), Dec. 9, 1941, in general records of the Department of the Treasury, office of the secretary, general correspondence, Secret Service, 1933–1956, in NA.

25. Press release No. 31–83, May 31, 1942, in Treasury records, Secret Service, in NA.

26. Press release No. S 170, Dec. 11, 1946, in Treasury records, Secret Service, in NA.

27. Daniel T. Goggin and H. Stephen Helton, *General Records of the Department of State* (Washington, D.C.: National Archives; General Services Administration, 1963), pp. 116–117.

28. David Kahn, *The Codebreakers: The Story of Secret Writing* (New York: Signet, 1973), pp. 176–177.

29. Henry L. Stimson and McGeorge Bundy, *On Active Service in Peace and War* (New York: Harper, 1947), p. 188.

30. Goggin and Helton, *General Records,* pp. 116–117.

31. Polk diary, March 16, 1920, in EMH.

32. Both quotations are from Sharp to Bannerman, July 1, 1925, in "Administrative File of Chief Special Agent Bannerman," situated in anachronistically labeled "Office of the Counselor" record section, which survived until June, 1927, in OC.

33. Sharp to Kinsey, July 13, 1925, in OC.

34. *Ibid.,* July 17, 1925.

35. *Ibid.,* July 13, 1925

36. *Ibid.,* July 13, 17, 1925.

37. Kinsey to Lane, July 20, 1925, in OC.

38. Kinsey to Sharp, July 11, 1925, in OC.

39. Sharp to Kinsey, July 13, 1925, in OC.

40. Penciled comments by Lane alongside the sentence quoted from Sharp to Kinsey, July 13, 1925.

41. See Selig Adler, *The Uncertain Giant, 1921–1941: American Foreign Policy between the Wars* (New York: Collier, 1969), pp. 90–92, 107, 107n.; Murphy, *Spying,* p. 109 and Chapter 12, below.

42. See Sidney Howard, *The Labor Spy* (New York: Republic, 1924); Edward Levinson, *I Break Strikes! The Technique of Pearl L. Bergoff* (New York: McBride, 1935); Clinch Calkins, *Spy Overhead: The Story of Industrial Espionage* (New York: Harcourt, Brace, 1937); Leo Huberman, *The Labor Spy Racket* (New York: Modern Age, 1937).

43. Calkins, *Spy,* p. 25.

44. William E. Leuchtenberg, *Franklin D. Roosevelt and the New Deal, 1932–1940* (New York: Harper Torchbooks, 1963), p. 217.

45. George S. Bryan, *The Spy in America* (Philadelphia: Lippincott, 1943), p. 13.

46. Quoted in Harry H. Ransom, *The Intelligence Establishment,* rev. and enl. ed. (Cambridge, Mass.: Harvard Univ. Press, 1970), p. 41.

47. Dulles, *The Craft of Intelligence* (London: Weidenfeld and Nicolson, 1963), p. 35.

CHAPTER 10

1. Washburn to secretary of state, May 26, 1925, in USDS.

2. Kellogg to "Amlegation, Vienna," May 27, 1925, in USDS.

3. *Ibid.*

4. *Ibid.*

5. David Kahn, *The Codebreakers: The Story of Secret Writing* (New York: Signet, 1973), p. 191.

6. *Ibid.*, pp. 2, 178–179.

7. The author is indebted to Judith Schiff, of Yale University library, who unavailingly searched the Stimson papers for relevant material, to C. Duncan Rice, of the department of history, Yale University, who acted as an intermediary in the search, to Deborah Neubeck (director of the Kellogg microfilming project), who searched without success the Kellogg papers, and to Ruby J. Shields, of the Minnesota Historical Society, who supplied advice and help in connection with the Kellogg search.

8. Clipping of review by Mark Brooke (chief, MI-4) of Walter G. Sweeney, *Military Intelligence: A New Weapon in War* (New York: Stokes, 1924), in *Cavalry Journal* (1924), enclosed in Brooke to W. V. Morris, Sept. 5, 1924, in MID.

9. As in the subfile on "Human Espionage Activities," Leland Harrison's file, in OC.

10. A. P. Niblack, *The History and Aims of the Office of Naval Intelligence* (Washington, D.C.: Government Printing Office, 1920), p. 24.

11. *Ibid.*, p. 6.

12. *Ibid.*, p. 12.

13. *Ibid.*

14. *Ibid.*, p. 4.

15. A. W. Johnson, "Duties of Naval Attaché" (Navy Department: n.d., but c. 1930), p. 63, in ONI.

16. *Ibid.*

17. *Ibid.*, pp. 28–30, 32, 44; Navy Department, Office of Naval Intelligence, "Sources of Information" (Washington, D.C.: Nov. 29, 1919), in ONI.

18. *Ibid.*, p. 64.

19. *Ibid.*

20. *Ibid.*, p. 68.

21. *Ibid.*, p. 13.

22. Niblack, *History*, p. 6.

23. Johnson, "Duties," p. 14.

24. *Ibid.*, p. 12.

25. *Ibid.*, p. 16.

26. *Ibid.*, p. 18.

27. Both quotations from *ibid.*, p. 16.

28. Niblack, *History*, p. 6.

29. *Ibid.*

30. Johnson, "Duties," p. 64.

31. *Ibid.*, p. 66.

32. E. R. Warner McGabe, "The Military Intelligence Division, War Department General Staff" (typescript of lecture delivered at the Army War College, Fort Humphreys, Washington, D.C., 1940), p. 1, in MID.

33. F. H. Lincoln (assistant chief of staff, G-2), "The Military Intelligence Division, War Department General Staff" (Fort Humphreys lecture, 1937), pp. 1–2, in MID; McGabe, "MID," p. 2.

34. McGabe, "MID," p. 2.

35. S. Heintzelman (assistant chief of staff, G-2), "Report of the Military Intelligence Division for the Fiscal Year Ending June 30, 1922," p. 4; Stanley S. Ford, "The Military Intelligence Division, War Department General Staff" (typescript of War College lecture, 1928), p. 6, both in MID.

36. Ford, "MID," p. 7.

37. *Ibid.*, p. 5.

38. McGabe, "MID," p. 5.

39. Ford, "MID," p. 14.

40. Notes for McGabe's lecture, dated Nov. 6, 1939; McGabe, "MID," p. 5; Lincoln, "MID," p. 3; all in MID.

41. McGabe, "MID," p. 5.

42. *Ibid.*, pp. 4–5.

43. *Ibid.*, p. 5.

44. Heintzelman, "Report," p. 4.

45. Both quotations from J. H. Reeves (assistant chief of staff, G-2), "The Military Intelligence Division, War Department General Staff" (War College lecture, 1924), p. 8, in MID.

46. *Ibid.*, p. 9.

47. Lincoln, "MID," p. 4; McGabe, "MID," p. 3.

48. Lanier Winslow to Leland Harrison, May 1, 1919, in file on "German Codes and Ciphers," in OC.

49. "Funds for Army–Navy Counter Espionage," *Army and Navy Journal* (June 1938), clipping in the Hanson Baldwin collection, Yale University library; (London) *Times,* July 1, Aug. 5, 1938.

50. "Funds" (above) and "Expansion of Intelligence Services," *Army and Navy Journal* (July, 1938), clippings in Baldwin collection.

51. Historical branch, G-2, "Materials on the History of Military Intelligence in the United States, 1885–1944" (unpublished document in the USA Center of Military History library, Forrestal Building, Washington, D.C., 1944), Part I, Exhibit B: "Headquarters Personnel and Funds Military Intelligence Activities (1885–1944)."

52. Barton Whaley, "Operation Barbarossa: A Case Study of Soviet Strategic Information Processing Before the German Invasion" (M.I.T. Ph.D., 1969), p. 40.

53. Kahn, *Codebreakers*, p. 5.

54. *Ibid.*, p. 273. See also Roberta Wohlstetter, *Pearl Harbor: Warning and Decision* (Stanford: Stanford Univ. Press, 1962), p. 176f.

55. See Emanuel V. Voska and Will Irwin, *Spy and Counterspy* (New York: Doubleday, Doran, 1940); Herbert O. Yardley, *The American Black Chamber* (London: Faber, 1931); Allen Dulles, *The Craft of Intelligence* (London: Weidenfeld and Nicolson, 1963); and Dwight D. Eisenhower, *Crusade in Europe* (London: Heinemann, 1948).

CHAPTER 11

1. Robert P. Browder, *The Origins of Soviet–American Diplomacy* (Princeton, N.J.: Princeton Univ. Press, 1953), p. 9.

2. Peter G. Filene, *Americans and the Soviet Experiment, 1917–1933* (Cambridge, Mass.: Harvard Univ. Press, 1967), p. 83.

3. James K. Libbey, "New Study Areas for Soviet–American Relations: The Case of Russian Gold," *The Society for Historians of American Foreign Relations Newsletter*, 6 (June 1975), 17.

4. Ernest R. May, *The World War and American Isolation, 1914–1917* (Cambridge, Mass.: Harvard Univ. Press, 1959), p. 38.

5. Confidential diary of Frank Polk, May 7, 15, 1917, in EMH.

6. Note by Wiseman, dated April 22, 1917, Wiseman papers, in EMH.

7. Filene, *Americans and Soviet*, pp. 28–30.

8. See Chapter 7 and Wilton B. Fowler, *British American Relations, 1917–18: The Role of Sir William Wiseman* (Princeton, N.J.: Princeton Univ. Press, 1969), pp. 114–118.

9. Lockhart, *Memoirs of a British Agent*, 2nd ed. (London: Putnam, 1934), pp. 222, 223, 256–258, 281–284, 313, 314, 322.

10. Political intelligence department, Foreign Office, "Memorandum on the Eve of the Counter-Revolution in Russia," Jan. 3, 1918, in Wiseman papers, and Polk diary, Jan. 18, Feb. 21, March 8, 1918, both in EMH; Richard O'Connor and Dale L. Walker, *The Lost Revolutionary: A Biography of John Reed* (New York: Harcourt, Bruce and World, 1967), pp. 223, 227; N. Gordon Levin, Jr., *Woodrow Wilson and World Politics* (New York: Oxford Univ. Press, 1968), p. 71.

11. Gordon Auchincloss diary, June 13, 1918, in EMH.

12. Betty M. Unterberger, *America's Siberian Expedition, 1918–1920: A Study of National Policy* (Durham, N.C.: Duke Univ. Press, 1956), p. 230, n.l.

13. Polk diary, Aug. 5, 1918, in EMH.

14. V. I. Lenin, "Beware of Spies!" *Pravda,* May 31, 1919, reprinted in Lenin, *Collected Works,* ed. George Hanna, 45 vols. (Moscow: Progress Publishers, 1965), vol. 29, p. 403.

15. Polk diary, June 13, 1919, in EMH.

16. Lenin, "The Third, Communist International" (speech in 1919), in *Collected Works,* vol. 29, p. 241.

17. Libbey, "Russian gold," p. 17.

18. W. L. Hurley, undated memorandum on "Shipment of Russian Gold from Sweden consigned to Irving National Bank of New York," in USDS.

19. Bureau of Investigation, Department of Justice, "General Intelligence Bulletin" (week ending Sept. 17, 1921), 12, in files of "Radical Division," situated in anachronistically labeled "Office of the Counselor" record section, National Archives, which survived until June, 1927, in OC.

20. James V. Compton, *The Swastika and the Eagle: Hitler, the United States, and the Origins of World War II* (Boston: Houghton Mifflin, 1967), pp. 254–259.

21. Bureau of Investigation, "General Intelligence Bulletin" (week ending Oct. 16, 1920), p. 15.

22. John P. Diggins, *Mussolini and Fascism: The View from America* (Princeton, N.J.: Princeton Univ. Press, 1972), pp. 262, 268, 414, 416.

23. Legend related by Joseph L. Minkiewicz, son of a Galician citizen of Austria and father-in-law of author, in spring of 1976.

24. Riga legation's paraphrase of intelligence report, translated as "Propaganda in Eastern Galicia," enclosed in each of two letters: from F. W. B. Coleman (legation of the USA, Riga, Latvia) to secretary of state, July 2, 1924, and anonymous (stamped "U-2") to J. E. Hoover, July 29, 1924, all in USDS.

25. Wiseman, "Note regarding Bertrand Russell," March 23, 1918, Wiseman papers, in EMH.

26. Polk diary, March 30, Dec. 6, 1918, in EMH.

27. Memorandum by N. G. Thwaites, Dec. 12, 1918, Wiseman papers, in EMH.

28. J. M. Winter, "The Social and Demographic Consequences of the First World War in Britain" (a paper delivered to the postgraduate seminar, department of history, University of Edinburgh, Scotland, Nov. 5, 1974).

29. Bureau of Investigation, "General Intelligence Bulletin" (week ending Sept. 25, 1920), p. 35.

30. *Ibid.*

31. See, for example, Bureau of Investigation, "Weekly Bulletin of Radical Activities" (June 26 and July 3 [two weeks in one because of the paper shortage], 1920), in OC.

32. See Frank Tannenbaum, *Peace by Revolution: An Interpretation of Mexico* (New York: Columbia Univ. Press, 1933).

33. Anonymous report from Mexico City (March 21, 1921), quoted in Mathew C. Smith, chief, negative branch, MID, to W. L. Hurley, April 6, 1921, in USDS.

34. *Ibid.*

35. Anonymous report from Mexico City (March 31, 1921), quoted in M. C. Smith to W. L. Hurley, April 18, 1921, in USDS.

36. *Ibid.*

37. Bureau of Investigation, "Weekly Bulletin" (June 26 and July 3, 1920), OC.

38. See Ronald Radosh, *American Labor and United States Foreign Policy* (New York: Vintage, 1970).

39. Selig Adler, *The Uncertain Giant, 1921–1941: American Foreign Policy Between the Wars* (New York: Collier, 1969), p. 96.

40. "B.A.B." to Alexander Kirk, Apr. 25, 1927, in USDS.

CHAPTER 12

1. See Merrill D. Peterson, *The Jeffersonian Image in the American Mind* (New York: Oxford Univ. Press, 1960).

2. Max Weber, *The Theory of Social and Economic Organization*, transl. A. M. Henderson and Talcott Parsons (New York: Free Press, 1947), p. 338.

3. Departmental order no. 414, June (17?), 1927, signed by Frank B. Kellogg, in anachronistically labeled "Office of the Counselor" record section, National Archives, which survived until June, 1927, in OC.

4. Kirk to Hoover, Hepburn, and Ford, June 22, 1927, in OC.

5. Departmental order no. 413, June 17, 1927, signed by Frank B. Kellogg, in OC.

6. Kirk to Hoover, Hepburn, and Ford, June 22, 1927, in OC.

7. "Officers Attached to the Office of Naval Intelligence" (list circulated in June 1927 among the six regional bureaus of the State Department), in OC.

8. Kirk to Hoover, Hepburn, and Ford, June 22, 1927, in OC.

9. Joseph C. Grew, *Turbulent Era: A Diplomatic Record of Forty Years, 1904–1945*, 2 vols. (London: Hammond, 1953), vol. 1, pp. 699, 705.

10. Kirk to Hoover, Hepburn, and Ford, June 22, 1927, in OC.

11. *Ibid.*

12. "Officers Attached."

13. Bruce W. Bidwell, "History of the Military Intelligence Division, Department of the Army General Staff," undisclosed number of parts, of which

only the first had been declassified by October 1975 (unpublished document issued by the Department of the Army, 1954, on deposit in the USA Center of Military History library, Forrestal Building, Washington, D.C.), Part I, X–24.

14. Historical branch, G-2, "Materials on the History of Military Intelligence in the United States, 1885–1944" (unpublished document: 1944), Part I, "Outline of Developments," p. 5.

15. *Washington Herald,* March 18, 1919.

16. Historical branch, G-2, "Materials," Part I, p. 23.

17. Adjutant general, by order of the sec. of war, circular on "Unauthorized Investigational Activities" (March 13, 1923), in MID.

18. E. R. Warner McGabe, "The Military Intelligence Division, War Department General Staff" (typescript of lecture delivered at the Army War College, Port Humphreys, Washington, D.C., 1940), p. 4, MID.

19. *Ibid.,* pp. 11–12.

20. *Ibid.,* p. 12.

21. *Ibid.*

22. Cordell Hull, *The Memoirs of Cordell Hull,* 2 vols. (London: Hodder & Stoughton, 1948), vol. 1, p. 495.

23. Beatrice B. Berle and Travis B. Jacobs, eds., *Navigating the Rapids 1918–1971: From the Papers of Adolph A. Berle* (New York: Harcourt Brace Jovanovich, 1973), p. 404.

24. *Ibid.,* pp. 448–450.

25. Berle, *Rapids,* p. 320.

26. *Ibid.,* pp. 320, 404.

27. *Ibid.,* frontispiece.

28. Corey Ford, *Donovan of O.S.S.* (Boston: Little, Brown, 1970), pp. 96–108.

29. Berle, *Rapids,* p. 351.

30. M. B. Powe and E. E. Wilson, "The Evolution of American Military Intelligence" (May, 1973: unpublished document prepared for use by the United States Army Intelligence Center and School at Fort Huachua, Arizona, kindly loaned by Delmar H. Finks), p. 43.

31. Berle, *Rapids,* pp. 337, 346; Powe and Wilson, "Evolution," p. 43.

32. R. Harris Smith, *OSS: The Secret History of America's First Central Intelligence Agency* (New York: Delta, 1973), p. 24.

33. *Ibid.,* p. 11.

34. *Ibid.,* p. 1; Ford, *Donovan,* p. 11.

35. Berle, *Rapids,* pp. 396–397.

36. Smith, *OSS,* p. 20.

37. Berle, *Rapids,* pp. 396–397. See also Fred J. Cook, *The FBI Nobody Knows* (London: Jonathan Cape, 1965), pp. 243, 258, 265–268, and Don Whitehead, *The FBI Story* (New York: Random House, 1956), p. 204.

38. Berle, *Rapids,* pp. 396–397.

39. Ford, *Donovan,* p. 337.

40. See William Stevenson, *A Man Called Intrepid: The Secret War* (London: Macmillan, 1976), and Francis L. Loewenheim, Harold D. Langley and Manfred Jones, eds., *Roosevelt and Churchill: Their Secret Wartime Correspondence* (London: Barrie & Jenkins, 1975).

41. Stevenson, *Intrepid,* p. 69.

42. Llewellyn Woodward, *British Foreign Policy in the Second World War* (London: Her Majesty's Stationery Office, 1970), vol. 1, pp. 334–335n.

43. Richard J. Whalen, *The Founding Father: The Story of Joseph P. Kennedy* (London: Huchinson, 1965), pp. 309–315, 513.

44. Stevenson, *Intrepid,* p. 109; Smith, *OSS,* pp. 208–209.

45. Stevenson, *Intrepid,* pp. 152, 180; David Hunt, "Looking-Glass War," *Times Literary Supplement* (May 28, 1976).

46. Stevenson, *Intrepid,* p. 153.

47. Hunt, "Looking-Glass War."

48. Smith, *OSS,* p. 20.

49. Smith, *OSS,* p. 210; Brian Murphy, *The Business of Spying* (London: Milton House, 1973), p. 77.

50. Smith, *OSS,* pp. 210–211.

CHAPTER 13

1. See Dwight D. Eisenhower, *Crusade in Europe* (London: Heinemann, 1948), p. 37; George C. Marshall quoted in Harry H. Ransom, *The Intelligence Establishment* (Cambridge, Mass: Harvard Univ. Press, 1970), p. 41; Allen W. Dulles, *The Craft of Intelligence* (London: Weidenfeld and Nicolson, 1963), p. 35; George S. Bryan, *The Spy in America* (Philadelphia: Lippincott, 1943), p. 13; Malcolm Muggeridge, "Book Review of a Very Limited Edition," *Esquire* (May 1966), p. 84, quoted in R. Harris, *OSS: The Secret History of America's First Central Intelligence Agency* (New York: Delta, 1973), p. 163.

2. Ransom, *Intelligence,* p. 70.

3. Smith, *OSS,* p. 35.

4. *Ibid.,* p. 163.

5. Eisenhower, *Crusade,* p. 37.

6. Smith, *OSS,* p. 12; Ransom, *Intelligence,* p. 68.

7. See Chapters 2 and 4, and Ransom, *Intelligence,* p. 68.

8. Smith, *OSS,* p. 245n.

9. Smith, *OSS,* pp. 38–43, 69, 74, 79–82.

10. Ransom, *Intelligence,* p. 65.

11. Ransom, *Intelligence,* p. 71, and the Pulitzer Prize-winning A. M. Schlesinger, Jr., *The Age of Jackson* (Boston: Little, Brown, 1945).

12. Ransom, *Intelligence,* p. 73.

13. Smith, *OSS*, pp. 127, 156, 159, and Louis Adamic, *Dynamite: The Story of Class Violence in America* (London: Jonathan Cape, 1931).

14. Smith, *OSS*, p. 263.

15. Charles E. Neu, *The Troubled Encounter: The United States and Japan* (New York: John Wiley & Sons, 1975), p. 198.

16. See Allen W. Dulles, *The Secret Surrender* (New York: Harper & Row, 1966).

17. Smith, *OSS*, p. 205.

18. *Ibid.*, p. 52.

19. Smith, *OSS*, p. 26, 26n; Richard Deacon, *A History of the British Secret Service* (London: Frederick Muller, 1969), p. 368.

20. William Stevenson, *A Man Called Intrepid: The Secret War* (London: Macmillan, 1976), p. 273n.

21. Stevenson, *Intrepid*, p. 362.

22. John L. Walford (search department, Public Record Office, London) to Jeffreys-Jones, July 16, 1976.

23. See H. Stuart Hughes (historian and former OSS researcher), "The Second Year of the Cold War," *Commentary* (Aug. 1969), quoted in Smith, *OSS*, p. 265; Franz Kafka, *The Castle*, trans. Willa and Edwin Muir (New York: Knopf, 1930); idem, *The Trial*, trans. Willa and Edwin Muir (New York: Knopf, 1937).

24. M. I. Gurfein to Jeffreys-Jones, July 19, 1976.

25. Gurfein to Jeffreys-Jones, July 19, 1976.

26. Stevenson, *Intrepid*, p. 208.

27. Gabriel Kolko, *The Politics of War: The World and United States Foreign Policy, 1943–1945* (New York: Vintage, 1970), pp. 136, 159.

28. Gurfein to Jeffreys-Jones, July 19, 1976.

29. Hugh Seton-Watson, *The East European Revolution* (London: Methuen, 1950), pp. 96, 102.

30. Eisenhower, *Crusade*, p. 251; Winston S. Churchill, *The Second World War* (London: Cassell, 1952), vol. 5, *Closing the Ring*, p. 254.

31. All quotations from Gurfein to Jeffreys-Jones, July 19, 1976.

32. "Memorandum of conversation: 'K' Project, November 13, 1943," in Adolph A. Berle diary, Berle papers, Franklin D. Roosevelt library, Hyde Park, New York.

33. Gurfein to Jeffreys-Jones, July 19, 1976.

34. "Memorandum of conversation: 'K' Project, November 13, 1943," in Berle diary.

35. Berle may have reflected the hesitation of his superiors. See John L. Gaddis, *The United States and the Origins of the Cold War 1941–1947* (New York: Columbia Univ. Press, 1972), pp. 76, 76n., 77.

36. "Memorandum of conversation: 'K' Project, December 30, 1943," in Berle diary.

37. Gurfein to Jeffreys-Jones, July 19, 1976.

38. Beatrice B. Berle and Travis B. Jacobs, eds., *Navigating the Rapids 1918–1971: From the Papers of Adolph A. Berle* (New York: Harcourt Brace Jovanovich, 1973), p. 400.

39. "Memorandum of conversation: 'K' Project, December 30, 1943," in Berle diary.

40. Sir Steven Runciman to Jeffreys-Jones, Aug. 12, 1976. Stancioff's widow intends to have her husband's papers cataloged and deposited in a U.S. library in the near future.

41. Gaddis, *Cold War*, p. 76.

42. Runciman to Jeffreys-Jones, Aug. 12, 1976; Julian Amery, *Sons of the Eagle: A Study in Guerrilla War* (London: Macmillan, 1948), p. 25; Paul Leverkuehn, *German Military Intelligence* (London: Weidenfeld and Nicolson, 1954), p. 144.

43. Gurfein to Jeffreys-Jones, July 19, 1976.

44. All quotations from "U-Mr. Stettinius, February 21, 1944," in Berle diary.

45. All quotations from *ibid*.

46. Gurfein to Jeffreys-Jones, July 19, 1976.

47. Eisenhower, *Crusade*, p. 224.

48. Eisenhower, *Crusade*, p. 222.

49. Churchill, *Closing the Ring*, p. 541.

50. An alternative point of departure for an Allied attack on the Balkans was to have been the northern Adriatic: see General J. C. Smuts to Churchill, Aug. 31, 1943, in Churchill, *Closing the Ring*, p. 114.

51. Smith, *OSS*, pp. 210–212.

52. Murphy, *Spying*, p. 79.

53. *Abwehr* memorandum on "Deutsche Interessenlage bei der Handhabung des Meerengenabkommens" (Nov. 17, 1943), and Count Moltke (Army headquarters, foreign intelligence) to Baron Steengracht (sec. of state), Nov. 18, 1943, in German Foreign Ministry Archives, on microfilm in the Foreign Office library, London.

54. It may well have been their preoccupation with Greece, rather than common sense, which preserved the British from confronting the Russians in the northern Balkans.

55. Smith, *OSS*, p. 239; Charles Whiting, *Gehlen: Germany's Master Spy* (New York: Ballentine, 1972), p. 107f.

CHAPTER 14

1. *Report to the President by the Commission on CIA Activities within the United States* (New York: Manor Books, 1975), p. 46, commonly known and hereafter cited as the *Rockefeller Report;* Hanson W. Baldwin, "Intelligence Arm Vital. Congressional Obstacles for U.S. Agency Thought to Ignore a Big Lesson of War," *New York Times*, April 24, 1946.

2. Corey Ford, *Donovan of O.S.S.* (Boston: Little, Brown, 1970), p. 343.

3. Departmental order 1351, in Department of State, *Bulletin,* 13, p. 739, quoted in *Documents on American Foreign Relations, 8, 1945–1946* (Princeton, N.J.: World Peace Foundation/Princeton Univ. Press, 1948: series hereinafter referred to as *DAFR*), p. 50; Victor Marchetti and John D. Marks, *The CIA and the Cult of Intellligence* (New York: Dell, 1975), p. 77; Baldwin, "Obstacles," *New York Times,* April 24, 1946.

4. *Rockefeller Report,* p. 47; R. Harris Smith, *OSS: The Secret History of America's First Central Intelligence Agency* (New York: Del/Delta, 1973), p. 363; H. W. Baldwin, "Inquiry for Intelligence," *New York Times,* April 7, 1947.

5. *Washington Post,* April 29, 1946, quoted in Ford, *Donovan,* p. 315.

6. Baldwin, "Obstacles," *New York Times,* April 24, 1946.

7. *Ibid.*

8. Smith, *OSS,* pp. 364–365; "Directive of the President [Truman] Establishing the Naval Intelligence Authority," January 22, 1946, in Department of State, *Bulletin,* 14, p. 174, reproduced in *DAFR, 8, 1945–1946,* pp. 506–507; Baldwin, "Inquiry," *New York Times,* April 7, 1947.

9. Durward V. Sandifer (State Department observer at the closed hearings conducted by the U.S. Senate Armed Services Committee and the House Committee on Executive Expenditures considering a bill drafted to create the National Defense Establishment) to Charles Fahy (State Department legal adviser), March 26, April 15, 30, 1947, in FDS; Richard M. Freeland, *The Truman Doctrine and the Origins of McCarthyism: Foreign Policy, Domestic Politics, and Internal Security, 1946–1948* (New York: Schocken, 1974), pp. 130, 202.

10. "Statement of Vice Admiral Forest Sherman, U.S.N., before the Senate Armed Services Committee," transcript dated Apr. 1, 1947, p. 1, in FDS.

11. Various transcripts of hearings in March and April of 1947, in FDS.

12. Paraphrase in Sandifer to Fahy, April 1, 1947, in FDS.

13. Patterson Testimony before House Committee on Executive Expenditures, in Sandifer to Fahy, April 30, 1947, in FDS.

14. Sandifer to Fahy, June 10, 1947, in FDS.

15. The National Security Act (1947), Title 50 U.S.C. Sections 403 (d) and (e), quoted in *Rockefeller Report,* p. 49.

16. "National Security Act of 1947" (chart accompanying first draft, n.d..), in FDS.

17. Braden to Fahy, Feb. 5, 1947, in FDS.

18. Sections 403 (d) and (e), in *Rockefeller Report,* p. 49.

19. Fahy, "Memorandum commenting on draft of Bill providing for a National Defense Establishment (Eighth Draft, 24 February, 1947)," p. 4., in FDS.

20. Hanson W. Baldwin, "Annex A: Outline of Testimony" (n.d.: typescript of testimony delivered circa 1955/1956, in closed hearings, possibly before senior members of the Senate's Armed Services Committee, chaired

by Mike Mansfield, or before the Hoover Commission's second Security Task Force—of which he was a member—chaired by General Mark W. Clark, or before a presidentially appointed group studying the secret operations of the CIA, under the chairmanship of General James Doolittle), p. 2, in Baldwin papers, Yale University Library, New Haven. Cf. *Rockefeller Report*, p. 51, and Lyman B. Kirkpatrick, Jr. *The U.S. Intelligence Community: Foreign Policy and Domestic Activities* (New York: Hill and Wang, 1973), p. 61.

21. Marchetti and Marks, *CIA*, p. 305.

22. *Rockefeller Report*, p. 49.

23. Baldwin, "Annex A," p. 1; Kirkpatrick, *U.S. Intelligence*, pp. 34, 61; *Rockefeller Report*, p. 51. Cf. James Forrestal, *The Forrestal Diaries: The Inner History of the Cold War*, ed. Walter Millis (London: Cassell, (1952), p. 110.

24. Baldwin "Annex A," p. 1.

25. *Ibid.*

26. *Rockefeller Report*, p. 51.

27. Smith, *OSS*, 364–365.

28. Kirkpatrick, *U.S. Intelligence*, p. 28; Baldwin, "Annex A," pp. 6–8.

29. Baldwin, "Annex A," p. 8. Cf. the incomplete accounts of the post-1947 intelligence community given in Marchetti and Marks, *CIA*, p. 106, and Morton H. Halperin, "N[ational] S[ecurity] A[gency] Spying: The Most Secret Agents," *The New Republic* (July 26, 1975) pp. 12–14.

30. *The Washington Post*, Oct. 11, 21, 1975.

31. Marchetti and Marks, *CIA*, p. 45; H. W. Baldwin, "Intelligence—V" *New York Times*, July 25, 1948.

32. Smith, *OSS*, p. 382.

33. Biographical data included in the Baldwin papers.

34. Baldwin, "Intelligence—I . . . V," *New York Times*, July 20–25, 1948; S. J. Rundt (Army intelligence veteran) to Baldwin, Aug. 1, 1948; E. A. Speiser (chairman of the department of Oriental studies, University of Pennsylvania, formerly OSS chief, Near East section, research and analysis branch) to Baldwin, July 28, 1948; Basil C. Walker (Army intelligence veteran) to Baldwin, July 20, 1948; George B. Cressey (chairman, department of geography, Syracuse University to Baldwin, July 22, 1948; Fred Robitschek (Army intelligence veteran) to Baldwin, July 20, 1948: all in Baldwin papers.

35. Baldwin, "Intelligence—I," *New York Times*, July 20, 1948.

36. Baldwin, "Intelligence—V," *New York Times*, July 25, 1948.

37. Baldwin, "Intelligence—III," *New York Times*, July 23, 1948.

38. *Ibid.*

39. *Ibid.*, Baldwin, "Intelligence—V," *New York Times*, July 25, 1948.

40. Baldwin to Jerome Doyle, April 16, 1947, in Baldwin papers.

41. Badwin to Dulles, July 6, 1954, in Baldwin papers.

42. Baldwin, "Annex A," p. 7.

43. Baldwin, "Intelligence—II," ". . . IV," July 22, 24, 1948.

44. Baldwin, "Annex A," p. 4.

45. Harry H. Ransom, *The Intelligence Establishment* (Cambridge, Mass.: Harvard Univ. Press, 1970), pp. 165, 172, 173.

46. Ransom, *Intelligence,* pp. 103–107.

47. *Ibid.,* p. 135.

CHAPTER 15

1. See R. Harris Smith, *OSS: The Secret History of America's First Central Intelligence Agency* (New York: Delta, 1972), lettered footnotes, passim.

2. Branch, "The Trial of the CIA," *New York Times Magazine* (Sept. 12, 1976), p. 126.

3. "Spies, Guerrillas & Violent Fanatics" (London, n.d. [c. 1971–1972]): summary of collective finding kindly supplied by author's godmother, Lily Pincus.

4. *Ibid.*

5. Charles La Salle (assistant operative, U.S. Secret Service) to Wilkie, Oct. 16, 1898, in RSS.

6. La Salle to Wilkie, Oct. 16, 1898, in RSS.

7. *Ibid.*

8. Opinion of Mrs. McDougall's brother, Al Heffley, paraphrased in La Salle to Wilkie, Oct. 16, 1898, in RSS.

9. Hill to ? ("Hon. Friend and Sir," possibly a congressman or Wilkie himself), April 30, 1898, in RSS.

10. *Ibid.*

11. See Daniel Defoe (1661?–1731), whose *Robinson Crusoe* (1719) was written while the author was an anti-Jacobite spy; William T. Le Queux (1864–1927; self-proclaimed English free-lance), *The Czar's Spy: The Mystery of a Silent Love* (New York: Smart Set, 1905), Robert Erskine Childers (1870–1922; World War I pioneer of British aerial intelligence), *The Riddle of the Sands* (London: Smith, Elder, 1903); J. Compton Mackenzie (1883–1973; director of British Aegean intelligence service in 1917), *Water on the Brain* (Garden City, N.Y.: Doubleday Doran, 1933); Graham Greene (1904– ; British intelligence, World War II), *Our Man in Havana: An Entertainment* (London: Heinemann, 1958); Ian Fleming (1908–1964; British intelligence, World War II, *Live and Let Die* (New York: Macmillan, 1954); and, on the short-story writer Cord Meyer (1920– ; with the CIA from 1953), see Peter Jenkins, "Cia Promotes a 'Dirty Trickster'," *Guardian,* March 22, 1973.

Three points should be noted in conjunction with the foregoing references: 1. American spy-fiction writers such as Robert W. Chambers seem to have been comparatively lacking in experience with real intelligence work. 2. The bibliographical citations are necessarily selective. 3. A future book on spy fiction (and one is much needed) might well address itself to the definition of the subject: does it include non-spy fiction which sheds light on its author, a spy?

12. Quoted in L. E. Sissman, "Raymond Chandler Thirteen Years After," *New Yorker* (March 11, 1972), p. 123.

13. Johannes Mario Simmel, *Gott Schützt Die Liebenden* (Munich: Heyne, 1959); Alistair Maclean, *Where Eagles Dare* (London: Collins, 1967).

14. See O'Flaherty, *The Informer* (London: Jonathan Cape, 1925); W. Somerset Maugham, *Collected Short Stories,* 4 vols. (Harmondsworth: Penguin, 1971), vol. 3 (originally published in 1928, in slightly different form, as *Ashenden*); Le Carré, *Tinker Tailor Soldier Spy* (London: Pan, 1975); Saunders Lewis, *Brâd* (Llandybie, Wales: Christopher Davis, n.d. [first performed in 1958]); Arthur Conan Doyle, *The Adventures of Sherlock Holmes* (London: Newness, 1892); John Buchan, *The Thirty-Nine Steps* (Edinburgh: Blackwood, 1915) and note 10 above on Childers, Greene, and Le Queux.

15. Conrad, *The Secret Agent: A Simple Tale* (New York: Harper, 1907).

16. Cooper, *The Spy; or, A Tale of Neutral Ground* (New York: Dodd, Mead, 1946 [originally published in 1821]).

17. Quoted in Christopher Lasch, *The New Radicalism in America (1889–1963); The Intellectual as a Social Type* (New York: Knopf, 1966), pp. 78–79.

18. Chambers, *The Red Republic: A Romance of the Commune* (London: G. P. Putnam's Sons, 1896); idem, *Lorraine* (New York: Harper, 1897); idem, *A King and a Few Dukes* (London: G. P. Putnam's Sons, 1904, originally published in 1896), idem, *The Conspirators: A Romance* (New York: Harper, 1899).

19. Chambers, *King,* pp. 10, 37, 72, 139.

20. *The Central Intelligence Agency* (Washington, D.C.: CIA, 1974), pp. 7–9.

21. Truman quoted in Charles Ashman, *The CIA–Mafia Link* (New York: Manor Books, 1975), p. vii.

22. Branch, "Trial," 116.

23. "Statement by W. E. Colby, Director of Central Intelligence before House of Representatives Select Committee on Intelligence August 6, 1975" (press release kindly supplied to the author by Angus M. Thermer, assitant to the director, CIA, on August 27, 1975).

24. *New York Times,* Sept. 16, 1976.

25. Schorr's own claim in his opening statement to the House Committee on Standards of Official Conduct (the Ethics Committee), reported in *New York Times,* Sept. 16, 1976.

26. *New York Times,* Aug. 16, 1976.

27. (London and Manchester) *Guardian,* Dec. 13, 1976.

28. *Guardian,* Dec. 21, 1976.

29. (London) *Observer,* Sept. 19, 1976.

30. (London) *Daily Telegraph,* Jan. 18, 1977; *Guardian,* Jan. 18, 1977. See Theodore C. Sorensen, *Kennedy* (London: Pan, 1965).

31. "Statement by W. E. Colby," p. 25.

32. Marchetti and Marks, *The CIA and the Cult of Intelligence* (New York: Dell, 1975), pp. 11, 14.

33. P. B. F. Agee, *Inside the Company: CIA Diary* (Harmondsworth. Penquin, 1975), p. 564.

34. Agee, *Diary*, pp. 599–624.

35. *Ibid.*, p. 558.

36. *Ibid.*, pp. 6–17.

37. *Ibid.*, p. 552.

38. *Central Intelligence Agency*, p. 8.

39. Branch, "Trial," 126.

40. Eric Goldman, *The Crucial Decade* (New York: Knopf, 1956), p. 106.

41. Goldman, *Decade*, p. 107.

42. John C. Smith, *Alger Hiss: The True Story* (New York: Holt, Rinehart and Winston, 1976), p. 393.

43. Smith, *Hiss*, p. 303.

44. Smith, *Hiss*, p. 142.

45. Goldman, *Decade*, p. 108.

46. Fred J. Cook used the phrase "American Dreyfus" to describe Hiss in *The Unfinished Story of Alger Hiss* (New York: William Morrow, 1958), quoted in Smith, *Hiss*, p. 436.

47. See Earl Latham, ed., *The Meaning of McCarthyism*, (Boston: D. C. Heath, 1965), and Robert Griffith, *The Politics of Fear: Joseph R. McCarthy and the Senate* (Lexington, Ky.: Univ. Press of Kentucky, 1970).

48. Hofstadter, "The Pseudo-Conservative Revolt—1954," in *The Paranoid Style in American Politics and Other Essays* (London: Jonathan Cape, 1966), pp. 41–65.

49. See Richard H. Rovere, *Senator Joe McCarthy* (London: Methuen, 1960), pp. 24–26; Richard M. Freeland, *The Truman Doctrine and the Origins of McCarthyism: Foreign Policy, Domestic Politics, and Internal Security 1946–1948* (New York: Knopf, 1972); and Athan Theoharris, "The Politics of Scholarship: Liberals, Anti-Communism and McCarthyism," in Robert Griffith and Athan Theoharris, *The Specter: Original Essays on the Cold War and the Origins of McCarthyism* (New York: New Viewpoints, 1974), p. 265.

50. Winks, "The Sordid Truth: Donald Hamilton," *The New Republic* (July 26, 1975), pp. 21–24. Donald Hamilton is the author of *Assignment: Murder* (New York: Dell, 1956), and several other spy thrillers.

51. Hayden, *Wanderer* (London: Longmans, Green, 1964).

52. *Ibid.*, pp. 291f, 386, and passim.

53. *Ibid.*, p. 310.

54. *Ibid.*, p. 391.

55. *Ibid.*, pp. 250, 418.

56. H. S. Commager, " 'Intelligence': the Constitution betrayed," *The New York Review of Books* (Sept. 30, 1976), p. 32–34.

57. Marchetti & Marks, *CIA*, p. 123.

58. Commager, "Intelligence," p. 33.

59. See the comments by Arthur Latham of the Tribune group of Labour party M.P.'s, reported in the (London) *Times,* Dec. 13, 1976.

60. *Guardian,* Dec. 9, 1976.

Bibliography

MANUSCRIPT SOURCES

Canada
Public Archives of Canada, Ottawa, Ont.: Sir Wilfrid Laurier papers.

England
Foreign Office Library, London: Microfilm of German Foreign Ministry Archives for World War II.
Public Record Office, London: Admiralty and Secretariat Files; J. C. Ardagh papers; Foreign Office files on "Spanish Espionage in U.S.A.," "Russia: War 1917," "1917 Maugham, Somerset," and "1917 Political, Russia (WAR)"; Records of the War Office Intelligence Division.

Scotland
Scottish Record Office, Edinburgh: Papers of Philip Kerr, Eleventh Marquess of Lothian.

United States
Library of Congress, Washington, D.C.: Josephus Daniels Papers; Leland Harrison Papers; Richard Olney Letter books; Woodrow Wilson Papers.
Massachusetts Historical Society, Boston: Papers of Henry Cabot Lodge.
National Archives, Washington, D.C.: General records of the Department of State: Charles Fahy's files, 1946–1947; records of the office of the counselor, Department of State: Leland Harrison's file, Edward Bell's file,

files on telephone taps and Indian revolutionaries, administrative file of chief special agent R. C. Bannerman, files of radical division; records of the under secretary, Department of State; general records of the Department of the Treasury, office of the secretary; records of the Office of Naval Intelligence; records of the War Department General Staff Military Intelligence Division 1917–1941.

National Records Center, Suitland, Md.: Records of the U.S. Secret Service.

Franklin D. Roosevelt Library, Hyde Park, N. Y.: Adolf A. Berle Papers.

State Historical Society, Madison, Wisc.: Charles McCarthy papers; records of the research division of the Commission on Industrial Relations, 1912–1915.

University of Michigan Library, Ann Arbor, Mich.: Joseph Labadie collection.

Yale University Library, New Haven, Conn.: E. M. House collection: diary and confidential diary of Frank L. Polk, Gordon Auchincloss diary; Hanson Baldwin collection; Papers of Sir William Wiseman.

UNPUBLISHED WORKS

Bidwell, Bruce W. "History of the Military Intelligence Division, Department of the Army General Staff." Undisclosed number of parts, of which only the first declassified by Oct., 1975. 1954. Unpublished document prepared for Department of the Army, in the USA Center of Military History library, Forrestal Building, Washington, D.C.

Brown, Giles T. "The Hindu Conspiracy and the Neutrality of the United States, 1914–1917." Univ. of California M.A., 1941.

Fisher, David. "Home Colony: an American experiment in anarchism." Edinburgh M. Litt., 1971.

Fraser, T. G. "The Intrigues of the German Government and the Gadar Party against British Rule in India, 1914–1918." London Ph.D., 1974.

Historical branch, G-2. "Materials on the History of Military Intelligence in the United States, 1885–1944." 1944. Unpublished document in the USA Center of Military History library, Forrestal Building, Washington, D.C.

McGabe, E. R. Warner. "The Military Intelligence Division, War Department General Staff." 1940. Typescript of lecture delivered at the Army War College, Washington, D.C.: National Archives.

"Spies, Guerrillas and Violent Fantasies." London: n.d. (c. 1971–1972). Summary of collective finding supplied by Lily Pincus of the Tavistock Institute of Human Relations, London.

Whaley, Barton. "Operation Barbarossa: a case study of Soviet strategic information processing before the German invasion." M.I.T. Ph.D., 1969.

Winter, J. M. "The Social and Demographic Consequences of the First World War in Britain." Paper delivered to the postgraduate seminar, department of history, University of Edinburgh, Scotland, Nov. 5, 1974.

Wriston, H. M., "Executive Agents in American Foreign Relations." Harvard Univ. Ph.D., 1922.

Zumach, W. "Report on Investigation of Detective Agencies." N.p.: 1914. In unpublished reports of the research division of the Commission on Industrial Relations, 1912–1915, State Historical Society, Madison, Wisconsin.

PUBLISHED OFFICIAL DOCUMENTS

Annual Reports of the Chief of the Secret Service Division. Washington, D.C.: Government Printing Office, 1907–1911.

Annual Reports of the Secretary for War. Washington, D.C.: Government Printing Office, 1892, 1893.

Documents on American Foreign Relations, VIII, *1945–1946.* Princeton, N.J.: World Peace Foundation/Princeton Univ. Press, 1948.

"Investigation in Relation to the Employment for Private Purposes of Armed Bodies of Men, or Detectives, in Connection with Differences between Workmen and Employers," *Senate Report,* 52 Cong., 2 sess., no. 1280 (Feb. 10, 1895).

Know Your Rights to Mandatory Review of Classified Documents. Washington, D.C.: Interagency Classification Review Committee, n.d. Pamphlet.

Naval Investigation. Hearings before the sub-committee of the Committee on naval affairs . . . Printed for the use of the Committee on naval affairs. Washington, D.C.: Government Printing Office, 1921.

The Pentagon Papers as Published by the New York Times. New York: Quadrangle, 1971.

"Report, Joint Committee on the Investigation of the Pearl Harbor Attack," *Senate document,* 79 Cong., 2 sess., no. 244 (July 20, 1946).

Report to the President by the Commission on CIA Activities within the United States. New York: Manor Books, 1975.

U.S. Commission on Industrial Relations. *Industrial Relations: final report and testimony.* Washington, D.C.: Government Printing Office, 1916.

U.S. Senate. Committee on Education and Labor, *Violations of Free Speech and the Rights of Labor,* part I, report no. 6. *Strikebreaking Services* (Jan. 26, 1939).

U.S. Senate Select Committee to Study Governmental Operations with Respect to Intelligence Activities. *Alleged Assassination Attempts Involving Foreign Leaders; Hearings Vol. I: Unauthorized Use of Toxins; Final Report Book 1: Foreign and Military Intelligence; Final Report Book 2: Intelligence Activities and the Rights of Americans.* Washington, D.C.: Government Printing Office, 1976.

PERIODICALS AND NEWSPAPERS

American Federationist
Army and Navy Journal
Boston Evening Transcript

Boston Sunday Herald
Chicago Tribune
Cigar Makers' Official Journal

The Detective
Edinburgh *Scotsman*
Fall River Globe
London *Observer*
London *Spectator*
London *Times*
Montreal Star
New York Sun

New York Times
San Francisco Chronicle
San Francisco Examiner
Toronto Star
Washington Herald
Washington Post
Worcester Post

MEMOIRS AND PUBLISHED PAPERS

The American–Spanish War: A History by the War Leaders. Norwich, Conn.: Chas. C. Haskell, 1899.

Baker, La Fayette C. *History of the United States Secret Service.* Philadelphia: L. C. Baker, 1867.

Beach, Thomas M. *Twenty-Five Years in the Secret Service: The Recollections of a spy, by Major Henri Le Caron, pseud.* London: Heinemann, 1892.

Bernstorff, Johann H.A.H.A. *The Memoirs of Count Bernstorff.* New York: Random House, 1936.

———. *My Three Years in America.* New York: Scribner, 1920.

Berle, Beatrice, and Travis B. Jacobs, eds. *Navigating the Rapids 1918–1971: From the Papers of Adolph A. Berle.* New York: Harcourt Brace Jovanovich, 1973.

Bryan, William Jennings and Mary Baird Bryan. *The Memoirs of William Jennings Bryan.* Darion: Bryan Memorial University, 1925.

Burns, William J. *The Masked War.* New York: George H. Doran, 1913.

Churchill, Winston S. *The Second World War,* vol. 5: *Closing the Ring.* London: Cassell, 1952.

Cronon, E. David, ed., *The Cabinet Diaries of Josephus Daniels, 1913–1921.* Lincoln: University of Nebraska Press, 1963.

Cuthbert, Norma B., ed. *Lincoln and the Baltimore Plot, 1861, from Pinkerton Records and Related Papers.* San Marino, Cal.: The Huntington Library, 1949.

Eisenhower, Dwight D. *Crusade in Europe.* London: Heinemann, 1948.

Forrestal, James. *The Forrestal Diaries: The Inner History of the Cold War,* ed. Walter Millis. London: Cassell, 1952.

Grew, Joseph C. *Turbulent Era: A Diplomatic Record of Forty Years, 1904–1945,* 2 vols. London: Hammond, 1953.

Hull, Cordell. *The Memoirs of Cordell Hull,* 2 vols. London: Hodder & Stoughton, 1948.

Lamon, Ward H. *Recollections of Abraham Lincoln, 1847–1865,* ed. Dorothy Lamon. Chicago: A. C. McClurg & Co., 1895.

Lansing, Robert. *The Peace Negotiations: A Personal Narrative.* Boston: Houghton Mifflin, 1921.

Le Caron, Henri. See Beach, Thomas M.

Lockhart, R. H. Bruce. *Memoirs of a British Agent,* 2nd ed. London: Putnam, 1934.

Maugham, W. Somerset. *A Writer's Notebook.* London: Heinemann, 1949.

Morison, Elting E., ed. *The Letters of Theodore Roosevelt,* vol. 1: *The Years of Preparation, 1868–1898.* Cambridge, Mass.: Harvard Univ. Press, 1951.

Papen, Franz von. *Memoirs,* trans. Brian Connell. London: André Deutsch, 1952.

Pinkerton, Allan. *The Molly Maguires and the Detectives.* New York: G. W. Carleton & Co., 1877.

Rintelen, Franz von. *The Dark Invader: Wartime Reminiscences of a German Naval Intelligence Officer.* New York: Macmillan, 1933.

Stimson, Henry L. and McGeorge Bundy. *On Active Service in Peace and War.* New York: Harper, 1947.

Trebitsch-Lincoln, Ignaz T. *The Autobiography of an Adventurer,* transl. Emile Burns. New York: Holt, 1932.

————. *Revelations of an International Spy.* New York: McBride, 1916.

Tunney, Thomas J. *Throttled! The Detention of the German and Anarchist Bomb Plotters, as Told to Paul Merrick Hollister.* Boston: Small, Maynard, 1919.

Voska, Emanuel V. and Will Irwin. *Spy and Counterspy.* New York: Doubleday, Doran, 1940.

Wilkie, John E. "Catching Spain's Spies," *Boston Sunday Herald,* Oct. 2, 1898.

Yardley, Herbert O. *The American Black Chamber.* London: Faber, 1931.

WORKS OF REFERENCE

Almanach de Gotha: annuaire généalogique, diplomatique et statistique. Gotha: Justus Perthes, 1764–.

Brockhaus Enzyklopädie. Wiesbaden: F. A. Brockhaus, 1967.

Dictionary of American Biography, 3rd supplement. New York: Charles Scribner's Sons, 1973.

Dictionary of National Biography. Oxford: Oxford Univ. Press, 1917, 1927, 1937, 1949, 1959, and 1971.

Dokumenty i Materialy po Istorii Sovetsko–Polskikh Otnoshenii. Moscow: Russian Academy of Sciences Institute of Slavonic Studies, 1963–.

Encyclopaedia Britannica, 14th ed., 24 vols. New York: Encyclopaedia Britannica, 1929.

Goggin, Daniel T. and H. Stephen Helton. *General Records of the Department of State.* Washington, D.C.: National Archives, 1963.

Polski Slownick Biograficzny. Wroclaw: Historical Institute of the Polish Academy, 1962–1964.

Who was Who in America, vol. 1. Chicago: A. N. Marquis, 1943.

OTHER BOOKS AND ARTICLES

Adler, Selig. *The Isolationist Impulse: Its Twentieth-Century Reaction.* London: Abelard-Schuman, 1957.

———. *The Uncertain Giant, 1921–1941: American Foreign Policy Between the Wars.* New York: Collier, 1969.

Agee, Philip. *Inside the Company: CIA Diary.* Harmondsworth: Penguin, 1975.

Allen, Harry C. *Great Britain and the United States: A History of Anglo-American Relations (1783–1952).* London: Odhams Press, 1954.

Amery, Julian. *Sons of the Eagle: A Study in Guerrilla War.* London: Macmillan, 1948.

Ashman, Charles. *The CIA–Mafia Link.* New York: Manor Books, 1975.

Auxier, G. W. "The Propaganda Activities of the Cuban *Junta* in Precipitating the Spanish–American War, 1895–1898," *The Hispanic American Historical Review,* 19 (1939).

Baden-Powell, Robert S. S. *My Adventures as a Spy.* London: Pearson, 1915.

Bailey, Thomas A. *Woodrow Wilson and the Lost Peace.* Chicago: Quadrangle, 1963.

Barraclough, Geoffrey. *The Origins of Modern Germany.* Oxford: Basil Blackwell, 1957.

Boorstin, Daniel J. *The Americans: The Colonial Experience.* New York: Random House, 1958.

Boyer, Paul and Stephen Nissenbaum. *Salem Possessed: The Social Origins of Witchcraft.* Cambridge, Mass.: Harvard Univ. Press, 1974.

Branch, Taylor. "The Trial of the CIA," *New York Times Magazine* (Sept. 12, 1976).

Broesamle, John J. *William Gibbs McAdoo: A Passion for Change.* Port Washington, N.Y.: Kennikat Press, 1973.

Browder, Robert P. *The Origins of Soviet–American Diplomacy.* Princeton, N.J.: Princeton Univ. Press, 1953.

Bryan, George S. *The Spy in America.* Philadelphia: Lippincott, 1943.

Buchan, John. *The Thirty-Nine Steps.* Edinburgh: Blackwood, 1915.

Calder, Robert L. *W. Somerset Maugham and the Quest for Freedom.* London: Heinemann, 1972.

Calkins, Clinch. *Spy Overhead: The Story of Industrial Espionage.* New York: Harcourt, Brace, 1937.

Calvert, Peter. *The Mexican Revolution, 1910–1914: The Diplomacy of Anglo–American Conflict.* Cambridge: At the Univ. Press, 1968.

Campbell, Alexander E. *Great Britain and the United States 1895–1903.* London: Longmans, 1960.

Carr, Raymond. *Spain 1808–1939.* Oxford: Clarendon Press, 1966.

The Central Intelligence Agency. Washington, D.C.: CIA, 1974. Pamphlet.

Chambers, Robert W. *The Conspirators: A Romance.* New York: Harper, 1899.

———. *The Crimson Tide.* New York: Appleton, 1919.

————. *A King and a Few Dukes*. London: G. P. Putnam's Sons, 1904 (originally published in 1896).

————. *Lorraine*. New York: Harper, 1897.

————. *The Red Republic: A Romance of the Commune*. London: G. P. Putnam's Sons, 1896.

Childers, Robert Erskine. *The Riddle of the Sands*. London: Smith, Elder, 1903.

Cline, Howard F. *The United States and Mexico*, rev. and enl. ed. New York: Atheneum, 1963.

Cook, Fred J. *The FBI Nobody Knows*. London: Jonathan Cape, 1965.

Cooper, James Fenimore. *The Spy: or, A Tale of Neutral Ground*. New York: Dodd, Mead, 1946 (originally published in 1821).

Cordell, Richard. *Somerset Maugham: A Biographical and Critical Study*. London: Heinemann, 1961.

Commager, Henry Steele, ed. *Documents of American History*, 5th ed. New York: Appleton-Century-Crofts. 1949.

Compton, James V. *The Swastika and the Eagle: Hitler, the United States, and the Origins of World War II*. Boston: Houghton Mifflin, 1967.

Conrad, Joseph. *The Secret Agent: A Secret Tale*. New York, Harper, 1907.

Curtis, Anthony. *The Pattern of Maugham*. London: Hamish Hamilton, 1974.

Davies, Norman. *White Eagle, Red Star*. London: Macdonald, 1972.

Deacon, Richard. *A History of the British Secret Service*. London: Frederick Muller, 1969.

Diggins, John P. *Mussolini and Fascism: The View from America*. Princeton, N.J.: Princeton Univ. Press, 1972.

Doyle, Arthur Conan. *The Adventures of Sherlock Holmes*. London: Newnes, 1892.

Dulles, Allen. *The Craft of Intelligence*. London: Weidenfeld and Nicolson, 1963.

Edwards, Bob and Kenneth Dunne. *A Study of a Master Spy (Allen Dulles)*. London: Housmans, 1960.

Edwards, O. Dudley. "James Larkin: Imprisonment in Sing Sing and a Challenge to Cosgrave." *The Irish Times* (April 21, 1976).

Ferrara, Orestes. *The Last Spanish War*, transl. W. E. Shea. New York: The Paisley Press, 1937.

Filene, Peter G. *Americans and the Soviet Experiment, 1917–1933*. Cambridge, Mass.: Harvard Univ. Press, 1967.

Flaherty, David H. *Privacy in Colonial New England*. Charlottesville: Univ. Press of Virginia, 1972.

Ford, Corey. *Donovan of O.S.S.* Boston: Little, Brown, 1970.

Foster, H. J. *A Study of the Strategical Considerations Affecting the Invasion of Canada by the United States*. London: War Office General Staff, 1904.

Fowler, Wilton B. *British American Relations, 1917–1918: The Role of Sir William Wiseman*. Princeton, N.J.: Princeton Univ. Press, 1969.

Freeland, Richard M. *The Truman Doctrine and the Origins of McCarthyism: Foreign Policy, Domestic Politics, and Internal Security, 1946–1948.* New York: Schocken, 1974.

Gaddis, John L. *The United States and the Origins of the Cold War 1941–1947.* New York: Columbia Univ. Press, 1972.

Gelfland, Lawrence E. *The Inquiry: American Preparations for Peace, 1917–1919.* New Haven: Yale Univ. Press, 1963.

Goldman, Eric. *The Crucial Decade.* New York: Knopf, 1956.

Greene, Graham. *Our Man in Havana: An Entertainment.* London: Heinemann, 1958.

Grenville, John A. S., and George B. Young. *Politics, Strategy, and American Diplomacy: Studies in Foreign Policy, 1873–1917.* New Haven: Yale Univ. Press, 1966.

Griffith, Robert. *The Politics of Fear: Joseph R. McCarthy and the Senate.* Lexington, Ky.: Univ. Press of Kentucky, 1970.

———— and Athan Theoharris, eds. *The Specter: Original Essays on the Cold War and the Origins of McCarthyism.* New York: New Viewpoints, 1974.

Gutman, Herbert G. "Five Letters of Immigrant Workers from Scotland to the United States," *Labor History,* 9 (fall, 1968).

Halperin, Morton H. "N[ational] S[ecurity] A[gency] Spying: Most Secret Agents," *The New Republic* (July 26, 1975).

Hammett, Dashiell. *The Maltese Falcon.* New York: Knopf, 1930.

Hayden, Sterling. *Wanderer.* London: Longmans, Green, 1964.

Hess, Gary R., *America Encounters India, 1941–1947.* Baltimore: Johns Hopkins Press, 1971.

Higham, John. *Strangers in the Land: Patterns of American Nativism, 1860–1925.* New Brunswick: Rutgers Univ. Press, 1955.

Hill, Larry D. *Emissaries to a Revolution: Woodrow Wilson's Executive Agents in Mexico.* Baton Rouge: Louisiana State Univ. Press, 1973.

Hofstadter, Richard. *Anti-Intellectualism in American Life.* New York: Knopf, 1963.

————. *The Paranoid Style in American Politics.* London: Cape, 1966.

Hogg, J. Bernard. "Public Reaction to Pinkertonism and the Labor Question," *Pennsylvania History,* 11 (July 1944).

Horan, James D. *The Pinkertons: The Detective Dynasty that Made History.* New York: Crown Publishers, Inc., 1967.

Howard, Sidney C. *The Labor Spy.* New York: Republic, 1924.

Huberman, Leo. *The Labor Spy Racket.* New York: Modern Age, 1937.

Hunt, David, "Looking-Glass War," *Times Literary Supplement* (May 28, 1976).

Hunter, Robert W. *Violence and the Labor Movement.* New York: Macmillan, 1914.

Jeffreys-Jones, Rhodri. "The Montreal Spy Ring of 1898 and the Origins of 'Domestic' Surveillance in the United States," *Canadian Review of American Studies*, 5 (fall, 1974).

————. "Profit Over Class: A Study in American Industrial Espionage," *Journal of American Studies*, 6 (December 1972).

————. "W. Somerset Maugham: Anglo–American Agent in Revolutionary Russia," *American Quarterly*, 28 (spring, 1976).

Jenkins, Peter. "CIA Promotes a Dirty Trickster," *Guardian*, March 22, 1973.

Johnson, Donald. *The Challenge to American Freedoms: World War I and the Rise of the American Civil Liberties Union.* Lexington, Ky.: Univ. Press of Kentucky, 1963.

Johnson, Walter, ed. *Turbulent Era: A Diplomatic Record of Forty Years, 1904–1945: Joseph C. Grew.* London: Hammond, Hammond, 1953.

Jones, John P. *The German Spy in America: The Secret Plotting of German Spies in the United States and the Inside Story of the Sinking of the Lusitania.* London: Hutchinson, 1917.

Kafka, Franz. *The Castle,* trans. Willa and Edwin Muir. New York: Knopf, 1930.

Kahn, David. *The Codebreakers: The Story of Secret Writing.* New York: Signet, 1973.

Kane, Harnett T. *Spies for the Blue and the Gray.* Garden City, N.Y.: Hanover House, 1954.

Kennan, George F. *Russia and the West under Lenin and Stalin.* London: Hutchinson, 1961.

Keynes, John M. *The Economic Consequences of the Peace.* London: Macmillan, 1920.

Kirkpatrick, Lyman B., Jr. *The U.S. Intelligence Community: Foreign Policy and Domestic Activities.* New York: Hill and Wang, 1973.

Kohn, Richard H. *Eagle and Sword: The Beginnings of the Military Establishment in America.* New York: Free Press, 1975.

Kolko, Gabriel. *The Politics of War: The World and United States Foreign Policy, 1943–1945.* New York: Vintage, 1970.

Lamon, Ward H. *The Life of Abraham Lincoln: From his Birth to his Inauguration as President.* Boston: J. R. Osgood & Co., 1872.

Langley, Harold D. *Social Reform in the United States Navy, 1782–1862.* Urbana: Univ. of Illinois Press, 1967.

Larkin, Emmet. *James Larkin: Irish Labor Leader, 1876–1947.* London: Routledge, 1965.

Lasch, Christopher. "American Intervention in Siberia: A Re-interpretation," *Political Science Quarterly*, 77 (1962).

————. *The New Radicalism in America (1889–1963): The Intellectual as a Social Type.* New York: Knopf, 1966.

Latham, Earl, ed. *The Meaning of McCarthyism.* Boston: D. C. Heath, 1965.

Le Carré, John. *Tinker Tailor Soldier Spy.* London: Pan, 1975.

Lenin, V. I. *Collected Works*, ed. George Hanna, 45 vols. Moscow: Progress Publishers, 1965.

Le Queux, William T. *The Czar's Spy: The Mystery of a Silent Love*. New York: Smart Set, 1905.

Leuchtenberg, William E. *Franklin D. Roosevelt and the New Deal*. New York: Harper Torchbooks, 1963.

———. *The Perils of Prosperity 1914–1932*. Chicago: Univ. of Chicago Press, 1958.

Levenstein, Harvey A. *Labor Organizations in the United States and Mexico: A History of Their Relations*. Westport, Conn.: Greenwood, 1971.

Leverkuehn, Paul. *German Military Intelligence*. London: Weidenfeld & Nicolson, 1954.

Levin, Jr., N. Gordon. *Woodrow Wilson and World Politics*. New York: Oxford Univ. Press, 1968.

Levine, Lawrence W. *Defender of the Faith: William Jennings Bryan: The Last Decade, 1915–1925*. New York: Oxford Univ. Press, 1965.

Levinson, Edward. *I Break Strikes! The Techniques of Pearl L. Bergoff*. New York: McBride, 1935.

Lewis, Saunders. *Brâd*. Llandybie, Wales: Christopher Davies, c. 1958.

Libbey, James K. "New Areas for Soviet–American Relations: The Case of Russian Gold," *The Society for Historians of American Foreign Relations Newsletter*, 6 (June 1975).

Link, Arthur S. *Woodrow Wilson and the Progressive Era, 1910–1917*. New York: Harper & Row, 1943.

———. *Wilson the Diplomatist: A Look at his Major Foreign Policies*. Baltimore: The Johns Hopkins Press, 1957.

Loewenheim, Francis L., Harold D. Langley, and Manfred Jones, eds. *Roosevelt and Churchill: Their Secret Wartime Correspondence*. London: Barrie & Jenkins, 1975.

London, John G. ("Jack"). "The Scab," *Atlantic Monthly*, 93 (January 1904).

Lowenthal, Max. *The Federal Bureau of Investigation*. New York: Harcourt Brace Jovanovich, 1950.

Leech, Margaret. *In the Days of McKinley*. New York: Harper, 1959.

Mackenzie, J. Compton. *Water on the Brain*. Garden City, N.Y.: Doubleday, Doran, 1933.

Maclean, Alistair. *Where Eagles Dare*. London: Collins, 1967.

Maddox, Robert J. "Woodrow Wilson, The Russian Embassy and Siberian Intervention," *Pacific Historical Review*, 36 (November 1967).

Mamatey, Victor S. *The United States and East Central Europe, 1914–1918: A Study in Wilsonian Diplomacy and Propaganda*. Princeton, N.J.: Princeton Univ. Press, 1957.

Mander, Raymond, and Joe Mitchenson. *Theatrical Companion to Maugham: A Pictorial Record of the First Performances of the Plays of W. Somerset Maugham*. London: Rockliff Publishing Corporation, 1955.

Marchetti, Victor, and John D. Marks. *The CIA and the Cult of Intelligence.* New York: Dell, 1975.

Marquand, John P. *Stopover Tokyo.* London: Tom Stacey, 1971 (originally published in 1957).

Mathur, L. P. *Indian Revolutionary Movement in the United States of America.* Delhi: S. Chand, 1970.

Maugham, W. Somerset. *The Collected Plays,* 5 vols. London: Heinemann, 1932.

———. *Collected Short Stories,* vol. 3. Harmondsworth: Penguin, 1971 (originally published in 1928, in slightly different form, as *Ashenden*).

———. *The Moon and Sixpence.* London: Heinemann, 1962.

———. *The Razor's Edge.* London: Heinemann, 1944.

May, Ernest R. *Imperial Democracy: The Emergence of America as a Great Power.* New York: Harcourt, Brace & World, 1961.

———. *The World War and American Isolation, 1914–1917.* Cambridge, Mass.: Harvard Univ. Press, 1959.

Mead, Margaret. *And Keep your Powder Dry: An Anthropologist Looks at America.* New York: Morrow, 1943.

Miller, John C. *Crisis in Freedom: The Alien and Sedition Acts.* Boston: Little, Brown, 1951.

Millis, Walter. *Armies and Men: A Study in American Military History.* London: Jonathan Cape, 1958.

Moore, R. J. *The Crisis of Indian Unity 1917–1940.* Oxford: Clarendon Press, 1974.

Morgan, H. Wayne, "The DeLome Letter: A New Appraisal," *The Historian,* 26 (November 1963).

———. *William McKinley and his America.* Syracuse, N.Y.: Syracuse Univ. Press, 1963.

Morris, Elting E., ed. *Turmoil and Tradition: A Study of the Life and Times of Henry L. Stimson.* Boston: Houghton Mifflin, 1960.

Mott, Frank L. *American Journalism: A History of Newspapers in the United States Through 250 Years, 1690 to 1940.* New York: Macmillan, 1941.

Murphy, Brian. *The Business of Spying.* London: Milton House, 1973.

Murray, Robert K. *Red Scare: A Study in National Hysteria, 1919–1920.* Minneapolis: Univ. of Minnesota Press, 1955.

Naidis, Mark, "Propaganda of the Gadar Party," *Pacific Historical Review,* 20 (August 1951).

Nelson, Anna K. "Mission to Mexico—Moses Y. Beach, Secret Agent," *The New-York Historical Quarterly,* 59 (July 1975).

Neu, Charles E. *The Troubled Encounter: The United States and Japan.* New York: John Wiley, 1975.

Niblack, A. P. *The History and Aims of the Office of Naval Intelligence.* Washington, D.C.: Government Printing Office, 1920.

Niebuhr, Reinhold. *The Irony of American History.* New York: Scribner, 1952.

O'Connor, Richard, and Dale L. Walker. *The Lost Revolutionary: A Biography of John Reed.* New York: Harcourt, Brace & World, 1967.

O'Flaherty, Liam. *The Informer.* London: Jonathan Cape, 1925.

O'Grady, Joseph P., ed. *The Immigrants' Influence on Wilson's Peace Policies.* Lexington, Ky.: Univ. Press of Kentucky, 1967.

Parish, Peter J. *The American Civil War.* London: Eyre Methuen, 1975.

Parkinson, C. Northcote. *The Evolution of Political Thought.* London: Univ. of London Press, 1958.

Peterson, Merrill D. *The Jeffersonian Image in the American Mind.* New York: Oxford Univ. Press, 1960.

Pinkerton, William A. "The Bolshevik Problem in America," *The Detective,* 35 (May 1919).

Preston, Jr., William. *Aliens and Dissenters: Federal Suppression of Radicals, 1903–1933.* Cambridge, Mass.: Harvard Univ. Press, 1963.

Radosh, Ronald. *American Labor and United States Foreign Policy.* New York: Vintage, 1970.

Ransom, Harry H. *The Intelligence Establishment,* rev. & enl. ed. Cambridge, Mass.: Harvard Univ. Press, 1970.

Rogin, Michael P. *The Intellectuals and McCarthy: The Radical Specter.* Cambridge, Mass.: MIT Press, 1967.

Rothwell, Victor H. *British War Aims and Peace Diplomacy, 1914–1918.* London: Oxford Univ. Press, 1971.

Rovere, Richard H. *Senator Joe McCarthy.* London: Methuen, 1960.

Rowan, Richard W. *The Spy Menace: An Exposure of International Espionage.* London: Thornton Butterworth, 1934.

————. *The Story of Secret Service.* London: John Miles, 1938.

Saxton, Alexander. *The Indispensable Enemy: Labor and the Anti-Chinese Movement in California.* Berkeley: Univ. of California Press, 1971.

Seton-Watson, Hugh. *The East European Revolution.* London: Methuen, 1950.

Seton-Watson, R. W. *Masaryk in England.* Cambridge: At the Univ. Press, 1943.

Simmel, Johannes M. *Mich Wundert, dass Ich so Fröhlich Bin.* Reinbeck bei Hamburg: Rororo, 1962.

Sinclair, Andrew. *The Available Man: The Life behind the Masks of Warren Gamaliel Harding.* Chicago: Quadrangle, 1969.

Sissman, L. E. "Raymond Chandler Thirteen Years After," *New Yorker* (March 11, 1972).

Smith, John C. *Alger Hiss: The True Story.* New York: Holt, Rinehart and Winston, 1976.

Smith, R. Harris. *O.S.S.: The Secret History of America's First Central Intelligence Agency.* New York: Delta, 1973.

Starkey, Marion L. *The Devil in Massachusetts: A Modern Enquiry into the Salem Witch Trials.* Garden City, N.Y.: Anchor, 1969 (originally published in 1949).

Stevenson, William. *A Man Called Intrepid: The Secret War.* London: Macmillan, 1976.

Stouffer, Samuel A. *Communism, Conformity, and Civil Liberties: A Cross-Section of the Nation Speaks its Mind.* New York: John Wiley, 1966 (originally published in 1955).

Sweeney, Walter G. *Military Intelligence: A New Weapon in War.* New York: Stokes, 1924.

Tannenbaum, Frank. *Peace by Revolution: An Interpretation of Mexico.* New York: Columbia Univ. Press, 1933.

Tuchman, Barbara W. *The Zimmerman Telegram.* London: Constable, 1959.

Unger, Irwin. *The Greenback Era: A Social and Political History of American Finance, 1865–1879.* Princeton, N.J.: Princeton Univ. Press, 1964.

United States Army in World War II Pictorial Record: The War against Germany and Italy—Mediterranean and Adjacent Areas. Office of the chief of military history, Department of the Army: Government Printing Office, 1951.

Unterberger, Betty M. *America's Siberian Expedition, 1918–1920: A Study of National Policy.* Durham, N.C.: Duke Univ. Press, 1956.

Walsworth, Arthur. *Woodrow Wilson: World Prophet.* New York: Longmans, 1958.

Ward, Alan J. *Ireland and Anglo–American Relations, 1899–1921.* London: Weidenfeld and Nicolson, 1969.

Weber, Max. *The Theory of Social and Economic Organization,* transl. A. M. Henderson and Talcott Parsons. New York: Free Press, 1947 (originally published in German in 1921).

Whalen, Richard J. *The Founding Father: The Story of Joseph P. Kennedy.* London: Hutchinson, 1965.

Whitehead, Don. *The FBI Story.* New York: Random House, 1956.

Whiting, Charles. *Gehlen: Germany's Master Spy.* New York: Ballantine, 1972.

Winks, Robin W. "The Sordid Truth: Donald Hamilton," *The New Republic* (July 26, 1975).

Wohlstetter, Roberta. *Pearl Harbor: Warning and Decision.* Stanford: Stanford Univ. Press, 1962.

Woodward, Llewellyn, *British Foreign Policy in the Second World War,* vol. 1. London: Her Majesty's Stationery Office, 1970.

Wriston, Henry M. *Executive Agents in American Foreign Relations.* Baltimore: Johns Hopkins Press, 1929.

Index